Forever Carnival

Also by Robert Lehane and published by Ginninderra Press
Irish Gold
W.B. Dalley

Robert Lehane

Forever Carnival

A story of priests, professors & politics
in 19th century Sydney

Forever Carnival
ISBN 978 1 74027 268 1
Copyright © text Robert Lehane 2004
Cover: St John's College, with high tower as originally envisaged

First published 2004
Reprinted 2016

GINNINDERRA PRESS
PO Box 3461 Port Adelaide 5015
www.ginninderrapress.com.au

Contents

Preface		7
1	Looking good	9
2	Out of Ireland	18
3	Sorting things out in Sydney	37
4	Progress	52
5	A bright start	64
6	Moving in	77
7	Disaster	93
8	Coming of the Irish	106
9	In Polding's absence	123
10	Difficult times	139
11	Parkes on the rampage	155
12	Moving on	166
13	A changing guard	180
14	Strong words	194
15	Exuberant charity	204
16	Preparing for the coadjutor	219
17	Out of St John's	236
18	More travels	253
19	At Balmain	263
20	One of the ugliest blots	279
21	Next door	288
22	Farewells	302
23	If only…	317
Sources		322
Picture credits		327
Index		345

Preface

Look up John Forrest in the National Library catalogue and you will find many references to the explorer, Premier of Western Australia and Federation 'founding father' of that name. You will also find a pamphlet, titled *Lecture on the Tendency of Modern Civilisation*, by a more obscure namesake. It is well worth reading. This Forrest's thoughts in 1870 on the dangers posed by extraordinary advances in science that he saw coming – 'when the impossible of our times will be the actual and the ordinary' – stand up remarkably well today.

The author, the Very Rev. Dr John Forrest, was recruited from Ireland in 1859 to set up the Catholic residential college, St John's, at Sydney University. A man of broad interests, high intelligence and irrepressible humour, he quickly became a popular figure in his adopted city – to the extent, according to one account, that 'no great public movement and no great social gathering were deemed perfectly representative in character without his presence'. Public lectures he gave on topics ranging from primary education to the Franco-Prussian War drew large and enthusiastic audiences, and he contributed frequently to the press. His friends included some of the colony's most notable politicians, lawyers, literary figures, academics and clerics, Protestant as well as Catholic.

Unfortunately, he was less well regarded by Sydney's Catholic archbishops, John Bede Polding and Roger Vaughan. These Englishmen, heading a colonial church that was overwhelmingly Irish, were somewhat isolated figures. Resentment of English rule, and of the leading role Polding gave to monks of the Benedictine monastery he established, produced continuing tensions. The archbishops' relations with Irish bishops appointed to country dioceses in the 1860s were usually cool and sometimes poisonous, and they viewed Forrest, a friend of the bishops from student days in Rome, in a similar light.

This book tells the story of Forrest and his friends against a backdrop of stirring events in Sydney, including the attempted assassination of Queen Victoria's son Prince Alfred by an Irish Catholic in 1868 and the tumultuous aftermath. It was an interesting period politically, as the new system of popularly elected government threw up colourful and sometimes unscrupulous combatants, among them Henry Parkes. The spirit of the times was optimistic; progress seemed unstoppable in the new land of opportunity.

For Forrest, establishing St John's College proved a thankless task. All available funds went into its grandiose building, leaving nothing for staff or scholarships. Students were scarce, and Archbishop Polding undermined recruiting by allowing Sydney's only Catholic secondary school, run by the Benedictines, to provide alternative lodgings for undergraduates. St John's under Forrest had just a few years of relative success – after a scandal at the school prompted an exodus of its students to the college.

Things became even worse for the Irishman after Vaughan, who had replaced him as Rector of St John's in 1874, succeeded Polding as Archbishop of Sydney in 1877. But he remained a popular and admired figure, and retained his good humour. He was 'one of the very few men in our midst who was such a shining example of perfect tolerance that the bitterest bigots exempted him from their animosities', wrote one newspaper after his death in 1883. His 'heart kept ever carnival', wrote another admirer in a memorial poem.

Principal sources for the story are the 'unofficial' Catholic newspaper *Freeman's Journal* and documents held at St John's College (including a valuable unpublished history of the college by R.A. Daly) and in Catholic archives. I am grateful for the generous access provided to the precious archival material. Most of the pictures of places and events are from the old *Illustrated Sydney News*, a publication whose files help bring the times to life.

1
Looking good

Sydney – what a town! On Boxing Day 1860, everyone seemed to be taking advantage of the perfect weather – 'out on steamboats, on yachts, on ferry boats, gigs, and cockle shells – out in four-in-hands, in family coaches, in gigs, in traps, and in milk-carts – out on horses, good, bad, and indifferent; and last and most pitiable state of all, out on Shanks's Mare'. The writer for *Freeman's Journal* found the setting intoxicating – 'the Eden laved by the waters of Parramatta River, …the roar of the sea out there at Coogee or Bondi'. He noted that Watson's Bay, just inside South Head, was a specially popular spot for picnics, and no wonder: 'The grandeur and sublimity of the scene from its stupendous cliffs is unequalled in the world – we will not attempt a description – it is too majestic to be sketched by a feeble hand…' Then there was the Australian sky, 'capable of inspiring hope in a heart oppressed with untold grief… The effects of nature's bounties are observable on our people, particularly in the native-born; and the consequence is that we are a pleasure-seeking, merry-making, light hearted, and perhaps we may say a glorious, offshoot from the parent trunks of the Emerald and the Trident Islands.'

Freeman's Journal was the Catholic paper, so most of its readers came from the Emerald Isle or were of Irish descent. It devoted most of its Boxing Day story to an outing to Middle Harbour by the 'St Mary's Literary Society', a Church-sponsored young people's group apparently with few literary pretensions. Some seven hundred, 'the most joyous lot in creation', set out from Circular Quay on the steamboat *Boomerang*. Upon landing on the 'beautiful silvery' beach, 'some ran, some jumped, and danced, and others scampered off into the bush'. After lunch, 'hearty, glorious, tumultuous sport' commenced and, when the band struck up, 'the votaries of Terpsichore were instantly desporting their figures…in the mazy whirls of the dance'. A game of 'Kissing in the Ring' began, but the Very Rev. Dean O'Connell 'put a "squasher" on the business in an instant. We have never seen an Irish Sunday "patron" disperse quicker at the sight of the priest than did the lads and lasses of Australia when ordered by the Very Rev. Dean.'[1]

The Catholic young, and Sydneysiders generally, were out in force again a month later, on Anniversary (now Australia) Day, 26 January 1861. Again parties of picnickers flocked to favourite spots, some offering views of the rowing and yachting regatta on the harbour. The outing for young Catholics, this time organised by the Young Men's Society attached to St Benedict's church, Broadway, began with a short train trip. Stop-off point on the line to Parramatta, opened in 1855, was Haslem's Creek, now a stormwater channel running into Homebush Bay. According to *Freeman's*, the three hundred and fifty excursionists first 'scampered' through Mr Smith's orchard, where they were allowed to pick the choicest fruit, and through the surrounding bush. Then 'old and young, husbands and wives, and we fancy very much innumerable sweethearts' danced in a clearing shaded by 'stakes and sylvan boughs' to music provided by the band of Sydney's Victoria Theatre. Those who preferred 'more manly exercises' played football and cricket.[2]

Among the older people present was the remarkable Caroline Chisholm, who 'seemed highly delighted at the proceedings'. Her eldest son, Archibald, was president of St Benedict's Young Men's Society and chief organiser of the excursion. By this time, illness had brought an end to the fifty-two-year-old Mrs Chisholm's extraordinary philanthropic work, over the past twenty years, for the immigrants – particularly young women – flocking to the colony.

With her at Haslem's Creek was the Very Rev. Dr John Forrest, recently arrived from Ireland to take up the post of Rector of St John's College at the University of Sydney. One can imagine that, as they watched the young at play, they talked about the changes Mrs Chisholm had witnessed in the colony since she arrived in 1838.

Then, although settlement was spreading rapidly and many people were doing very nicely, it was still a dumping ground for the felons of England, Scotland and Ireland; two more years were to pass before convict transportation to Sydney ended. Charles Darwin painted one side of the picture in his much-quoted description of the bustling town – population twenty-three thousand – in 1836: 'It is a most magnificent testimony to the power of the British nation... the streets are regular, broad, clean and kept in excellent order; the houses are of a good size and the shops well furnished.'[3] Writing a little earlier, the Rev. Dr William Ullathorne, the colony's first Catholic Vicar-General, saw things very differently: 'We have taken a vast portion of God's earth, and made it a cesspool; we have poured down scum upon scum and dregs upon dregs of the offscourings of mankind and we are building up with them a nation of crime, to be...a curse and a plague...'[4]

The contrasts were stark. While some prospered beyond their fondest dreams in the new land, the lot of the outcasts was bleak. But even before transportation ended, things were changing rapidly. While three times more convicts than free immigrants had arrived in the 1820s (about twenty-one thousand eight hundred compared with six thousand five hundred), in the 1830s free arrivals outnumbered convicts (forty thousand three hundred to thirty-one thousand two hundred). Most of the free settlers came in the second half of the decade, taking advantage of newly introduced assisted passage schemes (nearly twenty-five thousand assisted immigrants landed in Sydney between 1836 and 1840).

By 1860, more than a hundred and sixty thousand assisted immigrants had arrived in the colony, eager to seek their fortunes. This was double the total number of convicts sent to New South Wales. The European population of the colony had reached three hundred and fifty thousand, of whom about fifty-six thousand lived in Sydney.[5]

The gold rushes beginning in 1851 were a major spur to immigration and to the growth of colonial self-confidence. In 1856, the long campaign by locals for responsible self-government – an administration answerable to an elected parliament – achieved its goal when the New

South Wales Legislative Assembly met for the first time. Just two years later, the right to vote, until then restricted to landowners, was extended to all adult males (with a few exceptions, such as recent arrivals). Voting was by secret ballot, an innovation not introduced in England until 1872 (and the 'home' parliament did not extend the vote to all men until 1914).

The inauguration of the University of Sydney in 1852, despite well-founded doubts about the ability of the colony's rudimentary school system to produce a stream of candidates for degrees, was another sign of the optimistic spirit abroad. Two years later, provision was made for the establishment of church colleges, affiliated with the university, to accommodate students and give them religious instruction and help with their studies. Funds raised to build the colleges were to attract matching government grants of up to £20,000 – a large sum indeed in those pre-inflationary times when a cook or coachman might be paid less than £50 a year.[6] In addition, the government would provide a £500 annual stipend for the principal of each college.

The Catholic college, St John's, was launched with great enthusiasm. The initial appeal for funds, in 1857, brought promises of nearly £23,000, although actual takings fell considerably short of that sum.[7] The inaugural college Council, keen to obtain a Rector of the highest standing, asked four eminent clerics – Cardinal Wiseman, Archbishop of Westminster; William Ullathorne, the pioneer Sydney priest who was now Bishop of Birmingham; Archbishop Cullen of Dublin; and the famed ex-Anglican priest and theologian John Henry Newman – to make the choice. 'Attainments on a level with those of first class men of Oxford, or of Trinity College, Dublin, or of Cambridge, are what we should wish to secure', the churchmen were advised.[8]

Caroline Chisholm's companion on the Anniversary Day 1861 outing, Dr John Forrest, was the man chosen. A forty-year-old Irishman of sunny disposition and high academic accomplishment, Forrest stepped ashore in Sydney on 11 September 1860, ninety days after setting out from London on one of the fastest clippers sailing the oceans, the 939-ton *Cairngorm*. His adventurous twenty-three-year-old sister Maryanne accompanied him on what they reported had been a very pleasant voyage: 'the good ship did not experience rough seas or anything like tempestuous weather'.⁹

Early engagements included his introduction to the Archbishop of Sydney, John Bede Polding, formal acceptance of the Rector's job at a meeting of the St John's College Council, and being presented to the Governor, Sir William Denison. Forrest's main task was arranging for the college to open in temporary accommodation the following February. But he was also in demand for much else in the closing months of 1860 – including examining the pupils at three Catholic primary schools and the secondary boarding school, St Mary's College, Lyndhurst.¹⁰

Polding established Lyndhurst in a large house in Glebe in 1852. Its aim was to provide a traditional English education – centred on Latin, Greek and maths – for the sons of Catholics who had done well in the colony and for outstanding pupils from poorer backgrounds (who were to be given scholarships).¹¹ If young Catholics were to proceed to university, Lyndhurst was the most likely route. The university recognised this; in 1860, the examiners who put the students through their paces with Forrest were two of the three inaugural professors – John Woolley (Classics and Logic) and Morris Pell (Mathematics). The Irish priest's task was to quiz the boys on Xenophon and Roman history; he was impressed, finding they 'displayed great talent, great industry, and considerable knowledge'.¹²

Activities of the St Benedict's Young Men's Society – the group that organised the excursion to Haslem's Creek – also kept him busy. This was one of four or five such societies that flourished in Sydney in the early 1860s, connected with different Catholic churches; groups established in Ireland in the 1850s provided the model. *Freeman's Journal* gave extensive publicity to the lectures and excursions they organised, even when things went wrong. During a trip by steamer to Middle Harbour on Anniversary Day 1864, a drunken musician was pushed off the roof of the deckhouse and landed on an eighteen-year-old butcher, apparently

Queuing for harbour steamers – a mid-1860s Anniversary Day (26 January) scene at Circular Quay.

breaking his back. The report of the inquest into his death gives a feeling for the broad range of people involved in society activities. In addition to a priest, witnesses included a stonemason, another butcher, a plasterer, a scene painter and a grocer.[13]

Within days of his arrival in Sydney, Forrest was special guest at a St Benedict's Young Men's Society lecture on electricity, which attracted 'fully three hundred' to the church hall. The lecturer, Father Anselm Curtis, Prefect of Studies (head teacher) at Lyndhurst, amused the audience with demonstrations; to a 'continual roar of laughter', throngs lined up to receive electric shocks from equipment he had brought along. Forrest reportedly was most impressed.[14]

Two weeks later, he gave his first lecture in the colony at the same venue – on 'the state of education in the Pope's dominions'. 'On only a few occasions have we witnessed in this city so numerous and respectable an assemblage of Catholics,' gushed *Freeman's*. There were, indeed, many notables present.[15]

Heading the list was the seventy-year-old 'Archpriest' John Therry, a man whose exploits were already the stuff of legend. For most of the period from his arrival in Sydney in 1820 until 1832, this native of County Cork was the only Catholic priest in the colony. His tireless efforts to minister to a widely scattered, largely convict flock – which grew from around six thousand in 1820 to sixteen thousand in 1833 – made him a much loved figure. He initiated construction of Sydney's first Catholic church, which became St Mary's Cathedral; Governor Macquarie laid the foundation stone in May 1821. His career was replete with conflict with authority, which generally enhanced his reputation, and with fellow churchmen, which reduced it. In his last years, from 1856, he was the venerated parish priest at Balmain.[16]

Slightly junior to his friend Therry was sixty-six-year-old Archdeacon John McEncroe, from County Tipperary. A man of liberal views and moderate temperament, he came to Sydney in 1832 after spending seven years as a missionary priest in the United States. He was a key figure in the early development of the Church and of Catholic education in the colony.[17] McEncroe founded the long-lived (to 1942) Catholic *Freeman's Journal* in 1850, edited it for three and a half years and remained owner until 1857. In a fascinating talk to one of the Young Men's Societies in August 1860, he recalled with sympathy a conversation he had had in 1834 with an Aboriginal man who was an infant when Captain Cook sailed into Botany Bay in 1770. The Aborigine passed on what the old men of the Botany Bay tribe had told him about this first encounter. Their first thought was that the *Endeavour* was a huge bird, and the sailors large possums running up and down trees growing out of the bird. They became less alarmed when they saw that the strange figures were men, but were determined to follow the advice of the tribe's old women not to eat or drink anything offered as it might be poisoned. McEncroe went on:

> They [Captain Cook's men] wanted our people to drink, proceeded the native, but they refused, remembering the caution of the old women. They told them that grog did not injure themselves, and offered our people a tomahawk if they would but drink. They then agreed, provided that the

sailors would drink one half first – very ingenuous and very clever on the part of the poor natives. At length, as the native proceeded to tell, seeing that the drinking of the grog did no injury to the stranger, one of the natives drank the remainder. Immediately he called out 'fire, fire, fire in eyes, fire in nose, fire all over'…and becoming frantic at the idea he plunged into the water. These poor fellows, whose land we now enjoy, and who have disappeared from this country once their own, showed on this occasion a remarkable degree of caution and shrewdness.[18]

Another memorable man at Forrest's talk was the lawyer John Hubert Plunkett. He arrived on the same ship as McEncroe in 1832, at the age of thirty, to take up the post of Solicitor-General. Four years later, he was appointed Attorney-General, a job he held for twenty years. In Ireland, Plunkett had been an associate of the renowned Daniel O'Connell, 'the Liberator', in the agitation that finally achieved Catholic emancipation in 1829. He is said to have regarded Governor Bourke's Church Act of 1836 as his greatest contribution as New South Wales Attorney-General. This gave legal equality to the major Christian denominations, ending the privileged position of the Church of England.[19] Plunkett was an aficionado of Irish folk music, and Forrest moved the vote of thanks at a lecture he gave on the subject, assisted by a group of singers, at St Patrick's, Church Hill, in March 1861. Six months later, on what was probably his first trip to the interior, Forrest occupied the chair at a similar talk by Plunkett in Goulburn. This time, the fifty-nine-year-old lawyer provided the musical interludes, playing his violin.[20]

A younger lawyer who came along to hear Forrest, Edward Butler, will figure prominently later in the story. Born in County Kilkenny in 1823, Butler was active in the nationalist Young Ireland movement – sadly best remembered for a farcical armed rising in County Tipperary in 1848 – before setting out for Sydney in 1853. His major contributions to the cause were as a journalist, and after settling in the colony he employed his writing skills on Henry Parkes's *Empire* newspaper while studying law. He rose rapidly to prominence as a liberal-minded politician and barrister.[21]

On rising to deliver his lecture, *Freeman's* tells us, Forrest was greeted with 'several rounds of rapturous cheering' and applause that 'was again and again renewed'. In lively style, he produced figures to back his contention that education at all levels was much better provided for in Rome and the other parts of Italy still ruled by the Vatican than in England, Scotland and Ireland. He rejected the notion that the Church was, or ever had been, hostile to education: 'the light of faith and the light of knowledge have been kept burning together inseparably, ... twin lights in the same lamp, fed by the same hands, and protected by the same sanctuary.'

And what should education involve? Developing the reasoning faculty, the intellect, was just part of it, because 'reason is but one of the many faculties of the soul'. The 'moral faculties' were as important as the intellectual: 'Truth has splendid attractions for man; but the beautiful and the good take possession of his sentiments and his affections with a peculiar fascination.' As well as religious education – covering the 'ethical and doctrinal elements that lie concealed in the very foundations of European civilization' – the moral side should involve exposure to the 'ideal beauty' of great art. His closing message – 'Catholicism has nothing to fear from enlightenment; ignorance is its greatest enemy' – was greeted with prolonged enthusiastic applause.[22]

2

Out of Ireland

John Forrest was born near Buttevant, northern County Cork, in November 1820, the eldest of seven children of farmer Benjamin Forrest and his wife Sarah (née O'Connor). According to an apparently well-informed account of his life in the *Freeman's Journal*, his education began at a village school; then a Classics tutor in Buttevant prepared him for entry into the highly regarded high school at Bandon, also in County Cork. There, after 'carrying off the highest honours', he was urged to study for the bar at Dublin's Trinity College, his master 'predicting certain success and a brilliant career'.[1]

Instead, Forrest chose to study for the priesthood, and entered St Patrick's College, Maynooth, near Dublin, in August 1839. There, according to *Freeman's*, he won 'all manner of honours and distinctions'; the college records confirm that he was awarded prizes in logic, metaphysics and theology.[2]

His next destination, in 1845, was the Irish College, Rome. This was founded in 1628 to educate priests for Ireland, and following many vicissitudes – including closure by Napoleon in 1798 – was a flourishing institution in the 1840s. Its head from 1832 was the then twenty-nine-year-old Dr Paul Cullen, a priest of extraordinary influence who became Archbishop of Dublin and Ireland's first Cardinal. Although Cullen never visited the Australian colonies, he had a lasting impact on Catholic life there through, particularly, the influence he exercised in Rome on the choice of bishops.

Two of the bishops appointed to dioceses created in New South Wales in the 1860s and '70s – up to then, Polding had held sway over the whole colony – had been Cullen's students at the Irish College. They were Matthew Quinn, Bishop of Bathurst, who arrived in 1866, and Timothy O'Mahony, who took up his post at Armidale in 1871. The first Bishop of Brisbane, James Quinn, installed in 1861, was Matthew Quinn's older brother and another Irish College student. James Murray, Bishop of Maitland from 1866, was a cousin of the Quinns and their contemporary in Rome, although living at a different college. Patrick Moran, Cullen's nephew and another Irish College student, became Archbishop of Sydney in 1884. Earlier he had been Cullen's secretary in Dublin and a confidant of the Quinns and, especially, Murray.

Forrest was a contemporary of all these future bishops in Rome. The Irish College, built around a shaded courtyard off a narrow cobbled street only a few hundred metres from the papal palace, provided an ideal setting to contemplate the history and mysteries of the church. The Basilica of St Agatha, an evocative relic of ancient Rome, was attached to it. Under Cullen, life at the college apparently followed a strictly ordered and ascetic routine. According to the historian T.L. Suttor, with Cullen 'decorum was the keynote, a cold and distant correctness which [John Henry] Newman found such a trial'. One can imagine that Forrest and other students with a less rigid outlook on the world may also have found it trying. Whether or not they did, the careers of Forrest and his contemporaries suggest that they were strongly influenced by Cullen's strict 'Ultramontane' view of the Church's authority, teaching and practice.[3]

Forrest's Roman days ended in August 1847 after he celebrated his first Mass in the Tomb of the Apostle at St Peter's. Shortly before, he had been awarded his Doctorate of Divinity by the Gregorian University and ordained. The twenty-six-year-old was probably sorry to leave; Rome had made a big impression on him. In the Young Men's Society talk he gave soon after arriving in Sydney, he said the Popes, over seventeen centuries, had made the city

> the centre of attraction for men of every clime anxious to satisfy the intense craving of the artist for the realisation of that ideal beauty with which his soul is filled. Freely open to the stranger, and numerous as its fountains, are the collections of the immortal works of the greatest artists the world has seen. With its museums and galleries, its ruins of the past, its unrivalled

structures of later times, the works of Phidias and Praxiteles, rivalled by the genius of Michael Angelo and Canova, the whole city is one vast school of art, its four hundred churches alone exhibiting the choicest specimens of painting, sculpture, and architecture.[4]

The Ireland Forrest returned to could not have presented a more different picture. It was a land of disease, misery and death, in the grip of the potato-blight famine that had begun two years earlier. For about three years, he laboured as a curate in rural County Cork, mostly in parishes not far from his Buttevant birthplace. 'I never cooperated with so hard working and efficient a missionary,' wrote the priest of one of these parishes in a reference supporting Forrest's application in 1851 for the post of Professor of Theology at Maynooth. Another noted that he had 'had every opportunity of witnessing the zeal, piety, energy and perseverance [that Forrest] brought to bear...'[5]

Forrest failed to win the professorship, a disappointment that had at least one positive result: it provided the opportunity for him to win the friendly regard of John Henry Newman. In late 1850, James Quinn, the future Bishop of Brisbane, opened a Catholic high school, St Laurence O'Toole's Seminary, in Dublin and offered his Irish College contemporary, Forrest, a teaching job there. Forrest accepted, and was living in the Georgian mansion that housed the school when, in 1852, Newman also took up residence. The fifty-one-year-old Newman, renowned for his religious writings, had come to Dublin as Rector-elect of the Catholic University of Ireland, which opened in 1854.[6]

Newman led the high church Oxford Movement in

Dr John Forrest.

the Church of England in the 1830s. He converted to Catholicism in 1845, and three years later was ordained a priest in Rome. Cullen, initiator of the Catholic University, offered the rectorship to Newman. The university failed to flourish under his leadership, and he resigned in 1858 and returned to England. He had a chequered career in the Catholic Church, culminating in his elevation to Cardinal by Pope Leo XIII in 1879.

According to one of Newman's biographers, his interactions with the Dubliners in his circle offered 'something of the old fascination – social, spiritual, and intellectual combined – which had enthralled the elite of Oxford in the later thirties...' Newman often entertained groups to dinner; he 'talked especially freely and brilliantly with all these Irish friends, and keenly appreciated the wit and genius of some of them.'[7] Forrest most likely was in the latter category; a letter Newman wrote to the younger man in Sydney in 1862 is a sign of his friendly feelings:

> It rejoices me to hear that you are so happily situated at Sydney... It is my sincere wish and fervent prayer that your efforts may be prospered... It will be a great pleasure to me if you can have half an hour to tell me of yourself, your labours, and your trials and successes...[8]

Newman left St Laurence O'Toole's in October 1854, Forrest probably a little earlier. Matthew Quinn and James Murray had taught there with Forrest, strengthening his ties with these future colonial bishops.[9] Returning to the priestly coalface, he served in three parishes of Cullen's Dublin Archdiocese between 1854 and his departure for Sydney in 1860. He was ambitious for an academic career, and tried four times to win a professorship at Maynooth. After failing to obtain the theology chair in 1851, he stood soon after for professorships in logic and rhetoric. Then in 1857 he was one of four 'most accomplished scholars', according to the centenary history of Maynooth published in 1895, who competed for the again-vacant theology post. 'Rev. Gerald Molloy was the victor,' the book records. 'Those who know the Right Rev. Monsignor Molloy, now Rector of the Catholic University, will not be surprised at this result; and they will also be able to estimate the merits of the men who were able to meet him on no unequal terms...'

Molloy contributed recollections of Forrest to the centenary publication:

> He was a man of brilliant style and manner, and always carried the students with him. He had a great, and, I think, a deserved reputation in Logic and Metaphysics; but was weak in Moral Theology. He had immense elasticity and go, and I always regretted that he had not succeeded in gaining a place on the Maynooth Staff.[10]

The offer of the St John's rectorship came two years later. Whether Forrest viewed the position as second best is not recorded, but there is no sign from his career in New South Wales that – despite many setbacks – he ever regretted embarking on a new life in the colony.

Apparently the 'go' that Molloy saw in him was also a characteristic of his parish work, even though he was keen to leave it behind for academia. The farewell address presented by his parishioners at Kingstown before his departure for Sydney on 3 June 1860 promised that his name would long be revered and cherished there, and added,

> Your zeal in the mission, especially amongst the poor – your distinguished eloquence in the pulpit, added to your kindness and affability of manner, bespoke you the priest, scholar and gentleman.

Responding, a 'deeply affected' Forrest said the illuminated address would remain a 'memento of ties and affections that space cannot sever, and at the same time it will gently remind me not of what I am, but of what I ought to be.' A 'large concourse' accompanied him to the pier, and gave 'three hearty farewell cheers' as the boat pulled out.[11]

Meanwhile, in Sydney, controversy and rancour had replaced much of the initial enthusiasm as St John's College moved from fine idea to reality. The process of establishing the college began in mid-1857 with a stirring pastoral letter from Archbishop Polding. This lauded the 'new Australian world of ours whence all avowed inequality and injustice have been banished' and stressed the Church's commitment to the 'intellectual culture' with which university education would equip the future leaders of society. Polding concluded,

Strive, we entreat you, so to have your sons formed, that, in the noble spirit of Christians, they may have money as though they had it not; that they may look upon power as a sacred responsibility, only to be assumed, without ridicule and mischief, by men who are fortified by every intellectual and moral fitness.[12]

A preliminary fundraising meeting on 24 July 1857, chaired by Polding, brought in £5,500 in cash and promises.[13] Ten days later, Polding presided at a crowded and enthusiastic meeting at St Mary's Cathedral – the venue selected, said the Archbishop, not just because a very large hall was needed but also so 'our proceedings and our purpose may have the visible sanction and blessing of religion'. Speakers included Archdeacon McEncroe, J.H. Plunkett and Dean John Lynch, the missionary priest based at Maitland since 1838 and a consistent supporter of St John's. Also called to the podium was forty-four-year-old Peter Faucett, a prominent lawyer and member of the Legislative Assembly who came to the colony in 1852. He contrasted the civil and religious equality of his adopted land with the anti-Catholicism that still permeated his old university, Trinity College, Dublin. Barrister and politician William Bede Dalley, the twenty-six-year-old colonial-born son of Irish convicts, was the last speaker. His contribution, calling for scholarships that would open the college to the poor as well as the wealthy, displayed the eloquence that was already winning him renown as an orator.

The speech with the biggest impact was delivered by another lawyer, the fifty-seven-year-old Supreme Court Judge Roger Therry, who had migrated from Ireland in 1829, three years before Plunkett and McEncroe. Therry was a founding member of the university Senate. He described the meeting as a momentous event:

> It is the first occasion within the last three hundred years on which we, as Catholics, have met in grateful recognition of the favour and service of a truly parental government in conferring upon us an endowment of a college for the education of our youth in affiliation with an university established on the just basis of civil and religious equality... Truly, this is an occasion of great joy... Our liberty is now secured to us – but if ever

the day arrive when bad men by bad and arbitrary laws shall seek to disturb the religious equality with which our land is now blessed, the best bulwark against such an encroachment will be the college that you have this night met to establish. Knowledge is power, and it is strength, and there is not in the history of the world an instance of an enlightened people being an enslaved people. (Loud cheers.)[14]

Cash takings at this meeting exceeded £5,000 and promises brought the evening's total to nearly £12,000 – an extraordinary result. More soon flowed in from meetings at major country centres – Goulburn, Maitland, Bathurst, Armidale and Moreton Bay (Brisbane). Later in the year, the Bill formally establishing St John's College had an easy passage through parliament. The next step, as required under the legislation, was election of the college's governing Council by those who had subscribed funds, and this is when conflict began.

A meeting was called for 15 January 1858 to choose the Council Fellows – six priests and twelve laymen. Polding presided, but his hopes for the immediate election of a set of candidates who met his approval were dashed. Citing the small numbers present, Richard O'Connor, Clerk of the Legislative Assembly, moved that the election be delayed and a system adopted that would give subscribers throughout the colony a say in the choice. After a long discussion during which, according to *Freeman's*, 'some considerable warmth of feeling was exhibited,' the meeting adopted a proposal by Plunkett to set up a committee to devise a fair voting scheme.[15]

So began an extended period of upheaval in the Catholic community – a revival, with much rancour, of arguments with a long history. One issue was the respective roles of the clergy and laity in running the Church and its institutions. More basic was opposition to Polding's 'dream' that his Benedictine monastery at St Mary's Cathedral should be the centre of Catholic life in the colony, supplying priests to the various missions. There was a widely held view that, as the Catholic population was predominantly Irish or of Irish descent, the appropriate source of priests – and bishops when new dioceses were created – was Ireland. Anti-Benedictine and anti-English resentment found its main

Archbishop Polding.

target in Polding's right-hand man, the Vicar-General Henry Gregory, rather than the Archbishop himself.

Born in Liverpool, England, in 1794, John Bede Polding had joined the Benedictine community at the age of fifteen. After a notable twenty-year career in the monastery and school at Downside, near Bath, he was appointed Catholic Bishop of the Australian colonies in 1834. He arrived in Sydney, accompanied by a priest and five students (one of whom was Gregory), in September 1835.[16]

Polding was a dedicated missioner. He quickly arranged with Governor Bourke to be given charge for a few days of newly arrived Catholic convicts, so they could be instructed in their religious duties and given the sacraments. He was often away from Sydney on pastoral tours through his vast territories; Rev. Brian Maher's history of the Archdiocese of Canberra and Goulburn describes twenty-three visits to the southern districts, and he went north and west as well.[17] The earliest tours were on horseback; the later ones, as roads began to replace bush tracks, in vehicles ranging from gigs to carriages.

He sometimes complained of the discomfort – 'having travelled upwards of 1000 miles, in an open dogcart, under a broiling sun...worn out with labour of mind and of body', he wrote in January 1862[18] – but it is clear from his letters that he relished these breaks from the Sydney grind. Polding was no administrator, relying on the capable Ullathorne until 1840, when he returned to England, and then on Gregory, who was less well equipped for the task. As Ullathorne put it before he left, 'the Bishop is doing vast good as a missioner, and is idolised by the people as he is beloved as well as pitied by his clergy; only God never made him to govern or transact business.'[19]

The build-up to the turmoil that erupted in 1858 extended well back into the 1840s. Non-Benedictine (mainly Irish) clergy started displaying resentment at the preferment given to the Benedictines. Articulate laymen such as William Augustine Duncan, a Scot, and Jabez King Heydon, an Englishman, began objecting to the failure to offer the laity a meaningful role in church affairs. In 1851, Archdeacon McEncroe wrote to Pope Pius IX urging that new dioceses be carved out of Polding's territory and placed under Irish bishops. He argued that only Ireland could supply the priests the colony needed, but Irish priests were reluctant to come to an archdiocese run by English Benedictines.[20]

The rumblings extended to the monastery at St Mary's, to the extent that in early 1854 all but a few of the monks signed a petition to Rome calling for the removal of the unpopular Gregory as their superior. Polding proceeded to write a resignation letter, and then hurriedly departed, with Gregory, for Rome. The resignation was not accepted; evidently, Polding did not intend it to be. Polding's ambitions for the Sydney Benedictines received a setback when Gregory's behaviour at an audience with the Pope apparently convinced Roman officials that the complaints made against him had substance. The Archbishop was unmoved, however; on the pair's return to Sydney in January 1856, he announced that Gregory now had administrative responsibility for the cathedral as well as for the monastery and the archdiocese.[21]

As it appeared little had changed, McEncroe revived his campaign for new dioceses and Irish bishops and priests with a letter, in April 1856, to the influential Archbishop Cullen. He pointed out that, while the number of Catholics in Polding's 'immense mission' had doubled since 1851 (following the gold rushes that began that year), the number of priests was still virtually the same (about thirty-five).[22] Lay agitation intensified through *Freeman's Journal*, which McEncroe sold to J.K. Heydon in February 1857.[23] Beginning in May that year, the erudite W.A. Duncan, formerly a teacher and journalist and now Collector of Customs in Brisbane, submitted a series of pseudonymous letters that deplored the general ignorance of Catholics and their lack of political influence. He thought a college connected to Sydney University offered part of the answer, and so was pleased when Polding gave the go-ahead to St John's.[24]

How to elect the St John's Council was the question to be addressed when Polding convened a well-attended meeting of college subscribers on 25 January 1858, ten days after the abortive first meeting. The Archbishop would not have been pleased by Heydon's combative leader in *Freeman's* two days earlier calling for the selection of '*independent*' [his italics] men 'who, while they know their religion, and practise it, appreciate also their rights as citizens, and understand fully the relative positions of the clergy and laity in respect to each other'. Heydon also made the important point that subscribers had only one chance to choose the right people because the Council would elect the replacements for departing Fellows.[25]

The meeting passed peacefully enough, accepting with one minor change the election plan proposed by the committee appointed at the first meeting. This involved holding gatherings of subscribers at centres throughout the colony and aggregating the votes collected. It was when the local meetings began that feathers started to fly. One of the first was held at Parramatta; Richard O'Connor reported on what had happened there to the meeting at St Benedict's, Broadway, four days later. He said the Benedictine priest in charge, Bede Sumner, after announcing that Gregory had provided a letter recommending certain names for election, 'called upon the people to stand by their Archbishop, as there was a clique against him in Sydney, and to vote for the persons of his choice...' O'Connor heatedly denied that there was any such clique. To great applause, according to *Freeman's*, he added,

> Now that Dr Gregory has been so audacious as to attempt to crush down our throats his own nominees…it is our duty to vote tonight for those only who have been proscribed by Dr Gregory.[26]

The election process seems to have been something of a shambles. The committee that oversaw it reported to another meeting at St Mary's Seminary at the beginning of March that returns had come in from only seventeen out of forty-two districts, and seven of those had not been prepared properly. So it was back to the drawing board. Plunkett's proposal that the Archbishop be asked to convene a new meeting to elect the Fellows was carried by acclamation.[27]

This time, Polding was slow to act; the election was finally held on 16 June. In the meantime, tensions rose to new heights as the administration of the archdiocese came under sustained criticism in letters to *Freeman's*. McEncroe was caught in the middle – blamed by Polding for allowing the attacks to appear despite the fact that he no longer controlled the paper, and criticised by *Freeman's* for his appeals to editor Heydon to stop the onslaught.

Duncan, using the pseudonym Isidore, set the ball rolling with a long letter calling for the establishment of a Catholic lay association to cooperate with bishops and clergy in attracting priests and religious orders to the colonies and raising the Australian Church 'from the state of prostration in which it now lies'. Polding and Gregory were greatly displeased, apparently more with Heydon for publishing it than with the author, whose identity they did not know yet. 'For this, and for other delinquencies of a like nature, we have been deemed to have forfeited all title to be considered the "Catholic organ" for New South Wales,' Heydon told his readers the following week, 'and have been told to our face that "The *Freeman's Journal* must be put down".'[28]

A writer using the pseudonym Fidelior sprang to the defence of the hierarchy in the next issue: 'Far…from deploring the prostrate condition of our Church in the colony, I think we have reason to rejoice at the exalted position that she and her pastors command.' McEncroe also stepped into the debate. He said he had been charged with countenancing, at least indirectly, the Isidore letter and other criticisms of the hierarchy published in *Freeman's*. He denied this, reiterating that Heydon now controlled the paper. McEncroe said he was 'resolved to uphold and support the *Freeman's Journal*, until the Catholics of New South Wales can get another paper better deserving of their countenance and support.' But he urged Heydon not to publish any more letters or articles that 'may be fairly considered injurious to Catholic interests, or offensive to our ecclesiastical superiors'.[29]

Heydon did not take his counsel and the correspondence, pro as well as anti the Benedictine administration, continued with growing heat over the next two months. Richard O'Connor was one of Duncan's strongest supporters; he also had harsh words for McEncroe for urging Heydon not to publish the views of correspondents who 'express the wishes of the major part of the laity'.[30]

The controversy was not confined to the newspaper. In mid-May, *Freeman's* reported that a meeting had been called at the Sacred Heart church, Darlinghurst, to adopt resolutions declaring utmost satisfaction with the current ecclesiastical administration and condemning the paper. At least five hundred people turned up, but the result was not that intended. Instead, the crowd yelled 'no, no, we are not!' when asked whether they were prepared to accept the suppression of *Freeman's*. When the speaker suggested Catholics could not do without the paper, 'a scene of the most intense enthusiasm ensued; hearty cheers for the *Freeman's Journal* being renewed again and again for several minutes'. In the next issue, a letter writer reported on a meeting at St Benedict's at which Catholics were urged to 'put down' *Freeman's*. One speaker said he never read the paper, but 'as he had heard that something had appeared in it against the priest [the Benedictine Rev. Mellitus Corish], he could assure the meeting that if the writer were in Ireland there would soon be nothing left of him, but his feathers for the crows to pick'. The correspondent described the tone of the meeting as 'decidedly intolerant' and thought intimidation had prevented the intelligent portion of the audience from speaking up.[31]

Having fostered the agitation for two months, Heydon declared in a *Freeman's* leader towards the end of May that he contemplated 'the present state of things' with more pain than pleasure. He believed, though, that 'this present excitement is not only preferable to our previous lethargy and torpor, but is actually a necessary step between that death-like stillness and a new life'. He was in no mood for conciliation, claiming that the Benedictines in their current state 'stand as a wall between Catholicity and the country'.[32]

The focus now switched back to St John's and the Council election set down for 16 June. The college was a blessing that their fathers dared not dream of, Heydon wrote in the first of three pre-election leaders: 'this day, in an enlightened age, in a happy land, we are again emerging into day...' The second leader advised the election of fellows who 'to other fitness will join an independent mind, a resolute will, an unflinching firmness'. The third carried the argument further:[33]

> We have a large amount of available intelligence in the Catholic body – we have abundance of quick, shrewd, penetrating minds; and, what is not of less importance, independent ones. We have those to whom the vital question will be, not the views of this or that individual, but the interests of the college...

The same issue of *Freeman's* published, in smaller type and with cuts, a pastoral letter from the Archbishop on the St John's election. Polding's message was that voters should follow ecclesiastical advice:

> Confidence has been disturbed, where it ought to have rested, namely, in your Archbishop and Clergy, and that which should have been looked at only in the light of a responsibility has been thought of, and talked about, like the mere subject matter of vulgar party elections. Indeed, it is an affair of far other importance than the poor temporal interests and honours that form the objects of political schemes and strife. It is a matter of religion and conscience... And is it not the dictate of common sense, that your best advisers in such a business are your Archbishop and Clergy? When you listen to the voice of conscience and sound judgement in your own breasts, do you really find grounds for placing so deep a confidence in any as in them?... We exhort and warn you, then, Dearly Beloved, to proceed in this election as a matter of religious duty...[34]

Very large numbers of subscribers turned up for the Wednesday evening election in the St Mary's Seminary hall. Polding presided and, reported *Freeman's*, the proceedings, to select eighteen Fellows from fifty candidates, were conducted in a most becoming manner. 'The adherents of some of the aspirants to the dignity of Fellow evinced considerable ardour in their support, whilst the subscribers could be heard in all directions canvassing with the liveliest interest the relative claims of the various persons put forward; in fact, a rather excited anxiety was apparent in all, yet everything passed off in the best possible spirit of harmony and good-will.' The *Sydney Morning Herald* noted that, 'owing to the crowded state of the room, a good deal of crushing took place' as voters forced their way in batches to deposit their voting papers in the box provided. The voting took an hour and a half, and counting was not completed until 1 o'clock in the morning.[35]

The result pleased Heydon. It should satisfy the Catholic body, he editorialised in *Freeman's*, and 'speaks of approbation in the course we have pursued in our journalistic career.' O'Connor also was pleased, seeing the outcome as 'pregnant of hope for the future'. Whether Polding was pleased is not recorded, but the election was certainly not an overwhelming victory for his critics. While McEncroe and Archpriest Therry topped the list of clergy chosen, three of the other four were Benedictines. One was Gregory, the others Rev. Felix Sheridan from Sacred Heart church and Rev. Corish from St Benedict's. The sixth priest elected was Rev. Jerome Keating, a nephew of McEncroe. Heading the list of lay fellows were the lawyers Plunkett, Therry, Faucett and Butler. Heydon was elected, as were two other prominent critics of the Benedictines, O'Connor and schoolteacher Randal Macdonnell. Providing some balance was Thomas Makinson, a former Anglican minister who was now Polding's secretary. The other four lay fellows were lawyer William Curtis, a Sydney University graduate of 1856, the first year degrees were awarded, and businessmen Andrew Lenehan, J.V. Gorman and W.M. Davis.[36]

Within days, the Council met to elect a temporary Rector for the college. A Benedictine won the position, Dean Maurus O'Connell, the first Australian-born Catholic priest, who was ordained in 1848. He was selected ahead of Dean Lynch of Maitland and, by a narrow margin, Father Norbert Woolfrey, the English Cistercian priest in charge of St Charles' church, Waverley.

The process of finding a permanent Rector began soon afterwards. First, a letter was drafted to the Pope advising him of the college's establishment and of the Council's desire to appoint a man of eminent learning as Rector. Probably at the urging of Revs Therry and McEncroe, the letter noted that it would be most pleasing if a Jesuit Father could undertake the task and requested the Holy See's assistance in pursuing that goal.[37] Therry had long wanted to see the Jesuits established in Australia, and left most of his substantial estate to the order. McEncroe also admired the Jesuits; his will provided funds for a professorship of logic and theology at St John's and expressed the wish that a Jesuit be appointed. As etiquette demanded, Polding sent the letter to Cardinal Barnabo, Prefect of the Vatican's Congregation of Propaganda Fide (in English 'Propagation of the Faith', but commonly referred to simply as 'Propaganda'), with a request that he present it to the Pope 'in the manner which may be most acceptable'.[38]

Polding also signed the letter (chapter 1) sent about the same time – early July 1858 – to the eminent ecclesiastics Wiseman, Ullathorne, Cullen and Newman asking them to jointly select a suitable priest as Rector. This, too, expressed a preference for a Jesuit, noting that if one could be prevailed upon to accept the office his appointment would be welcomed 'with great delight'. It advised that McEncroe would soon proceed to England as the Council's 'accredited agent', his role 'not… to share the responsibility of the selection, but to give such information and assistance as may be desired'.[39]

The sixty-four-year-old Archdeacon, no doubt wearied by the Sydney excitements, departed in November 1858 and reached Rome early the following January.[40] Days before he left, the St John's Fellows prepared a letter setting out what was expected of him. They assumed he would wait on Cardinal Wiseman in London as soon as possible to see if a Rector had already been chosen. In the likely event that nothing had happened, he was to do everything he could to facilitate correspondence between the four ecclesiastics. They went on,

> As these gentlemen are already sufficiently acquainted…with the literary and educational standing which the Council would desire their Rector to possess, they will expect from you only that you afford to his Eminence and his colleagues the advantage of your experience of our social conditions as amongst ourselves and in relation to our fellow colonists of the other denominations so that their choice may fall, if possible, upon a gentleman who, in addition to the highest educational attainments, may also by his personal bearing and accomplishments be able to sustain with dignity and grace the prominent position he will be called upon to occupy on public and social occasions in this colony.[41]

McEncroe was also to make it known that the Council would not hesitate, if necessary, to supplement the £500 a year salary provided by the government – an offer that would have caused wry amusement to any Council member (or St John's Rector) who thumbed through the old minutes in later years.

As expected, McEncroe found nothing had been done towards choosing a Rector. His inquiries in Rome about obtaining a Jesuit proved fruitless. Replying in April 1859 to the letter from the St John's Fellows, the Pope advised, 'We have notified the General of the Society [of Jesus] that it is Our wish that he should

Archdeacon McEncroe.

send some of his Religious to your City. The General, however, though anxious to comply with Our wish with all speed, was regretfully compelled to state that at present it is impossible for him to send members of his Society there, since in fact he has none to whom he could commit this office.'[42]

McEncroe left for England in February, visited Wiseman in London and travelled to Birmingham where he consulted Ullathorne, a friend since his Sydney days, and Newman. Wiseman held out the prospect of securing 'an Oxford man of high literary standing' who was currently a professor at Dublin's Catholic University to serve as Rector until the Jesuits could provide a suitable man. After this idea fell through, McEncroe advised Polding that a former professor at the Irish seminary Carlow College 'whom your Grace once wished to go to Sydney', Rev. Dr Kane, would probably accept the rectorship. Presumably he also declined because the search continued, culminating in Forrest's acceptance of the post in August 1859.[43]

It seems that Archbishop Patrick Leahy of Cashel, the ecclesiastical province in which Forrest worked as a curate during the famine years, recommended him. McEncroe was returning to old haunts when he visited the Archbishop at Thurles, County Tipperary; he was born not far from the Rock of Cashel, ancient seat of the Kings of Munster, which is about twenty kilometres south of the cathedral town. Leahy's role in Forrest's selection comes to light in an exchange of letters between McEncroe and Leahy in 1867. 'As you directed me to find a Rector for St John's I hope you may know of some good and well educated Priest as V-Rector of that College,' McEncroe wrote, adding that he was setting up a permanent endowment to support the vice-rector's position. Leahy replied that he would be most happy to suggest a fit person.

Both letters contain friendly mentions of Forrest. McEncroe says he told the Rector 'you expect a subscription from him towards the expense of improvements in your Cathedral' (this was the present Romanesque cathedral at Thurles, which Leahy initiated and his successor, Thomas Croke, a friend of Forrest's from his Irish College days, consecrated in 1879). Leahy's reply begins by thanking McEncroe for having conveyed his message to Forrest; it does not reveal whether a subscription eventuated.[44]

Not surprisingly, then, it was McEncroe rather than the eminent ecclesiastics who found a rector for St John's. The clerics were happy to endorse the choice. Wiseman and Ullathorne wrote that they did not know Forrest, but were impressed by the testimonials from Cullen and Newman. Cullen described Forrest as 'an excellent theologian, a good philosopher and well versed in classics and science. He is also a ready and able preacher, and a zealous and edifying ecclesiastic. …I am convinced that Dr Forrest will discharge with zeal and energy the duties of any office that he may accept, and that he will be unceasing in his exertions to promote the interests of science and literature, and to hallow them by making them subservient to the great end of man's creation.' Newman was just as glowing in his praise:

> I have the pleasure of knowing Dr Forrest personally, and though I have no experience of his literary and scientific attainments, yet I have seen and heard enough of him to be able to speak confidently about him, though not, I am sure, to the full extent of his merits. I should consider that he was an energetic man, allowing himself no rest when he had an object in view, and very zealous in doing his duty to the utmost. I am informed, and have every reason for believing, that he is a good logician, both from turn of mind and from reading. I know also that he has devoted his attention to literature in the wide sense of the word, and knowing the vigour of his mind, such diligent attention cannot have been without proportionate results. From the interest I have taken in him ever since I knew him, it will please me much to hear that he has been put in charge with work so important as that to which the duties of your University will call him.[45]

Forrest signed an agreement with McEncroe on 1 September 1859,[46] and before the end of the year set off on a continental tour, visiting Rome and inspecting universities and colleges in France and Belgium to help prepare himself for his new job.[47] His sister Maryanne, who had been at a convent in Belgium, joined him in Paris, anxious, according to a newspaper account,[48] 'to share the hardships of the long journey to far-off Australia'. News of Forrest's appointment preceded his arrival in Sydney by nearly ten months; his final departure from Ireland was delayed by the need to sort out family affairs 'disarranged' by the death of an uncle as well as by his European travels.[49] *Freeman's* was pleased with the choice: 'He is a gentleman of rare learning, *and a thorough Irishman* [the paper's italics],' reported its Dublin correspondent.[50]

3

Sorting things out in Sydney

As well as a Rector, St John's College needed a building on its eighteen acres within the university site at Grose Farm, three kilometres from the city. Still imbued with the grand hopes for the project expressed at its launch, the Council determined that nothing but the best would do. In February 1859, it commissioned the London-born William Wilkinson Wardell, architect of many churches in England in the 1840s and '50s, to produce a suitable design.[1]

Wardell had worked for, and was strongly influenced by, Augustus Welby Pugin, famed for his 'gothic revival' architecture and artefacts. Like Pugin, he was a convert to Catholicism, and after migrating to Melbourne in 1858 he became the architect of choice for grand Catholic buildings. Polding was moved to remark in 1868 after the bills started coming in for the present St Mary's Cathedral, Sydney, 'Wardell, though a good, is a most expensive architect; so much so that a proverb goes: if you want to be ruined put yourself in W's hands.'[2]

As well as St Mary's, on which work began in 1866, Wardell designed St Patrick's Cathedral, Melbourne. He received the commission for that project in September 1858, and in March 1859, a month after being awarded the St John's contract, was appointed chief architect for the Victorian government.[3] So he was a very busy man when he drew up general plans – which were accepted by the St John's Council in September 1859 and by the university Senate a month later – for two of the proposed three wings of a grand gothic-revival sandstone building. Only twenty-five students' rooms were included, but the chapel, dining hall, library, lecture rooms and apartments for the Rector, Vice-Rector and professors were on the scale required for the completed building,

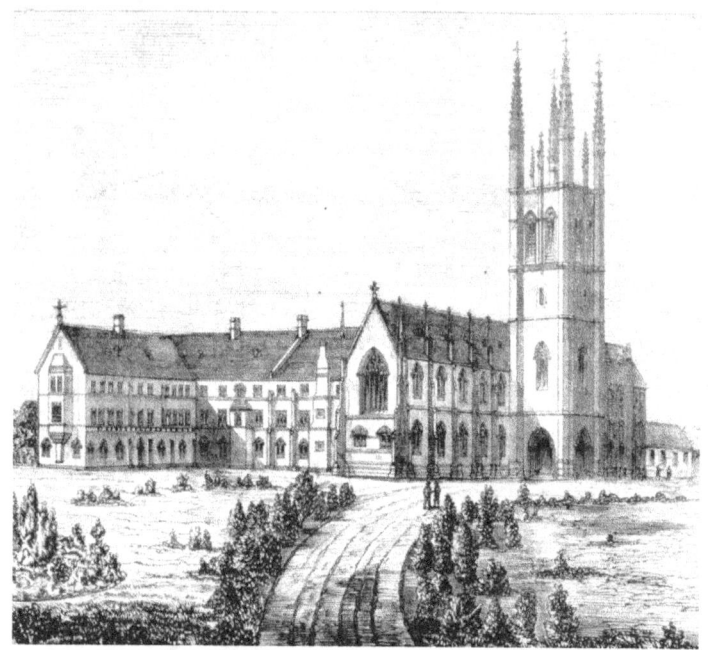

A sketch of St John's College as originally envisaged by the architect Wardell.

with a third wing providing much more student accommodation. Among other imposing features were the entrance hall, stone stairway and, especially, the tower.[4]

Plans were made quickly for a ceremonial foundation stone laying by Polding on 27 December 1859, but before this could take place the Council's relations with Wardell started to sour. The Fellows registered their concern when the architect advised in October that his Victorian government work was cutting into the time he had available for the project.[5] In early December, with time running out to prepare for the ceremony, they despatched a telegram demanding that he come to Sydney at once:

> Archbishop requires outline of building on ground and certain foundations laid or he will not perform ceremony – you must do this – we won't – if your engagement with Victorian government prevents your proper attention to our work it will be a breach of engagement with us…[6]

Disputes followed over payments and delays in supplying working plans for the building's construction. Then, in June 1860, the Council demanded that Wardell explain 'serious defects' that the clerk of works had found in the plans – including 'the apparent want of sufficient light in the vestibule' and inadequate provision of water closets in the building. A month later, it accepted Wardell's resignation.[7]

Edmund Blacket, architect of the main university building, was quickly invited to take over, and happy to accept. He had designed the first college on campus, the Anglican St Paul's, the first stage of which was ready for occupation two years after its foundation stone was laid in January 1856.[8] The Council instructed Blacket to generally adhere to Wardell's design; any changes made should be with 'a view to diminish the expense of the proposed structure and not in any way to increase it'.[9]

By this stage, finding the necessary funds had become a major concern. The original appeal produced cash and promises totalling £22,805.[10] If all the money promised had been delivered, the maximum government contribution of £20,000 would also have been available, giving the Council a very healthy sum to spend. However, the amount actually paid up by October 1860 was only £14,907[11] – so, with the matching government grant, a sum of just under £30,000 was available. This was well below the projected cost of Wardell's design, and even after Blacket made cuts that saved an estimated £1,689 – including substitution of Australian hardwood for Pitch Pine and omission of a fountain – the funding challenge remained large. The tender accepted from builders Young and Williams at the end of 1860 was for £35,754, so thousands of pounds remained to be raised before payment became due.[12]

The Council had other matters to deal with in its first years. A special meeting in May 1859 considered the style of dress to be worn by the Fellows, and concluded that a black hood lined with purple would be appropriate, together with a cap 'according to the pattern now produced by Mr Plunkett'.[13] In July 1859, attention turned to a key question that seems to have been largely ignored up to then: where were students to come from?

The university had hardly got off to a flying start. Between its opening in 1852 and 1860 only one hundred and nine young men (women were not admitted until 1881) qualified for entry by matriculating, and between 1856, when the first degrees were awarded, and 1860 only thirty-three earned their Bachelor degrees.[14] In 1859, just one student was in residence at the newly opened St Paul's College.[15] In September that year, a select committee of the Legislative Assembly chaired by Terence Aubrey Murray, an Irish-born landowner with broad intellectual interests, began an inquiry into the state of the university. Reporting in June 1860, the committee said it seemed clear that the university had not yet realised the expectations of the public, and great mistakes had been made – in particular 'a large amount of unnecessary expenditure' on grandiose buildings. The establishment of affiliated colleges was a 'grievous mistake', Murray and his colleagues added, violating the intended 'strictly secular' nature of the university. State support for them constituted a useless, and injurious, expenditure of public money.[16]

No action was taken to end the government funding. It is hardly surprising, however, that concern was growing that St John's might attract few students and prove a pale shadow of the institution promised to subscribers. J.K. Heydon addressed the issue in *Freeman's* in March 1860.[17] It was 'absolutely impossible' for the existing Catholic education system to provide 'a score' of students for the college, he wrote.

> St John's College will be useless – or rather worse, an expensive toy – unless we prepare feeders for it… *We MUST have Catholic Grammar Schools, conducted by skilled and competent teachers*, all over the country…

Peter Faucett may have had similar ideas in mind when he moved at the July 1859 meeting of the St John's Council that a committee be formed to inquire into the state of the principal Catholic schools and suggest how the Council might help secure 'the highest attainments in Catholic candidates for admission to St John's College and the University'. This idea was rejected, perhaps because the Fellows expected Polding would be offended by the Council taking on such a task and by the implication that they might have something useful to say about how Lyndhurst was run. Instead, the Council decided to seek advice from the Archbishop, as the college's official Visitor, on the best means of obtaining students.[18]

After a meeting with six of the Fellows, who included Abbot Gregory and one of his chief critics, Richard O'Connor, Polding wrote the Council a long letter. He began by insisting that the Council's only role was to govern the college; it should not seek to involve itself in broader educational questions. Then he rejected the idea that setting up secondary schools around the country would produce more students for St John's. In fact, more potential candidates were already emerging (presumably from Lyndhurst) than the Council credited: 'Some time ago five were ready to matriculate, and by next Xmas five or six again will be ready; but an obstacle existed and still exists to their proceeding. Our St John's College does not yet live practically. I cannot in conscience send our young men to the lectures of non-Catholic professors unattended by a Catholic tutor.' Polding probably had the recent turmoil in the Church on his mind as he explained his belief that increasing these numbers – with St John's there to provide the necessary religious framework – could only be a gradual process:

> When the homes of our young men shall have been somewhat changed in point of cultivation, when the social condition of our whole community, Catholic and Protestant, shall be somewhat different, so that money alone, and vulgar effrontery of statement and invective, as you must often, gentlemen, have observed them with grief, shall less influence our public assemblies; and when, on the other hand, honour and power, if not profit, shall attend the men of solid, accurate, refined, laborious intellect, then our Universities will be valued, and our families will send to them the flower of their sons. I am convinced that we can but favour this natural growth; we cannot, gentlemen, force it.[19]

Polding reiterated his expectation that it would take time to fill the college when he laid the foundation stone on 3 January 1860 (a week after the originally intended date). The 'noble building we propose to erect will...be capacious beyond the arithmetically estimated needs of the present hour,' he said. But this would be beneficial; the 'greatness of the provision' would 'speak eloquently of its object', and help create a desire for the 'treasures of intellectual wealth and accomplishment' offered by university education.

Nearly two thousand people attended the ceremony, despite 'thick, drizzling' rain. The Governor, Sir William Denison, was there to offer his best wishes for the college's success. With due ceremonial, Polding blessed the foundation stone and sprinkled it with holy water. Then a colourful procession formed comprising: master of ceremonies; bearer of the archiepiscopal cross supported by acolytes carrying candles in glass lanterns; acolytes bearing censer and incense; two cantors; clergy in cassocks and surplices and wearing birettas; the college Fellows in academic costume; two assistant priests; and the Archbishop with four train bearers. A choir chanted psalms as they slowly made a circuit of the future building, sprinkling holy water on the soil.[20]

As 1860 began, the sixty-five-year-old Polding had reason to hope the turmoil that had afflicted the Church over the past few years was at last subsiding. It had risen to new heights over the previous eighteen months, fanned by a series of extraordinary events. In June 1858 Polding, in company with his fellow bishops Robert Willson of Hobart and James Goold of Melbourne, issued a 'pastoral admonition' vehemently attacking *Freeman's* and the laity who used it to publicly discuss matters that, in their view, belonged to church authorities. They condemned the 'insolent and most foul liberty' that saw laymen 'commit to public print what each one may think concerning faith, discipline, authority and ecclesiastical individuals'.

> For men of little wisdom invade the citadel of Zion, and corrupt the fountains of wholesome knowledge, for the destruction of the Christian community. They have become execrable in their undertakings… Following in the footsteps of Luther and other authors of heresy… These roaring lions, in their audaciousness, usurp every thing to themselves; every thing must be examined; every thing must be weighed by minds, perhaps, but lightly imbued with Catholic truth and discipline; and nothing at all reserved for Episcopal authority and loving obedience of the faithful and confiding soul…[21]

John Hubert Plunkett.

Shortly afterwards, apparently as a conciliatory gesture, Polding invited the laity to submit their suggestions to him through Archpriest Therry. A meeting selected seven prominent men – St John's Council members Plunkett, Butler, Heydon, O'Connor, Davis and Macdonnell plus lawyer James Hart (who joined the Council in March 1859) – to draft a statement. This invited Polding to head a lay organisation that could assist in matters including obtaining clergy, the introduction of religious orders to the colony and the establishment of new dioceses. The Archbishop dismissed the proposals; Butler later complained that the 'respectable deputation' had been 'repelled with deliberate insult and rudeness'.[22]

In a move that presumably he hoped would provide support for his stand, Polding then called his clergy to a conference at Campbelltown on 31 August. Thirty-eight priests turned up – and backed the establishment of new dioceses and lay participation in Church government. An isolated Polding forwarded the recommendations to Rome without comment.[23]

The next major excitement came in February 1859, when Heydon heard that Gregory had proposed the appointment of a Protestant, Dr Bassett, to the board of the Catholic Orphan School at Parramatta, to replace Plunkett who had resigned twelve months earlier. *Freeman's* broke the news in its 23 February edition – under the headline 'Treason'. Appointing a Protestant was 'treason against Holy Church and the lambs of her flock!' the paper fumed. '…we are an army with a general watching every opportunity to betray us to our enemies…'[24]

Three days later, a public meeting at the Victoria Theatre – attended by nine hundred people according to *Freeman's*, although others claimed the number was much smaller – adopted a set of fighting resolutions.[25] One proposed the appointment of a 'provisional committee' that would take on the task of nominating candidates for vacancies on the boards of government-supported Catholic institutions – such as the Orphan School – 'until the ecclesiastical administration of Catholic affairs be committed to dignitaries of the Church in whom the Catholic community can have confidence'. Another called for the transmission to Rome of 'a concise account of the progressive mismanagement on the part of our ecclesiastical authorities…'

Those present included six St John's College Fellows – Heydon, O'Connor, Faucett, Butler, Davis and Macdonnell – and James Hart, who was about to join the Council. Not all supported the resolutions. Faucett thought they went much too far, and proposed that the meeting just note its deep regret at Gregory's conduct in recommending Dr Bassett's appointment. Butler wanted ecclesiastical maladministration condemned, and claimed 'the authorities at St Mary's had repelled the laity until they stood isolated from their confidence and the relations that would otherwise have existed and grown strong between them'. Nevertheless, he was against the idea of the proposed provisional committee.

The thirty-year-old lawyer, politician, writer and orator Daniel Henry Deniehy delivered the speech that ensured the resolutions were carried with little dissent. 'Brilliant Dan Deniehy', the man who coined the phrase 'bunyip aristocracy' to help sink W.C. Wentworth's proposal for a hereditary upper house in New South Wales, did not spare Polding in his much-cheered performance. One word from the Archbishop would have stopped the 'grave scandal' of Bassett's nomination, Deniehy said. 'If His Grace chose to abdicate his governing functions' in favour of Gregory and 'content himself with a titular position', that did not relieve him of responsibility.

Having adopted the resolutions, the meeting elected six men to the provisional committee – Deniehy, O'Connor, Macdonnell, parliamentary librarian W. McEvilly, solicitor W. Reynolds, and the French consul, Louis de Sentis. Copies of the resolutions were sent to Polding and the head of the colonial government, Charles Cowper. The Archbishop wasted no time in responding. Letters, signed by

Gregory, were dispatched on 2 March threatening the six committee members and Heydon with excommunication unless they renounced the Victoria Theatre proceedings within eight days. To ensure that what was happening was widely known, Gregory had the letters published as advertisements in the *Sydney Morning Herald*.

All but Deniehy quickly complied, but under protest, and an appeal to Rome was organised. In *Freeman's*, Heydon claimed that the Archbishop, by an improper use of his spiritual powers, had deprived the seven of their civil rights; at no time had they intended to interfere in any purely ecclesiastical matter.

> We have yielded, but…it has been only for a time – only as though while in company with a madman we humoured his follies for fear of his madness; or as though, when awakened by a thief in the night, we should be compelled to write him a cheque on our banker…[26]

The appeal, signed by all except Deniehy and Sentis, claimed Polding and Gregory had misunderstood the Victoria Theatre resolutions – unintentionally, they hoped. It criticised the 'indiscreet and capricious behaviour' of Gregory, 'believed to have been for the last 20 years the main cause of the stagnation in our religious and educational institutions and discontent in the minds of our people'. The appellants noted that Polding had sent them private letters displaying 'a strain of paternal affection, for which we would be more grateful if they had not been preceded by a vituperative address levelled against ourselves' to be read from pulpits. They also noted that O'Connor had now been appointed, on Gregory's recommendation, to the position that was to be filled by the Protestant Dr Bassett, and Deniehy had 'received publicly from the Archbishop the highest possible mark of respect, and has delivered, under ecclesiastical patronage, a lecture to the Catholic Young Men's Society'.[27]

Polding also immediately wrote to Rome. He had a simple explanation for the origin of the turmoil – 'hatred harboured by some against my Vicar General, who sometimes has had of necessity to uphold ecclesiastical discipline'. 'That,' he told Cardinal Barnabo of Propaganda, 'is the hub of the mystery.'[28] More letters followed, in which the Archbishop displayed little charity for any of the miscreants except Deniehy. 'We have the testimony of a priest that he has made satisfaction verbally even more fully than all the others have,' he wrote. 'He was disgusted at his confreres, and abandoned the clique, and for this they wish now to denigrate him.'[29]

Polding's attacks on the five who signed the appeal, in letters to Barnabo in April and May 1859, sought to show that, as well as being of dubious character, they occupied posts of little standing. O'Connor, Clerk of the Legislative Assembly, was just 'one of the secretaries' working there. He had been a 'deplorable drunkard', and after an attack of delirium tremens had 'left his family and a dying infant to assist at a public banquet'. Subject to bouts of vanity and excessive pride, he had openly confessed that 'the true object that he and his dupes have in mind is to take over the management of Church revenues'. Parliamentary Librarian McEvilly was, 'it is true, in charge of the books, but he no more resembles what is called in Europe a librarian than a Swiss Guard resembles the dean of a Cathedral. He was once a convict.' Heydon had made his money as a pawnbroker [in fact, it was probably his role as agent for the cure-all Holloway's Pills that made him financially secure.][30] 'He is at present Editor of the *Freeman's Journal* and that is to say enough.' The lawyer Reynolds was 'a small-time advocate with little reputation or public standing'. Macdonnell called himself 'Master of the High School' in Paddington – 'The truth is, he himself has given this grandiose title to a certain little boarding school.' He was a 'man of savage temper and unrestrained bearing'.

In case anyone in Rome should be impressed by the fact that three of the five were Fellows of St John's College, Polding explained, 'when the College began, it was necessary to choose by public nomination any man who could win over the votes of the crowd. At this time, this title has absolutely nothing in common either in meaning or in reputation with the title Socius Collegii [Fellow of the College] used in Europe.' Summing up, the Archbishop advised Barnabo that the appellants were men of 'coarse and brutal sentiments'. Therefore, in responding to the appeal, it would be wise for the authorities in Rome to carefully avoid 'the mild expressions by which the Church usually tempers, in its forbearance, the severity of its censures'. Any expressions that were not strongly condemnatory were liable to be turned 'to their own profit – even to their own praise'.

Barnabo's response, which reached Sydney in September, disappointed Polding. The appeal had been examined and found to have not followed correct canonical procedure. The appellants appeared, however, to be good Catholics, and there would be no obstacle to their making a just appeal, in canonical form, at any time.[31] As the Archbishop had foreshadowed, O'Connor and his colleagues took this as implicit recognition of the strength of their case. Polding complained that the weak response had left them 'confirmed in malice'.[32]

For Polding, the crises just kept coming. May brought an extraordinary episode at St Vincent's Hospital, Darlinghurst, run since its establishment three years earlier by the Irish Sisters of Charity. The hospital catered for Catholics and Protestants alike, but during his rounds one day the Catholic chaplain, Father Kenyon, removed a Protestant Bible and prayer book from one of the wards. The hospital's superior, Sister de Lacy, and a recently appointed Protestant surgeon, Dr Robertson, protested. Apparently with Polding's authorisation, the books were soon restored.

The sequel – including the resignations of de Lacy and Robertson and attacks on the Church's handling of the affair by prominent laymen including Plunkett and Butler – seems to have been wildly out of proportion to the event that sparked it. The Sisters of Charity had come to the colony in 1838, and a history of difficult relations with Gregory may partly explain the uproar. Polding viewed what had happened as 'one of the most convincing instances of the folly of lay persons, however good [he was referring to Plunkett], mixing in Church matters'.[33]

Shortly afterwards, Polding was confronted with a scandal at St Mary's monastery. News broke that one of the monks, a Frenchman, Jean Gourbeillon, had been receiving a female visitor who entered via a window. An overheard cough betrayed what was going on. 'O horrible! horrible!' wrote Polding to the Bishop-elect of Adelaide, Patrick Geoghegan. 'To palliate his own guilt he has told... infamous things about his brother priests... I have reason to know that he has been one of the principal suppliers to the [Freeman's] Journal of the calumnies against the Vicar General.'[34]

News from Rome in the second half of 1859 and early 1860 compounded the Archbishop's trials. With the establishment of new dioceses under active consideration, in late 1858 he first proposed Gregory as bishop of Moreton Bay, and then an English Benedictine, Norbert Sweeney, for that post and Gregory as Bishop of Maitland.[35] Instead, the July mail brought news that James Quinn, protégé of Archbishop Cullen, had been appointed Bishop of Brisbane. So an Irishman would lead the Church in the new colony of Queensland, separated from New South Wales in 1859; Rome had supported McEncroe's argument, not Polding's. And what about Gregory? Polding wrote to Barnabo expressing sorrow that his Vicar-General had not been raised to episcopal dignity and seemed unlikely to be in the near future. The Cardinal's reply may not have brought much comfort:

> I should like you to bear in mind that the election of Bishops depends entirely on the will and discretion of our Most Holy Father and, in matters of the gravest import, he is often influenced by the wisdom of his own mind and by the light of God's grace with which he must be held to be illumined in such a way that there is nothing for us to do but to follow and revere his commands...[36]

Much more upsetting news arrived the following March in a letter from Bishop Ullathorne: Rome had decided that, to restore peace in Sydney, Gregory must leave. Ullathorne was well informed about events in the colony – from recent discussions with McEncroe and Bishop Goold of Melbourne as well as letters from Australia – and had advised the Roman authorities on the matter. Cullen may also have had a hand in the decision.[37]

Writing to Barnabo, Polding did not attempt to hide his 'inexpressible sorrow'. For twenty-five years, Gregory had 'led a most pure life as a priest, a most saintly life; as Vicar General he has been blameless, and successful. But he has had the misfortune to provoke the hostility of a certain clique, as has also his Archbishop…' Gregory's recall would have 'disastrous' consequences; the faction would appear to have triumphed. 'They naturally persuade themselves that they have…caused the deepest humiliation to the ecclesiastical authority… They have heard that this authority was not consulted, and no matter what may be the motive of the Holy See, those who judge by externals find, in the actual fact of Fr Gregory's departure, a flagrant disgrace for the local authority.'[38]

The news of Gregory's recall reached Sydney about three weeks after McEncroe returned from his travels.[39] Many friends greeted him at the wharf, but his reunion with the Archbishop must have been strained. Before and during his absence, Polding had criticised his alleged complicity in the *Freeman's* controversies in letters to Barnabo, Cullen and others. One letter to Barnabo revealed Polding's fear that McEncroe might be made a bishop; he claimed no Australian bishop 'would wish to assist at his consecration – unless forced to do so by an express order'.[40] Now he had another major ground for complaint – McEncroe's supposed support for Gregory's removal. He told Ullathorne, 'I have not heard a single person except McEncroe who does not deplore the retirement of Dr Gregory as a grievous misfortune.'[41] Not surprisingly, McEncroe was not welcomed back to his old quarters at St Mary's; Polding transferred him to St Patrick's, Church Hill, and wrote a year later, 'I see very little of McEncroe now.'[42]

For his part, McEncroe apparently had been distressed by the news he received from Sydney during his travels. In an echo of his earlier attempts to persuade Heydon to exercise more discretion in what he published in *Freeman's*, he wrote to the editor from Ireland in October 1859 urging, 'in the name of goodness do all you can to reconcile matters in Sydney'.[43] He was then at Kingstown, near Dublin – most likely for talks with Forrest. He probably briefed the St John's Rector-elect on some of the personalities and issues he would encounter in Sydney.

The newly returned McEncroe may have influenced the tone of a *Freeman's* leader at the end of March 1860. This looked forward to a renewal of peace in the local Church – 'a peace based on true zeal in the cause of religion and the union of priests and people'. Heydon went so far as to acknowledge past errors, although without much conviction:

> We sometimes allowed feeling to be exhibited in the correspondence columns of our paper. This was wrong. We should have obliged our correspondents to keep to facts, or direct reasoning, and not allow them to impute improper motives or use harsh expressions, particularly in reference to ecclesiastics. For the slight dereliction of duty – of which we publicly accuse ourselves – we are sincerely sorry.[44]

Two months later, he announced that his proffered olive branch had been 'scornfully' spurned and he was leaving *Freeman's* – 'solely for the sake of peace'. For two years 'there has been no toleration exhibited towards us,' Heydon wrote. 'We have been denounced; the sacrifice of our journal has been proclaimed as a necessary expiation to appease the dignity we had offended.' A letter from McEncroe in the next issue offered no sympathy. He said he had advised Heydon 'against inserting any letters or articles of a personal, irritating or uncharitable tendency; and it would have been well for the interest of the *Journal*, as well as for the peace of the Catholic community, that this advice had been followed'.[45]

The new editor and part-proprietor, William Dolman, was another Englishman. Polding was very pleased, reporting to Barnabo that 'the bad tool of a semi-Protestant proprietor and its editor who is an Apostate – I mean the *Freeman's Journal* – has passed into hands truly Catholic, and in future we shall be able to look forward to seeing our affairs reported to the people in a suitable manner'.[46] His joy was short-lived; in March 1863, he told Gregory that *Freeman's* was becoming an ever more wretched rag, pandering 'to the lowest prejudices of a mere Irish Mob… I have threatened Dolman not to take it, and unless it alters, I will not.'[47]

More than ten months passed between the arrival in Sydney of news of Gregory's recall and his departure on 5 February 1861. Hoping for a change of mind, Polding first announced, in April 1860, that his Vicar-General was to spend a year in Europe on archdiocesan business. Public acknowledgment that he would not be returning finally came in December.[48] 'This separation must wound the sensitive heart of the venerated prelate, and inflict a wound that time cannot heal upon the heart of the Right Rev. Abbot,' observed the new *Freeman's*. 'Whatever difference of opinion exists upon the wisdom of some of his official acts, there is none upon his motives – his sincerity – his earnest piety – his stainless honour.' Forrest joined more than thirty other priests, including McEncroe, at a farewell gathering at St Mary's on the morning of Gregory's departure. Reported *Freeman's*, 'We can confidently state that no one ever left the shores of New South Wales with such an ovation.'[49]

4

Progress

By September 1860, when Forrest and his sister stepped ashore in Sydney, at least a semblance of normality had returned to relations between the Archbishop, clergy, and prominent laymen. The departure of Heydon from *Freeman's* was a major calming influence, and the impending return to England of Gregory, though a sad blow to Polding, meant the main target of complaints against the ecclesiastical administration would soon be gone.

Prospects for good relations between Polding and the St John's College Council were also improving with changes in its membership; he would have been pleased to see the resignations of Heydon and Macdonnell (the schoolmaster of 'savage temper and unrestrained bearing').[1] W.A. Duncan, now Collector of Customs in Sydney, was one of the new Fellows. His letters to *Freeman's* had started the commotion leading up to the Council election in June 1858, but he later offered some sort of apology to Polding. The Archbishop wrote to him in March 1859 saying his approach had brought consolation. To err was human, and much honour abounded in acknowledging 'in deference to lawful authority that a wrong step has been taken'; there was no hint of acknowledgment that his own intransigent approach might have been part of the problem.[2]

At meetings in the last months of 1860, the Fellows finalised plans, with Forrest, to bring the college into operation in temporary accommodation at the beginning of 1861. They rented (for £190 a year) a house in Newtown Road near the university, and agreed that up to £200 should be spent on furnishing the reception room, dining room and kitchen with items that could be taken to the new building.

One domestic servant was to be hired to look after the Rector, students and visitors.³

The Council accepted an ambitious program of studies proposed by Forrest in philosophy, modern history and Catholic doctrine. Also, tuition was to be provided to help students with their university studies in mathematics, classics, French and German, and instruction would be available in English language and literature and two languages not taught at the university, Spanish and Italian. The devotional program would involve morning and evening prayer, instruction, and regular celebration of Mass.⁴

Advertisements announcing the opening of St John's College and inviting parents to enrol their student sons appeared in the press from early January 1861:

ST. JOHN'S COLLEGE IN AFFILIATION WITH SYDNEY UNIVERSITY

> The Council of St. John's College have rented a large house close by the University Buildings, to serve the double purpose of temporary College and residence for the Rector.
>
> The College of St. John will be commenced immediately, and finished within two years. In the mean time, the advantage of an University Education, with protection for the faith and morals of the students, are provided in the temporary College under the Rector's superintendence. As the College is for the benefit of Catholic people, the expenses shall be as moderate as may be compatible with the comfort and suitable maintenance of the students.
>
> The next Session of the University commences early in February, 1861. Parents and guardians of those students who intend to matriculate in the coming Session, and to begin their University studies in St. John's College, will please to communicate with the Very Rev. John Forrest, D.D., Rector of St. John's College, Sydney.⁵

Later advertisements provided more information. The annual payment – the 'pension' – required per student would be £50. 'For this each student will be furnished with board, a separate room, and the assistance of a tutor in preparing for the University Lectures in addition to the special collegiate course.'⁶

Forrest sent a circular, addressed to the clergy and laity, to major centres around the colony to explain the role of the college and assist recruitment. St John's would provide 'a suitable residence' for Catholic students in which their religious education would be attended to and 'their morals protected from the corruption and vice inseparable from a large city'. Through 'regularity, discipline and tuition', the college would help students with their university studies. And it would provide lectures in subjects involving Catholic principles – such as modern history, metaphysics and ethics – that 'cannot be safely entrusted to any teachers except men of undoubted orthodoxy'. The circular offered encouragement to those who might feel daunted by the prospect of university study: 'An extensive school course, and some ambition and ordinary industry, will enable an intelligent youth to go through his University Studies with success and with honour.'[7]

As the start of the university year drew near, the college advertisements began to betray anxiety at the lack of response to date. 'Parents and Guardians will please to communicate immediately with the Rector, as the University Session commences on the 12th FEBRUARY', *Freeman's* readers were advised on 9 February. The first day of term came and went with no enrolments. Shortly afterwards – no doubt to the huge relief of Forrest and the Council – eighteen-year-old Patrick Joseph Healy signed in. Healy, who was starting the second year of his BA studies, came from Maitland. Perhaps the Maitland-based Dean Lynch, long an advocate and fundraiser for the college, encouraged him to enrol. Some weeks later, William Charles Browne, a first-year student from Singleton – also within Lynch's territory – entered the college.[8]

Dean John Lynch.

With interest so sparse, the Council decided in May 1861 to ease admission requirements. Only students who had matriculated or were about to do so could be formally enrolled in the college. But under the new rules young men could be admitted earlier as 'temporary' residents to prepare for the matriculation exam if the Rector thought that, with tuition, they had a reasonable chance of success. Within days of the Council's decision, the third and last student of 1861, Andrew Browne, entered the college on that basis. The Act establishing St John's made no provision for this additional role, and protests were lodged with the university Senate. After lengthy negotiations, the arrangement received the go-ahead in February 1862. A similar scheme was introduced at St Paul's – also short of students – two years later.[9]

Archbishop Polding was taking a keen interest in what the Rector and Fellows were up to. In January 1861, two weeks before Gregory's departure, he wrote a long letter to Bishop Goold of Melbourne – mainly on the injustice of the abbot's recall and the difficulty of judging, in the present 'selfish' age, whom to trust. Of Forrest, he observed, 'I must say I am most agreeably disappointed. He is not the man the O'Connors and Heydons expected – a flash Cleric. Far from this, his manners are most homely.' Forrest 'thinks well and will uphold Ecclesiastical authority', Polding added.[10]

The question of ecclesiastical authority over St John's seems to have been much on his mind. Having failed to control the election of the college Council, he now sought to ensure that he would have the last word on the rules governing its operations. St John's was a Catholic institution established at his direction and so, on the face of it, his desire seems reasonable. On the other hand, as a college affiliated with the University of Sydney, it had to be sanctioned by legislation. The Bill incorporating the college, enacted without objection from the Archbishop, stated clearly that the power to make, alter or revoke by-laws and rules governing 'all things in and connected with the College and the discipline thereof' rested with the Council.[11]

Polding wrote to Cardinal Barnabo in Rome in February 1861 asking whether, 'according to canon law or customs approved by the Church', such by-laws and rules required the approval of the Archbishop, as Visitor to the college, before taking effect.¹² In a letter written the next day, he asked the just-departed Gregory to try to ascertain the powers of the Visitor to the Catholic University, Dublin.¹³ Whether Gregory discovered anything helpful is unknown, but the response from Barnabo pleased Polding; the word from Rome, he told Gregory in July, was that no laws made by the St John's Council were valid until approved by the Visitor.¹⁴

Polding conveyed this news to the Council in August 1861 in a letter to Forrest. He said that, because it had always seemed obvious to him that approval of the college's laws and rules fell within the Visitor's functions,

> I have felt some surprise at not having been called upon by the Council itself to fulfil the duty. Supposing however that the propriety and obligation of what seemed to me the natural course might not appear so distinct as they did to myself, I preferred to be silent until I should have consulted the Holy See and obtained its explicit direction. The answer which I have now received affirms positively, as I expected, the obligation of submitting all By-Laws and Rules to the Visitor in the first instance, and expresses surprise that I should have thought it necessary to propose a query on the subject.¹⁵

The Fellows considered Polding's letter at their September meeting and rejected his demand. They adopted a resolution saying the powers at issue were clearly derived from the Act 'and it is the duty of the Council not to allow room for any doubt on the matter'. Provocatively, they noted that Polding had given the legislation his 'fullest consideration and total approval' before it was presented to parliament. They would concede only that

> although the right of the Council is so clearly evident, nevertheless, wishing the same Council to obtain the cordial co-operation of His Grace in the important duty in which they are involved, they are disposed and have always been disposed, to pay honour to His Grace's dignity in so far as it is consonant with their duty under the Act of Incorporation, and they will always deem themselves fortunate in having received his advice in everything that bears upon the interests, moral and religious, of the College.¹⁶

Polding's reply, in a letter to Forrest, was a mildly worded, but firm, rejection of the resolution. 'It is my conviction that it is essential to the true idea of a Catholic College that in the final analysis the Archbishop would be superior in everything that relates to [it]', he wrote. He and the Council had a single aim, and the Fellows' contribution – which involved putting 'their time, their experience and their social status' at his disposal – was greatly appreciated. He could not understand how any Catholic prelate, in such circumstances, could 'do other than…refrain from lightly making his own individual judgements in opposition to theirs'. But he could also 'in no manner understand how [the prelate] could renounce under any pretext whatever his final supremacy…'[17]

Another early sign that relations between Polding and the St John's Council would remain strained – and that his opinion of Forrest might be changing for the worse – came in March 1861 when Dean Lynch was elected to the vacancy caused by Gregory's departure. Polding objected to the failure to consult him, noted in a letter to Gregory that Forrest's casting vote had secured the outcome, and told Lynch that if he wanted to remain a St John's Fellow he would have to leave Maitland, where he had been based for twenty-two years. Lynch protested, but chose to resign from the Council.[18]

At the end of April, Bishop James Quinn of Brisbane, the first of the Irishmen appointed against Polding's wishes to dioceses carved from his territory, arrived in Sydney en route to his new posting. Polding presided at a High Mass at St Mary's to celebrate his arrival, which had been delayed by a smallpox scare requiring a month's stay at Melbourne's quarantine station.[19] Three of the six priests in Quinn's party – 'a queer lot…four French, one Irish, and one Italian!' Polding told Gregory – reached Sydney before the bishop. Apparently, Polding felt insulted by the informal manner of their arrival. 'Without any letter to me and making first for Dr Forrest, the Irish and two of the

Bishop James Quinn.

French came on Saturday last,' he wrote, adding that he did not know when Quinn was coming.[20] In a minor way, this was perhaps a foretaste of later events that Polding interpreted as intriguing by the Irish bishops and Forrest, their friend from Irish College days, against him.

On 24 May, in his capacity as Rector of St John's, Forrest attended the Queen's Birthday Levee hosted by the Governor, the newly arrived Sir John Young; apparently he was the only Catholic priest to do so. Polding had decreed a boycott because, acting on orders from London, the Governor had told him the Anglican bishop would have precedence over him in the proceedings.[21] Whether Forrest's attendance annoyed Polding is not recorded, but his non-appearance at St Mary's on 29 June, the feast of St Peter and St Paul and twenty-seventh anniversary of the Archbishop's consecration as bishop, certainly did. 'He never comes near me,' Polding complained to Gregory. 'He did not pay his respects on SS Peter and Paul, and of course I did not ask him to dinner with the Clergy.' Elsewhere in the letter, Polding said he and his secretary, Thomas Makinson (a St John's Council member), thought Forrest 'finds the duties above his stretch and will not be sorry to have a pretext for resigning'.[22] On the basis of such incidents and scuttlebutt, Polding's opinion of Forrest may have already changed to the extent that he hoped this would happen. It seems a pity that he did not make the effort to initiate a dialogue with the Rector.

There is no other indication that Forrest was having second thoughts about the wisdom of his decision to leave Ireland to take up the St John's post. He wrote what must have been a cheerful letter to John Henry Newman in May 1861 asking for his help in implementing a Council decision to appoint, if possible, a 'distinguished graduate of Oxford' as college lecturer in classics and mathematics – at a salary of £300 plus board. Newman did not reply until July 1862. 'You must have thought I had forgotten you and your wishes,' he wrote. 'This is anything but the case. I have continually thought of you.' The problem he had encountered in finding someone for the job was that the salary offered was too low. Newman went on, 'It rejoices me to hear that you are so happily situated at Sydney. There is a peculiar satisfaction in belonging to a young country, and to be laying the foundations of great institutions. It is my sincere wish and fervent prayer that your efforts may be prospered...'[23]

Forrest continued to contribute to, as well as enjoy, the life of Sydney. In February 1861, he was on the platform for a St Benedict's Young Men's Society lecture by Caroline Chisholm in favour of early closing of shops (6 p.m. instead of 10 p.m.). A week later he was the lecturer – the subject, 'progress'.[24] Distinguished figures present included J.H. Plunkett, Peter Faucett and Dr Kevin Izod O'Doherty, a Young Ireland nationalist exiled to Tasmania in 1849 who, following his pardon in 1854, completed his medical studies in Dublin and then, in 1860, migrated to Australia. O'Doherty had become friendly with James Quinn in Dublin[25] and in 1862 followed the bishop to Queensland where he remained a staunch supporter of the controversial prelate.

Freeman's published Forrest's talk in full – five and a half packed columns of type. Perhaps carried away by the occasion, the reporter observed, 'The absorbing attention with which the audience received this learned, eloquent and argumentative discourse could not be surpassed by any assembly in the world.'

Every century, if not every generation, was characterised by some dominant idea, Forrest began, and currently it was 'progress'. This embraced industry and science – fleets of merchant vessels sailing the seas, cities lit up at night, 'gigantic machinery of Titanic power', messages flashed by telegraph from one hemisphere to the other. 'Far be from me to undervalue the triumphs of genius, the discoveries of the age... I enjoy them as you do,' he said.

> But...this progress, great as it is, is over-estimated as an element of human advancement, and by a false judgment of this age it is usurping the place of a higher and nobler progress – the progress of morality and virtue. For with all our boasted enlightenment and progress, is it not a melancholy truth that in this age wealth is more prized than virtue? Man's higher nature, his nobler faculties, are neglected...

True progress, Forrest said, 'must embrace all the faculties of man', ennobling the intellect and expanding the heart. 'This is the secret of education, which is the commencement…of all human progress.' He spoke of the importance of art to civilisation: 'Love of the beautiful – deep, lasting and enthusiastic – is incompatible with a love of vice.' A nation lacking in virtue was ready-made for slavery: 'The less men govern themselves, the greater the necessity for external coercion.'

He peppered his talk with light touches. For example, the Church, while in favour of industry and material progress, had good reason not to become involved in commerce and manufacturing: 'It is as unjust to expect the Church to take human industry under its care as to expect the College of Surgeons to elaborate a new set of quadrilles. It is not her business.'

He ended with a rousing exhortation to his young Catholic listeners:

> Your country calls upon you to be ready to discharge the duties of true citizens; you have a noble mission. You have inherited a land rich in everything that makes a nation great and powerful. You have free institutions, freedom of education, of religion, civil rights, and perfect equality with your fellow citizens; guard them faithfully, jealously; your own rights are best secured by respecting and protecting the rights of others. Be true to your principles, of truth, justice and integrity; be moral men practising the virtues of the Christian, following the maxims of the Gospel, and the honour and liberties of your country will be safe in your keeping, and the flag which you bear in the future, the standard of progress, will deservedly bear the cheering inscription ADVANCE AUSTRALIA.

St Patrick's Day, 17 March, fell on a Sunday in 1861, and at McEncroe's invitation Forrest delivered the sermon for the occasion – on 'the Life and Virtues of the glorious Apostle of Ireland' – at St Patrick's church.[26] The following evening he, along with 'most of our leading citizens' according to *Freeman's*, was at Sydney's St Patrick's Day dinner. Terence Aubrey Murray, Speaker of the Legislative Assembly, took the chair, and Forrest, the only priest named in the paper as having attended, said grace before the banquet began.

As usual on such occasions, there were many speeches and toasts. Murray, who had left Ireland at the age of sixteen in 1826, proposed the toast to the 'Fatherland' in an emotional speech contrasting ancient times when Ireland 'was foremost among civilized nations' with its present unfortunate state. Dr O'Doherty responded, regretting that the 'brotherhood and kindly feeling' that existed in the colony between the English and Irish still seemed far off 'at home'. His sympathy for 'the national existence of Ireland' was as strong as ever, he said, and he could not conceive why this should be incompatible with good feelings between the two peoples. He went on, 'To us there are no hills so grand as the hills of old Ireland – no rivers so bright, no valleys so green; we worship her ruined shrines, her dismantled castles, and fondly linger over the romantic history of the past embodied in them…' Daniel Deniehy was among the many other speakers (part of his contribution 'unfortunately was inaudible from the popping of the corks from the champagne,' *Freeman's* reported).[27]

Forrest had school examining duties in late June, before the mid-year break, at Lyndhurst and St Mary's Seminary; according to *Freeman's*, he was impressed by the students' achievements.[28] In late July, he delivered another lecture on 'progress', this time under the auspices of the Young Men's Society at Sacred Heart church, Darlinghurst. The hall reportedly was 'completely crowded in every part', and Forrest was warmly applauded as he spoke and 'most enthusiastically cheered' at the end.[29]

It was a powerful talk – one can imagine it provoking a strong response. Baldly stated, his message was that the immense power that the rapid progress of science and industry was placing in human hands would lead to ruin – unless there was corresponding moral progress. Looking back from 2004, his view from 1861 seems remarkably prescient. The following extracts give the flavour of the talk, but cannot do it full justice.

> …unless some strange and unforeseen obstacle be interposed – and there is no reason to think there will be – the progress of science, and the knowledge of the laws and forces of the material world, will increase man's power to such an extent that in a few years he will employ motive power and machinery so vast, so gigantic, that the mechanical wonders of our time, which astonish even those who called them into existence, must appear as little better than the toys of children.

...the progressive increase of the forces which man can employ baffles all the calculations of sober thought, and even the powers of the wildest imagination. The future of science, invention, discovery cannot be contemplated seriously without grave apprehension; for in the midst of the accumulated forces of nature which the genius of man is destined to combine, man himself becomes helpless and insignificant...

And when [man] shall have multiplied a thousandfold his conquests, and combined the irresistible forces of nature to an extent that imagination cannot picture, what if he should become the enemy of his kind and convert the vast and varied elements under his control into engines of destruction? Do not mistake my meaning. I do not say that science is of necessity a fatal weapon, and material progress and the discovery of the secrets of nature an evil or an advance to ruin – far from it. Science is noble – it is good – it is from heaven, from the Father of Lights – it is His gift to his children; but it is a power, and who will deny it is a formidable one? Formidable even now in its infancy; but in the future when matured and augmented to an extent we may conjecture without realising, when children will smile at our ignorance, when the impossible of our times will be the actual and the ordinary, when the secrets of Nature mysteriously concealed from us shall be revealed to our children, when men shall see, and know, and touch, what is not even conjectured as possible by the philosophers of this time – how formidable is it not destined to become? A formidable power – for good or for evil, for man or against him, according to the use or abuse of human liberty.

Bad and wicked and perverse men have ruled the destinies of mankind as long as we can follow them by the light of authentic history. Are the rulers and the nations of the future more likely to act otherwise? What is Babylon – butchered in the dead of night, in the midst of its drunken debauch? What are revolutions – accomplished in a few hours – dynasties of a thousand years crushed in a day and swept away forever? What are these facts of history to the possible catastrophes of the future, when the spirit of destruction shall seize upon the irresistible powers of Nature to exterminate, perhaps, an entire nation by the agency of a few civilized men? There is nothing extravagant in such anticipations.

I maintain then, without hesitation, that the material progress of our day menaces civilization, and is destined to be fatal without the protection to be found in the moral progress of nations... A man without any idea of moral obligation – without a sense of duty, obedience, respect for the rights of others – without love of his kind, or fear of an overruling Providence

– without virtue or religion – is a formidable barbarian when armed with the inventions of civilization. The simple savage is but a child compared with him...

...virtue, conscience, religion are alone capable of protecting society, and preventing a gigantic material progress, the triumph and glory of our age, from becoming the scourge of mankind, and plunging the world into an abyss of barbarism.

5
A bright start

Freeman's loved Sydney's summers. In 1861–62, the weather was hot and dry, but with a balminess 'sufficient…to temper the genial warmth of the sun'. How fortunate the colonists were, blessed with 'the beautiful – we might almost say the unparalleled – climate enjoyed by this land, throughout which Nature has scattered her choicest gifts with such boundless profusion.' And they showed no lack of appreciation, enjoying the summer 'with an éclat almost unprecedented in the annals of holiday-making'.

The biggest excitement this summer was the first tour by an All-England cricket team; 'to witness the interest which their play excites, one would imagine that cricket, and cricket only, was the be-all and the end-all of our sublunary existence'. The tour started in Melbourne, and arrangements were made to allow Sydneysiders to follow the game there. Reported *Freeman's*,

> the eagerness with which the telegrams from Melbourne, which are stuck up outside the *Herald* office and Tattersall's for the information of the public, giving an account of the state of the game at intervals throughout the day, [are read] reminds one of the memorable occasion when all the newspaper offices in London… were besieged by expectant crowds anxious to know the issue of the pugilistic contest between the respective champions of Old England and Young America.[1]

The Australians were no match for England, captained by H.H. Stephenson, so New South Wales was allowed to field twenty-two players against England's eleven in their four-day game at the end of January. Sydney suspended business for the entire week 'in order to keep carnival', *Freeman's* reported. Tens of thousands watched as the wickets

A harbour regatta, January 1865.

tumbled – England made 241 in its two innings and New South Wales 192. The local team did better in its second innings than its first, but only one player contributed a two-figure score (15) to the total of 127, and five of the twenty-two made ducks. Reporting the last day's play, *Freeman's* commented, 'The magnificent fielding of the Eleven attracted universal admiration throughout the day, and at the conclusion of the game they were loudly cheered by the immense crowd – not less certainly than 25,000 persons – who had assembled to witness one of the most exciting spectacles ever presented to the people of this colony.'[2]

The university year started a week after the end of the cricket with the matriculation exam on 11 February. Back from spending part of his vacation in Melbourne, Forrest would have been pleased with enrolments – two continuing students (Healy and William Browne) and six new ones, five of whom were in the last year of their BA.[3] Those five were non-residents, attending the college lectures but living at Lyndhurst.

Forrest's trip south came at an interesting time. Dr John Barry, principal of the Melbourne boarding school St Patrick's College, fled the colony in disgrace on Christmas Day 1861 following a financial scandal. Polding reported to Gregory, 'A report goes about that Dr Forrest… has offered to take charge of [the college]. I do not think the Bishop would accept his services.'[4] If for no other reason than that St Patrick's was mired in debt, this sounds as unlikely as the earlier rumour that he would already welcome a pretext to resign from St John's.

The enrolment at St John's of students who lived at Lyndhurst may have been an outcome of major changes that were occurring at the school. Through nearly all of Forrest's time as Rector, Lyndhurst offered itself as an alternative residence, and source of instruction, for undergraduates who had completed their secondary studies there; these students had no involvement with St John's. This severely inhibited the capacity of St John's to obtain enough students to cover costs and to develop a collegiate spirit. *Freeman's* readers had a rare glimpse of the competition at the end of March 1861, less than two months after the college opened. A paragraph noted 'with satisfaction' that St John's student Patrick Healy had won a university prize. In the next issue, the following letter appeared.[5]

> In your last issue you express the pleasure you felt in seeing the name of Patrick Healy, a Student of St John's College, among those who were distinguished at the University Commemoration. Of course sir, you are in your private capacity at liberty to be pleased at what you like. It was a source of pleasure to more than you, that the Student of St John's took a prize. But, surely as a Catholic Journalist, you might just have mentioned that another Catholic young gentleman, Mr Joseph Meillon, of St Mary's, Lyndhurst, took first class in two subjects. No doubt there will be some in the community who, being glad at Healy's success in one subject, will be doubly glad of Meillon's in two. There is one at least who is very glad, and he is
> A LYNDHURST BOY.

The secondary school established by Polding at Glebe – within walking distance of the university – could not have taken on this additional role without the Archbishop's concurrence, if not blessing. So, for whatever reason – his objection to the make-up of the Council or to Forrest, or his lack of control over the college – he contributed to making it very difficult for St John's to succeed. There is one glimpse in his correspondence of temporary reservations about the extra role Lyndhurst had assumed. Writing to Gregory in September 1863, he referred to a first-year university student, Edmund Fitzgerald, who did not want to transfer from Lyndhurst to St John's: 'It is a nice feeling, still we must persuade him to go there.'[6] Fitzgerald remained at Lyndhurst.

The school's own struggle to keep numbers at an economically viable level may have been another reason why it allowed its students to stay on when they proceeded to university. Since its opening in 1852, Lyndhurst had catered only for boarders and provided only a 'classical education' aimed at those with aspirations for higher studies. The seminary at St Mary's Cathedral had catered for day students; its star pupil was the brilliant lawyer and politician William Bede Dalley, who was called to the bar in 1856.[7]

Lyndhurst had prospered in its early years, but Polding told Gregory in June 1861 that student numbers had fallen to twenty-nine, 'we are running fast into debt', and 'we must take day scholars or shut up'.[8] So in August 1861 St Mary's Seminary closed – to be replaced by a 'model school' to train primary school teachers – and Lyndhurst opened its doors to day students. It also began offering an alternative educational program for pupils intending to undertake 'commercial pursuits'.[9] The changes were immediately – but, as it proved, only temporarily – successful. By May 1862, enrolments had risen to about forty boarders and thirty day boys.[10]

In the meantime, healthy student numbers were producing bustling activity in the temporary St John's. And on the opposite side of the university grounds the grand new college building was rapidly taking shape. Work started, under the architect Edmund Blacket's supervision, in February 1861, and the foundations were completed around the middle of the year. By early September 1861, reported the *Empire*, the walls had reached a height of about twenty feet.[11]

They are of massive construction; and although the buildings are very extensive, and the workmanship of a very elaborate character, all parts appear to be proceeding simultaneously. This result is facilitated by means of powerful cranes, which traverse the building by means of a railway carried on a strong framework, about thirty feet high, from end to end of the works. With all of this machinery the heaviest blocks of stone are lifted into their places with almost as much ease as if they were no larger than bricks, and wall, buttress, arch, and clustered column are growing as if by enchantment… Young men interested in mechanics, and desirous of seeing how the latest adaptations of machinery are capable of superseding the slow and cumbersome system of manual labour hitherto, almost exclusively, in use in the building trade, will be well repaid by a visit to St John's College at Grose Farm.

The St John's Council had brought the 'very disagreeable matter' of the departure of the college's original architect, William Wardell, to a conclusion three months earlier with a £450 termination payment.[12] Another lingering issue was settled in November 1861 – how much Forrest should be paid for the period between his agreement with McEncroe in September 1859 and taking up the job a year later. Apparently, McEncroe had overstepped instructions in agreeing that the Rector should receive his £500 a year salary from the day of the agreement. On the other hand, McEncroe had expected Forrest to leave for Sydney many months sooner than he did. The compromise reached, deducting about four months' pay, seems to have left no hard feelings between the two men.[13]

Outside the college, Forrest was in demand as a school examiner again at the end of 1861, at Catholic primary schools as well as Lyndhurst. At the reorganised Lyndhurst, he again shared the duty with Professors Woolley and Pell, and had kind things to say about the students' progress and the skill of their teachers.[14] In February 1862, he was one of many priests who took part in the solemn consecration of St Benedict's church by Polding – the first time this elaborate ritual, which included the placing of holy relics in the altar, had been performed in the colony. Bishop Quinn – in Sydney for a synod of bishops that Rome had instructed Polding to call – sang High Mass at the end of the ceremony.[15]

Quinn's seven-week stay in Sydney did nothing to improve his relations with Polding. Only one other bishop, Patrick Geoghegan from Adelaide, turned up for the synod, and he was three weeks late because of problems with coastal steamers. Bishops Goold of Melbourne and Willson of Hobart chose not to come – Goold because of fallout from the Barry scandal and Willson 'on account of the heat and his health', Polding told Gregory. Of Quinn, Polding wrote, 'With me he is disappointed.'[16]

That seems to have been an understatement. Quinn reported to Cullen that he, Polding and Geoghegan had agreed that, because the other bishops were absent, they should merely nominate topics for a full synod in Melbourne at the end of the year and set out their views on these. They would meet twice a day until business was completed. Instead, wrote Quinn, they had met only four times in four weeks; meetings had been 'adjourned and deferred on the most frivolous pretexts'. After the last meeting, held an hour before he left for Brisbane, Polding had bade him 'a most affectionate farewell – told me I should accept his little carriage or his buggy as a present.' Quinn implied that he saw this as an attempt to persuade him to endorse Polding's recommendation of Rev. Austin Sheehy, who had replaced Gregory as Vicar-General, and Geoghegan for appointment as bishops of two proposed new dioceses. Having withheld his endorsement, 'I have never heard of the buggy since,' Quinn told Cullen.[17]

Quinn was present, but not called on to speak, at a meeting in early March 1862, chaired by Polding, to raise funds for the debt-burdened and still incomplete St Mary's Cathedral. Speakers included McEncroe, Dean Lynch and Richard O'Connor. Some pointed to the success of the appeal for St John's College in 1857 as an example that Catholics should now emulate in the cause of St Mary's. Forrest seconded one of the resolutions moved at the meeting, and donated a very generous £50. The meeting was not a success: 'The number of persons present was not near so large as we should have anticipated,' said *Freeman's*. Takings on the night and up to August 1862 totalled just under £2,000.[18]

In July, Forrest gave a lecture on the Cowper government's proposal, then before parliament, to phase out payments in support of the colony's clergy.[19] Governor Bourke's Church Act, which established the principle of equal recognition for the major denominations, introduced this 'State aid' in 1836. The official Catholic view was strongly in favour of its continuation, but some prominent laymen – one was Edward Butler – thought it should be abolished.

The tack Forrest took in his talk at a St Patrick's Young Men's Society meeting, chaired by McEncroe, should have pleased Polding – although some of his arguments read like debating points designed to entertain his young audience rather than serious contributions to the discussion. He said the cost of the aid – 1 shilling and 7 pence per head of population – was trifling compared with the benefits derived from the inculcation by clergy of the various denominations 'of the duties of morality and the fear of a judgment to come'. Withdrawal of the payments would greatly reduce this activity because priests would have to spend much of their valuable time 'in going about to collect dues'. The consequences could be dire, for clergy as well as those they ministered to. Such a mode of living 'dried up the finest springs of human nature,' *Freeman's* reported him saying,

> and in many instances compelled the priest to take from the poor what he knew they could not afford to give, but which his own necessities compelled him to accept. Another evil was that it engendered sordid habits; and customs grew upon a man so that what was originally a necessity became at last a pleasure, and he who was naturally generous and liberal grew by the practice of such a system avaricious and hard hearted. [This] contrasts unfavourably with a system which provides him with a decent permanent endowment, and does not compel him to seek for a dinner when he ought to be attending to his duties, hearing confessions, or writing his sermon.

Forrest noted also that 'some of the laity were generous, some stingy, some large-hearted, some close-fisted'. Under a voluntary system, a priest 'would be compelled to meet the whims of every one, and re-echo their political sentiments in order to make a living for himself'. His arguments, and those put by Polding and, among others, J.H. Plunkett and the *Freeman's Journal*,[20] failed to carry the day and State aid for clergy was phased out from 1863.

Much else outside the college was occupying Forrest's time. Shortly after his State aid talk he gave 'a most eloquent and impressive sermon' at Mount Carmel church, Waterloo, to help raise funds to improve the church grounds. A week later, he attended a St Benedict's Young Men's Society talk at which the Governor had planned, but was unable, to preside. Forrest's distinguished company on the platform included the Governor's wife, Lady Young; the Premier, Charles Cowper; and Caroline Chisholm, who had recently opened a school for girls in Newtown. The speaker was Terence Aubrey Murray, and the subject 'Tombs and Tumuli and the Tales They Tell'.[21]

In August and October, he was one of the priests who assisted the Archbishop in ceremonies connected with the entry of future nuns into the Convent of the Good Shepherd in the city.[22] October also brought a trip across the harbour to preach at the Catholic church at St Leonards; Forrest's presence attracted a large congregation, *Freeman's* reported, helping raise funds to pay off the church's debt. A month later he was back at St Leonards with Bishop Quinn, who was making a brief visit to Sydney on his way to the synod in Melbourne.[23] According to *Freeman's*, Polding had asked Quinn to perform confirmations there because his health was 'not equal to the fatigue'. All went well – including a 'sumptuous entertainment' provided for Quinn, Forrest and other clergy after the ceremony – until the time came to return to Sydney. It was only half past three, but

> no steamer was to be found; both were plying in some other part of the harbour… Will the Government – will not some gentleman of influence – save the North Shore from the disgrace attached to it on account of its ill-regulated ferry? The road from the North Shore is the direct road to the Northern Districts of the colony and to Queensland; and yet it can be rendered absolutely useless when the owners of a couple of wretched steam boats choose to let them out for some other purpose…

The main issue demanding the attention of Forrest and the St John's Council from mid-1862 was the college's difficult financial situation. June saw a flurry of activity to cut costs and solicit funds. Blacket was told to stop work on parts of the building including the first portion of the tower (a tower ten metres shorter than that in Wardell's plan was eventually built in the 1930s).[24] Forrest was busy writing letters, mostly appealing for financial help. Copies of two dated 17 June 1862 survive.[25] One was a cheerful note to Sir Charles Nicholson, recently returned to England after playing a prominent role in establishing the university and serving as Chancellor from 1854:

> I am instructed by the Council of St John's to apply to you for the amount of your subscription to our College. The roof is on. The contractors are working almost double time and our funds are daily growing "beautifully less". The College is really an ornament to the City. I send you the Circular that the Council have directed to all the Subscribers who owe anything. It will supply you with information up to the date it was issued.
>
> On Monday next Mr Wentworth's statue is to be inaugurated in the Great Hall of the University. Mr James Martin delivers the "oration". Scarcely any news. The clergy of all denominations are in trouble. State aid is doomed – by a Bill before the House, sure to pass. The Church and School Lands are also on the table, and are likely to be declared waste lands of the Crown, the opinions of the Home Government notwithstanding. An Education Bill promised by the Government has not been introduced as yet.
>
> Your successor, the new Chancellor [Francis Merewether], is going on well. The Tower is rising gracefully over the University. The walks are planted, the Bridge is completed, and your bookshelves and oil paintings are furnishing the Halls and Corridors.

The other was to John Henry Newman; it would have crossed with the letter Newman wrote to Forrest in July (chapter 4). Forrest said he had been instructed by the St John's Council to 'request that the appointment of a Tutor, if not already made in compliance with our letter of May 1861, be postponed'.

> The difficulty in collecting the outstanding contributions to the building fund renders this step necessary and the Council have adopted this course most reluctantly. The entire contract amounts to nearly Forty Thousand Pounds. On the 4th June 1863 we will be called upon to meet the balance due to the contractors and we will be obliged to draw upon the £1000 set apart to provide a Tutor at a time when our hopes were higher than they are just now.
>
> In fact many of those who promised large subscriptions have left, or become unable from altered circumstances to keep their promises on the faith of which the contract was made by the Council.

Allow me to thank you in my own name, and in that of the Council, for the kind interest you have taken in St John's College, and at the same time to apologise for all the trouble we have given you.

Two days after writing these letters, Forrest was one of five hundred guests on the inaugural cruise of the 'splendid' steamer *Morpeth* on Sydney harbour. The only other priest mentioned in *Freeman's* as taking part was the principal of Lyndhurst, Rev. Anselm Curtis; perhaps this outing was a sign of currently good relations between the college and school. It was quite an event, with the Governor, Sir John Young, the chief dignitary on board. After lunch, the passengers disembarked at Middle Harbour, where a band performed and 'quadrilles, polkas and other dances followed each other in quick succession.'[26]

The college's parlous financial state was apparently not public knowledge yet. William Dolman, editor of *Freeman's*, seemed unaware of it when he wrote enthusiastically in June:

> Twelve months have scarcely elapsed since that portion of Grose Farm devoted to a Catholic College within the Sydney University was a camping-ground for bullock-drays and a commonage for the cattle of Camperdown. On this day it is the site of one of the most graceful and artistic structures in Australia... We congratulate the Catholics of New South Wales...

Ten days later, after being given a tour of inspection, Dolman declared that the completed college would be 'by far the most magnificent structure in New South Wales'.[27] The message was very different in December 1862 when he wrote about the failure of many intending donors to pay up:

> It is with regret and surprise we learn that some of the subscribers who took credit for their liberality, and were proud of their generosity, have refused to redeem their promises. The sum of £5000 promised to the College remains unpaid and cannot be got after repeated applications. To call this ungenerous would not express our sentiment – it is morally, perhaps legally, unjust... This is not creditable to us...[28]

Despite some generous donations, including £100 each from Edward Butler and a Mrs Smidmore, only an additional £826 was collected by late October 1862.²⁹ Sir Charles Nicholson was one of those who did not respond to the call. In a letter to Forrest, he denied having promised money but said that if he returned to the colony he would be disposed to contribute because he had a kindly feeling towards the college.³⁰ Sir Charles remained in England, where he died at the age of ninety-five in 1903. Sydney University's Nicholson Museum with its remarkable collection of antiquities, including many he collected in Egypt, stands as a monument to his contributions to the colony.

Polding was informed of the college's financial plight in July 1862, in a letter from Forrest on behalf of the Council. He told the Archbishop that, following the poor response to circulars sent to indebted subscribers, the Council had made cost savings totalling some £2,300, but still had to find between £4,000 and £5,000. The Fellows 'deemed it right to submit the whole matter to your Grace, who, as the originator of the College, must feel even greater solicitude than themselves for its completion, as affording, in connection with the elevating purposes to which it is dedicated, a memorial as appropriate, beautiful, and enduring, as could be desired in honor of the first Archbishop of Sydney'.

Replying two months later, Polding assured the Council of his sympathy in the matter. He undertook to issue another pastoral letter 'urging upon the clergy and the people a revival of the truly admirable and characteristic devotion' shown when funds were first sought for St John's. This eventually appeared in March 1863, three months before payment was due. 'The object is as noble, the good is as permanent, the credit is as bright and substantial as it ever was, and will be,' Catholics were advised. 'We will not contemplate a failure, a falling off from your first spirit and design. It is not the Catholic way…'

A report from Edmund Blacket, published at the same time, gives an interesting picture of the building that Forrest and his students would soon occupy – including the drastic effects of the relatively minor savings that had been made as the work approached completion. The 'Main Front' wing contained the Rector's and Vice-Rector's quarters, the Visitors' room and a room for professors, and above them the 'philosophical instrument room', the library and twenty-five students' rooms. Downstairs in the 'North Wing' were the kitchen, apartments for the porter, housekeeper and servants, lecture and class rooms and vestibules, and upstairs the chapel and ante-chapel, refectory, sacristy and infirmary.

'When the works were far advanced, the deficiency of funds became evident, and I was instructed to suggest some means for reducing the cost of the building,' Blacket wrote.

> I suggested the omission of so much of the Tower, Scullery, Cloister, and Refectory stairs as were not positively in hand, thus making a saving of about £1,700. This proving insufficient, I was again desired to make further deductions, and the only parts I could omit without leaving the Building useless were the internal finishings of the Library – and the floors, doors, plastering &c, of the Chapel, Sacristy, Lecture and Class Rooms, Servants' Rooms, Kitchens, Infirmary and Refectory – with a further saving of £900. By this plan, the Chapel and Refectory, two of the finest apartments of their kind in the Colony, are thus left useless, and temporary arrangement had to be made, by appropriating the Library to the use of a Chapel – the Visitor's Room for Lectures, and the Professors' and Vice-Rector's Rooms to domestic purposes.[31]

An ill-looking Polding – he told Gregory he had been suffering from a severe jaundice attack – chaired a fundraising meeting at St Mary's a few days after the pastoral letter appeared.[32] Plunkett, McEncroe, Faucett and Archpriest Therry were among those who made rousing speeches. To demonstrate the personal commitment of members of the college Council to the project, Edward Butler noted that they had subscribed about a quarter of the total sum collected to date, nearly £4,000.

The response was meagre; £352 was handed in at the meeting and Therry promised another £100. Commenting on this failure, and the disappointing response to the appeal for funds for the cathedral a year earlier, *Freeman's* observed sardonically, 'The people of this colony cannot be accused of lukewarmness in anything they undertake; generally speaking their enthusiasm glows with white heat at the commencement of any enterprise, only that it may be more certainly extinguished by descending several degrees below zero.'[33]

Subsequent strenuous fundraising efforts included wide distribution of Polding's pastoral, the resolutions adopted at the meeting at St Mary's, and a letter from Forrest. This sought help in raising the funds needed to complete the building contract, and noted that considerably more would be needed to place the college 'in a state of efficiency such as its founders would desire'.

> For example, the Chapel and other principal apartments must be decently furnished, a Library must be provided... But there is another matter which the Council of St John's consider of still greater moment... [They] anxiously hope that the present appeal will not only enable them to meet their actual liability to the builders, but that there will be a surplus sufficient at least to establish two or more scholarships... As the Council have spared no exertions to make the College what it is admitted to be – the finest architectural structure in this hemisphere – so they are determined to leave nothing undone to bring its benefits within the reach of all, whatever their circumstances, who give evidence of their aptness to profit by a liberal education.[34]

This appeal lifted collections to £1,460, leaving available funds still considerably short of the sum required just to pay the builder. The upshot was that the Council had to arrange a substantial cash credit with a bank, with the Fellows accepting liability, to cover the deficiency. Blacket advised that the cost of works to November 1863 was £38,645.[35] Despite the savings made, this was nearly £3,000 more than the original contract price; part of the explanation lies in additions that the Council ordered before the funding crisis – including installation of a large rainwater tank and purchase of the contractor's workshops for stables and other uses.[36]

The Council made further fundraising efforts, and in February 1864 Archdeacon McEncroe circulated a letter asking people to contribute to the college 'as a personal favour' to him. He said he had never made such an appeal before, but did so now because he was 'so anxious' to see the college able to realise the high expectations that Catholics held for it.[37] Again takings were meagre, and in May 1865 Forrest and the eighteen Fellows were obliged to each contribute £53 to finally settle the accounts.[38]

6

Moving in

In the summer of 1862–63, after undertaking his usual examining duties at Lyndhurst with Professors Woolley and Pell,[1] Forrest set off to see some more of the country – whether by coach or on horseback is not recorded. He visited the Lambing Flat goldfields, discovered in 1860 and now well past their roaring peak. He also called on relatives at a sheep station, Coppabella, west of Yass. Fifteen-year-old William Lehane, son of the owner of Coppabella, Jeremiah Lehane, was Forrest's cousin and a Lyndhurst student. William's mother, a sister of Forrest's mother, had died two years before. Perhaps one purpose of Forrest's trip was to persuade William and his father that it would be a good idea if the young man proceeded to the university and St John's. He did so in 1864, but only fairly briefly.[2]

If Forrest attempted any other recruiting on his travels, it had no immediate effect. Student numbers in the temporary college were down again to two when it reopened in February 1863. All the previous year's students had left, most of them – including the first student, Patrick Healy – having completed their BAs. Both the new entrants were first-year undergraduates. One, John Gorman, came from Lyndhurst; he was a son of one of the original college Fellows, J.V. Gorman. The other was an Irish-born youth bearing the famous name Daniel O'Connell; his places of education are recorded on the college roll as 'various'.[3]

Keeping up his Irish associations, Forrest was a prominent figure at Sydney's 1863 St Patrick's Day dinner, seated at the top table next to the chairman, Peter Faucett. In April, he joined in efforts, led by J.H. Plunkett, to raise funds for a monument in Dublin to Daniel O'Connell, 'the Liberator'. At a packed meeting to launch the fundraising, Plunkett recalled that he had enjoyed the friendship of the great campaigner for Catholic emancipation. Others who displayed their oratorical prowess included W.B. Dalley and the lawyer James Martin, who succeeded Cowper as Premier in October. Forrest was one of a committee of ninety formed to promote the plan, which won strong support across the colony.[4]

Also in April, Forrest presided at the marriage, at St Mary's Cathedral, of his twenty-five-year-old sister Maryanne to a thirty-four-year-old Irish-born medical doctor, James Gilhooley. Plunkett was a witness.[5] In August, Dr Gilhooley stood for election to a vacancy on the St John's Council caused by the resignation of Faucett. He lost to a young English Catholic engaged in the wool trade, Henry Austin. The vote was 11 to 3, Polding informed Gregory. 'It was quite unbecoming, Forrest to go about electioneering. He has lost ground with the Fellows.'[6]

For whatever reasons – he seemed happy to keep discovering new ones – Polding was now fixed in his poor opinion of Forrest. He told Gregory that only two students would go with the Rector to the new building, which would be ready for occupation in September. 'With Forrest at the Head, it will be a failure. So much for McEncroe's choice. The Coll. is a splendid structure. It surpasses the University in appearance. But what is a beautiful body without a Soul?' Gilhooley, as it turned out, was quite acceptable to the Fellows as a Council member; he was elected in 1864 and remained on the Council for twenty years.[7]

If Polding had wished to be fair to Forrest, he would have noted that no students matriculated from Lyndhurst in 1861 or 1862 and only two did in 1863.[8] As one of those stayed on at the school, St John's did well to have two, rather than one, student enrolled in 1863. Polding's comments show that McEncroe was still out of favour; it is interesting that the Archbishop now attributed the choice of Rector to him rather than to the eminent ecclesiastics enlisted for the task.

Surprisingly, Forrest was chosen to preach at St Benedict's on the anniversary, in July, of the church's consecration. Polding, accompanied by Bishop Willson of Hobart, celebrated the High Mass. *Freeman's* described the sermon as 'a very eloquent discourse' in which Forrest dwelt in a forcible manner on the duties of Christians living in the world, proving that, so far from being exempt from the practices of piety, erroneously supposed by some to be only necessary in the cloister, they were, if possible, still more bound to a strict observance of the duties of religion, in order that they might obtain grace to preserve them from the dangers and temptations incidental to their state of life.[9]

Two weeks later, he was one of thirteen priests at a meeting of clergy convened by Polding to consider an education Bill recently introduced into Parliament by Premier Cowper. This aimed, among other things, to bring all government-supported schools under a single overseeing body rather than the current separate denominational and national schools boards. The meeting declared the measure 'fraught with…many injustices to the Catholic community' and decided that a petition setting out the Church's view should be presented to the Legislative Assembly. The danger passed, at least temporarily, two months later when the government fell.[10]

In early September, shortly before Forrest and his two students moved into the new building, Polding accompanied Bishop Willson as far as Melbourne on his trip home to Hobart. He aimed to be back in Sydney by 29 September, the date set for the ceremonial inauguration of St John's. Advertisements announced that the Archbishop would solemnly bless the chapel and celebrate High Mass, Forrest would deliver an address, and a collection would be made for the building fund. *Freeman's* said it understood Bishops Goold of Melbourne and Quinn of Brisbane would be present.[11]

On 21 September, Polding wrote to Gregory from Melbourne. He said he had been very unwell since his sea trip; bile had been 'stirred up by the sea' and he was experiencing symptoms similar to those of his illness earlier in the year, but not nearly as bad. 'I shall be quite well in a day or two and then comes the return – for I cannot delay – the opening of St John's Coll. being fixed for the 29th. A beautiful edifice it is – if it only had a soul! There are only two students with Forrest… For my own part, I do not think the Coll. will ever make way in public confidence under its present Head. Perhaps not under another, unless

St John's College in Forrest's time as Rector.

greater activity prevails amongst Caths.' In apparent contradiction of the view he expressed in 1859 (chapter 3), he added, 'There ought to be large Classical Schools at the principal towns to serve as feeders to Lyndhurst and to St John's...'[12]

Previewing the coming ceremony, the *Sydney Morning Herald* described St John's as a 'truly beautiful and commodious Gothic pile – beyond all doubt the most magnificent collegiate structure in the Australian colonies'. It said the 'learned and energetic' Forrest, in his address, would describe 'the precise end and object of the collegiate establishment over which he presides, and the nature of its relation in a religious, social and educational point of view, with the University of Sydney'. The Archbishop would 'set apart the building to its intended use with all the ceremonies provided for such an occasion by the Roman Ritual'.[13]

Unfortunately, the ceremony did not occur. Polding told Gregory on his return to Sydney in December that he had accepted strong advice to travel overland from Melbourne.[14] Forrest was forced to place advertisements announcing that, 'in consequence of the illness of His Grace the Archbishop, the inauguration of the college is postponed until further notice'.[15]

Polding's letter expressed no regret that the opening had to be called off, or remorse for any inconvenience or disappointment caused. Mostly it was a happy account of his slow trip from Melbourne doing what he enjoyed most, ministering to his humble flock. Bishop Goold accompanied him much of the way to Albury, driving the buggy. Then in towns and settlements as he headed north from the Murray he performed hundreds of confirmations, and at one place baptised a converting Unitarian.

He spent four days in the Weddin Mountains near Grenfell, haunt of Ben Hall's bushranger gang, 'in the hope of meeting with the gang'.

> I had received notice that they were about to cross the Lachlan to me, but unfortunately just at the crossing place 7 troopers came on them, and they scampered off in a different direction. However, my great object was to see and instruct those of their families who might be tempted to join them. These I saw and instructed, and never met with persons so ignorant of the first truths, just as our prisoners used to be. I spent 10 hours in the days I was there in instructing some 7 or 8 young persons.

In mountainous country further east, people 'came pouring out' from the isolated valleys having heard he was coming; 'you would wonder whence they came to meet and welcome me. We had a most happy time, enjoyed from morning till night and more, the people so good and simple, so fervent.'

The tone of the last part of the letter could not be more different. On arriving in Sydney he had found a critical letter from Cardinal Barnabo in Rome. 'If the Card. has no respect for our rank in the Ch. he should not forget that we are entitled to common courtesy,' he complained to Gregory. '[To] be hoisted up into the pillory and to be pelted by [some]one's representation and slander, he seems to consider a matter for no account... I would not treat a Schoolboy as he treats Bishops...' Polding also had more to say about St John's (it was 'in a fix'), Forrest and McEncroe. 'McEncroe has many ways hampered this mission, but this Forrest infliction is worse than all,' he wrote, again with no explanation of what was wrong with the man. 'How to get rid of him no one knows except by closing the College, and this is perilous.'

That last line probably was prompted by the fact that the St John's Council had despatched a deputation to the Archbishop, on his return, to again discuss the funding crisis. The group of three – McEncroe, Plunkett and solicitor Eyre Ellis, who had joined the Council in 1861

– mentioned the possibility of closing the college. Polding told them they should persevere in trying to raise the necessary funds, adding that closure would be neither wise nor fair, as much money had been subscribed generously towards it.[16]

Two of the St John's lay Fellows, William Curtis and John Donovan (a lawyer elected to the Council in 1862), joined the usual team – Forrest, Woolley and Pell – as examiners at Lyndhurst at the end of 1863.[17] In the New Year, two of the school-leavers matriculated, and both entered the college, lifting its undergraduate enrolment to four. Another five students moved in during 1864 to prepare for the matriculation exam the following February. So things were starting to look up.

At a Council meeting at the beginning of February 1864 – just before studies resumed – Forrest was thanked by the Fellows after offering to take personal responsibility for the college's running expenses, beyond those covered by income from fees, in the first university term.[18] A circular issued about the same time detailed the student charges. In addition to the £50 a year 'pension', these were: washing, two guineas per term; candles, one guinea per term; coals at cost price when required. The charge for students staying in college during vacations was one guinea per week. All students were to have 'exclusive use of a room, board, and attendance of servants'. They would be expected to 'provide their own rooms, according to their taste and means, with the necessary furniture'.[19]

Provision was made for recreation as well as study. The minutes of a Council meeting at the end of February reported that Forrest 'read a letter from the Students of St John's College requesting the Council to allow them to use one of the rooms in the College for a billiard room, stating that it was not their intention to put the Council to any expense should this request be sanctioned.' The Council agreed.[20]

The billiard table that Forrest and the students acquired became an institution at St John's. In a letter to a Benedictine confidant in Rome in 1868, Polding described the Irish suffragan bishops enjoying Forrest's hospitality at the college, drinking whisky and playing billiards. Polding seemed to regard the presence of the billiard table as a symbol of the college's degeneration, commented the historian A.E. Cahill.[21] The table was mentioned again in the 'St John's College Magazine' of December 1921 in an article about an old student, Charles Coghlan, who enrolled in 1869. 'He delights in recounting stories of the old days when the students were few and when the famous "patriarch" billiard table, which so honourably expired last year, was the pride of the Common Room,' the magazine reported. 'He mentions that it was originally bought for the use of the Rector.'[22]

Also in February 1864, Forrest wrote a long letter to Archbishop Cullen.[23] He noted that his 'leave of absence', presumably from Cullen's Dublin archdiocese, was about to expire; this is the only reference encountered to the possibility of his Sydney appointment being curtailed by a recall to Ireland. He had no wish to return, telling Cullen,

> The climate – the people – the country – I like… I will with pleasure continue in St John's until it is fairly started and in full work… I never enjoyed better health and was never more constantly occupied.

To help familiarise Cullen with the current state of the colony and Sydney University, Forrest enclosed some newspapers and the latest university calendar. He told the Archbishop that about thirty per cent of the colonial population of three hundred and fifty thousand were Catholics, 'and are with few exceptions Irish or the children of Irish. They are excellent people…' He also praised the Protestants, saying members of all denominations were 'most anxious to attend the services of the Catholic Church – there is no vulgar bigotry – no ascendancy – there is not in the world a finer field for able and zealous priests'.

The letter also contained criticism – some of it echoing that of McEncroe in the 1850s. There were not enough priests in New South Wales, 'and there probably will not be until the vast territory…is divided into five or six dioceses.' Forrest continued,

> I wish we had the Vincentians and other orders to help the good work. It is impossible for the few priests that are, to do much in the way of public instruction and preaching; they are overworked… The congregations in Sydney are very intelligent – and complaints are constantly made of the very

defective system or style of instruction given. The Cathedral here would be thronged with Protestants if there were solid and systematic instruction given on Catholic doctrine and practice.

Schools for 'intermediate education' had yet to be established, he told Cullen: 'We want the teaching orders, and we want the Christian Brothers.' Also theological conferences for the clergy were much wanted. 'I have wearied Your Grace, but what can one do?' he went on. 'This is the first time I have written a line on matters relating to this Diocese. I have endeavoured to mind "my own business" – if I have succeeded it is well.'

Forrest reported that Bishop Quinn was well and succeeding beyond all expectation in Queensland. He also had some up-to-the-minute news for Cullen. 'Our venerable Archbishop has not been well lately,' he wrote, and

> his illness has been aggravated within the last few days by the conduct of a member of his order who left the monastery or college of Lyndhurst in which he was principal and took with him the housekeeper, a married woman, to Melbourne where they are now living together. There are two others of the order, one of them a deacon, married in this city. It is a grievous scandal – everyone knows it – it is in the public prints and could have been prevented. It is a heavy visitation.

The priest who took off to Melbourne with the Lyndhurst housekeeper, Mrs Granger, was thirty-four-year-old Anselm Curtis. Apparently the two had been living together for some time.[24] Polding's sad response is preserved in a letter to Gregory bearing the same date, 20 February 1864, as Forrest's to Cullen.[25] He wrote 'with a heart well-nigh broken and head downcast in shame, for must I tell you, my dear Child, what will so deeply grieve you – unfortunate Anselm has gone off from Lyndhurst with the housekeeper to Melbourne'.

Polding said the news had been kept out of the press, except for 'some mysterious lines' in the sporting paper *Bell's Life in Sydney*. *Bell's* had planned to publish a long account, but some laymen had 'bought the proprietors off – £20 – so nothing will appear'. He went on,

This is the heaviest blow we have yet sustained... We have reason to fear he has been leading a life of sin and going on with his duties for a long time... We must pray for him, and how much do we not stand in need of prayers for our unworthy selves! I continually pray that God would send us those he himself has chosen, but alas! I receive no response. Would that I could surrender my trust into the hands of another. I feel strongly tempted to place my mitre at the feet of the Holy Father and entreat him to select my successor, for surely my sins and my unfaithfulness have much to do with these dreadful calamities... I am sometimes inclined to envy your happy escape.

Four months later, Polding told Gregory, 'We have struck at the root of the evil by having F. Felix [Sheridan] appointed Prior...and no women employed about the house.' The finger of blame was now firmly pointed at the supposed temptress, Mrs Granger, about whom he had harboured doubts from the outset: 'I did not like her appearance. I thought she was too young, but so much was said of her reservedness and discretion, that I was over-ruled and it was only after the catastrophe that I learnt she was living separated from her husband – the most dangerous of characters.' By this stage, more had appeared in the press after, according to Polding, McEncroe imprudently alluded to the scandal while addressing his St Patrick's congregation. The upshot was that 'our Sydney pious moral Scavengers were busy scattering their filth with their pens'.[26]

From a long-term perspective, these events were possibly bad news for St John's as they lowered the reputation of Lyndhurst. Fewer students at the school would mean fewer candidates for university studies. Immediately, though, the impact was probably positive. If all had been running smoothly, the two 1864 matriculants from Lyndhurst might not have come across to St John's, and the four ex-Lyndhurst boys who prepared for matriculation at the college might have completed their studies at the school. These four – who included Forrest's cousin William Lehane – matriculated in February 1865 and carried on at the college.

The annual university commemoration ceremony, at the beginning of April 1864, provided confirmation that those were quite healthy numbers in the context of the progress of the institution as a whole. Only five students received their first (BA) degrees; one was

Archpriest John Therry.

William Browne, who was at the temporary St John's in 1861 and 1862. Another six took second or third degrees – MAs or LLBs. The dignitaries on the dais in Edmund Blacket's Great Hall – including the Governor, Sir John Young, and his entourage, university staff and Fellows of the two colleges – probably outnumbered the student body. Forrest was there, seated between the Warden of St Paul's College, the Rev. W.H. Savigny, and the eminent geologist and Anglican priest, the Rev. W.B. Clarke. *Freeman's* described the event, which included speeches by the Governor and the Chancellor, as a celebration of the triumph of intellect and an occasion for pride.[27]

For Catholics, and many others, the next month was an occasion for mourning – and for reflection on the colony's rapid progress. Archpriest Therry, a prominent and much loved figure since Governor Macquarie's time, died at the age of seventy-three in the early hours of 25 May; his funeral three days later was reportedly 'the most numerously attended' seen in Sydney up to then.[28] Commented *Freeman's*,

> As the veterans of the colony pass away from the living the mind reverts to the early days, when scrub and bush covered many a spot now populous. What an immense change has taken place within the last fifty years, and from what a depth have we risen to our present position! The biography of Father Therry, indeed, will be an intimate history of the colony…[29]

Archdeacon McEncroe delivered the memorial address at a service in St Mary's the day before the funeral. It was a moving occasion; the sixty-nine-year-old broke down as he spoke of his old friend. Reported *Freeman's*, 'When we saw this unbending, determined spirit, this living embodiment of the sterner virtues, this brave general of the church melting into tears…, overcome by his deep grief, we as all others present could not refrain from mingling out tears with his…'

McEncroe recalled first seeing Therry in 1815 when he was a student at Maynooth; Therry was celebrating Mass in the college chapel. 'Little did I think that so slender and apparently delicate a young priest was destined to come and labour at the extremities of the earth, and that amidst the outcasts of society.' He recounted episodes from Therry's early years as the colony's only priest – building St Mary's and ministering, often in the face of official opposition, to the Catholic convicts. On one occasion, at a time when he was barred from visiting gaols, hospitals and other public buildings, Therry arrived at a hospital to attend a dying Catholic and was stopped at the door by a soldier…

> Father Therry remarked, 'What will you do if I force my way in?' The soldier said he couldn't help it if he did and then placed his musket with a fixed bayonet across the door, when Father Therry with the quickness of lightning stooped down under the musket and disappeared in the prisoners' hospital. He really had many very severe trials and difficulties to encounter at this time in the discharge of his duties, and being alone and unaided showed wonderful firmness and presence of mind.[30]

The Archbishop led the funeral observances at St Mary's, which was 'densely thronged in every part'. McEncroe and Forrest were among the six pallbearers. A long procession of marchers and mourning coaches, followed by 'upwards of one hundred and fifty carriages', accompanied the coffin to the Devonshire Street cemetery (now the site of Central Railway Station). There, the Fellows of St John's lined the pathway leading to the vault, where Polding performed the final rites.

Reminiscences were again the order of the day when McEncroe preached at the funeral of Father Michael Brennan at St Patrick's church, Parramatta, the following October. A St John's Fellow since 1861, Brennan had died at the age of fifty-four after twenty-six years in the colony. Forrest and three lay members of the college Council attended the burial at Penrith, where Brennan had been based for many years.[31]

His first posting, in 1838, was to the frontier village of Yass. From there, according to a contemporary newspaper report, 'without a hut of his own', he travelled 'through the forests instructing blacks and whites scattered over hundreds of miles of country'.[32] McEncroe praised the work of Brennan and the other missionary priests who had helped bring about a 'great and consoling change' throughout the colony:

> On my first visit to Parramatta a prisoner's bark hut occupied the site of the present beautiful church of St Patrick in which we are assembled. I had then to celebrate mass in the upper story of a watch-house, while the clanking of chains and the turmoil of prisoners was going on underneath. Having been to Wollongong last week…I noticed the weather worn ruins of the old prison stockade, in which I celebrated the first mass about thirty-one years ago. What a contrast to the excellent church of St Francis Xavier, that now stands prominent not far from those ruins. All these changes for the better are no doubt the work of the right hand of the Most High, carried out during a course of years under the judicious direction of our indefatigable Archbishop.

In December, Forrest again joined Professors Woolley and Pell in examining the students at Lyndhurst, and being impressed by their performance. Studies at the school were now under the direction of Rev. Norbert Quirk, a thirty-three-year-old Benedictine priest who was born in Ireland, came to Australia as a boy, and gained arts and law degrees at Sydney University. In his examination report, Forrest generously wished Quirk and his 'fellow-labourers in Lyndhurst a continuation of the success that crowns your exertions for the past year'.[33]

None of the Lyndhurst school leavers of 1864 matriculated, but that did not prevent undergraduate enrolments at St John's reaching their highest number yet – ten – when studies resumed in February 1865. Six students, including all those who prepared for matriculation at the college in 1864, began their BA studies, and there were two in second year and two in third year.[34] *Freeman's* noted that St John's had more students than the Anglican St Paul's College, and attributed this to 'the untiring exertions of the accomplished Rector', and perhaps even more to 'the homage which we as Catholics pay to education'.[35]

Forrest must have been feeling pleased with the way things were going when at the end of February he joined McEncroe on the platform

Public holiday fun at Manly beach, 1865.

for a St Patrick's Young Men's Society talk by Rev. James Conway on 'The Bible, its friends and its foes'.[36] An Irishman who quickly won repute as a preacher after arriving in Sydney in 1863, Conway had been elected to the St John's College Council in late 1864. Apparently he was a priest who enjoyed life in the sunny capital; Polding reprimanded him in June 1864 for hosting a picnic at Manly Beach at which women were present.

The Archbishop acknowledged in his letter to Conway that they were ladies 'very much indeed to be respected'. But he was not aware that they were 'entitled in any way, according to the discipline of the church and consequently to the usages of this jurisdiction, to such a very marked distinction' as being the 'principal parties' at such a picnic. 'I request that there may not be a repetition of yesterday's festivity,' he wrote.

> And whilst I am drawing your attention to these matters, permit me to say it is quite at variance with the usages of the mission, to pass the evenings in conviviality. If a missioner has discharged his duties, as I am sure you, Dear Fr Conway, would desire him, he will be too glad to have his evenings to himself. So much as regards himself to attend to – so much to be done in preparation for others. God forbid, that it should be said amongst us, as it has been said elsewhere, that the priest of God is the chief ornament of the festive board. He is the life of the Confessional – of the Pulpit – the ornament of the Sanctuary – the Consoler of the sick chamber – Elsewhere what is he? What will he be? In the abundance of paternal love I thus write.[37]

This letter, so revealing of Polding's character, helps us understand why he had formed a poor opinion of Forrest. The witty Rector was an 'ornament of the festive board' – for example, at St Patrick's Day dinners – from his arrival in Sydney, and undoubtedly passed many evenings 'in conviviality'. Presumably, Polding considered such socialising just as incompatible with his role as head of St John's College as with that of a parish priest.

Polding reprimanded McEncroe in May 1868 for chairing another lecture by Conway at St Patrick's. He said Conway had disgraced himself as a priest, and had been placed on the St John's Council by the 'party in Sydney who take the part of every priest whose conduct Superiors cannot approve'. He added, 'I know not how it is – there are so many mysterious doings. I scarcely know whom to trust.'[38] Conway died the following October; Polding attended him at the end.[39] Nine years later, weeks after Polding's death, Forrest demonstrated his high regard for Conway by advertising in *Freeman's* for donations towards a monument with which 'a few friends who loved him in life' wished to mark his grave.[40]

Forrest, frequently McEncroe's guest at St Patrick's, preached at a retreat at the church in the lead-up to St Patrick's Day 1865. On the day itself, the Archbishop was present, in his pontifical robes, for a Grand

High Mass in the church – joining McEncroe, Forrest, Conway, the Vicar-General Father Austin Sheehy, and a number of other priests. The celebrant was forty-year-old Father Joseph Garavel, a French priest recently arrived from New Zealand where he had earned high regard for his work with Maoris.[41] Garavel, a man 'loved and reverenced for his… genial charity of heart and mind',[42] will make further appearances in the story. Apparently one of Forrest's closest friends, he also maintained good relations with Polding and his successor, Archbishop Vaughan.

Chancellor Edward Deas Thomson was the bearer of good news when the university's annual commemoration came around again in early April 1865. It had never been in a more flourishing condition, with forty-six students, including twenty-one new matriculants. Students honoured at the commemoration included Matthew Maher, in his second year at St John's, who was awarded prizes in classics and mathematics.

Maher was also the principal recipient of prizes at a ceremony held in the St John's chapel – now in use, but in a far from finished state – immediately after the commemoration. McEncroe presided; *Freeman's* stated that the Archbishop had been unable to do so. Eight other college Fellows were present, including Very Rev. Felix Sheridan, Prior of Lyndhurst, and Rev. Conway. Summarising the state of St John's, Forrest said the students' progress and prospects for the college were satisfactory, discipline was good, and studies, 'both general and special in the University and College', were most satisfactory. He hoped student numbers would rise further soon.

He announced that Polding had kindly sent a silver medal with the Pope's image to be awarded to the best divinity student, and Conway had given a prize for the same subject. Both went to Matthew Maher, who also took the main history award. Lesser prizes were presented to five other students.

Forrest noted that the college now had a 'splendid' library – thanks to donations from James Hart, who had given 3,964 volumes, Rev. Conway (823 volumes), Archdeacon McEncroe (333), W.A. Duncan (219), J.H. Plunkett (222), and the executors of the late Dean Grant of Bathurst

(227). He thanked the Fellows for their 'labour and liberality', and 'hoped soon to see some charitable Catholics make some endowments to St John's'.

McEncroe ended proceedings with a few words of exhortation to the students. They should remember the blessings they were enjoying, which had been denied to their forefathers, *Freeman's* reported him saying. They should be proud of them and put them to good purpose.

> In no part of the British Empire were Catholics better circumstanced than they were. They had a college affiliated to the University where they could take all their degrees, while their countrymen at home had built a University at very great cost, and were unable to obtain a royal charter to confer degrees. In Canada the Catholics possessed a University, but which was principally indebted for its existence to the liberality of one ecclesiastic, the Bishop of Quebec, whilst in this colony they owed their position to the munificence of the Legislature.

He added that he hoped to see St John's prosper, and 'each year have an accession to its inmates'. After the meeting broke up, visitors inspected the college building. Then Forrest entertained the Fellows 'and a few friends' to dinner.[43]

7

Disaster

Thursday 29 June 1865, the feast of St Peter and St Paul, was the thirty-first anniversary of the consecration of Polding as a bishop. The seventy-year-old Archbishop was visiting Bathurst, but at St Mary's the bells began pealing before daybreak to mark the occasion. In the evening, Father Garavel officiated at the Benediction of the Most Blessed Sacrament. The large congregation left the cathedral at about 8.30, the gaslights were extinguished, the doors were closed, and Garavel returned to the priests' quarters nearby.

The peace and quiet was short-lived. About forty-five minutes later, a passer-by noticed fire in the cathedral and urgently raised the alarm. Garavel, reported *Freeman's*,

> immediately hastened to the sanctuary of the Cathedral and removed the Blessed Sacrament. The casementing of the semi-circle running round the sides of the high altar, the archiepiscopal throne, the roof and upper portions of some of the columns springing from the sanctuary were at this time in sheets of flame. There was but just time for the Rev. gentleman to accomplish his mission and speed back from the high altar through the Cathedral fast filling with fire and blinding smoke, and seek refuge in the cloisters; and from this moment no attempt could be made to enter the Cathedral, for the purpose of saving anything.

Garavel was not the only hero that evening. W.B. Dalley was one of several men soon on the scene who rescued 'large quantities of robes, plate, altar furniture, paintings and missals' from the sacristy and vesting rooms, which were soon engulfed by flame. Also rescued were the relics and shrine from the cathedral's chapel of St Felician. As the night wore on, the fire brigade, police and many volunteers, including sailors from a French naval ship then in port, did their best to contain

Fire destroys St Mary's Cathedral.

the flames. 'Amidst suffocating clouds, showers of sparks falling like luminous hail around, the toppling over of beams, the sinking in of sheets of plaster, and the darting out of forked fire on all sides, these heroic men discharged their duty in a way to move admiration even to tears,' *Freeman's* observed.

The sight the next day was a 'roofless blackened mass'. Inspection of the wreckage revealed that the heat had been so great the metal pipes of the organ had apparently 'altogether disappeared'. Chalices and other gold and silver objects kept in safes behind the altar had melted and fused together. Objects stored in a press in the sacristy were also damaged – with, according to *Freeman's*, one fortunate exception. This was an old chalice that had once belonged to Oliver Plunket, the Archbishop of Armagh who was martyred during the anti-Catholic repression of the late seventeenth century and created a saint by Pope Paul VI in 1975. The chalice had remained in the family; ironically, the then owner, J.H. Plunkett, had arranged for it to be kept at St Mary's for greater safety.

The inquest into the fire – which 'destroyed everything beautiful and imposing, pictures, statues, the grand organ, the carved throne, the holy tabernacle' – was unable to pinpoint a cause. St Mary's had cost more than £50,000 to build, but was not insured. With memories fresh of failed efforts to raise funds for the cathedral and for St John's, one could imagine that despair would be the prevailing feeling. But that seems to have been far from the case.

On the evening after the fire, McEncroe presided at a meeting in the St Mary's Seminary hall; despite the lack of notice, the room was crowded and more than £6,000 was subscribed on the spot. *Freeman's* was pleased to note that, as well as most of the Catholic clergy and a strong lay contingent, 'many of our Protestant friends' were present. Two more fruitful meetings were held there, and healthy collections made at the city churches, in the lead-up to a 'Great Public Meeting' convened at the Prince of Wales Opera House a week after the fire. Polding was back from Bathurst, and pleased to welcome to the stage the Governor, Sir John Young, leading politicians including James Martin (now opposition leader; Cowper was again, briefly, premier), and many other notables, Protestant as well as Catholic. McEncroe and Forrest were among the large contingent of clergy present.

Opening proceedings, Polding told the gathering – 'one of the largest…meetings that ever took place in the colony', according to *Freeman's* – that when informed of the fire he was 'prostrate – stunned – at first, by the blow'. But then word of the public response, as people of all denominations mingled 'their sympathies with our own', immediately raised him up. Good had come from the calamity and a new cathedral would rise from the old. To continuous cheering, he proclaimed, 'Resurrection, my friends, is not a creation, and though St Mary's now lies lowly as it were, in her tomb, yet she shall rise again more glorious and more stately…'

The Governor followed with a speech that was widely praised at the time, and in later years, for its eloquent repudiation of sectarianism and religious bigotry. He urged people to take heed of the religious crimes and sorrows of the past, and 'shun the false lights...of intolerance and persecution'.

> In this country all Churches are equal and all men are free... There is no need...to import the passions of bygone ages, or the hatreds of another hemisphere. I trust that the union displayed at this meeting will raise up one other effectual barrier against their admission, and that as your Cathedral rises – as rise it will, in renewed grandeur – the sense of the calamity which has overtaken you will be lost in the joy of the successful restoration, or only be recalled in association with pleasant memories of the goodwill and the active sympathies which have been elicited by the occasion from all classes of your fellow citizens.

Subsequent speakers – Catholic and Protestant – reinforced this message. W.B. Dalley moved a resolution thanking the press of Sydney for its role in 'calling forth and expressing the general sympathy'. Since September 1864, Dalley had been editor of *Freeman's*, combining this role with frequent court appearances as a barrister. The paper became more readable and interesting under his guidance, and again won Polding's approval.

A leader of the Jewish community, Saul Joseph, spoke at the end of the meeting, praising Polding and describing the afternoon's proceedings as a 'triumph of reason, intellect and intelligence over bigotry, intolerance, and oppression'. The Archbishop's response, which brought loud cheering and much laughter, suggests the meeting had further raised his spirits. He said the reason he had not made a long speech at the beginning was that 'he intended to make a longer one at the end on a very important subject, and that was: Give proof of your gratitude, my friends, by coming forward and putting your money down.'

The meeting added about £3,000 to the subscription tally, lifting the total for the first week to £15,000. Fundraising had scarcely begun yet outside the city, Dalley noted in *Freeman's*. He urged that no exertion be spared 'to raise a sum that will enable us to erect a building which will rival in architectural beauty and grandeur the magnificent cathedrals in the old country'. A succession of fundraising meetings quickly followed, in Sydney and country centres. A pastoral letter by Polding was read from pulpits on 16 July. 'How truly rich and wonderful is the mercy of God', he declared.

> How quickly and surely…the tenderness of His mercy has followed the stroke!… [A] work of faith is set before us to do… Your Archbishop comes to you, not in tears, but in hope and confidence, and asks you to do it… Let our very mourning turn to festival in view of the good dispositions which the re-building of a temple for God shall have excited, and sustained, amongst us…

Plans were quickly made to build a temporary weatherboard pro-cathedral, able to accommodate two thousand people, on a site close to the ruins; this was completed in about two months. At the same time, William Wardell, original architect of St John's College, was commissioned to produce the design for a new cathedral. *Freeman's* felt confident that the result would be 'something very handsome', and was encouraged by the progress of the building fund, predicting that at least £20,000 would be in hand by the end of the year.[1]

For St John's, an inevitable effect of the destruction of St Mary's was to kill off any remaining hope of substantial fundraising to complete the building and provide for scholarships or even for repairs and other running expenses. *Freeman's* had appealed in April 1865 to 'generous minded Catholics' to 'at once contribute out of their ample means' to the college, noting its unfinished state and, despite this, its current success – due to the 'unwearied zeal' of Forrest and the 'assiduous attention' of the Fellows. This apparently produced little response, and after the disaster of 29 June nothing could compete with the cathedral for Catholic donations.[2]

A court report in *Freeman's* a week after the fire provides a glimpse of the college's unfinished state. Thomas Pickering appeared at the Central Criminal Court charged that on 20 March 1865 he did 'burglariously break and enter the dwelling-house' of Forrest 'and did then and there steal therefrom one watch of the value of £10, one watch of the value of £15, and 25s in money'. He had been arrested after trying to sell one of the watches to a pawnbroker.

Forrest told the jury he had been disturbed during the night and heard steps in the corridor, but when he got up to investigate found nobody. Next morning, he discovered the watches and money had gone from the table in his room. Inspection of the college revealed that the burglar had entered the cloister through an unglazed window. Pickering was found guilty and sentenced to three years' hard labour.[3]

A development in 1865 that could have improved the college's prospects was a decision by the university Senate, announced by Chancellor Deas Thomson at the annual commemoration in April, to excuse some students from attending lectures. He said the aim was to spread the benefits of the university more widely. Young men who established 'a fair claim to exemption' would be free to study privately and then participate in 'the general competition for degrees, honours, prizes and scholarships'.[4]

This would be the making of the colleges, predicted J. Sheridan Moore, a former Benedictine monk and headmaster of Lyndhurst who had become a prominent figure in Sydney literary circles. Giving a public lecture in July, he said he envisaged their empty rooms filling with young men who worked in the city during the day and studied for degrees in the evening. This new class of students would associate with the 'regular University men…in the refectories, in the billiard rooms, at the special lectures in the halls, and otherwise socially…' The result would be the start of 'a real University life'.

> Will this not be better than have the affiliated colleges as they are now 'full of emptiness', or with only a few pupils who actually make them look more desolate than they are? When the hum of student life is heard about them, when the tread or trample of student feet make their corridors and halls resound, when the glow of student faces and the light of rapt student eyes shed a radiance where all now is gloom, worse than total, then will the affiliated colleges be of real public service…

Moore was not at all impressed by the current state of St John's and St Paul's. He said they had cost about £100,000, but all they had succeeded in doing was give vent to religious rivalries in architecture; 'they have lent an artistic turn to polemical controversy by exhibiting it in pointed arches, imposing columns, floriated mullions, and pinnacled towers!'[5]

Moore's prediction proved a pipedream; as it turned out, enrolments at St John's were at a peak in 1865 that would not be reached again for more than a decade. If the atmosphere in the corridors and halls was gloomy in 1865, it must have been much more so a few years later. For the university as a whole, the change in admission conditions had virtually no effect on student numbers through the remainder of the 1860s, and in the early 1870s things actually went backwards. Only eighteen young men matriculated in 1870 (compared with twenty-one in 1865), fourteen in 1871 and thirteen in 1872. Numbers rose again to the low twenties from 1873.[6]

St John's lost one of its six first-year students of 1865 in the September vacation. Perhaps Forrest travelled with his cousin William Lehane when he returned to the family property near Jugiong on the main road to Melbourne. William's father had recently bought a second grazing run and the eighteen-year-old was to take over as manager, so university studies had to end.[7] Those who bemoaned the failure of successful Catholics to send their sons to university often cited stories like this; the fathers had work for their sons to do.

Forrest, who seems to have liked to get away from Sydney in the vacations, went on to the Victorian goldfields. Possibly one purpose was to visit David Croke, younger brother of his friend from Irish College days, Rev. Thomas Croke – later Bishop of Auckland and Archbishop of Cashel. David had migrated to Victoria in 1855, married, and settled with his family at Ballarat where he was registered as a miner.[8] Forrest probably also called on the senior priest at Ballarat since 1859, the 'amiable and urbane' Archdeacon Laurence Sheil, whose appointment as Bishop of Adelaide had just been announced. He assisted at Sheil's consecration by Bishop Goold at St Francis's Church, Melbourne, in August 1866.[9]

Other business on the goldfields trip included buying shares in two mining companies. The man he consulted about this was Andrew J. Forbes, manager of the United Extended Band of Hope Company, Ballarat. Forbes reported in a letter to Forrest that he had secured for him four shares in that company for £110 and five in the Great Extended Gold Mining Company, Bald Hills (north of Ballarat), for £55.[10]

Some time in the second half of September Forrest met up with Father Patrick Smyth, based at Castlemaine from 1856. This forty-one-year-old Irish priest had, like Sheil, come to Victoria in 1853, two years after the first big gold discoveries. The following year Goold posted him to Ballarat, where he witnessed the tensions build that culminated in the brutal attack early in the morning of Sunday 3 December on the primitively armed miners defending the Eureka Stockade.

Father Smyth was a hero of Eureka. In the weeks leading up to the bloodshed, he took on the task of peacemaker, trying both to persuade the authorities to be less provocative in enforcing the hated mining licence system and to cool the passions of the protesting miners. His efforts were to no avail. Austin McCallum's Eureka Commemoration Address delivered in Ballarat on the 127th anniversary, 3 December 1981, told Smyth's story and painted a vivid picture of events on the fatal morning. Awakened by the sound of gunshots, Smyth had immediately ridden to the stockade.

> Inside the stockade he saw a scene of carnage; all had been destroyed. Tents, carts and stores were burning and even bodies were lying in the flames. Hideously wounded men were groaning on the ground as they bled to death from bayonet wounds. The priest could see that the victors had gone berserk and had behaved with terrible savagery… He knew his own men only too well; it seemed to him that almost all of the dead and dying were Irishmen.

Smyth attended the dying, delivering the last rites. He did what he could for the wounded, and called on the help of others. One of these was Raffaello Carboni, a miner whose first-hand account is a key source for the Eureka story. McCallum quoted from Carboni's book:

> Catholics! Father Smyth was performing his sacred duty to the dying, in spite of the Troopers who threatened his life, and forced him at last to desist. Protestants! Spare us in future with your Sabbath cant. Not one of your ministers was there, helping the digger in the hour of need.

Smyth is said to have engineered the escape of the wounded Peter Lalor, leader of the Eureka rebels, from the stockade – providing his horse, and clothes for a disguise. The next evening, Lalor, whose condition was deteriorating rapidly, was taken to Smyth's presbytery. There the priest was among those who helped as a doctor amputated the fugitive's left arm at the shoulder. McCallum noted that, having assisted a rebel leader with a price on his head, 'the failed peacemaker was now a successful lawbreaker'.[11]

At his next posting, Castlemaine, Smyth was popular among his largely gold-mining flock. He was also a builder, founding an orphanage and starting work on a large church, which was completed under his successor in 1866. By September 1865, Smyth was dying of consumption. *Freeman's* reported that, as a last resort, he had been advised 'to try a change of air to the more genial climate of Sydney'. He had, accordingly, come to Sydney 'in company with the Very Rev. Dr Forrest'. We have no information on how they accomplished the long journey – possibly it was by the recently completed railway from Castlemaine to Echuca, on the Murray, and then by Cobb and Co. coaches. Despite Forrest's good company, travelling must have been difficult for the sick man. He died within weeks of reaching Sydney, on 14 October 1865.[12]

Back in Sydney, the ever-pressing question of college finances was on the agenda again when the St John's Council met in early October. Forrest presented a statement showing that keeping the college going since the beginning of 1864 had left him £107 out of pocket and said he hoped the college would reimburse him 'as soon as it should be in funds'. In the meantime, he was prepared to keep paying the domestic bills if the Council would fund any necessary repairs and the municipal rates (£27 a year). The Fellows were grateful, carrying a motion thanking the Rector 'for the very handsome manner in which he has met the Council in the matter of the moneys advanced by him from his private funds, and for the kind offer to carry on the College, on the old terms, until further notice'.[13] The following month the Legislative Council received a petition from the St John's Council seeking an exemption from rates; nothing came of it.¹⁴ Only a big increase in student numbers or some generous donations could put the college 'in funds', and no prospect of either was on the horizon.

On 22 November, Polding departed on a hastily arranged visit to Rome, England and Ireland that was to keep him away from Sydney until August 1867.¹⁵ Left in charge was Father Austin Sheehy, the thirty-eight-year-old Vicar-General. Sheehy, from County Cork, immigrated with his parents in 1838, studied at St Mary's Seminary, entered the Benedictine monastery at St Mary's and was ordained a priest in 1852. He was teacher in charge at St Mary's Seminary during the 1850s, Prior of Lyndhurst from 1861 up to the shake-up that followed the Anselm Curtis scandal at the beginning of 1864, and a member of the St John's College Council from 1863 to 1870.

Disturbing news from Rome most likely prompted the trip. Polding had heard in August that candidates acceptable to him had been selected as Bishops of Goulburn and Armidale, and thirty-seven-year-old James Murray, Archbishop Cullen's secretary, was to take charge in Perth. But then there was a change of plans. Following objections, a meeting of cardinals in September decided the Goulburn and Armidale appointments should be suspended pending review and Murray appointed Bishop of Maitland, a post that Polding had hoped Gregory would fill. Official notification of this unwelcome turn of events reached Sydney after Polding's departure, but earlier mails had provided hints, at least, of what was happening and, by the time he left, the men named for Goulburn and Armidale had decided to decline appointment. The mail may also have brought the news that an influential cardinal was suggesting an additional role for Murray – as Polding's coadjutor, to assist him for the remainder of his term and then succeed him. This idea was quickly rejected, doubtless to his great relief.¹⁶

The seventy-one-year-old Archbishop arrived in the Eternal City in January 1866 to find not only the new Bishop of Maitland there to greet him but also Murray's cousin, forty-four-year-old Matthew Quinn, who had been appointed Bishop of Bathurst. Cullen had consecrated his two protégés at a ceremony in Dublin eight days before Polding left Sydney.[17] Polding's meetings with the new bishops were strained. Quinn remarked unkindly in a letter to Cullen that he needed to see the Pope caress Murray to convince himself that the Irishman was really Bishop of Maitland. Murray told Cullen that he hoped in time the Archbishop would come around to accepting his new suffragans.[18]

(In a letter to Sydney written soon after arriving in Rome, Polding complained of another 'great disappointment' – his mail from the colony had not arrived yet. *Freeman's* reported that it had been sent 'by some stupid post office clerk to a distant town in Queensland' – presumably Roma!)[19]

Always looking for a way to bring Gregory back to the colony, Polding tried to secure his appointment to one of the again-vacant bishoprics, Goulburn and Armidale. Again no success – another priest he put forward as a candidate, Rev. William Lanigan, was appointed to Goulburn at the end of 1866 and the Armidale post remained unfilled. Lanigan had been pastor at Berrima for most of the period since McEncroe recruited him for the colony in County Tipperary in 1859.[20]

On the matter of a coadjutor, Polding lobbied for the appointment of an English Benedictine. His first preference was Herbert Vaughan, one of six brothers in an old Catholic family of landed gentry who had entered the priesthood; his distinguished career culminated in appointment as Archbishop of Westminster in 1892 and Cardinal the following year. Finding Herbert, the eldest of the six, definitely unavailable, Polding turned his attention to the second brother, Roger Bede. Again the initial answer was a firm no, but he persisted and eventually, seven years later, had his way.[21]

Polding did win Rome's consent to his fallback option – appointment of his Vicar-General, Austin Sheehy, as Auxiliary Bishop. News of Sheehy's selection reached Sydney in January 1867.[22] Those unimpressed by the appointment included the retired judge Roger Therry (who failed to notice Sheehy was to be Polding's auxiliary rather than coadjutor, and so would not have the automatic right to succeed him). Therry wrote to McEncroe from his new home in England,

> I cannot help saying that Mr Sheehy must have risen greatly in estimation for talents and general ability to fit him for the office of Coadjutor Archbishop... I hardly think he is the person whom one would expect or desire to see at the head of the Australian Mission for probably the next 25 years... In the Bishops of Maitland and Bathurst you have, I believe, the right men in the right places.[23]

Critics in the colony, including Murray and Matthew Quinn (who arrived in Sydney in October 1866), responded more harshly, passing on serious unsubstantiated allegations against Sheehy – including that, as Prior of Lyndhurst, he had connived at the transgressions of Anselm Curtis. On his return in August 1867, Polding received instructions from Cardinal Barnabo in Rome to defer Sheehy's consecration, if it had not already occurred, until the complaints had been investigated. Sheehy chose to resign his new appointment, and remained Vicar-General.[24] The Archbishop commented to Gregory, 'Calumny and misrepresentation once more have prevailed. He is the fourth recommended by me and so set aside... Really it is dangerous for me to propose anyone. A storm of slander is sure to fall upon him.'[25]

Polding's trip had had its excitements. In Turin, en route to England, he and his travelling companion, the Benedictine Rev. Edmund Athy, were arrested and 'kept in strict confinement' for several hours. 'In vain did he expostulate; in vain did he state who he was and what was his mission, and claim the protection of an Englishman,' *Freeman's* reported. Brought before magistrates, the pair underwent 'a short but impertinent investigation', and were then allowed to depart, 'a sort of apology' having been made.[26]

In early 1867, Polding visited Dublin. Cardinal Patrick Moran, Archbishop of Sydney from 1884 to 1911, recorded in his 'History of the Catholic Church in Australasia' that Polding dined with Archbishop (now Cardinal) Cullen on the evening of 5 March, Shrove Tuesday. A long-threatened Fenian uprising against English rule of Ireland had been fixed for that night, wrote Moran, who was Cullen's nephew and now secretary, and probably present on the occasion.

Dr Polding trembled with alarm whilst such matters were spoken of at the Cardinal's table. He feared that every instant the scenes of the Paris revolution would be renewed, and that for an Englishman in particular short shrift would be the order of the day. He went direct to the steamer and sailed at once for Liverpool.

As it turned out, Polding had little to fear that evening. 'Poor deluded men, full of ardour and ready to lay down their lives for their long suffering country, were bidding good-bye to their friends and hurrying off to the Green Hills,' wrote Moran. But a heavy snowfall 'prevented the Fenians from mustering in any considerable number, and in great measure cooled their revolutionary ardour.'[27]

Fortunately, Polding's travels had their pleasant interludes. He sent McEncroe a happy note from Ireland saying old friends had been asking after him, and concluding, 'I hope, dear Father John, you take good care of yourself'. He enclosed a pressed shamrock spray and small green flag.[28]

However, the trip – twenty-one months away from Sydney – could certainly not be counted a success. Irish bishops had been installed in three of the colony's new dioceses. Gregory would not be returning. And there was no prospect that an English Benedictine coadjutor would arrive soon to lighten the old Archbishop's load and take over when he was gone.

8
Coming of the Irish

'Here, in this beautiful Australian land, we have had much to be grateful for during the past year,' *Freeman's* reminded its readers, in typically optimistic fashion, in a leader ushering in 1866. Wars and rumours of wars had disturbed the tranquillity of the great nations of the earth, but

> How different has it been with us! Our march has been onward, peace has been with us... Australian progress has a rapidity and a steadiness about it that distances, beyond competition, the advances made by the older countries... Population is increasing, commerce rushing onwards impetuously... Education is fast permeating through the masses, to an extent that...in a very few years the Australian colonies will be one of the best educated sections of the habitable globe...[1]

Education proved to be the big issue of 1866. In September, Henry Parkes, Colonial Secretary in a new government led by James Martin, introduced legislation seen as undermining the Church's authority in the schooling of Catholic children. His Public Schools Act, which took effect at the end of the year, probably lifted the general standard of primary education in the colony, but it was implemented in a way that ensured continuing controversy and a reigniting of sectarian bitterness.

At the close of 1865, however, there was no sign that major changes to the schools system, although canvassed in earlier years, were imminent. Six days before Christmas, Forrest and McEncroe were among the clergy who examined the pupils at St Vincent's School, conducted by the Sisters of Charity at Darlinghurst. They expressed themselves highly pleased with the results. A few days earlier Forrest had examined again at Lyndhurst, and disappointed *Freeman's* by suggesting the students could do better. The examiners had found, said the paper,

Their classics are unexceptionable – their mathematics highly satisfactory – their knowledge of constitutional history, and their general conduct uniformly excellent. The only subject in which our young Crichtons appear to be at all deficient is that of logic, as to their proficiency in which Dr Forrest, one of the examiners, regrets that he cannot say much. We only wonder why after such a long list of excellencies he should have thought it necessary to say anything... The [examiners'] reports are doubtless no more exaggerated than such documents usually are, or than is easily explainable by the natural desire of generous minds to encourage good boys, and perhaps also to some slight extent by the near approach of the Christmas holidays.

Freeman's lamented that, despite Lyndhurst's excellence, student numbers were lower than they had been for many years. All speakers at the awards ceremony – McEncroe, who stood in for Polding as presenter of prizes, Prior Sheridan and the headmaster, Rev. Norbert Quirk – noted the problem and wondered why it was so. McEncroe told the gathering that Catholics should not begrudge the expense of a 'good, sound, liberal' education for their sons. It would be bad for the country if 'all its youth were hurried away to earn money before their minds were properly stored with religious principles, and before their intellects had been enlarged by such a liberal education as best tended to develop their latent faculties and individual talents'.

Quirk made special mention in his speech of Edmund Fitzgerald, a boarder at Lyndhurst who had just completed his university studies. This was the young man who Polding thought in 1863 should be persuaded to move to St John's even though his reluctance to do so created 'a nice feeling' (chapter 5). Fitzgerald had remained at Lyndhurst where, said Quirk, he had 'endeared himself to the many generations of students who have been his contemporaries'.[2]

No longer, it seems, was any doubt held about the propriety of Lyndhurst serving as a residence for university students – in competition with St John's College – as well as a secondary school and training institute for priests (a role it had been given in 1857).[3] The only student from the school who matriculated at the beginning of 1866 followed Fitzgerald's example and stayed at Lyndhurst. This had little immediate effect on numbers at St John's; although no new students entered the college in 1866, enrolments remained relatively healthy at eight. However, it was an ominous sign for the future.[4]

Notable absentees from the Lyndhurst examinations at the end of 1865 were Professors Woolley and Pell, who had shared the task with Forrest every year since 1860. Woolley was in England, about to embark on his return journey to Sydney after a year's leave. In March 1866, news reached the colony that he was one of the many who had drowned when the Sydney-bound steamer, the *London*, foundered in the Bay of Biscay on 11 January.

Freeman's devoted many columns to articles eulogising the university's foundation Principal and Professor of Classics; in fact, it boasted that it had 'paid the best tribute to his memory that has appeared' even though Woolley was not a Catholic (he was a Church of England minister). The paper praised his commitment to popular education through frequent lectures at the School of Arts in Newtown, and recalled his visits to Lyndhurst as 'festival days' during which he had stood among the students 'scattering kindly words, like flowers, inspiring hopes, effacing disappointments…' At the university, he had 'taught those students…who had mind enough to follow him, to soar to the higher regions of aesthetics'.[5]

Possibly Forrest wrote parts of the Woolley tribute. According to the fiftieth anniversary issue of *Freeman's* published in 1900, Forrest contributed regularly to the paper from soon after his arrival in the colony in 1860 until well into the 1870s.[6] By-lines were virtually unknown in those days, so it is impossible to identify his contributions – except for a few pieces in 1870 and 1871 that were signed JF. Among articles that Forrest may have written in 1865 and 1866 were leaders marking the death of Cardinal Wiseman and the appointment of Archbishop Cullen as the first Irish Cardinal.[7]

As editor, W.B. Dalley explained in 1865 why *Freeman's* did not name its writers. One reason was that people gave more weight to a 'newspaper's opinion' than to that of an individual, even though 'a leading article is not after all the production of many heads, but of one'. Another was that lack of attribution protected the authors. A contributor would derive some benefits from being named:

> It would give him what all men must have who would work well, an individuality in his work – it would give him a real, personal stimulus to exertion, and ensure him whatever honour or praise his productions might merit. On the other hand it would expose him to the malice of his enemies – to the hatred, possibly to the revenge, of those whom his denunciations of wrong, of imbecility, or corruption in high places might offend... The privilege of anonymous authorship is essential to the existence of an independent press, and nowhere more so than in a country like our own, where power unfortunately is not always found allied with honour.[8]

The fiftieth anniversary *Freeman's* published a long list of people who had contributed over the years. As well as notable Catholic laymen and priests, it included such well-known literary figures as Henry Kendall, Victor J. Daley and Henry Lawson. From the following vignette, relating to the early 1870s, it seems Forrest was part of the paper's inner circle (the proprietors then were Thomas Butler, younger brother of the lawyer Edward, and a former teacher, Michael McGirr).

A BRIGHT CIRCLE

> The *Freeman* never had a 'round table' or a weekly meeting of its lightweight and heavyweight fighting men after the fashion of old *Sydney Punch*. Yet there was many a brilliant gathering in the dingy backroom overlooking the little lane. Shy, nervous Kendall has sat there amidst a bright company. The effervescent Dalley is telling a story, seated with him the witty Dr Forrest, the buoyant-hearted Dean O'Connell, Frank Hutchinson, and Tom O'Mara – Editor Butler, temporarily evicted from his chair, leaning against the window leisurely puffing his Henry Clay, and jovial Michael McGirr, with his robust form and broad expansive smile, effectively screening off from general view the ancient but unpicturesque book-shelves.

The sociable Forrest had formed friendships extending well beyond the Church and university, and beyond *Freeman's*. In April 1866, for example, he attended farewell functions for the wealthy financier, philanthropist and politician Thomas Holt, who was leaving on a visit to Europe. This fifty-four-year-old Yorkshire-born Congregationalist had

Fun and games at Thomas Holt's mansion, The Warren, overlooking Cook's River.

made money from pastoral interests and lost it on ventures including scientific oyster farming and coal mining. One purpose of his trip was to collect works of art for the gallery in his 'Victorian Gothic' mansion, The Warren, at Marrickville, overlooking Cook's River.

Forrest joined a large group of politicians, lawyers, clerics and others at Holt's farewell dinner at the School of Arts, and four days later was a speech-maker – his contribution was able and humorous, said the *Sydney Morning Herald* – at a picnic in Holt's honour at Sans Souci, at the mouth of George's River. 'A more picturesque and tranquil scene could not well be found, though the length of the journey and the roughness of the road were obstacles which nothing but the most warm and disinterested friendship could have surmounted,' the *Herald* observed. About seventy gentlemen of 'influence and social distinction' sat down to a sumptuous luncheon in a spacious marquee, and cheered and applauded as many speeches were made and toasts drunk.[9]

Forrest's associations with Holt continued after his return to the colony two years later. A letter from Holt to the sometimes virulently anti-Catholic Rev. John Dunmore Lang in September 1870 provides a happy insight into the Irishman's character. Apparently Holt, the seventy-one-year-old Lang and Forrest had been on a journey together – perhaps to Sans Souci. Wrote Holt,

> You certainly showed a considerable amount of courage in coming so long a distance. I assure you that the pleasure of the trip was greatly enhanced by your good company. I was never more amused in my life than at the pleasantry between you and Dr Forrest. What would one of the bigots say if they had happened to overhear Dr Forrest humorously proposing to you to cast lots whether he should turn Presbyterian or you should turn Roman Catholic? However great the religious differences may be, and however firmly we may believe in our religious creeds, I do delight to see men of every creed meet together on the most friendly terms.[10]

Less denominational harmony was evident at a big event in Sydney shortly after the Sans Souci picnic. This was the inauguration, on St George's Day, 23 April 1866, of Prince Albert's statue in Hyde Park, facing Macquarie Street. Public subscriptions collected after the death of Albert, the Prince Consort, in 1861 had paid for the statue. The day of its inauguration, by the Governor, Sir John Young, was declared a public holiday, and a crowd claimed to be the biggest so far seen in Sydney – upwards of forty thousand – witnessed the ceremony.

An entertaining leader in *Freeman's* wondered if many of those who watched and cheered could name any particular distinction of Albert's that warranted the honour paid him. It doubted that 'any general definition of the object of the gathering would have amounted to much more than a repetition of the old joke – "In honour of Prince Albert – a great man, Sir; but what did he do?"'. Nevertheless, the statue was a great ornament for the city, and 'all must unite in the hope that we may never see erected in Sydney the statue of a less worthy man'.

A long and colourful procession led by the eight-hundred-strong Volunteer Artillery and Rifles and including representatives of many organisations, including the Fellows of St John's College, began proceedings by marching from the Domain to Hyde Park. When all had settled, Bishop Barker of the Church of England read a prayer for the

Inauguration of Prince Albert's statue.
The crowd was said to be the biggest yet seen in Sydney.

Queen. The Governor made his speech, then eight young ladies unveiled the statue by drawing strings that raised the flag that had covered it.

> A loud shout from the assembled thousands immediately burst forth, which was repeated over and over again, and simultaneous with it was heard the booming of the artillery from Fort Macquarie. The Lyster opera company,

who had a stage erected especially for them, on the right of the statue, sang the national anthem, after which the German choir sang their own national hymn. His Excellency, amidst the cheers of the throng, then left the ground, after which the crowd gradually dispersed.[11]

Absent from the ceremony were Sydney's Catholic clergy, apparently as part of the long-running protest over the precedence granted on official occasions to the Anglican bishop over his Catholic counterpart (chapter 4). Another reason given was that many, including Vicar-General Sheehy, were attending the funeral of a pioneer priest, Rev. Patrick Magennis, at Appin, near Campbelltown. Magennis, who came to the colony in 1839, had been a St John's College Fellow since 1864.[12]

Freeman's thought it 'perhaps as well' that the clergy were not at the inauguration, because Bishop Barker's reading of a prayer as part of the ceremony was an insult to Catholics. The program for the event had contained no mention of the prayer reading, and Edward Deas Thomson, Chancellor of the university and chairman of the organising committee, should have recognised its impropriety and prevented 'the insult that has been offered to a large section of the community'.

At its meeting in early May, an indignant St John's Council directed Forrest to protest on its behalf to Deas Thomson.[13] The addition of the prayer to the ceremony seemed 'very like a breach of faith towards all public bodies and all persons of religious denominations who do not think it right to have prayers offered for them in public by the Bishop of the Church of England as their representative', Forrest wrote. He asked for an explanation of Barker's unexpected appearance.

Deas Thomson took the letter as an insult, claiming to be 'at a loss to conceive by what authority the Council of St John's College have thought proper to constitute themselves the catechists, as well as censors', of the statue committee in the matter of the prayer. He denied that he had been party to any departure from the published program, and claimed the Council was aware that an explanation of the events had been given to the 'present head of the Roman Catholic Church in the colony' (Sheehy) through J.H. Plunkett.

Forrest's reply was in part conciliatory, but objected to the 'discourteous tone' of Deas Thomson's letter and his failure to explain what had happened. He said the Council did not know Sheehy had been offered an explanation and added that 'public acts, especially acts affecting public bodies, are not usually explained by private personal communications'.

Freeman's published the correspondence a month after Forrest sent his second letter, giving Deas Thomson's failure to reply as justification. The paper said it had still not heard what Sheehy had allegedly been told. 'We can only hope,' it added, 'that the explanation, whatever it may have been, was not only a little more satisfactory but also a little more ordinarily polite than the extraordinary terms in which Mr Thomson has thought fit to reply to a body of gentlemen, his equals in every respect, and whom as a member of the Statue committee he had already, intentionally or unintentionally, knowingly or only foolishly, been instrumental in insulting.'[14] So ended a singularly unedifying episode.

As they had done for years past, the Catholic clergy boycotted the Queen's Birthday levee at Government House on 24 May because of the precedence issue. Forrest was the exception, attending as he had done in previous years as a representative of St John's College. Council members Edward Butler, Eyre Ellis and J.V. Gorman accompanied him.[15] The order from London granting precedence to the Anglican bishop had been in force for five years now; it reached Sydney within months of Sir John Young taking over as Governor in 1861.[16] Polding had confided to Gregory shortly before that, as Young had Catholics in his household, he hoped 'very amicable relations' would be established with the Governor, 'though I hate the consequence – dining at Govt House'.[17] Probably, despite his indignation at the precedence 'insult', the socially shy Archbishop had been glad of an excuse to avoid the levees.

Forrest, of course, was a much more sociable priest, and in late July joined the Samoa-based Coadjutor Bishop of Central Oceanica, Dr Elloy, Archdeacon McEncroe and others at a dinner hosted by Rev. George Dillon of St Augustine's church, Balmain. Earlier, the French bishop had confirmed a hundred and fifty children and adults at the church; islanders being educated for mission work by Marist Fathers stationed at Villa Maria, Hunter's Hill, took part in the service. McEncroe preached after the confirmation and, as had become his habit, recalled times long past. Reported *Freeman's*,

> He remembered the days when but one log hut existed on the scrubby headland that now formed the beautiful and increasing suburb of Balmain... He remembered too when the first French Missioner came to Sydney on his way to the South Sea Islands over thirty years ago... These missionaries...lived only for the good of the people of Christ. They went leaving father and mother and riches and honours and pleasures and even food and raiment to save the savages...[18]

Two days later, McEncroe and Forrest were among guests of Father Garavel, hero of the St Mary's Cathedral fire, at and after the blessing by Vicar-General Sheehy of the foundation stone for his new church at Newtown.[19] Garavel had been appointed pastor of Newtown and Camperdown in late 1865, and had lived at St John's while searching for a suitable house for a presbytery.[20] In January 1866, McEncroe chaired a meeting of the committee formed to select a site for the Newtown church – and recalled the days 'when Newtown contained only a few slab cabins, and when Camperdown was composed of only a few huts and uncleared land'.[21]

Clearly, Sydney and its surrounds had undergone great changes since McEncroe arrived in 1832. In June 1866, *Freeman's* published a detailed description, from the just-published 'Bailliere's Gazetteer of New South Wales'.[22] Latest population estimates, as at mid-1864, were 60,299 for the city and 41,698 for the suburbs – total 101,997. That is just over half the present population of Hobart. The city had a 'fine appearance' from its 'magnificent harbour':

> Densely packed round Sydney cove and Darling Harbour with stores, warehouses, and wharves, it stretches out to the southward in long rows of substantial dwelling houses and shops, and spreads out in the distance in suburban villas and gardens and costly and substantial mansions.

Gas produced at the Australian Gas Light Company's works

on Darling Harbour lit the city. The water supply, 'of the very best quality', came from Lachlan Swamp, 'an extensive basin, surrounded by sand hills, extending from Paddington to the shores of Botany Bay'. Most government offices were temporary structures, built by the early governors; the city's finest buildings belonged to banks and insurance companies. Notable examples were the 'rich and handsome edifices' erected side by side in George Street by the Commercial Banking Company and Bank of New South Wales.

Vehicles 'of every description' plied Sydney's streets. Omnibuses travelled from Wynyard Square and Queen's Wharf in Lower George Street 'to all parts of the city and suburbs: to Petersham, Camperdown, Newtown, Randwick, Waverly, Paddington, the Glebe, Balmain, Pyrmont, the South Head, and Botany Bay'. Cabs could be had at numerous stands at any hour of the day or night. Horse-drawn trams conveyed passengers along Pitt Street between the railway terminus at Redfern and Circular Quay (this tramway closed in December 1866 after other road users complained about the protruding rails). On the harbour, steam ferryboats plied from Circular Quay and Miller's Point to the North Shore at regular intervals. Other ferries ran to Balmain, Manly Beach, Watson's Bay, and various points on the Parramatta River.

The Botanic Gardens were the pride of Sydney: 'It would be difficult to say whether nature or art has the larger claim on the gratitude of society for all the beauties that are collected here.' The Museum contained a large, valuable and interesting collection of objects of natural history. The Mechanics Institute in Pitt Street had an excellent library. There were three theatres – the Prince of Wales, the Victoria and the Lyceum – and many first class hotels and restaurants. At the observatory on Flagstaff Hill the time ball dropped daily (except Sunday) at 1 p.m., enabling ships' captains and others to set their timepieces. Electric telegraph linked the flagstaff with the signal station on South Head, so when a vessel approached the Heads the news could be conveyed immediately and flags hoisted to announce the impending arrival and indicate the type of ship and where it had come from.

There was another side to Sydney. In 1864, *Freeman's* wrote of evil smells encountered in parts of Pitt, George and King Streets; 'we have an invigorating sea-breeze, …but it would require a continual hurricane to sweep away all the noxious and poisonous vapours that emanate from the stinking slums of various parts of the city, and from the rotten carcases that encumber our waste allotments'.[23] The paper returned to the theme four years later in a leader headed 'The horrors of Darling Harbour'.

In the first place, the whole of the sewage from Brickfield Hill to Redfern is deposited in the shallow water at the foot of Liverpool street. In the second place, the surface drainage from the same extensive quarter is carried and left to putrefy there. Add to this the debris from the miserable tenements as well as from the large factories and saw-mills about, and you will be able – no doubt inadequately – to realise some of the worst horrors of the place… It is not extraordinary that where dead dogs and cats – and in some instances dead horses – are allowed to lie on the dull-green ooze of the beach, under a blazing sun, till the full tide carries them out to the middle of the Harbour – fever and other fearful diseases should be rife.[24]

The description of Sydney's government-supported schools in Bailliere's Gazetteer also presented only a partial picture. They were said to be 'numerous, well attended and well managed'. Since 1848, funding for schools across the colony had been provided through two boards – the Denominational Schools Board for those run by the churches and the National Schools Board. One consequence was that schools were certainly numerous in some places – more so than necessary as 'national' schools and those of the various denominations competed for limited numbers of children. Whether schools were well attended is another matter; an inquiry in 1861 found pupils at a sample of Catholic schools spent on average less than two years there.[25] Probably the general standard of management had improved since the mid-1850s when an inquiry found teachers in Catholic schools were 'quite unfit and wholly incompetent' and the children 'in a deplorable state of ignorance'.[26]

Henry Parkes's Public Schools Bill of 1866 established a Council of Education to take over the functions of the two boards. That feature, at least, of the proposed legislation was public knowledge by mid-1866 when a meeting of priests convened by Sheehy prepared a list of points that they wanted the government to take into account in drafting the Bill. Their demands included adequate Catholic representation on the new Council; without this, they said, the principle of religious liberty and equality would be violated. McEncroe headed a deputation that presented the document to Parkes in late July. Parkes assured them 'there was not the slightest danger of placing the Roman Catholic children at a disadvantage'.[27]

Freeman's begged to differ when details of the Bill were revealed in September. Its main initial objection was that the Colonial Secretary (Parkes) would chair the new Council of Education and appoint the other five members, each to come from a different religious denomination.[28] This would give Parkes far too much control over the entire school system, the paper thought. A 'justly constituted' Council would have the churches represented in proportion to their strength in the community – and the Catholic members would be chosen by the bishops in council, not by Parkes. Later issues of *Freeman's* found much more to object to, and argued that the Bill sought to destroy the denominational schools. Despite denials, a highly provocative comment by Parkes in his second reading speech gave strength to this assertion. 'The clergy of the various churches…are the most inveterate, and the most powerful, enemies that popular education ever had,' he said.[29]

Protests against the legislation gained momentum over subsequent weeks. In early October, Sheehy chaired a 'very numerous and influential meeting', which he said had been called not so much to consider the Bill as to enter a 'deliberate and united' protest against it. A week later, J.H. Plunkett told a meeting chaired by McEncroe at St Patrick's that passage of the legislation would be a 'calamity and disgrace'. As Plunkett had chaired the National Schools Board for ten years from its establishment in 1848 – in the face of much Catholic criticism – his views attracted considerable interest. He argued that churches had the right to educate their people as they thought fit, and saw no justification for the proposed 'violent' change to the existing dual system. Forrest proposed the vote of thanks at the end of the talk 'in few but happy words'.[30]

Bishop Murray. *Bishop Matthew Quinn.*

He, no doubt, was looking forward to the arrival, any day now, of the Irish bishops Matthew Quinn and James Murray. The 2,500-ton clipper *Empress*, which carried a large company of priests and nuns as well as the bishops, was first sighted from South Head about 3 p.m. on Sunday 21 October and the news promptly telegraphed to the city. 'Joy-bells' immediately began 'pealing merrily' at the Sacred Heart church and St Benedict's, and Irish flags were raised at two prominent locations to help spread the glad tidings. 'A stir was at once perceptible through the city and from all quarters hundreds flocked in the direction of the Circular Quay,' *Freeman's* reported.

There many boarded a steamer bound for the Heads, but hopes of greeting the bishops and party that evening were dashed by a lack of wind that kept the *Empress* well out to sea. A southerly change during the night enabled a speedy entry, and by morning she was anchored between Bradley's Head and Watson's Bay. Vicar-General Sheehy hastened out to greet the party. Then another steamer set out from the Quay, 'crowded as she could possibly be' with priests – including McEncroe and Forrest – and laymen.

On arriving alongside the *Empress*, three hearty cheers arose from the steamer, which were responded to by those on board the vessel. The clergy and [lay welcoming] committee proceeded on board the *Empress* and welcomed their Lordships... So eager was the crowd to obtain the blessing of their Lordships that they all knelt down and thus received the first Episcopal blessings from the newly arrived bishops. The band kept up a series of enlivening airs while the company, including the newly arrived, stepped on board the steamer which then slowly returned to Circular Quay.

There, despite pouring rain, an 'immense multitude' greeted the bishops, priests and nuns. They then proceeded to the packed pro-Cathedral where 'a solemn Te Deum was chanted in thanksgiving to Almighty God for their safe voyage'. Next stop was St Mary's Seminary, where the bishops received and responded to addresses of welcome. The ceremonies ended shortly before 1 p.m.; then, reported *Freeman's*, 'their Lordships proceeded with the Very Rev. Dr Forrest to St John's College, where they are at present residing'.

No doubt the three old friends found much to talk about. Matthew Quinn's brother James, Bishop of Brisbane, joined them during the week, and on the Friday afternoon all three bishops were present at an awards ceremony in the college chapel. Guests included most of the lay members of the college Council. J.H. Plunkett, who had been appointed Vice-Chancellor of the university the previous year, gave a prize, as did Rev. Conway. The efforts of two students in theology and three in logic were rewarded; all 'received a round of hearty applause' after receiving their awards. Forrest gave a very satisfactory account of the progress of St John's, *Freeman's* reported, 'and expressed a confidence that the arrival of the Bishops of Bathurst and Maitland would still further stimulate its progress'. All present, the paper added, were 'apparently much interested in the welfare of St John's'.[31]

That evening, Forrest gave a lecture on the Public Schools Bill at the city's Masonic Hall. Bishops Matthew Quinn and Murray joined him on the platform; others present included Rev. William Lanigan, soon to be appointed Bishop of Goulburn. Plunkett took the chair, and about four hundred people paid a shilling each to attend – proceeds to the building fund for Father Garavel's new church at Newtown.

Forrest proceeded to entertain the audience as well as provide a critical commentary on the legislation. The state had a duty to ensure the people were educated, he said, and there were parts of the Bill 'that every fair man must welcome heartily'. He approved of replacing the two boards with a single Council of Education, and was not concerned about its denominational composition – so long as it had the 'capacity and honesty to do justice to every class'. It was right that the Council should control teachers' salaries and training courses because those who made the laws

> were not always the best judges of these matters. (Laughter.) He was sure people would be very sorry to entrust a child to such a schoolmaster as some of these men would make. (Laughter.)

Forrest argued forcefully that the state had no role in religious education; its sole concern should be secular teaching. He rejected the Bill's proposal that the public school curriculum include 'general religious teaching as distinguished from dogmatical and polemical theology'. There was no such thing as this 'common Christianity', he said.

> Why, there were controversies about the very basis of the moral virtues. There was a controversy as to whether there was a heaven or hell, or whether God would punish our actions… How could these men who talked such drivelling nonsense as that undertake to legislate for our children?

He was not impressed that an hour a day was to be allowed for religious teaching by visiting clergy at public schools. This was scarcely practical, and 'if five or six of them did not come into the school and make a rattle with their conflicting creeds, there was no religious education to be given in any other way under the bill'.

He disputed the notion that the teaching in denominational schools was uniformly poor; he knew of some excellent teachers. To abolish these schools because there were inefficient teachers in some of them 'would be more unreasonable than to abolish the Legislature because there were people in it who ought to be somewhere else. (Loud laughter.)'

The provisions for limiting proliferation of schools, which strongly favoured public schools, drew his derision. A public school could be established at any location where it would attract twenty-five pupils. But for denominational schools the minimum attendance was thirty, and such a school could not be sited within two miles of a public school unless their combined regular attendance exceeded two hundred. And no denominational school could be established more than five miles from the nearest public school. Said Forrest,

> you could put one of these public schools anywhere you pleased – at the door of the Church, or at the back of the priest's house – as they did at Balmain some time ago… But suppose there were 80 or 100 stanch Church of England people with a fine grown up flock as they often had; or 80 or 100 sturdy old Papists on whom the primeval blessing had descended also? (Laughter.) One would think they ought to have a school, if 25 other persons were entitled to have one, with books and maps, and all the most delicate appliances? Oh! don't dream anything of the kind! (Laughter.) Catch the Colonial Secretary doing that! (Laughter.) If those 80 or 100 people were within two miles of the 25, they couldn't have a school at all.

And what of the provision to prohibit denominational schools more than five miles from the nearest public school?

> The object of this clause appeared to be to garrison the country with public schools by gradually extending their lines, but taking good care that no one was there before them. (Laughter.)[32]

9

In Polding's absence

Bishops Matthew Quinn and Murray spent a week in Sydney, based at St John's, before heading off to their new bush dioceses. Austin Sheehy joined Quinn's party on the long journey over the Blue Mountains to Bathurst. Crowds of well-wishers in carriages and on horseback greeted them as they approached the town and accompanied them in. Then members of the local Catholic Young Men's Society, bearing colourful banners, joined the cavalcade as it proceeded up the main street, lined with spectators, to an enthusiastic welcome at the church of Saints Michael and John, now raised to cathedral status. Sheehy returned to Sydney after inducting the new bishop at the cathedral.[1]

Murray's travelling companion on the steamer to Morpeth, on the Hunter River downstream from Maitland, was Archdeacon McEncroe, who was to preach three days later at the bishop's installation ceremony at his cathedral, St John's, Maitland. 'Rounds of hearty cheers' greeted them as they stepped ashore in the late afternoon before setting off by carriage on the fifteen-kilometre road trip to the cathedral town. Murray wrote home,

> A number of horsemen, and horsewomen too, followed us at full gallop and kicked up a tremendous dust, so much so that when we looked back, we could hear the noise of the horses and see the dust rising mountains high, but neither horses nor men nor women could be seen, they were all hidden in the cloud of dust. They cheered us all most vehemently, and, you may be sure, old Ireland too.[2]

Within days of taking possession of their dioceses, both bishops returned to Sydney for a conference of clergy on the Public Schools Bill, which was now before the Legislative Council, having been passed by the Assembly. Bishop James Quinn of Brisbane also attended; he presumably had remained in Sydney after greeting his brother and cousin less than two weeks earlier. The meeting, chaired by Sheehy, drew up a petition for Plunkett to present to the upper house. The two new bishops announced their intention to follow suit by, *Freeman's* reported, 'calling their clergy in conference to take the necessary steps to petition against the obnoxious measure'.

The day before the meeting, Forrest hosted a gathering of 'distinguished Catholics' – which most likely included the three bishops – at St John's College. At least one non-Catholic was also present – the Anglican lawyer Robert Johnson, who was a member of the Legislative Council and a Fellow of St Paul's College. Probably much discussion took place about prospects for improving the Public Schools Bill in the Council. If the fifty-four-year-old Johnson reached agreement with the Catholics on amendments to pursue, he had no opportunity to put his intentions into effect because, unfortunately, he died suddenly the next day. Forrest, McEncroe and Plunkett joined the funeral procession to Randwick Cemetery – perhaps a sign of good relations between the university colleges as well as personal regard for Johnson.[3]

The Legislative Council secured some welcomed amendments, including easing the restrictions on establishing denominational schools and removing the provision making the Colonial Secretary ex-officio chairman of the Council of Education. The Bill was signed into law in late December. A few days later, Parkes appointed the members of the Council – himself, Premier James Martin, two more politicians, and Sydney University's Professor of Chemistry and Experimental Physics, John Smith. All were Protestants except Martin who, although from an Irish Catholic family, did not practise the faith and had strongly supported Parkes's legislation. They chose Parkes as their chairman – achieving the Colonial Secretary's original aim by a different means. An educational administrator who had long advocated a unified state school system, William Wilkins, was appointed the Council's full-time secretary, charged with giving effect to its decisions.[4]

Freeman's initial response had a 'more in sorrow than in anger' ring to it.

> There are no people in New South Wales more tolerant than the Catholics, there are none who seek less for anything in the shape of ascendancy, they are perfectly satisfied with fair play, but that they are not at all likely to get from the present ministry. They have had many proofs of this, and it only required the nomination of the Council of Education to put the climax on them.[5]

A month later, after speeches by McEncroe and Parkes at a dinner given by teachers from denominational schools, the paper's tone became optimistic. McEncroe had expressed confidence in the Council of Education, and Parkes had assured the gathering that this would prove justified. 'We have no reason to doubt the sincerity of Mr Parkes, and we have much reason to believe that his confreres are anxiously disposed to do their duty fairly to church schools and common schools alike,' said *Freeman's*. The tide turned quickly again. By July the paper was accusing Parkes of 'clerico-phobia' and a 'crafty, insidious' attack on the Catholic faith.[6]

As a secondary school attracting no government funds, Lyndhurst was unaffected by the changes. It had a relatively successful year in 1866; pupil numbers doubled and three scholarships were established to provide opportunities for less wealthy boys.[7] Forrest was again an examiner at the end of the year, praising the performance of the best students in Latin. From a report in *Freeman's* in early January 1867, it seems he expected several of the final year group to matriculate and enter St John's in February.[8] Unfortunately, this was not to be; three matriculated but stayed on at Lyndhurst. As a result, Lyndhurst was now home to four undergraduates and St John's had just six students.

If the St John's Fellows had wished to conciliate Polding and persuade him to stop Lyndhurst undermining the college, they might not have carried one of the resolutions put at their December 1866 Council meeting. Moved by Duncan and seconded by McEncroe, this formalised the understanding that the suffragan bishops would stay at St John's on their visits to Sydney. Forrest was asked to write 'to the different Bishops of the Province placing the rooms of the College at their disposal during their visits to the Metropolitan City' as it would be 'for the interests of the College that a good understanding should exist between the Australian Hierarchy and the Council'.[9] Polding, who distrusted the Irish bishops as he did Forrest, viewed their many meetings at St John's over the next seven years with much suspicion.

Another development that would have displeased the Archbishop was the election of Rev. Michael McAlroy as a college Fellow in August 1866. This forty-five-year-old had won a great reputation as a pastor and builder of churches and convents in the Yass and Goulburn regions.[10] However, with two long-time associates, Revs Patrick Dunne and Patrick Bermingham, he was in Polding's black books. Bermingham won particular notoriety for taking twelve boys from southern New South Wales to Ireland for secondary schooling – an action interpreted as aiming to undermine Lyndhurst. They sailed from Sydney in February 1861 on the same ship as Henry Gregory. McAlroy was seen as leader of this 'clique', and Polding managed to prevent his appointment as a bishop on at least two occasions.[11]

Reduced student numbers meant that by 1867 the financial position of St John's had become even more difficult than before. At its first meeting after studies resumed the Council appointed a committee, chaired by Forrest, to look for solutions. This recommended against increasing fees – because subscribers had been promised that the 'cost of education in the College should be within every man's reach' and there were comparatively few 'persons of wealth' among Catholics. Instead, the 'most legitimate remedy' lay in greater student numbers, coupled with such 'aid as may flow from the bounty of individuals'. Recognising that relief from these sources was not in prospect, the committee concluded that it could not 'suggest any immediate remedy for the present state of things'.

The report detailed the college's running costs. Weekly household expenditure was £8 10s, comprising: baker, 15s; butcher, £1 15s;

grocer, £2 5s; vegetables, £1; sundries, 15s; plus, for wages: butler and cook, £1; and two other servants, £1. For a year, that amounted to £442. In addition, £27 had to be found for municipal rates and £7 10s for insurance, bringing total expenses to £476 10s. Income from six students each paying £52 10s a year was £315, leaving a deficit of £161 10s. The committee noted that these figures included no provision for building repairs, 'the necessity for which is becoming painfully manifest'. It suggested £100 was the minimum requirement per year. Also, the college had 'never been properly furnished, even with articles that are purely essential'.[12]

The committee recommended that a memorial 'stating explicitly and fully the present position of the College' should be placed before the Archbishop and Bishops. This would invite 'their influence on its behalf, as well as towards an increased supply of students'. The three-page letter, signed by Forrest on behalf of the Council, was not sent until after Polding's return to Sydney in August.[13]

It noted that a 'much larger annual accession of students than the College has yet received' had been expected. If this could be realised, not only would St John's become self-supporting but it would 'so much the more extend its sphere of usefulness'. One unfortunate consequence of the shortage of funds was that the chapel had 'not been furnished with a due regard to the solemn offices to which it is dedicated'. Also, the 'fine hall intended for the refectory' remained useless, the library had insufficient shelves and tables, and 'in other portions of the building the absence of suitable furniture is painfully manifest'.

'The Council cannot believe that the spirit which prompted the generous contributions of the Catholic people in aid of the founding of this Institution has become so deadened as to leave it to perish from the want of support in the main essential to its existence, the supply of students,' the memorial stated. It suggested a good way individuals or groups could assist was by establishing 'foundations or exhibitions' to enable the sons of poorer Catholics to enter the college.

The suffragan bishops sent sympathetic responses, but with pressing financial demands in their dioceses could offer no immediate assistance. Matthew Quinn hoped the high school he had founded in Bathurst, St Stanislaus' College, would increase student numbers at St John's, and said he would consult with his brother bishops on other possible ways to help.[14] Polding apparently did not reply, but again offered his thoughts to Gregory. The college seemed 'like a farce', he wrote; 'I wish indeed I had F. Bede Vaughan [the English Benedictine he wanted, and eventually obtained, as his coadjutor (chapter 7)] for this important establishment. Dr Forrest has the confidence of the Bishops who find St John's a convenient lodging point but I believe neither clergy nor laity look upon him as the right man in the right place.'[15]

Forrest, meanwhile, was seeing a lot of the new bishops. At the end of February 1867, he travelled to Bathurst with James Quinn, one of Quinn's senior priests Dr John Cani, and Rev. Garavel of Newtown. Matthew Quinn, his Bathurst clergy and 'a few respectable laymen' met the party 'down the Sydney road' and escorted them into town. The main purpose of the visit was to take part in religious ceremonies marking the third anniversary of the death, at the age of forty-eight, of Dean John Grant, a pioneer priest who for many years had ably headed the Bathurst mission. The popular Grant had been out of favour with Polding since joining in the criticism of the Benedictine administration in the late 1850s and early '60s.[16] *Freeman's* reported that two thousand people packed the Bathurst cathedral for the High Mass celebrated by James Quinn, and large crowds also attended two subsequent services.

Matthew Quinn took the opportunity to show Forrest St Stanislaus' College, which he had opened at the beginning of the year. According to *Freeman's*. Quinn told the Rector that it had about twenty pupils preparing for university matriculation, 'some of whom would, he hoped, be able to go down in twelve months'. Forrest congratulated Quinn 'on this fact', and 'complimented the teachers on the efficiency of their system of teaching which he promised to test more fully before his departure from Bathurst'.[17]

The school's head teacher (president) was Rev. James McGirr, who had previous associations with both Lyndhurst and St John's College. McGirr arrived in Sydney in early 1856 having completed most of his studies for the priesthood in Ireland.[18] The young man was soon appointed 'Principal' of Lyndhurst, but apparently was dismissed the following year.[19] Just when he went to St John's, and on what basis, is unclear; certainly the college was not in a position to fund a salary. It seems he was there in 1864 and the association continued for two more years.

Bishop Quinn met McGirr at St John's shortly after arriving in the colony in October 1866. Clearly impressed, Quinn soon ordained him and put him in charge of St Stanislaus', which initially occupied a room in the Bathurst denominational primary school run by his cousin Michael McGirr (Michael later became part proprietor of *Freeman's*). W.A. Duncan claimed in 1877 that James McGirr had been expelled from Lyndhurst after speaking out against Benedictine abuses there: 'poor McGirr, bound to the Divine Office and to celibacy, would have gone to ruin and died of hunger had he not been taken in by Doctor Forrest, and ordained by Mgr. M. Quinn'.[20] This act of Forrest's probably earned him another black mark from Polding.

In a reminiscence published in 1905, one of the first pupils at St Stanislaus', James Callaghan, wrote that McGirr, while at St John's, had been particularly successful at preparing students for matriculation. 'One of his most distinguished students' was a New Zealander, Joseph Tole, one of five schoolboys who entered the college in 1864 and matriculated at the start of 1865. 'Mr Tole had come to St John's wholly unacquainted with Latin, and in nine months made a brilliant pass,' Callaghan recalled. He also remembered Forrest examining at St Stanislaus', describing him as 'the most terrific [presumably meaning terrifying] of examiners, but kindest of men'.[21]

It seems that McGirr had less success in Bathurst than at St John's in giving boys the grounding they needed for university study. Quinn's confidence that St Stanislaus' would soon begin sending a stream of students to St John's proved unfounded. Only one old boy,

John Shorthill, matriculated and entered St John's during Forrest's remaining seven years as Rector. He enrolled in February 1869, but left the following August.[22] A contemporary of Shorthill at St Stanislaus', Thomas Murray, recalled him as being 'of a good age' and 'the "daddy" of all the boys'. 'He came in for some money, and cut a great dash in Sydney. He paid us a visit – I really do believe – for the express purpose of showing how great a man he had become.'[23]

St Patrick's Day fell on a Sunday in 1867, and Forrest and James Quinn were among those who took part in celebrations of 'unusual splendour' at McEncroe's St Patrick's Church, Sydney; Quinn had not hurried back to Brisbane after the Bathurst trip.[24] News of William Lanigan's appointment as Bishop of Goulburn reached Sydney the following month, and plans were quickly made for James Quinn, assisted by his brother and James Murray, to consecrate him on Pentecost Sunday, 9 June. Polding surmised, probably correctly, that the three Irish bishops were keen to formalise this addition to their ranks while he was away. 'Dr Lanigan was consecrated in all hurry,' the Archbishop told Gregory in his first letter after returning to Sydney on 7 August.[25]

For Forrest, an important engagement three weeks before the Goulburn consecration was the first Sydney University annual commemoration addressed by Dr Woolley's successor as Professor of Classics, Charles Badham. Like his predecessor, Dr Badham was a Church of England minister, but his speech left *Freeman's* confident that he had 'left behind him all religious prejudices if ever he had any'. Forrest would have endorsed this sentiment; praising the Sydney professors in 1873, he said none had ever sought to impose his religious views on students.[26] No doubt Forrest also enjoyed the striking oratory that quickly won Badham renown in Sydney.

He may have felt less happy when the list of matriculants, graduates and prizewinners was read out. Two St John's students were awarded their BAs, and another won a prize for his efforts in classics in second year. But the college was not represented among the matriculants, while one of the three residing at Lyndhurst won a university scholarship.

Bishop Lanigan.

The trip to Goulburn for Lanigan's consecration by the clerical party from Sydney – which included McEncroe, Sheehy and Forrest – must have been cold and uncomfortable. The roads were in a wretched state due to rain, *Freeman's* reported. A downpour the night before the ceremony had made the Wollondilly River crossing impassable, preventing latecomers from reaching the town on the Sunday morning.

Despite the weather, only people who had purchased tickets could be accommodated in the small brick church of Saints Peter and Paul, completed in 1848, that was to serve as Goulburn's cathedral for the next five years. The elaborate ceremony began with Lanigan's robing in episcopal vestments; at this point the absence of a mitre distinguished him from the bishops. Forrest, as notary to the Presiding Bishop (James Quinn), read the Apostolic Mandate authorising the consecration, then a kneeling Lanigan took the Oath of Obedience. Following much further ceremonial and the celebration of Mass, the three bishops jointly placed the mitre on Lanigan's head, completing his consecration. Proceedings ended with Lanigan delivering his first Pontifical Blessing to the congregation.

In the evening, the new bishop hosted a banquet – a magnificent affair, according to *Freeman's* – for all the clergy present and a large number of laymen, Protestant as well as Catholic. About a dozen toasts were proposed and responded to with much applause. The biggest ovation, for Lanigan's speech of thanks in reply to James Quinn's toast to his health, demonstrated 'such a genuine burst of feeling that we began to imagine ourselves again a resident in the green isle', wrote the *Freeman's* reporter.

The visiting bishops had interesting things to say. James Quinn said two principles guided him in his work. He saw it as his duty, not an 'affectation of liberality', to be equally kind to those outside the Church as those inside. And he 'never was and never would be a politician'; if the clergy mixed in party politics, much evil was likely to result. Nevertheless, where questions of religion or education were concerned, it was a bishop's duty to speak out and he would never shrink from doing so 'any more than he would shrink from the stake or the scaffold'.

Matthew Quinn said he had 'laid down for himself the rule not to open his mouth on any public question until he had had a year's experience' in the colony. But he could not keep this resolution on 'the subject of most importance', education. Catholics had no wish to 'obtrude their opinions upon others', nor would they 'take any mean advantage of them'. All they demanded was 'freedom of education' – which required that the heads of the Church select the books used in Catholic schools, teachers be appointed by the Church's pastors, and school property be 'vested in the Catholic body'. For this, *Freeman's* reported him saying, 'had he struggled, would he continue to contend, and if necessary for the accomplishment of this object should he be prepared to shed his blood'.

James Murray endorsed Quinn's views on education. Avoiding emotive language, he said he had expected to find in New South Wales 'that freedom of education which is consonant with the liberty enjoyed by the people', but unfortunately he had been mistaken. Murray injected a touch of humour into the proceedings in his praise for Lanigan's appointment. Having worked as a priest in the district for many years, the new bishop was 'known to and loved by all – not a lately imported bishop like some of his friends'.

Forrest responded to two toasts proposed by Lanigan. In the first, to the clergy, Lanigan singled out four of the priests present for special mention – his Vicar-General Michael McAlroy, Sheehy, McEncroe and Forrest. The Rector of St John's, he said, headed 'one of the highest of the literary institutions of the colony', and his 'great learning would

qualify him to preside over the highest literary institution in the world'.
Replying, Forrest was similarly effusive. He believed

> there were not in the world a body of more hard-working clergy than those of this colony. The services they performed even in the worst weather and under the most unfavourable circumstances were feats that were never elsewhere exceeded; and he might be excused for saying this as he could not claim to belong to the ordinary ranks of the clergy, being, as they knew, at the head of an educational establishment.

Responding to Lanigan's toast to the laity, Forrest noted that many present had been educated at universities. While all wished success to the University of Sydney, they owed much to the universities of the old countries. He proposed a toast to 'our ancient universities', which provided the cue for Walter M. Adams BA, a 'late Fellow of New College, Oxford', recently arrived in the colony, to make a long speech extolling the vital role of these institutions in producing men of pluck, endurance, courtesy and honour. His contention that the intellect of Europe now had a rival in the intellect of Sydney University drew 'great applause'.

Forrest then proposed the last toast of the evening, to the press of New South Wales. A free press in a free country was one of the greatest of blessings, he said. He believed

> the press of Australia would bear favourable comparison with that of any other country in the world. Its liberty never degenerated into licentiousness. No doubt it happened that now and then its position was abused by individuals who availed themselves of its columns, but this was not the fault of the press, but of individuals.

On this positive note, the gathering wound up at about 10.30 p.m.[27] Over the next three days, the four bishops – Lanigan, James and Matthew Quinn, and Murray – conferred on matters including education and diocesan boundaries. Most likely, Forrest was involved in the discussions. He and Murray remained in Goulburn until the Thursday following the consecration; the Quinns stayed a few days longer. Sheehy left on the Monday; he was invited to take part in the discussions as Polding's representative, wrote Cardinal Moran in his history of the Church, but 'excused himself as being obliged to return to Sydney on matters of importance'.[28]

According to the well-informed Moran – he was in regular contact by mail with the Irish bishops, especially Murray, his predecessor as Cardinal Cullen's secretary – the bishops wanted to 'devise some method of united action' to secure modifications to the Public Schools Act. Sheehy, before he left, had promised to concur in any resolutions that were adopted.

The two Bishops Quinn and Lanigan travelled to Sydney in time to take part in Corpus Christi celebrations at St Mary's on 20 June.[29] The following day Matthew Quinn, Lanigan and Sheehy presented themselves as a deputation to Parkes bearing a document setting out the views of the New South Wales bishops on primary education. This demanded that four 'principles' be accepted as a basis for their cooperation. One was that it should be no more difficult to set up a Catholic school, in terms of pupil number requirements, than a public school. Another was that Catholic pupils in mixed schools should not be given religious instruction with other children or by a non-Catholic teacher. The others dealt with control of the training, appointment and dismissal of teachers.

The statement requested some further changes, including 'fair representation' of Catholics on the Council of Education. But the bishops also sought to conciliate, noting that they had no objection to government inspection of schools to ensure teaching was up to standard or to 'strict supervision over the expenditure of the public money'. And they did not require separate schools for Catholics in thinly populated places.

Parkes gave the deputation no cause for hope of any concessions. He pointed out that meeting the bishops' demands would require changes to the law, and as the government had just succeeded in having the legislation enacted 'it would be almost an act of puerility on their part if they were to ask the Legislature to undo what it had deliberately done'. He said the government would consider it 'a great misfortune if the Roman Catholic clergy stood aloof from assisting to work out a scheme of education for the children scattered over this large country'.[30]

Matthew Quinn presided at a large public meeting at St Mary's Seminary five days later, called to consider what to do next. All speakers condemned the legislation. Lanigan thought it would be disastrous for Catholic children. Plunkett said that from a Catholic viewpoint the Act was a 'penal one and as long as it remained upon the statute book he could not look upon this as a free country'. McEncroe acknowledged that he had said earlier he would give the legislation a twelve-months trial, but he had now seen enough to know it was objectionable. He thought that, when 'the whole of the Catholics, who were one third of the population, expressed their opinion', change could be achieved. The meeting decided to appoint a committee to 'watch the working' of the Act and call a public meeting when necessary.[31]

The Quinns were still (or again) in Sydney, presumably staying at St John's, on the afternoon of 8 July when Forrest held another prize-giving ceremony in the chapel. The *Freeman's* report indicates that only Forrest, the students and the bishops were there; the students must have been thoroughly used by now to the presence of the suffragans at the college.

The New Zealander Joseph Tole, in his third year, won the two prizes awarded, for theology and philosophy. He went on to take arts and law degrees, was admitted to the New South Wales bar in 1871, and returned to Auckland where he had a successful legal career. Forrest was full of praise for his star student, confident that he would continue to 'so conduct himself as to be a credit to his country and honour to his college'. James Quinn, who presented the prizes, told the gathering he was happy to find that studies of theology and philosophy were 'warmly appreciated and earnestly pursued' in the college.[32] The students were very fortunate

> in the opportunity which they all enjoyed at St John's in having such a professor as Dr Forrest for their direction in these and all other branches of their scholastic studies. His friendship for that reverend gentleman had now extended over a period of more than twenty years, and he had never but one opinion as to his estimable qualities as a man, and his abilities as a scholar.

That, no doubt, was a genuine compliment from an old friend. It is hard to believe, though, that Quinn was serious when he went on to say 'the Archbishop would, he knew, have been pleased if he could have been present'. Polding had apparently never visited the college. In December 1866, the Council directed Forrest to communicate with the Archbishop after he returned to the colony to try again – following the failed attempt in 1863 – to arrange for him to formally open St John's.[33] The college remained unopened for another eight years.

The Quinns, Murray and Lanigan were in Sydney to greet Polding, now nearly seventy-three years old, when he arrived on the afternoon of Wednesday 7 August aboard the coastal steamer *Alexandra*. He had sailed from Liverpool in late April on the clipper *Chariot of Fame*, which reached Melbourne in the last week of July after surviving terrifying storms off the Cape of Good Hope.[34] During a ten-day stopover in the southern capital he laid the foundation stone for St Ignatius church, Richmond, another work of the architect William Wardell.

Enthusiastic harbour welcome for Archbishop Polding on his return to Sydney in August 1867.

A gentle breeze blew, the sun shone warmly and the sea was 'calm as a mirror' for the Archbishop's arrival, *Freeman's* reported. A flag hoisted at St Mary's shortly before midday signalled that the *Alexandra* was off Kiama. This provided the cue for 'an immense number of people' – including a large contingent of clergy, among them Forrest – to hasten to three steamers that had been booked to escort her in. First off was the *Morpeth*, with four to five hundred on board. She headed out to sea, and on the first sight of smoke from the *Alexandra* 'people who were rather dull from the gentle heaving of the steamer became more lively, and the music of the German band, which was on board, seemed to impart life to all'.

> In a very short time, the *Alexandra* came up, and as both steamers neared each other a tremendous cheer rose from the *Morpeth*, and immediately his Grace could be seen on the deck of his steamer waving his hand in acknowledgement of the compliment. The band played 'Home, Sweet Home,' 'See the conquering hero comes,' and both steamers abreast of each other made all speed possible.

The second welcoming steamer met the *Alexandra* off Bondi, and 'cheer upon cheer followed with the waving of handkerchiefs'. The three boats steamed through the Heads side by side, and were greeted by the third packed welcoming vessel, which lined up beside the others.

> It was a beautiful sight… As they neared Sydney the various headlands were seen to be crowded with spectators waving hats and handkerchiefs… As the steamers neared the wharf the sight was truly wonderful, every available space was crowded with people and the streets leading to the water were all but impassable… There could not have been less than 10,000 persons in the neighbourhood waiting to catch a glimpse of his Grace.

Because the crowd was so large, plans for a procession from the wharf to St Mary's were abandoned. Instead, 'after a considerable delay', a passage was cleared to allow Polding, Sheehy and McEncroe to make their way to a coach, which proceeded to the pro-Cathedral at a slow pace amid continuous cheering. There the greeting party included the four bishops. The organist struck up 'See the conquering hero comes' as Polding entered the building. Then, after a short religious ceremony, the Archbishop thanked the people for their welcome, noted that it was now thirty-three years since he first landed in Sydney, and said he had never felt better in his life.

> In fact he felt as if he could labour amongst them for another thirty years, but whether the time was long or short he was determined to labour at his post till the last.

Polding returned to St Mary's the following evening for the formalities of receiving and responding to presentations. He told the gathering he had felt homesick during his travels and, if it was God's will, 'would desire never again to leave these Australian shores, so dear to me in a thousand ways'.[35]

10
Difficult times

'All you tell me, except one thing indeed, is matter of congratulation and hope,' said Polding in response to the clergy's account of the state of religion in the colony at the presentation ceremony the day after his return to Sydney. That thing, of course, was the new education regime. 'Our liberty of education has been assailed and impaired,' he said. 'It is indeed deplorable.'[1]

As well as the Public Schools Act itself, rules laid down by the Council of Education were causing consternation. These included an insistence that all schools receiving government funding use textbooks published by the Irish Board of National Education. The objections gained added strength after Matthew Quinn drew attention to recently revealed private thoughts of the late Anglican Archbishop of Dublin, Dr Richard Whately, who had been heavily involved in setting up the Irish system. Whately had expressed confidence that the education provided was gradually 'undermining…the vast fabric of the Irish Catholic Church'.[2]

Polding's pleasure at returning to Sydney seems to have faded swiftly as he surveyed the political and ecclesiastical scene. 'What a sea of troubles I am in,' he wrote to Gregory two weeks after his arrival. 'An infidel system of education is now established by law… Religious animosity studiously fostered by persons in authority, and I do not see I shall receive any very efficient aid from my Epl [Episcopal] confreres.'[3] Writing again two months later, he appeared to place much of the blame for what had happened on the new bishops.

> Just as I expected and as I forewarned them at Rome, this importation of Irish Bps, as Parkes & the Ministerial party term the coming of Mgrs Quinn & Murray for Bathurst & Maitland, has been the unfortunate cause

of, or pretext for, raising a No Popery cry, and has been used to influence the votes for the passing of this most obnoxious Education Bill. At the Consecration of Dr Lanigan at Goulburn, there was a dinner and of course, speeches after, which I am sorry to say contained much to inflame. It might have suited the atmosphere of Dublin, but here was sadly out of place.[4]

He was probably referring to James Quinn's statement that he would not avoid speaking out on questions of religion or education 'any more than he would shrink from the stake or the scaffold', and Matthew's that he would be 'prepared to shed his blood' in the cause of freedom of education. In fact, though, the statement on education drawn up by the Irish bishops was mild compared with views Polding put to a packed meeting at St Mary's in early November. While the bishops did not insist on separate schools for Catholics in thinly populated places, implying that children in those areas could attend public schools, Polding declared that public schools could not 'in conscience be used by Catholics'. He went on to say the government seemed determined 'to put an end, if possible', to Catholic denominational schools, and added:

> We believed that our religion was in this colony free and safe from any loss of freedom, but we see it now hampered… I do not hesitate to say I feel myself as much a bond slave, after being thirty years in the country, as those bond slaves whom I saw and endeavoured to comfort when they had their chains about their feet. (Cheers.)[5]

The object of the meeting was to establish a 'Catholic Association' to raise funds to build new Catholic schools, set up teacher training schools, and bring teachers to New South Wales. Speakers included Plunkett, McEncroe, Sheehy and Dalley. The former *Freeman's* editor J.K. Heydon, apparently back in favour, moved the resolution establishing the Association. Polding told Gregory the idea was for every Catholic to contribute a penny a week, and this seemed to have been 'taken up very warmly' by the people. 'If it will only last,' he added in a display of the world-weary pessimism that increasingly characterised his letters. As he had feared, after a few successful years the Association faded away in the early 1870s.[6]

In September 1867, a month after Polding's return, Bishop Murray visited Sydney to greet a party of eight Dominican teaching nuns just arrived from Kingstown, near Dublin, to establish a convent at Maitland. 'We found our dear Bishop, thin and worn and delicate and low enough, for besides the effects of his sea voyage, this business of Education is weighing heavily on him,' wrote one of the nuns, twenty-four-year-old Sister M. Hyacinth Donnellan.[7] Probably the recent record Hunter River floods had also contributed to his fatigue. 'I suppose £40,000 would not compensate for property, crops, etc., that were completely lost,' Murray told Moran in a letter that also described relief efforts in which Catholics and Protestants worked 'most cordially' together.[8]

The nuns reached Sydney a few days before Murray, and were shown the city and surrounds. At St Patrick's, McEncroe was moved to tears 'to see another band of Missioners come to aid them in their labours', Sister Hyacinth wrote in her lively account of their voyage and arrival in the colony. She said schools and education were 'the topics of the day' everywhere they went, and quoted McEncroe as saying Australia was 'in a worse state than it was 35 years ago'.

Their excursion the day Murray arrived was a steamer trip up the Parramatta River – 'the scenery…could be compared with nothing else but fairyland,' wrote Sister Hyacinth – and visits to convents at Rydalmere (Subiaco) and Parramatta. The bishop was waiting at their lodging house when they returned and 'welcomed us most heartily'. Forrest, whom they knew from his time in the Kingstown parish, was also there, 'as droll and as hearty as ever'. A few days later, with Murray, they visited St John's College where

> Dr Forrest made us take a glass of Australian wine and also gave us the first good laugh we have had since we left dear St Mary's [Kingstown]. Nothing could equal his kindness…

She added that it was owing to Forrest's 'kind influence' that Dean Lynch, a long-time friend of St John's and its Rector, had donated a block of land adjacent to the Maitland convent building.[9] Murray noted in a letter to Moran that this was worth probably £200 or £300.[10]

It is not surprising that Murray and Forrest got on well; the bishop's letters and speeches reveal a man of positive outlook, calm good sense and gentle humour. He told the Dominican sisters before they left Ireland that the building they were to occupy in Maitland had been owned by a parson, 'but don't be afraid of that for we will say Mass in it and banish all the evil spirits, should there be any'.[11] He could not promise, though, that Maitland's mosquitoes would leave them alone 'since they have not spared the Bishop'. On the day they left Sydney for Maitland, Forrest was one of several priests who joined Murray and the nuns for midday dinner. 'Champagne in abundance' was served, 'as well as fruit which the archbishop sent over to us', recorded Sister Hyacinth.[12]

In December, Forrest gave another public lecture on the education issue; McEncroe was one of the 'very numerous and most respectable audience' at Sydney's Masonic Hall. People wanted to know why the Catholics were 'so noisy' on the question 'when others appear to be satisfied', he began. Essentially it was because Catholics 'cannot give up their children to be taught religion by those who cannot teach them according to the dogmas of the Roman Catholic Church'. To expose them to lessons in scripture 'interpreted by every untaught, conceited and self-opinionated man who happened to be appointed a public school teacher' would be 'to submit to the subversion of the very principle of the Roman Catholic Church – the principle of authority'.

Forrest's talk is revealing of his outlook on life, which combined strict religious orthodoxy with a liberal and democratic spirit and, apparently, friendly feelings for all. He said Catholics were entitled to think for themselves on any matter not concerned with dogma.

> They vote at elections; they are divided on the railway loan, on the land question, and on the Treasurer's budget. Who of the Church says 'O, you're in danger!' It was only questions of doctrine on which they must have no doubt; and in those doctrines they must be taught by apostolic authority.

He was pleased to note that the Council of Education had reversed its original decision that Catholic schools must use the Irish Board's scripture textbooks; however, their continued use in public schools was an 'injustice which Catholics cannot submit to'. In line with the bishops' statement, he said Catholics in mixed schools should receive no religious instruction unless their parents requested it. He noted that the 'many' Protestant pupils at the schools James Quinn had established in Queensland attended religion lessons only if their parents had given written consent.

Forrest hoped the people's 'sense of justice and fair play' would prevail, resulting in parliament's removal of the objectionable features of the legislation. He believed both Protestants and Catholics valued religious liberty too much 'to fall together by the ears', and was confident the attempt apparently being made to promote discord between them would prove futile.

> Any cry of that sort must inevitably fail. (Hear.) We know each other too well to be deceived by the trickery of politicians. (Cheers.) We love one another too well as friends and neighbours to consent to adopt an imaginary howl, at the wish of those who have other objects to serve than education.

Winding up his talk, Forrest noted that Polding had departed from his 'usual conciliatory, delicate course' in denouncing the government's education measures.

> And what was the reason? His rights and his duties and the privileges of his people had been tampered with; and he's not the man to allow it. (Cheers.) Popular as he is, he is not an Irishman. But Dr Polding is a sturdy Englishman, and therefore not hot-headed; not a man in the community could allege that he had displayed anything but a conciliatory spirit during his thirty years' career in this colony, and what could have effected such a change? When he found upon his arrival that the welfare of his flock had been assailed, what wonder that the venerable old man had been goaded into indignation...[13]

Freeman's commended Forrest for having put the Catholic position 'calmly, temperately, logically, without the use of a single word or phrase which could fairly be supposed to convey offence to the members of any denomination'. It hoped his talk, and a pastoral letter by Bishop Murray that gave 'a detailed exposition of the Catholic doctrine on education', would help quell 'the many false and exaggerated versions of our demands' that the 'foes of free education' were circulating. It called Forrest and Murray 'two master minds', and noted that both had detected 'the same weaknesses in their adversaries' position'.

In the same issue, *Freeman's* again urged wealthy Catholics to donate or bequeath money to St John's for scholarships. It noted that the 'noble Catholic College', presided over by a 'learned divine…of amiable and most persevering character', continued to have 'a paucity of students'. By failing to take advantage of the higher education on offer, Catholics were putting themselves at serious disadvantage when issues such as the schools controversy arose. 'Is it not easy to see that if one third of the members of the Assembly had been highly educated Catholics – that if there had been even half a dozen Catholics of this calibre in the Assembly – no Minister would have dared to inflict upon us such a series of wanton insults?'[14]

These are sentiments that might have appeared in *Freeman's* under any of its editors. However, the departure of Dalley as editor at the end of 1866 and his replacement by a twenty-eight-year-old Irishman, Richard O'Sullivan, had changed the paper. Its coverage of Catholic events was as detailed and respectful as ever, with internal controversy carefully sidestepped. But like his older brother A.M. Sullivan, owner and editor of the Dublin *Nation* co-founded by the Young Irelander and later Premier of Victoria, Charles Gavan Duffy, O'Sullivan was an Irish nationalist, and he used *Freeman's* to stridently promote the cause of Irish independence.[15]

His period as editor coincided with the rise of the Fenians, committed to the violent overthrow of British rule of Ireland. O'Sullivan insisted in *Freeman's* that he never encouraged, applauded or endorsed Fenianism.[16] However, it was easy for his critics to blur the distinction between support for the Fenians' methods and for their nationalist goals, which he shared. Polding was among those who did not recognise the difference; 'The *Freeman's Journal* has been the cause of immense mischief, by its Fenianism and anti-English tirades,' he told Gregory in October 1867.[17]

Prince Alfred, Duke of Edinburgh.

News of the impending visit to the Australian colonies of Prince Alfred, Duke of Edinburgh, second son of Queen Victoria, reached Sydney that month. Rather than respond with another biting commentary on English–Irish relations, *Freeman's* published an amusing leader sympathising with the twenty-three-year-old prince. He would be received by people who had taken great pains 'to make themselves look outrageously ridiculous' and addressed 'in the stilted conventional phraseology with which his ears are already but too well acquainted'. He would have little chance to enjoy himself at the ball in his honour; on the other hand, its organisers would be 'in a state of ecstatic delight the whole evening'. Those who had 'the happiness of touching the royal hand' would 'there and then take out patents of nobility for the rest of their lives'.[18]

After visits to South Australia and Victoria, the prince arrived in Sydney Harbour captaining HMS *Galatea* on a rainy Tuesday 21 January 1868. Nineteen packed steamers escorted the ship to its anchoring point off Mrs Macquarie's Chair. Thousands of cheering spectators thronged the prince as he came ashore for a brief visit to Government House; he 'acknowledged the somewhat rude welcome…with great good humour', reported the *Empire*. In the evening, back on the *Galatea*, Alfred witnessed – along with crowds of Sydneysiders on shore who braved the rain – a display of fireworks set off from Fort Denison, Fort Macquarie, Dawes' Battery and boats on the harbour. One attraction was a small steamer 'fitted up and illuminated as a fiery dragon'. This

A steamer fitted up as a fiery dragon added extra sparkle to the 'harbour illumination' staged to welcome Prince Alfred to Sydney.

was 'propelled through the fleet, discharging fiery combustibles from its mouth, roman candles and squibs'.

The official welcome took place at noon the next day. A lavish triumphal arch had been erected at Circular Quay for the prince's ceremonial greeting by Sir John Young's recently arrived successor as Governor, the Earl of Belmore, and Premier Martin, Colonial Secretary Parkes and other ministers and dignitaries. Martin and some of his colleagues turned up in 'court costume' – cocked hats, laced coats and swords. The *Empire* (no longer owned by Parkes) noted the contrast

James Martin.

between the prince's 'youthful look, comparatively small stature, and plain dress' and the 'bulky forms and gaudy trappings of most of those by whom he was received'.

When the speeches were over, a lengthy procession escorted the prince up George Street, along Bathurst Street to Hyde Park, past the statue of his father, Prince Albert, and down Macquarie Street to Government House. In one of the last carriages – behind the Chancellor, Vice-Chancellor, Senate, professors and officers of the university – sat Forrest, in company with the Warden of St Paul's College, Rev. Savigny. Cheering spectators lined the route despite continuing rain; 'in some places even chimney tops were occupied'.[19]

Freeman's greeted the prince warmly: 'Of one thing we are quite sure, that there is not in New South Wales a man of any creed or nationality on earth who does not wish the Duke of Edinburgh a pleasant stay here and a safe voyage home'. The paper was impressed by the good humour of the crowd, which, it noted, 'hailed with much merriment' the ministers 'tricked out in all their finery'. A 'universal spirit of toleration' characterised the colony's people; 'in the name of everything we hold dear let us not allow the demon of religious intolerance or of party strife to raise its head here'.[20]

Knowing what was just around the corner – the attempted assassination of Prince Alfred by an Irishman, Henry O'Farrell, and the subsequent anti-Irish, anti-Catholic frenzy fanned by politicians, particularly Henry Parkes – those words seem sadly naive. Possibly the same can be said about a leader in the same issue of *Freeman's* that condemned the hanging in England of three Fenians – 'the Manchester

Martyrs' – convicted of murdering a policeman while freeing two of their colleagues from police custody. Among other provocative statements, the paper declared the crime 'altogether a political matter'; it was 'monstrous to class these men among murderers'. Articles such as this provided powerful ammunition for those choosing to see the shooting of Alfred as more than the unforeseeable act of a solitary madman. The *Sydney Morning Herald* had no trouble finding a potent series of quotes to back its claim that *Freeman's* had preached treason and 'inspired an assassin'.[21]

The royal visit was still proceeding peacefully when studies resumed at Sydney University in February. Forrest would have been pleased to welcome the first new undergraduate to enrol at St John's since 1865 – Henry Sullivan, a sixteen-year-old from Bathurst. A former Lyndhurst pupil, Sullivan had completed his matriculation studies at the college. He joined three other university students there, all with their BAs and now studying for second degrees. One other Lyndhurst student matriculated in 1868 – and stayed on at the school while studying for his BA. At least one candidate for matriculation in 1869 – possibly there were two or three – entered St John's during 1868.[22]

Within a week or so of term beginning, Forrest set off for Bathurst to join Bishops Matthew Quinn and Murray at the laying of the corner stone for the town's Sisters of Mercy convent. This was a gathering of old friends – not just Forrest and the bishops but also the head of the convent, Mother Ignatius, who was a sister of their colleague from Irish College days, Rev. Thomas Croke. She and a team of eight adventurous women from the Convent of Mercy, Charleville, County Cork, had come to the colony in 1866 with Quinn and Murray.[23]

The 'largest congregation of Catholics ever remembered' in Bathurst turned out for the ceremonies, which began with Mass in the cathedral; Quinn was celebrant and Forrest preached. Murray performed the stone-laying formalities and then addressed the gathering. He praised the sisters, who had 'abandoned friends, country, home and their endearing associations' to devote their energies to the education of young women on the other side of the world. He said the vast numbers present, 'many of whom had travelled from the towns in the interior and the remote bush', demonstrated the 'astounding effrontery' of those who claimed the laity did not support the bishops' position on the education issue. The schools of the Bathurst diocese were famed 'far and near', he added.

> I was somewhat sceptical myself on this matter, but I am so no longer. The learned Rector of St John's College examined [at] the boys' school in my presence and that of your Bishop and his clergy on Friday last… They had no superficial examiner on that occasion in Dr Forrest, but a thorough searcher, who spared no pains to find how solid had been the foundations of their acquirements. They were put through a searching ordeal, but I am glad to say they came off successfully.[24]

Murray praised the 'thrilling eloquence' of the sermon Forrest had delivered. That this was no idle compliment is apparent from the fact that Moran referred to the 'most touching and eloquent' sermon in his history of the Church in Australasia.[25] Most likely, Murray was his informant. Two months after the Bathurst ceremonies Murray mentioned in a letter to Moran that Forrest had just visited Maitland and preached 'a magnificent sermon' on Holy Thursday.[26]

Freeman's published the Bathurst sermon in full over two pages, describing it as a 'brilliant discourse'. Forrest's theme, as in talks he gave soon after arriving in the colony (chapter 4), was the perils of material and scientific progress without corresponding moral progress. He linked this with the current education debate and the push for purely secular education. The presence of so many people at the stone-laying ceremony and their generous donations to the convent showed there was a strong demand for education combined with religion, he said. However,

> The spirit, tone and temper of politicians, and writers of unquestionable ability, of the great masses of men, in almost every country, point to the opposite – education without religion. In fact, this is only one aspect of a most pernicious error, influencing unfortunately too many in our age and time. This world – the laws that regulate it and the means of succeeding in the acquisition of wealth – are made the great end of existence. As if there were no higher destiny for man than to extend commerce, develop industry, and construct machinery.

The melancholy truth, he said, was that despite 'our boasted enlightenment' wealth was more prized than virtue. Man's higher nature, his nobler faculties, were neglected. The 'indefinite augmentation' of wealth brought 'a proportionate increase of cupidity and selfishness', he added, and 'the fabulous riches of a few may be consistent with the abject misery of the multitude'.

> Wealth, no doubt, will provide ships and arsenals, fortresses and cannon – everything, in a word, that can save its possessors, except one thing – brave hearts, full of resolution and heroism, ready to become the living ramparts for the defence of truth, justice, and social order. Exorbitant and exaggerated wealth is a social cancer: it corrupts those who possess it, and degrades those whom it impoverishes.

He said the Church was in favour of material progress, but as a means, not an end. 'The world has nobler instincts and higher ambitions. The progress of the age includes the advancement of science, of the arts, legislation, government, and social institutions. I maintain that without moral progress, without virtue in the Christian sense, the onward march of mankind in these departments is impossible.'

He praised the 'illustrious' Sisters of Mercy, who had renounced their possessions, torn themselves away 'from all the endearments of home and friends', and come to a land 'at once strange and distant'. The convent would be 'a nursery of every virtue' for the 'future women of the district'. 'Their intellect will be cultivated, their affections will be directed according to the teaching of the Gospel…'[27]

Back in Sydney, Forrest was again McEncroe's invited preacher at St Patrick's on St Patrick's Day. The service went ahead in a packed church – five days after the shot rang out at Clontarf that wounded Prince Alfred, fortunately only superficially, and sparked frenzy in the colony. Other St Patrick's Day celebrations were cancelled; *Freeman's* noted that Catholics were 'anxious to go through the religious ceremonies of the day although they were unwilling to take part in any national demonstration under the sad circumstances in which the colony is placed'.[28]

The first *Freeman's* report of the shooting at the royal picnic was written before the attacker's identity became known. 'The prayer which was fervently uttered by thousands of our countrymen on their learning the sad affair was – "Pray God, that he be not an Irishman!"' it observed.

> We need not say that in that prayer we heartily concur. For if the atrocious ruffian be of our race, then Irishmen must bow their heads in sorrow, and confess that the greatest reproach which has ever been cast upon them, the deepest shame that has ever been coupled with the name of our people, has been attached to us here in the country where we are so free and prosperous.[29]

Unfortunately, O'Farrell was an Irishman and, as people flocked to meetings called around the colony to express indignation at what had happened, sympathy for the prince and loyalty to the Queen, the cry went up that Fenians were behind the crime. Speakers in the Legislative Assembly the day after the shooting promoted the theory. 'Hear, hear', MPs called, when Robert Wisdom claimed there was not a member of the Assembly, or a person in Sydney, 'who was not satisfied that the crime was the result of Fenian organisation'. Wisdom accused *Freeman's* of sedition; he was one of many speakers who attacked the paper. The Rev. John Dunmore Lang told the Assembly O'Farrell was probably 'only the agent of a gang associated for the vilest and most atrocious purposes'.

Prominent Catholics rushed to declare their abhorrence of what had happened. Dalley told the crowd, estimated at twenty thousand, at the indignation meeting in Hyde Park that the attempted assassination was 'the most awful calamity that has befallen this country'. Duncan told a hastily called meeting of civil servants that he had 'scarcely yet recovered from the shock of the atrocious crime'. At St Patrick's on the Sunday following the shooting, McEncroe said no crime during his more than thirty-six years in the colony could be compared with it 'in wickedness and infamy'. He exhorted the congregation to 'join in humble prayer to Almighty God to restore [Alfred] speedily to health, and also to avert from them the calamities which they had reason to apprehend would fall upon the colony as the consequence of such enormous guilt'.[30]

A special meeting of the St John's College Council was held the next day, and for the first, and probably only, time the press was invited to witness proceedings. The object was to formally adopt an address to the prince, signed by Forrest as Rector. This read,

> To his Royal Highness Alfred Ernest Albert, Duke of Edinburgh, Earl of Kent, Earl of Ulster, Duke of Saxony, and Prince of Coburg and Goths. May it please your Royal Highness, – We, the Rector and Fellows of St John's College within the University of Sydney, beg to approach your Royal Highness with the expression of our deepest sympathy, and at the same time of our horror of the atrocious and cowardly attempt which has been made on your Highness's life. The gloom which this crime has cast over the whole colony will, we fervently hope, by God's blessing, be soon dispelled by your speedy recovery and restoration to perfect health. We desire also to convey to your Royal Highness the earnest assurance of our attachment to the person of her Most Gracious Majesty your Royal Mother, and to the laws and institutions under which we live, and our warm appreciation of the kindly and estimable qualities which have won for you personally the affection and good-will of the whole community.

Solicitor Eyre Ellis instigated the meeting, prompted, he said, by repugnance at the notion being advanced by some that Catholics and the Irish had a special responsibility to publicly disavow any sympathy with O'Farrell or his motives. It was 'an intolerable insult to them as Catholics to ask them to disclaim sympathy with a murderer', he said. Catholics 'joined heart and soul with the rest of the community' in denouncing the crime, but he could never sanction 'the idea that, because a vile assassin happens to be of the same religion or country, a man is necessarily bound to disclaim sympathy with him'.

One of those who had called on O'Farrell's co-religionists and countrymen to speak up was the Speaker of the Legislative Assembly, William Arnold. He was loudly cheered at the civil servants' meeting addressed by Duncan when he said Irishmen and Roman Catholics should 'come forward and deny anything approaching to sympathy not only with this act but…with the feelings of disloyalty of which it was only an open and insolent manifestation'. All speakers at the St John's Council meeting echoed Ellis's objection. Edward Butler 'burned with indignation to find it thought by any man in the slightest degree necessary that Catholics should come forward and disclaim their sympathy with murder'. John Donovan said the shooting had provided the opportunity for a venting of the 'bigotry and intolerance that had long prevailed' in the community. He had long felt Catholics were regarded as aliens, and 'the climax had arrived when they were asked to exculpate themselves from a charge of such an insulting character'.

Two speakers, Duncan and Vicar-General Sheehy, criticised *Freeman's*. Duncan said its 'disloyal writings' had provided a pretext for the suspicions aroused against Catholics. Sheehy said he had 'always repudiated the notion that it represented the Catholic body'. He maintained, with the Archbishop, that 'no paper could represent the Church except under the censorship of the Church'.[31]

Polding was visiting the southern regions of the archdiocese when Alfred was shot. The only reference to the dramatic events of the past fortnight in his first letter to Gregory after his return, dated 27 March, was apparently an afterthought, written at the top of the first page.

> I saw the Prince today at Govt House. He very kindly sent for me. He has the appearance of perfect health.

Much of the letter was a glowing report of his travels in the Monaro: 'A glorious campaign we have had; a great harvest of souls… A fine open country with a people altogether fitted to it, untainted by Sydney Vice & grumbling, simple and ready to be moulded to good Christian life.' He thought this southern district was just the place for Gregory to take charge as Vicar-General, and issued another fruitless invitation to his friend to return: 'Come, dear Gregory, once more to the field of your early labours'.[32]

In later letters, Polding had more to say to Gregory on the events that followed Alfred's shooting, and on Henry Parkes who, as Colonial Secretary, had ministerial responsibility for the police investigation. 'Sydney has been in fearful commotion,' he wrote on 22 April. 'Parkes and Martin have made great capital out of this most miserable affair. Of all hateful men, the first named is to the fore. I cannot repress my dislike. His being the supreme power in NSW, for such he is though Martin is nominally Premer, is the heaviest curse that could befall this country.'[33]

The previous October, referring to the new education arrangements, Polding described Parkes as 'a determined, unscrupulous enemy to Catholics and to Irishmen'. The Archbishop was perhaps not always a good judge of character, but this time he seems to have been pretty right.[34]

11

Parkes on the rampage

The story of Henry Parkes's role in investigating the crime, and of his determination to demonstrate that a Fenian gang was behind it, is an extraordinary one. Parkes, then aged fifty-two, was a self-made English migrant. His business ventures, including the *Empire* newspaper, which he launched in 1850, generally failed, but his life in politics kept him at the forefront of colonial affairs from the late 1840s until his death in 1896.[1] His early political instincts were of the liberal/radical variety, and at a Sydney dinner in honour of the Young Irelander Charles Gavan Duffy in 1856 he proclaimed that, had he been in Duffy's position, he 'would have been a rebel also'.[2] If any idealism remained twelve years later, it was matched by a singular lack of scruple.

Then, as now, when a crime was committed, no matter how exalted the victim, customary procedure was for the police to investigate. Parkes, though, took matters into his own hands. Soon after O'Farrell was lodged in Darlinghurst Gaol, the Colonial Secretary and a political friend, James Byrnes, turned up to interview him. Then, with two police officers, the pair visited two hotels where O'Farrell had stayed, interviewed people who had spoken to the assailant, and took possession of items including loose pages apparently from a diary kept by O'Farrell. Parkes made further visits to the gaol over the next two weeks with a shorthand writer who, out of view of the prisoner, recorded the Parkes-O'Farrell conversations.[3]

The day after the shooting, the government offered a £1,000 reward for information leading to the apprehension and conviction of accomplices of O'Farrell, and a free pardon to any who turned informant.[4] These generous inducements produced no results, but the committal hearing provided support for the conspiracy theorists. One policeman claimed O'Farrell had said as he was arrested, 'I'm a Fenian – God save Ireland.' Another reported the words as, 'I'm a bloody Fenian, and I'll die for my country.' At the conclusion of proceedings, O'Farrell said, 'I have nothing to say but that the task of executing the Duke was sent out and allotted to me.'[5]

The transcripts of Parkes's gaol interviews, eventually made public in December 1868, show O'Farrell elaborating on that story.[6] Tip-offs to the newspapers provided exciting hints of what was emerging. Readers were told that O'Farrell was one of a band of ten Fenian agents who had cast lots for the task of shooting the prince. Fenianism was said to be rampant in Sydney, and disclosures had been made implicating many people. Why then, wondered *Freeman's*, had none of the accomplices been traced? Editor O'Sullivan never wavered in his conviction, which proved correct, that in fact O'Farrell had no more connection with the Fenians 'than the Editor of the *Sydney Morning Herald*'.[7]

A week after the shooting, parliament hurriedly passed, with only one dissenting voice, a colonial version of Britain's Treason Felony Act. Less than three weeks earlier, by remarkable coincidence, an official request had arrived from London for New South Wales, along with the other colonies, to adopt this legislation, which the House of Commons passed in 1848. The Act was being used successfully to suppress Fenianism in Ireland and England; it had 'succeeded in filling Irish gaols', said *Freeman's*.[8] The New South Wales version, with intimidating new clauses added by the colonial government, was effectively an

Henry Parkes.

open invitation to informers to come forward with allegations of disloyal acts and statements, however trivial.

Newspaper advertisements emblazoned with 'God save the Queen!' and signed by Parkes called on all 'loyal subjects' to help enforce the Act by providing information and exercising 'the powers conferred upon every person' to arrest offenders. People were urged to look out for those using language disrespectful to the Queen or 'factiously avowing' to refuse to join in any loyal toast or demonstration in her honour. Provisions banning the expression of sympathy with any felony committed under the Act or with perpetrators, alleged as well as convicted, offered even more scope to informants.[9]

Many responded, and *Freeman's* advised its readers to take care: 'In the present excited state of the public mind a jest or loose expression might be seized upon and a prosecution ensue.' A number of drunks were reportedly taken into custody after declaring themselves Fenians, and at Gundagai a racegoer who exclaimed 'Hurrah for the green' was arrested; the magistrates released him after he said green was the colour worn by a winning horse. More seriously, the respected detective who tracked down the bushranger Frank Gardiner in 1864, Daniel M'Glone, lost his job after failing to arrest a man he allegedly overheard saying 'What a fuss about the Prince; if he was a poor man with four or five children there would not be so much about it'.[10] No accomplices of O'Farrell, or others who could pose a genuine threat to society, were found; the Treason Felony Act proved as ineffective as the £1,000 reward.

O'Farrell was brought to trial before Judge Cheeke and a Supreme Court jury at the end of March. Martin, as Attorney-General, prosecuted. A prominent Victorian barrister, B.C. Aspinall, and W.B. Dalley appeared for the defence, arguing that O'Farrell was insane when he committed the crime and therefore should be found not guilty. O'Farrell's sister, Caroline Allen, was their main witness, recounting episodes of drunken delirium, suicide threats and other 'strange and peculiar' behaviour. The jury was not swayed, and the judge pronounced the expected death sentence.[11]

This was carried out at Darlinghurst Gaol just three weeks later. The government had rejected a request by Prince Alfred that O'Farrell be spared until the British government was consulted. Rumours that the prince, who left for England a week after the trial, did not want his assailant executed had appeared in the press within days of the shooting.[12] Another sign that he was keen to calm matters was Polding's prominent place at the top table at his farewell luncheon.[13]

Parkes, though, was in no mood for peace. On 9 April, he offered a further £250 reward for informers. The announcement said there was 'good reason to believe that certain persons, disaffected towards her Majesty's Government, meet together for seditious and illegal purposes'. This reward was for information leading to the apprehension and conviction of any such people.[14]

About the same time, rumours began circulating that police had intercepted a letter written by Bishop Sheil of Adelaide to O'Farrell in Sydney shortly before the shooting. This reportedly wished him success in what he was about to undertake and promised that, if successful, he would receive the Church's absolution. Parkes was almost certainly the source of this sensational intelligence. In a letter to the *Sydney Morning Herald*, Bishop Quinn of Bathurst said the Colonial Secretary had shown him the letter, but not to read. 'Mr Parkes' remarks, at the time, left me under the painful impression that he wished to connect the Bishop with Fenianism, through O'Farrell,' Quinn wrote. It turned out that the letter was Sheil's reply, sent to a Victorian address, to one from O'Farrell in April 1867 expressing a desire to resume studies for the priesthood. Sheil wished him well.[15]

Possibly a report a few weeks earlier that letters had been sent to O'Farrell in Sydney care of McEncroe and Forrest shortly before the shooting was the result of another unsubtle attempt to link the Church with the crime. However, this story, in the *Illustrated Sydney News*, absolved the clerics, saying neither 'had the most remote idea of what O'Farrell's true character was'. A similar item mentioning McEncroe and 'some person connected with St John's College' appeared in the *Sydney Morning Herald*.[16]

The origin of these stories became clear when the transcripts of the Parkes-O'Farrell conversations were released. O'Farrell told Parkes that, to please his sisters, who wanted him 'to study for the Church', he had applied for employment at St John's, but had not been taken on. He had arranged for letters from relatives to be sent there, care of Forrest, and to McEncroe. On the morning of the shooting, he had gone to the college to collect one from his sister in Melbourne.

Parkes: Did you fetch that letter yourself?
O'Farrell: Yes; I walked in and took it.
Parkes: It was on the table?
O'Farrell: Yes.[17]

At the trial, O'Farrell's sister, Mrs Allen, said she had received a string of letters from him from Sydney in which he asked her to send him money. All but one of her replies, with money enclosed, had been sent to the hotels where he was staying. The other – apparently the last – was addressed to St John's (she did not mention McEncroe).[18]

Parkes paid O'Farrell another visit in gaol the day before his execution, at O'Farrell's request. The prisoner had a written statement to give the Colonial Secretary, which he did not want read until after his execution. Parkes arranged for a visiting magistrate to sign it and have it delivered to him.[19]

The next two days' proceedings in parliament were dramatic. William Macleay, an opponent of Parkes who had earlier accused him of exciting 'an anti-Catholic feeling and cry' to make political capital for himself, took the starring role. At the sitting on the day of the execution, 21 April, Macleay asked Parkes if he had received a communication from O'Farrell. Yes, said Parkes, but as Cabinet had not considered it the contents could not be made public yet. He went on, according to the newspaper report,

> As it happened there had come to the hands of the Government another communication, which was opened at the same time as that of O'Farrell. This other communication was of the very highest importance, from a source demanding the highest consideration, and one of these could not,

without detriment to the public service, be considered apart from the other. The Government had evidence of a new kind of crime that was deeply seated in the colony, and which it would take all the power of the Government to grapple with; and until the information which came to hand was well considered by the Government, it would weaken their hands if they were compelled to make that letter public.

What was the 'new kind of crime', and the evidence for it? Parkes provided no information, leaving people to imagine what they chose. Having given the Colonial Secretary the opportunity, eagerly accepted, to make a fool of himself, the next day Macleay produced a copy of O'Farrell's declaration and read it to the amazed MPs. In it, the condemned man expressed 'heartfelt sorrow for the grievous crime' he had committed and added,

> I have hitherto said that I was one of many, who were prepared to do the deed had I not done it. I had not the slightest foundation for such a statement. I was never connected with any man or any body of men who had for their object the taking of the life of the Duke of Edinburgh. Never was I in any other than an indirect manner connected with that organization in Ireland and elsewhere which is known by the name of the Fenian organization. I wish moreover distinctly to assert that there was not a human being in existence who had the slightest idea of the object I had in view when I meditated on and, through the merciful providence of God, failed in carrying into effect the death of the Duke of Edinburgh...[20]

Parkes and his supporters refused to accept that O'Farrell had now told the truth; Rev. Lang put their view colourfully, claiming the statement had been 'concocted for him by the Romish priesthood'.[21] Polding, who had visited O'Farrell twice as he prepared for his end, sought to allay such notions by giving Macleay a statement to read in parliament. The Archbishop said he could confirm, from his own knowledge, that, though advised to make it, the declaration was O'Farrell's 'free, voluntary act'. He had written it 'in order to make some atonement for his crime', and 'for the express purpose of its being published'. In order to secure its publication, he had placed 'in the hands of a confidential person a duplicate, written and signed by himself'.[22]

That person was the prison chaplain, Father John Dwyer, grandson of the 'Wicklow Chieftain' Michael Dwyer, a leader of the Irish rebellion of 1798. Dwyer, confessor and spiritual adviser to O'Farrell in his last weeks, gave the document to Dalley who passed it on to Macleay, most likely after discussing how it could best be used to discomfort Parkes.[23] In a letter to Gregory describing the events, Polding said O'Farrell had made the duplicate because he had no confidence in Parkes. 'It is the universal belief that for his own purposes to keep up the diabolical excitement, Parkes would either have suppressed or mutilated or modified for his own ends that declaration,' he wrote.[24]

Dwyer was sacked as chaplain at Darlinghurst Gaol, and Parkes stepped up the hunt for Fenians. For example, he secretly placed on the government payroll a man named Harry Benedict who promised to expose Fenians he knew in Melbourne; Benedict proved another charlatan.[25] In early May, a dinner arranged by Rev. George Dillon of St Augustine's church, Balmain, to raise funds for his new school building took on the appearance of a protest meeting. Forrest, several other priests and 'not a few influential laymen' joined Dillon on the platform. *Freeman's* reported that more than five hundred people packed the hall.[26]

The main speaker was Walter M. Adams, the 'late Fellow of New College, Oxford,' and Catholic convert who spoke at Bishop Lanigan's consecration dinner (chapter 9). Adams had become well known for his criticisms of the government in letters to the *Sydney Morning Herald*, collated in late 1867 as a pamphlet titled 'The Rhinoceros Ministry' (the title page explained that the rhinoceros is a 'very thick-skinned animal').[27] He spoke of

> religious animosity sedulously fanned, every slanderer's report that can add fuel to the flame carefully heaped up, the uncorroborated statements of a possible madman and a proved assassin eagerly seized upon to inflict a stigma on the whole community, and his dying declaration removing the stigma converted into an instrument of fresh suspicion.

However, his conclusion was hopeful. In spite of the most strenuous efforts to divide the people, they refused to be divided. He looked forward to the day 'when the interests of the nation shall no longer be made the mere footstool for the ascent of a demagogue'.

He had only a few months to wait for Parkes's resignation as Colonial Secretary. This occurred towards the end of September, according to Parkes in protest at the sacking of W.A. Duncan as Collector of Customs following a dispute with the Treasurer, Geoffrey Eagar. *Freeman's* was not alone in suggesting other motives, even including trying to regain Catholic sympathy by backing a prominent layman in conflict with the government.[28]

Parkes was increasingly becoming a figure of ridicule in some circles, not only Catholic. What, asked *Sydney Punch*, was the never explained 'new kind of crime' that he revealed in April? It was to be found in

> fostering sectarian animosities, conjuring up the hatred of rival races, invoking the damnable and meaningless antagonisms of foreign parties, making capital out of condemned cells, and transforming the gallows into a hustings.[29]

In late August, the mysterious murdered Fenian, soon immortalised by a Sydney wit as 'the Kiama ghost', made his entrance. Parkes called a meeting at the Kiama courthouse to report to his constituents on the government's achievements. The hall was packed and, as the crowd cheered, he claimed for the first time that the police had been informed before Prince Alfred landed in Sydney that 'an outrage would be attempted upon his life'. He went on,

> I can produce evidence, attested by affidavit, which leaves no doubt in my mind that not only was the murder of the Prince planned, but that some person who was in the secret, and whose fidelity was suspected, was foully murdered before the attack was finally made upon the Prince.[30]

If it was known that Alfred was in danger, why, sceptics immediately asked amid calls for the affidavit to be produced, wasn't a greater effort made to protect him? And where was the body of the murdered Fenian? As usual, Parkes offered no answers. 'The Colonial Secretary cannot exist without…avowing his knowledge of some mysterious fact calculated to make most people's hair stand on end,' commented *Freeman's*.

Parkes, now a backbencher, repeated his Kiama claims at a meeting at Jamberoo in October and added another extraordinary statement:

five hundred special constables had been sworn in to guard Alfred on his arrival.[31] Within weeks the government fell, to be replaced by an administration headed by John Robertson, a staunch critic of Parkes. It soon emerged that the former Colonial Secretary had taken possession of the O'Farrell file, including the assailant's diary sheets and the transcripts of the interviews at Darlinghurst Gaol. Eventually, on 18 December, he tabled the documents in parliament and the shaky basis of his claims was revealed.[32] Supporting the notion of a Fenian conspiracy were such quotes from the gaol conversations as

> Parkes: But I understood you to say that you had great compunction in shooting him at all – that you did not like it?
> O'Farrell: Who would?
> Parkes: But you felt compelled by the instruction from the Fenian Government?
> O'Farrell: We were under oath. As to the matter of fear, I did not care a fig. I took the oath to shoot any man that did not fulfil the particular obligation which devolved on him – all did.
> Parkes: I think you said there was a band of ten?
> O'Farrell: Yes.

Giving rise to the Kiama ghost story was this strange passage in O'Farrell's diary:

> Woe to you England, when the glorious 'nine' carry out their programme. There was a Judas in the twelve – in our band there was a No. 3 as bad, but his horrible death will I trust be a warning to traitors. Such another I am confident is not among the nine. Oh, that I were with them! For after all, this thing I have to do for vengeance, and to rouse the Irish here, will cost too dear, as I know I could have done so much more in England. But it is my duty to the R., and I will, if able, do it.

There was no support for Parkes's claimed foreknowledge of a threat to the prince. And the five hundred special constables? It turned out that Parkes had given the police chief authority to swear in a brigade of specials to keep the peace at a parade of Orangemen planned to coincide with the prince's arrival. The march was called off, so this plan lapsed. The proposal had nothing to do with intelligence of a Fenian assassination plot.[33]

The conclusion drawn by many from the diary and gaol conversations was that they confirmed O'Farrell's insanity. 'A more rambling, disjointed, incoherent, wild and aimless piece of composition never proceeded from the mind of man,' *Freeman's* observed of the diary. An important question arose: why were these documents not presented at O'Farrell's trial? Wrote *Freeman's* in relation to the diary,

> We very much fear that people who have no very high opinion of the then existing Ministry will declare it was not produced because it would tell strongly against the case for the Crown; because in the hands of Mr Aspinall, or Mr Dalley, it would be turned into a powerful argument to establish the insanity of the prisoner.[34]

To Dalley, normally one to see the best in people, the actions of Parkes were unforgivable. When his political star rose again in 1872, remarkably with Catholic help, the lawyer was scathing in his denunciation. In a speech, subsequently published as a pamphlet, Dalley denounced the former Colonial Secretary, now Premier, as one of those characters 'so repulsive as to make silence upon the part of honest men a crime'. Referring to Parkes's 'new kind of crime' and 'Kiama ghost' speeches, he said their deliberate falsehoods had

William Bede Dalley.

> alarmed and convulsed the country, ...sent a thrill of horror through our whole political and social systems, ...split up into sections a community that had existed in peace and harmony so long. These were the statements upon which sprang into existence everywhere all kinds of associations for the creation and encouragement of bitter sectarianism and national animosities... These were the statements to which we undoubtedly and directly owe the revival and perpetuation here of feuds which have even died out in that beautiful but unhappy country which was their savage birthplace.

From the moment 'these astounding statements' were made, he continued, 'rumours arose, suspicions were excited, the very air of our social life was poisonous with alarms and apprehensions; bloody conspirators were suspected in the persons of the most inoffensive citizens, and organizations dangerous to life, directed against loyalty, and menacing the constitution, were looked for everywhere.' He praised the 'brave and bold' Scottish Protestant William Macleay, who had taken Parkes on in parliament 'for the vindication of the character of the country, and to place beyond all shadow of doubt the loyalty of its people'.[35]

Prince Alfred made two more visits to Sydney as Captain of HMS *Galatea*. On his second arrival, in March 1869, a year and a day after the shooting at Clontarf, well-wishers packed on to steamers greeted him on the harbour and crowds lined the shore. Then he was 'allowed to go about like any other commander of a ship of war', *Freeman's* reported. 'Every day he takes a drive to some of the suburbs of the city; in the evening dines at Government House with a select few and afterwards usually visits one of the Theatres.'

The paper was amused to hear that he had worn a large bunch of shamrocks on his breast on St Patrick's Day, and his horses had been 'bedecked' with green ribbons. 'There can no longer be any doubt that Fenianism of the greenest hue is rampant in the colony,' it joked. 'Oh, that a prince of the blood royal should set the example!' His third visit, in October and November 1870, also passed without fuss or incident.[36]

12

Moving on

On 22 August 1868, two days before Parkes delivered his 'Kiama ghost' speech, the much-loved Archdeacon McEncroe died at the age of seventy-three. It is sad that his end came at a time when the denominational harmony he had always promoted seemed to be fracturing. But his funeral, probably the largest yet seen in Sydney, presented a different picture; Protestants and Catholics mingled in a massive display of respect and affection. An estimated forty thousand gathered outside the Devonshire Street cemetery to witness the arrival of the procession. Wrote *Freeman's*,

> All classes were there, all ages were there, all creeds were there, brought together by the universal wish to pay to Archdeacon McEncroe the last token of esteem which men pay to a departed friend. Well did he deserve it from them.[1]

By remarkable coincidence, the chief advocate in the 1850s for the creation of new dioceses with Irish bishops died surrounded by five such bishops after receiving their blessings. Polding, who had delivered the last rites, was also present. Meetings with the Archbishop to plan a provincial council of bishops in 1869 had brought the Quinns, Murray, Lanigan and Daniel Murphy, Bishop of Hobart since 1866, to Sydney. Their first session was on the day McEncroe took to his bed, four days before he died. In a touching letter to Gregory, Polding described daily visits to the old priest as congestion of the lungs developed, religious observances with the 'dear good man', and the moment 'his purified, holy soul obeyed the summons of its Creator and went forth to meet Him whom he had so long and so earnestly served'.[2]

As McEncroe died on a Saturday, *Freeman's* had nearly a week to prepare its elegantly written tribute, which gave a detailed account of his life and noted the 'sturdy independence in his character' and his lack of interest in rising in rank in the Church; 'he preferred to live in the sphere of active usefulness'. The much briefer *Sydney Morning Herald* obituary was also to the point:

> His hearty devotion to his own Church and his fearless vindication of what he deemed the unalienable rights of his co-religionists never embittered his social relations with those who were conscientiously opposed to the Roman Catholic faith; his unswerving independence, sterling friendliness, and manly candour being thoroughly appreciated by all... [He had] a homely quiet earnestness, and integrity of purpose, which clothed all his acts with a singular naturalness, and dignity, of which he seemed wholly unconscious.[3]

After a succession of solemn ceremonies in a crowded St Patrick's on the Sunday and Monday, the final Dirge and Requiem Mass were celebrated at St Mary's on the morning of Tuesday 25 August. The five visiting bishops were there with Polding, as well as more than forty priests, including Forrest. Thousands unable to be accommodated in the pro-Cathedral waited outside to join the slow procession to the cemetery. At the tomb, also that of Archpriest Therry, Polding recited the last prayers. 'His words could scarcely be heard, owing to the grief which weighed him down,' *Freeman's* reported, 'and hundreds were heard to sob audibly around the vault'.

Polding's sorrow at losing his comrade of thirty-three years is moving. He undoubtedly felt affection for McEncroe, as shown, for instance, by the note enclosing a shamrock spray that he sent him from Ireland in early 1867 (chapter 7). But from his side it had not been a trusting relationship; the Irishman was too often seen as a hindrance to his plans for the archdiocese or an outright opponent. Examples are numerous, including McEncroe's association with *Freeman's*, his supposed support for Gregory's recall, and even the selection of Forrest as Rector of St John's. As recently as March 1868 Polding had named McEncroe to Gregory as one of those — Forrest was another — not backing him on the issue of Sheehy's appointment as auxiliary bishop (chapter 7),[4] and in May he reprimanded him for chairing a talk by Rev. Conway.[5]

Polding was McEncroe's age (he was born two months earlier), and noted in his letter to Gregory, 'My turn must now come; may I be as well prepared and have some if not all the Consolations our dear friend received in his last moments.' He was a lonely figure – even more so now even though McEncroe had not been a confidant. Apparently Gregory, although long gone from Sydney, was still the only one who filled that role. Polding told him in January 1868 that Sheehy was very good as Vicar-General but 'I cannot talk over things with him as I could with you… he is so cold & will not bend when he ought'.[6] The following October, he confided,

> I feel how incompetent I am to meet the exigencies of my position. I have underhandedness to contend against. I have none to help me and I feel the powers of my mind in abeyance under increasing depression, nervousness, indecision, and reluctance to all mental exertion… I am paralysed. If I had only someone to encourage me – rouse me, scold me, [to] do what I know ought to be done. I am unhappy – oh how unhappy…[7]

Just a month before McEncroe died, he and Polding had undertaken a pleasant task together, welcoming into the Catholic fold one of the most remarkable early colonists, Dr William Bland. This honoured medico, philanthropist and fighter for representative government arrived in Sydney as a convict in 1814 having killed a man in a pistol duel on the naval ship he was serving on as surgeon. A man of wide interests, Bland's extracurricular activities in the colony included editing the report of the explorations of Hume and Hovell, proposing a way to prevent spontaneous combustion of wool in ships' holds, and publishing a design for a propeller-driven hydrogen-filled balloon (an Atmotic Ship!).[8]

A life-long Anglican, the seventy-eight-year-old received Holy Communion when a Church of England minister visited him two days before his death. The next morning he sent for Polding, McEncroe and Forrest, and all answered the call. According to the *Freeman's* account, 'obtained from the very best authority' (most likely Forrest), Polding arrived first and at Bland's request prepared him for reception into the Catholic Church. Then McEncroe baptised him 'in the presence of a few Protestant friends of the doctor and Mrs Bland'. Polding returned in the afternoon and 'continued his pious exercises with the sufferer'. In the evening, seeing Bland sinking rapidly, he administered Extreme Unction.[9]

An article from Goulburn's *Southern Argus*, described accurately by the *Empire* as 'usually well posted up in matters relating to the Roman Catholic Church', provided interesting additional information.[10] It reported that for several years Bland had been in the habit of conversing with Forrest 'on the many occasions on which they met in the Sydney University'. Probably they talked about the progress of science as well as religious matters. The *Argus* said Bland regarded McEncroe as 'an old and tried friend', and *Freeman's* noted that the old priest had visited him frequently in his last months.

This episode is a striking illustration of the capacity of the Irishmen McEncroe and Forrest to build friendly connections across the community – an ability that Polding, although always ready to answer the call of those seeking the consolations of the Church, did not share. Another example in Forrest's case is his baptism at St John's College in November 1869 of three- and seven-year-old sons of the freethinking Terence Aubrey Murray, President of the Legislative Council. It also suggests he could be very persuasive.[11]

In October 1868, Forrest spoke at another packed fundraising event at St Augustine's, Balmain – his subject again the Public Schools Act and the way the Council of Education was implementing it. He elaborated on points in the bishops' statement on primary education presented to Henry Parkes in June 1867 (chapter 9), and as usual sought to amuse as well as inform his audience. Addressing the demand that Catholics not be given religious instruction with other children, or by non-Catholics, in 'mixed' schools, he ridiculed the notion that a 'common Christianity' satisfying everybody could be taught. And a teacher presenting lessons contrary to his own religious views would be 'a liar and a hypocrite in his teaching'.

If he disbelieves in the existence of God, how can he teach God's existence?

Or invoke His sanction? Or appeal to His justice or His sanctity? How, in short, can he speak of God's omnipresence as witnessing the offences even of public school children? (Applause)... But suppose the teacher does believe in God: then we really have something in the shape of sanction for his lessons on morality. Yet this man may ridicule the divinity of Our Lord as a Popish folly, or as a Protestant fable. He may, and he ought if it be his view, laugh at the Trinity as a contradiction in terms, and blaspheme the Incarnation as a great deal worse. (Hear, hear)...

A teacher might be an expert in geology, or have a smattering of chemistry; no matter what his expertise, he would be required to lecture on 'common Christianity', Forrest said. But in the public schools there were

> Jews, Unitarians, Socinians, Muggletonians – (Laughter) – Congregationalists, Wesleyans, Chinese, Church of England, and Papists. (Roars of laughter). What Christianity is common to all these? The Jews abhor it, common or uncommon. (Laughter). Christ is not God according to the Unitarian... The members of the Council of Education have divers religious views, but they have never yet enlightened the world as to what they held, or what they rejected – that is, the public have not yet been favoured with any specific statement of their views. But, of course, they know what 'common' Christianity is, for they are the Council of Education enforcing it – enforcing it even upon Jews and Chinese, who both hate it, as the devil does holy water. (Roars of laughter.)[12]

The end of the year brought an event that briefly lifted Polding's spirits – the blessing and laying of the foundation stone of the new St Mary's Cathedral.[13] Normally such a ceremony marks the beginning of construction, but this time it celebrated completion of the building's massive foundations. The next contract, taking the walls of the choir, transepts and nave to a height of forty feet, had been let, with work to start soon.

For most participants the ceremony, on 8 December, was an open air one, although a large tent was provided for the invited guests. Two other structures had been erected – a massive wooden cross close to the site of the future High Altar and a platform on which the Archbishop and clergy took their seats. Four bishops joined Polding there – Murray, Lanigan, Matthew Quinn and fifty-eight-year-old Pierre Bataillon,

'Gentlemen of the press' record the laying of the foundation stone of the new St Mary's Cathedral.

based in the South Pacific since the 1830s. Forrest was one of nearly fifty priests with them.

After the religious observances and sermon, the Archbishop performed the ceremonial laying of the stone with a trowel with a carved ivory handle and solid gold blade embossed with images of the old and new cathedrals. Then Plunkett led a deputation on to the platform to read an address from 'the Catholics of Sydney' to the Archbishop, and noted that, within yards of the same spot, he had presented the first such address to the newly arrived Polding thirty-three years earlier.

Referring to events following the shooting of Prince Alfred, Plunkett and his fellow signatories said Polding's character and public services as head of the Church provided 'ample refutation of the calumnies of those unhappy people who would represent our faith as a conspiracy against loyalty and human liberty'. Responding, the Archbishop said he took comfort from the fact that 'our noblest fellow citizens' had quickly rejected the 'shamefully foul and cunning calumnies' that had been 'cast into the air, like a deadly miasma'. Now people were starting to wonder 'what the fuss of anger and suspicious hate' had all been about.

He said he hoped to travel to Rome towards the end of 1869 for the Vatican Council called by Pope Pius IX, and would like to take a picture of the new cathedral in its completed state and a photograph of the walls risen to fifteen, twenty or twenty-five feet. Displaying a lighter side that sometimes emerged on public occasions, he added,

> You see I am confiding to you a secret, but there is neither treason nor felony in it, so mind you keep the secret; and, that it may be more safely kept, tell it at once to everyone, man, woman, and child, that you know. It will be well kept then, and I shall have many to help me to realise my project, to build up [the] five and twenty or thirty feet I speak of. I shall be, if I go, almost, if not quite, the oldest Archbishop of that Council, and I should dearly like to boast a little about you at Rome, and to hear them say, 'what a fortunate Archbishop that is, he comes one year with a sad history of a Cathedral destroyed, and then almost the next he comes with the picture of a tenfold more magnificent one already built,' – for well begun, you know, dear friends, is half done.

At the luncheon afterwards in the St Mary's Seminary hall, Forrest had a place at the top table with Polding, the four bishops, Plunkett and the consuls of France and Spain. Polding proposed toasts to the Queen and the bishops, and Matthew Quinn proposed Polding's health. Replying, he said he was 'going down the hill of life', but was greatly consoled by the conduct and zeal of his clergy on whom he depended to 'steady his tottering steps'.

Exactly four weeks later, another blow struck – the destruction by fire of the temporary cathedral.[14] Fanned by a northwesterly wind, the conflagration, which began in the early hours of Tuesday 5 January 1869, destroyed the wooden edifice in less than an hour. The loss was almost total; the vestments, church plate and pictures – and the relics of St Felician – saved from the Cathedral fire of June 1865 were destroyed. The Archbishop's crosier and mitre were consumed, as was a treasured gift from the Countess of Shrewsbury, a set of vestments that included 'a cope of cloth of gold, set with precious stones and jewels'. Among recognisable items found 'completely fused by the heat' in the smouldering wreckage was the silver trowel Polding had used to lay the St John's College foundation stone in January 1860.

Fortunately, important items kept in offices attached to the pro-Cathedral, including the church registers and plans for the new cathedral, were saved. And, unlike the old cathedral, this building was insured, although for only £1,500 – not enough to rebuild the temporary cathedral let alone replace the other losses.

Hundreds more than the hall could accommodate gathered at St Mary's Seminary the evening after the fire. Greeted by loud cheering, a 'deeply moved' Polding told the gathering that, difficult as it was to understand, they must recognise the 'ever merciful providential hand of Almighty God' in what had happened. 'What He has given to us in the way of chastening has been in mercy,' he said. 'What He has done to us must have been for our good.' He wondered whether

> too much complacency may have intermingled with our purpose in seeking to erect that new cathedral which we still hope to see one of the glories of the Southern Hemisphere. (Cheers.) We may have failed in the singleness of heart in which all ought to be dedicated to God, and therefore have been called upon to suffer.

The main message of the other speakers, who included Dalley and Edward Butler, was sympathy for Polding. 'To us it is a matter infinitely more to be deplored than the loss of the building burnt this morning, that you should suffer as we know and feel you have suffered under this visitation,' said Dalley. Butler referred to rumours that the fire was the result of arson, and said if an incendiary was responsible he should be pitied. The true incendiaries were those who had 'excited religious dissensions' and 'tried to burn up the happiness' of their country and people. The inquest into the fire found no reason to suspect that it had been deliberately lit.[15]

More than £400 was collected at this meeting, and as much again the following evening at gatherings at the Seminary and at St Patrick's and the Sacred Heart church, Darlinghurst. A new, larger, temporary cathedral – this time built of brick, with iron girders – rose quickly, and Bishops Murray and James and Matthew Quinn joined Polding for its blessing and opening on the last Sunday in May.[16]

Three new students took up residence at St John's College at the beginning of 1869, out of a total of seventeen who began their university studies that year. They came from three schools – Lyndhurst, Sydney Grammar, and St Stanislaus', Bathurst. The Lyndhurst student, and probably one or both of the others, had studied for matriculation at St John's. Forrest's efforts appeared to be reaping some rewards again, with five resident students and another non-resident enrolled.[17]

Lyndhurst could not make a similar claim at the start of 1869 as no new students joined the group of undergraduates living there. However, 1868 had been a successful year for them; *Freeman's* reported that a first year student, three in second year and another in third year had done well at the end-of-year university exams.[18]

It would be intriguing to know what influences resulted in one Lyndhurst boy enrolling at St John's in both 1868 and 1869 while the rest of the university contingent stayed at their old school. Even more interesting would be a record of what Forrest and the Fellows had to say about Lyndhurst's undermining of the college. Unfortunately, nothing on this is recorded in the Council minutes.

Polding told Gregory in November 1868 that 'St John's College is lingering on in the same way – lost confidence, a sad pity'.[19] There was no acknowledgement that, by allowing – probably encouraging – Lyndhurst to usurp the college's role, he had put it in an impossible position. *Freeman's* noted in December 1868 that all but two or three of the Catholics who had passed through the university up to then had received their schooling at Lyndhurst. If Lyndhurst students were dissuaded from enrolling at St John's, what hope could the college have?

Correspondence in the lead-up to the provincial council, arranged for April 1869 following the August 1868 bishops' meeting in Sydney, throws further light on Polding's attitude to St John's under Forrest. Writing to Lanigan in February, he first proposed that the council be held in Melbourne in conjunction with the consecration of St Patrick's Cathedral, but when that ceremony was postponed he wrote 'our only recourse would perhaps be...St John's College here in Sydney'.[20] His preference, though, was for the bishops to call off their gathering until after the Vatican Council, to begin later in the year – a suggestion that brought a stinging response from James Quinn in Brisbane. Quinn told Polding he could not entertain the idea as it would breach 'the most decided instruction' from Rome, and added that St John's was the only venue available 'where the Bishops and other ecclesiastics taking part in the synod can live together'.[21]

Matthew Quinn offered Polding a way out, telling him James Murray had suggested the new Bathurst convent would be a very appropriate location for the meeting.[22] Polding wrote to Bishop Goold in Melbourne,

> Dr Quinn of Brisbane writes strongly in favor of St John's College. To this I have personal objection. We shall have there intrigue upon intrigue. Quinn of Bathurst has just completed a splendid Convent large enough for all purposes and communicating with the Church. He has very strongly urged our meeting there and I am inclined to believe it will be well. We shall be removed from Sydney & Forrest's intriguing, and the trip over the Blue Mountains will be of advantage to all of us. The rail takes us two-thirds of the way. My carriage will go before and we shall then go together – self, you and Adelaide. We shall travel delightfully.[23]

Five days later, this nice idea had been abandoned; Polding told Lanigan that, 'all things considered', Melbourne would be the best location.[24] The council opened in Wardell's still far from finished St Patrick's Cathedral on Sunday 18 April with eight bishops present – Murphy of Hobart, Sheil of Adelaide, Goold of Melbourne, James Quinn of Brisbane and Polding and the three New South Wales suffragans.

The two Quinns, Murray and Lanigan had travelled to Melbourne together by steamer from Sydney. Also on board were various priests who were to take part in proceedings, including Forrest, Dean Lynch, Garavel and Sheehy, so if intrigue was to occur this sea voyage provided the perfect opportunity.[25] Polding had arrived a few days earlier, probably accompanied by his chaplain, Father Vincenzo Coletti. The Italian priest was one of two masters of ceremony for the opening rituals.[26]

There can be little doubt that Coletti, who had become an increasingly influential adviser, fuelled the Archbishop's sense of being under siege. He wrote to a priest while travelling with Polding in the Monaro in February 1868, 'from what I have heard and experienced, I tell you that there is a real plot or conspiracy against the Archbishop, not personally directed but in the sense that they want an entirely Irish Church which would be equivalent to virtual Fenianism… My friend, you cannot believe the two-faced attitude these Irish priests have…'[27] Coletti, who himself seems to have been a master of intrigue, will make further appearances in the story (chapters 18 and 21).

Proceedings of the weeklong council were not reported, but Polding gave a light-hearted account of them at a 'grand dejeuner' afterwards hosted by the Melbourne laity. There had been, he said,

> meetings of the Bishops with theologians, and meetings of the Bishops without theologians, during the week, and no doubt the ladies would like to know what they had been doing (laughter). There had also been meetings of the Bishops, theologians, clergy, and laity in the magnificent Cathedral opposite, for religious purposes. At one stage of their proceedings they had been obliged to turn even the ladies out of church, who, no doubt, thereupon came to the conclusion that there was a freemasonry among the Bishops. They had now a meeting of Bishops, theologians, clergy, and laity outside the church, and he was glad to see that the ladies were well represented on this occasion.

Polding's next comments sparked responses from most of the bishops when their turn to speak came. He described the man chairing proceedings, the former Premier of Victoria, John O'Shanassy, as setting 'an example of noble-heartedness such as should always be given by an Irishman'. Apparently trying to retrieve his words, he added, according to the *Freeman's* report, that he 'used the word Irishman without regard to distinct nationality, for he ignored distinction of country. The moment we touched Australian soil we became Australians, and he thought it would be wrong to introduce the misfortunes and prejudices – the cause of party spirit – of other countries into discussion here.'

Bishop Murphy of Hobart was first to react: 'while we were all Australians we should never at any time forget the country of our birth', he said. James Quinn joked that he had made up his mind, when about to become an Australian bishop, that everything Australian was the best in the world, but added that he thought 'a man who was afraid to own his country should be ashamed of himself'. Murray thought it impossible 'for a man to be a good citizen of his adopted country unless he loved his native land'. Lanigan said he quite concurred that they were all Australians, but added that he 'would as soon forget the mother that bore him as cease to remember the land that gave him birth (great applause)'.

O'Shanassy sought to calm tensions, saying he thought the Archbishop had been 'misunderstood in some of his remarks about nationality; what he understood him to mean was that it was most unwise to be continually parading one's nationality in an offensive manner before his neighbours'. Polding apparently remained unfazed, proposing two toasts in cheerful fashion and, at the end of proceedings, 'bestowing upon each lady and gentleman as they left the high compliment of shaking hands with them'.[28]

The pastoral letter issued at the end of the council, signed by all the bishops, condemned 'indifferentism' as the 'deadliest of all errors'. It dealt at length with 'mixed schools' – 'Catholics cannot without detriment to conscience avail themselves of the public schools'; and 'mixed marriages' – to be strongly discouraged and, where allowed, to occur without solemn benediction.

It also contained a powerful statement on the situation of Australia's

Aborigines. The settlers, professing to be Christians, should have sought 'to protect, and teach, and make disciples of Christ those poor children of the soil', the bishops said. 'Alas! It is shocking to think of what has, in fact, been done. With very little, with short-lived, exception, injustice, neglect, cruelty, and a million times worse, the actual teaching of vice, have branded the annals of white men. The stain of blood is upon us – blood has been shed far otherwise than in self-defence...'

While many colonists had exhibited a humane Christian spirit in their relations with Aborigines, others had, 'in justification of a great crime, striven to believe that these black men are not of our race, are not our fellow creatures'.

> We Catholics know assuredly how false this is; we know that one soul of theirs is, like one of our own, of more worth than the whole material world... By which means the Christian regeneration of the aboriginals may be best attempted we can scarcely yet determine in detail... Still, some little has been done, enough to show how utterly false is the assertion that our aboriginals are irreclaimable... What is wanting is not capacity in the aboriginals, but apostolic self-devotion in the followers of Christ... The Fathers of this Council... desire solemnly to lay upon the conscience of all who have property in these colonies the thought that there is blood upon their land, and that human souls, to whom they are in so many ways debtors... are perishing because no man cares for them. It is a thought not for the clergy alone, but for the whole Church, laity and clergy too. No one of us must dare to say with Cain the murderer, 'Am I my brother's keeper?'[29]

Perhaps J.H. Plunkett's hand can be seen in this; he participated in the council as its lay secretary. As New South Wales Attorney-General in the 1830s, '40s and '50s, Plunkett had fought hard, in the face of much opposition, for equality before the law for Aborigines. The example best remembered is his success in securing the conviction, followed by hanging, of seven white men for the 'Myall Creek massacre'. Their crime was the unprovoked killing of about thirty Aboriginal men, women and children on Dangar station, west of Inverell, in 1838.[30]

Plunkett died in Melbourne, aged sixty-six, two weeks after the provincial council closed. Polding, still in Melbourne, attended him, and reported to Gregory that his death was 'just what each one might envy'.[31] In accordance with Plunkett's request that his remains lie near those of his old friend McEncroe, the body was brought to Sydney. Polding returned on the same steamer, and took part in the Dirge and Requiem Mass at McEncroe's old church, St Patrick's. Forrest was among the large contingent of clergy present.[32]

Mourners included the Premier, John Robertson, many prominent politicians and lawyers, including a few who were Plunkett's contemporaries for more than thirty years, and Sydney University's three professors. The recently knighted Sir Terence Aubrey Murray, President of the Legislative Council, perhaps deserves special mention. He had demonstrated his admiration for the man they were honouring by naming one of his sons, baptised by Forrest in November 1869, John Hubert Plunkett Murray. (This was 'Hubert' Murray, administrator of Papua from 1908 until his death in 1940.)

'An immense concourse' lined George Street for the procession to the Devonshire Street cemetery. Those marching in front of the hearse included the Fellows of St John's College in academic dress. About a hundred and fifty carriages followed; noting the procession's length, *Freeman's* observed that when the Archbishop's carriage, at its head, reached the cemetery, the last carriage 'was only as far as Bathurst Street'. Polding, again 'much affected', read the prayers at the grave. Among the glowing tributes, probably the most eloquent appeared in *Sydney Punch*. Most likely the work of Dalley, then a frequent contributor to *Punch*, it praised Plunkett's work as chief law officer in the years before responsible government:

> Just, when to be just was to be heroic – liberal, when intolerance was mistaken for firmness – uncorrupted and incorruptible amidst great and constant temptations – what remains to be said of one whose life adorned the service of his Queen and the history of his country?[33]

13
A changing guard

The deaths of McEncroe and Plunkett deprived the St John's College Council of two members it could ill afford to lose. When the first Fellows were elected in June 1858, McEncroe topped the vote for clergy members and Plunkett for the lay positions.[1] Both were as highly regarded in the general community as among Catholics for their honesty, moderation and good sense, and for the roles they had played in developing the colony's primary schools – McEncroe in charge of the Catholic system and Plunkett chairing the old National Schools Board.

Plunkett was a founding member of the university Senate, and Vice-Chancellor from 1865 to 1867. Demonstrations of his commitment to St John's included donating more than two hundred books to the college library. He seems to have had a good relationship with the Rector. For example, in late 1866 Forrest proposed the vote of thanks at a lecture he gave on the Public Schools Act, and two weeks later he chaired one on the same subject by Forrest (chapter 8).

From their many associations, it is clear that McEncroe also got on well with Forrest, and he gave numerous practical demonstrations of his concern for the college's success. In early 1867, he bought a hundred acres in Queensland 'as a permanent endowment toward the support of a Vice-Rector' and sought the help of Bishop Leahy of Cashel in finding a suitable candidate for the position (chapter 2). His will, drawn up in February 1868, six months before his death, provided for the rents and profits from three houses he owned in Sydney to go towards the salary of a professor of logic and theology in the college. It expressed the wish that, 'if practicable', the professor should be a Jesuit.[2]

McEncroe bequeathed the remainder of his library to St John's – he had donated more than three hundred volumes in 1864 – together with his small chalice and missal. Another provision in the will shows he hoped the college would take on the additional role of training priests. The income from three hundred acres he owned at Jamberoo was to support ecclesiastical students for the Archdiocese of Sydney, in colleges in Ireland and Rome 'until arrangements are made for the education of such students in St John's College itself'.

Apparently Forrest lost little time in contacting the Superior of the Jesuits in Australia, Father Joseph Dalton of St Patrick's College, Melbourne, about implementing the provision to appoint a professor to the college. Dalton expressed interest; a letter in March 1869 inquired whether a supplementary salary would be available to top up the income from McEncroe's estate.[3] The wheels turned very slowly, however. The college Council did not consider the Forrest–Dalton correspondence until February 1870, when it instructed Forrest to seek Polding's agreement 'to the Jesuits being invited to take office in the College'.[4] The Archbishop quickly said yes,[5] but another two months passed before the Council received Dalton's assurance that he would urge the Jesuits' Father General in Rome to 'name a Professor at once'.[6]

After hearing nothing more, the Council moved in late 1870 to fill the post itself. The Fellows invited Rev. David D'Arcy, a priest of the Bathurst diocese, to take up the position if a Jesuit had not been appointed by the following May.[7] D'Arcy, aged about forty, was a relative of McEncroe and had been a St John's Fellow since 1865. He moved in to the college, as Vice-Rector and professor of logic and theology, in August 1871, three years after McEncroe died.[8]

Two years earlier, in his 1869 annual report to the Council, Forrest had made clear his frustration at still having to run the college on his own and cover expenses from his salary. The report began with good news. After a 'brilliant examination', a St John's student, John Dillon, had become a barrister at the end of 1868. Three students had matriculated in 1869 and the college roll stood at six, including a non-resident who came to the two lectures in theology and two in philosophy, each an hour long, given every week. Discipline was satisfactory, and the students attended regularly at morning and evening prayer and meditation, and Mass on Sundays, holidays and Thursdays. There was a sermon every Sunday after Mass. Forrest continued,

> I request the Council of the College to make arrangements for next year, say February 1870, to relieve me of the responsibility of maintaining the College, and superintending every detail of its management. For more than six years I have discharged what I voluntarily undertook, with the permission of the Council, and I find I cannot longer continue to meet these demands. The large dining room is still useless; an outlay of £100 would suffice to fit it up for the present and one half of this sum can be had from the government. The immediate appointment of a Vice-Rector is necessary; one man cannot fairly be expected to do the work of many.[9]

The situation at St John's would only get worse, but fortunately Forrest had many interests and friendships outside the college. It seems that Rev. Garavel at St Joseph's, Newtown, was among his closest friends, and Forrest was a guest at the opening of a school there in February 1869 and the blessing of the church by Polding three months later. In July, Forrest chaired a meeting to arrange a testimonial to Garavel, who was about to leave on a visit to France and Rome. He was there, he said, not as a brother priest 'but as one of the parishioners, sharing their feeling of reverence for their pastor'. Two weeks later, he was master of ceremonies at the presentation of an illuminated address and a 100-guinea purse to the popular Frenchman.[10]

In May, Forrest spoke at a well-attended meeting called to initiate fundraising for a memorial chapel over the graves of McEncroe and Archpriest Therry. He regretted the public's 'apathy in showing devotion to the dead'; there was 'too great a desire of display upon funerals, and too little upon that holy and wholesome thought of praying for the dead', he said.[11]

His judgement of the public mood seems to have been correct; nothing came of this proposal. *Freeman's* certainly didn't help. A week after reporting plans for the McEncroe/Therry memorial, it launched an appeal on behalf of thirty-four Fenians who had been transported to Western Australia in late 1867 – in the last shipment of convicts to Australia – and had now been freed. *Freeman's* devoted so much space to its own appeal, to raise funds for the Fenians' passage home, that any attempt to collect for another cause through its columns would have been drowned out.

Freeman's could justly boast of the success of its appeal; by mid-August about $1,400 had been raised. Editor O'Sullivan wrote that the 'would be leaders of the Irish in these colonies' took no part, and accused them of lacking moral courage.[12] Dalley and Butler were among the notables who steered clear; many more were horrified when, in October, O'Sullivan announced plans for a grand welcome for the Fenians at Clontarf, scene of the shooting of Prince Alfred. Vicar-General Sheehy prepared a circular to be read in all churches calling on Catholics not to attend. The organisers were, he wrote, 'most childishly playing into the hands of men who are, at this moment and in this city, striving to represent Catholics as in every country the sources of imbecility, degradation, and crime'. Premier Robertson settled matters by banning the event.[13]

O'Sullivan's fellow proprietors soon gave him his marching orders from *Freeman's*. In a generous parting letter the thirty-one-year-old thanked those who had supported and encouraged him 'during the severe crises which the paper had to undergo within the last two years'. He praised his successor as editor, Thomas Butler, as 'in every way worthy of confidence and support', and hoped the paper would long enjoy 'the favour and support of the Irish body in Australia'.[14]

O'Sullivan moved to San

John Robertson.

Francisco where, after working as a newspaper editor and barrister, he died of pneumonia in 1880. *Freeman's* noted that his 'memory was still warmly cherished' by many old friends of the paper, and offered well deserved praise for his journalism during the Fenian scare of 1868:

> When it was 'treason' to defend an Irishman or a Catholic in this country, Richard O'Sullivan, as editor of the *Freeman*, bravely risked his fortune, aye, his life, for justice. No threats, however powerful, no legislative machinery, however subtle, could transform that brave Corkman into a renegade or time-server.[15]

Polding made up his mind in July 1869 to go to Rome for the great meeting of bishops, the Vatican Council, to begin on 8 December.[16] James Quinn and Lanigan were among other Australian bishops who decided to attend; Matthew Quinn and Murray stayed home. A few priests arranged to visit Rome while the Council was in session. One was fifty-three-year-old Dean Lynch, the pioneer priest at Maitland who had taken charge of the Armidale mission in 1862. Apparently he hoped to be appointed the first Bishop of Armidale,[17] but when he arrived in Rome he found the post had already been filled. Forrest's contemporary at the Irish College, forty-four-year-old Timothy O'Mahony, was consecrated bishop in Cork, Ireland, eight days before the Vatican Council opened.[18]

Preparing for his departure, Lynch came to Sydney in September, staying at St John's as Forrest's guest. This may explain the Rector's presence at a picnic arranged by the St Francis Total Abstinence Society in early September; Lynch was a noted temperance campaigner. At least three thousand people took part in this lively event, across the harbour near the site now occupied by Taronga Park Zoo. *Freeman's* reported that while some were 'tripping it on the greensward' to jigs and reels played by an 'indefatigable fiddler', others occupied themselves with football and athletic sports.[19]

James Quinn also arrived in Sydney around this time. Towards the end of September he, Forrest and Lynch crossed the Blue Mountains to join Matthew Quinn at the opening and dedication of a new church at O'Connell Plains, on the Fish River twenty kilometres south-east of

Bathurst. 'The glens and the windings' of the river resounded with the cheers of six or seven hundred people as the bishops and priests arrived, *Freeman's* reported. When the ceremony was over, all joined in a 'truly sumptuous dinner... It spoke abundantly for the Fish River district to see such an array of turkeys, geese, fowl, &c...'

The following evening, the Mayor of Bathurst took the chair and the Bishops Quinn and Dean Lynch were among the large and appreciative audience when Forrest gave a lecture to inaugurate the town's new St Aloysius' Reading Room and Circulating Library. Education was the 'instrument of civilization and the protection of liberty'; throughout one's life, 'every step... should be one of education,' he said. The Catholic library would provide the means for people, after their day's work, to 'refresh their minds, enlarge their thoughts', and thereby become better citizens.

He advised people to focus their studies. While 'no sportsman himself', he had been told that 'if you fired at a flock of birds you were likely to kill nothing, whereas if you shot at one in a crowd you were nearly sure to kill three or four'. They should choose a course to pursue, but he had no objection to their reading light literature as well. He urged them to imitate children in their eagerness to learn:

> A child is full of enquiry. He will poke his finger into your eye; he will snatch at your spectacles if you wear them; he will take hold of your nose, or your beard if you have a good one, all for the sake of gratifying his curiosity, or obtaining knowledge.

Mankind's journey of discovery had scarcely begun, he added. What was already known was the equivalent of a few shells gathered at the seashore compared with 'the contents of the great ocean'. It was 'but the other day' that Lord Rosse's telescope had penetrated the depth of the sky; why shouldn't they look into the night sky and pursue similar studies? There were many thousands of suns, some created 'ages before man was brought into being', that could be revealed by careful and conscientious study. 'Nature...enriches those only who pursue a course of industry,' he advised.[20]

The following week, the Quinns, Forrest and Lynch travelled to Maitland for the laying of the foundation stone of a new residence for Bishop Murray. Forrest delivered the sermon at High Mass in St John's Cathedral before the ceremony.[21]

Four days later he was back in Sydney attending a dinner at Lyndhurst to farewell Polding. This was a clergy-only affair, with the exception of the Archbishop's secretary, Thomas Makinson – a 'magnificent entertainment which was enlivened throughout by a beautiful band of music', *Freeman's* reported. There must also have been a reporter present, who noted that, on rising 'to a perfect avalanche of applause', Polding 'playfully remarked that as there were no reporters present he could unbosom himself with more freedom'.

After praising his 'beloved priests, his dearest children in Jesus Christ', the Archbishop said too much had been made of his advanced age: 'it was no impediment…as long as a man is able to be efficient in his missionary life. (Applause).' He entertained only 'one little apprehension' about setting out for Rome,

> he might be 'sea sick' for a while – that was a malady which, no doubt, the Holy Father himself had once suffered, for he was on a distant mission early in life; but there were, he averred, some cardinals in Rome, who never got tossed on the 'briny wave' and who, if they did, never after perhaps think it a light matter to travel several thousand miles of ocean.

The next evening, the pro-Cathedral was 'crowded in every part' for the presentation of farewell addresses to the Archbishop by the clergy and laity. Polding and his chaplain Rev. Coletti, James Quinn and Dean Lynch departed the following morning, 9 October, on the Royal Mail steamer *Malta*. Two harbour ferries accompanied the *Malta* to the Heads, but numbers on board were 'scanty'; *Freeman's* attributed this to the timing – the early hours of a Saturday.[22] It would be intriguing to know how Polding and Quinn, men apparently with little regard for each other, got along as travelling companions.

The Archbishop's absence proved brief. Ill on arrival at Aden, he disembarked and, with Coletti, caught the next steamer home, arriving 'in perfect health' the day before Christmas.[23] In letters that suggest his public cheerfulness before leaving bore no relation to his true feelings, he told Gregory in the new year that he much regretted returning. 'I live…in a cold unsympathising atmosphere,' he wrote in March 1870.

> I never committed a greater mistake than when I retrograded at Aden… Whatever difficulties I might have met with, they could not be so great as those I am in… I cannot say that Religion is in a more flourishing state for the increase in the number of Bishops. There is now abroad a feeling of bitterness more intense than words can express, outside of the Church; and within, a spirit of nationality and party we should be better without. So, my dear Gregory, my old age has not fallen in pleasant places. I begin to long for a release from this life, though I contemplate the after judgement in fear – great fear…[24]

In his next letter, he complained that he had nobody 'to take counsel with'. Sheehy was 'so reserved', and Coletti brought him 'all sorts of reports and statements which do not add to my peace of mind'. He was convinced 'there is some secret party against me', and had never done a more foolish thing than when he 'yielded to advice' and returned to Sydney.[25]

Polding arrived in the midst of parliamentary elections that started badly for those hoping for an end to sectarian division in the colony. Parkes topped the poll for the four-member electorate of East Sydney, the first contested. Martin – now Sir James, having been knighted earlier in the year – came next. Third was a Scotsman, David Buchanan, notorious for his anti-Catholic rhetoric.

Buchanan did not let his followers down in his acceptance speech, claiming the question at issue in the election had been 'whether they would be governed by an ecclesiastical or civil power'. He said 'a great struggle was going on', not between Catholics and Protestants, but between Catholics and their 'priestly and arrogant rulers'. Parkes's message was similar. He spoke of the danger to liberty posed by persons who controlled others 'for sinister objects to serve themselves'; from the context it was clear he was referring to Catholic bishops and priests.

Dalley responded with a powerful show of oratory in a speech supporting Rev. John Dunmore Lang's candidature for the other four-member electorate, West Sydney. (Like Forrest, Dalley was a long-time admirer of Lang despite his many anti-Catholic pronouncements.) Dalley marvelled at the patience with which Catholics had 'borne every insult and contumely that had been put upon themselves, their religion, and their clergy.' But, 'damned with a Parkes and cursed with a Buchanan', it was time to speak out. When he finished doing so the 'entire meeting rose and cheered for several minutes,' *Freeman's* reported. Lang subsequently withdrew from the contest, but Dalley's speech had made quite an impression. It was 'as noble a burst of eloquence as ever came from the lips of man', said the *Evening News*. 'It was an oration that conquered prejudice and evoked all generous instincts.'[26]

The opposition, led by Parkes and Martin, had less success as polling continued. *Freeman's* was pleased with the election outcome, which saw Charles Cowper replace Robertson as Premier of a government otherwise similar to its predecessor. The paper was glad to see many of Parkes's strongest supporters during the Fenian scare lose their seats, and noted that in a number of electorates Protestant votes had helped return Catholic candidates. Edward Butler, elected unopposed for the seat of Argyle, centred on Goulburn, was the best known of the new Catholic members of the Legislative Assembly.[27]

Butler told electors in his nomination speech that he belonged to the 'great liberal party', which comprised those 'who made their roads and their railways, who promoted settlement on the lands of the colony, and who encouraged education'. In what was probably an oblique reference to Parkes, a close friend in earlier years, Butler said it was 'a terrible mistake for those still claiming to be liberals to try to drive the Roman Catholic population into a position of antagonism. If they succeeded in doing so they would strike off the right arm of the liberal party.'[28]

Butler, at the end of 1869, was one of only five of the original eighteen St John's College Fellows who remained on the Council.[29] Among the new members was lawyer Patrick Healy, the college's first student, who was awarded his BA in 1863 and elected to the Council

Rev. Callaghan McCarthy.

in 1868. A year later, Dalley filled the spot vacated by Plunkett, but he took little part in Council deliberations and was required to resign in 1872 after missing three consecutive meetings.[30] McEncroe's replacement, Rev. Callaghan McCarthy, elected in late 1868, took a much greater interest in the college.

This forty-seven-year-old Irish-born priest, ordained by Polding in the early 1850s, served at Mudgee up to the formation of the Bathurst diocese. Then he came to Sydney, choosing to stay under Polding's jurisdiction.[31] His actions on the St John's Council suggest he may have been influenced by the Archbishop's attitude to Forrest. And unlike other members who probably held similar views, notably Polding's secretary Thomas Makinson and the Benedictine Father Sheridan, both foundation Fellows, he was prepared to speak up.

At Council meetings between August 1869 and the end of the year, he moved a raft of resolutions that implied criticism of Forrest's management of the college.[32] One sought a return from the Rector giving the names of all St John's students, past and present; the dates of their entrance, matriculation, graduation, and departure; and details of any who had failed to graduate at the usual time. Forrest reported that there was only one student in the last category – Daniel O'Connell, who entered in 1863 and left in 1866 without a degree. McCarthy foreshadowed, but quickly withdrew, another resolution asking a more-easily-answered question: how often and when had the Archbishop, in his capacity as Visitor, visited the college, and what had been his recorded remarks? Presumably someone let him know there had been no such visits.

The Council adopted McCarthy's proposal that the students face annual *viva voce* examinations, in the presence of the Fellows, on the subjects taught at the college. His motion that a committee of Fellows – comprising Butler, Sheridan, W.A. Duncan, Richard O'Connor (another of the original Fellows), Eyre Ellis and himself – be appointed to enquire into present and past discipline at the college was also adopted. Forrest's brother-in-law Dr Gilhooley seconded this motion, probably a sign that Forrest was happy to cooperate.

McCarthy's account of the establishment and proceedings of this committee, in the Sydney Archdiocesan Archives, reveals his disappointment at what happened.[33] Apart from himself, only Duncan, Gilhooley and Forrest attended the meeting that set up the committee, he wrote. With so few Fellows present, he was disinclined to proceed, 'but urged by the Rector', he did. He hoped the next Council meeting, in early December, would be well attended, providing the opportunity for extensive discussion of how best to address the subject. But, again, few turned up.

Shortly afterwards, wrote McCarthy, Forrest left for New Zealand on vacation. As the Rector 'was personally interested in the prosecution of the enquiry', he thought it best not to proceed until Forrest returned. However, advised otherwise by some members, he convened a meeting of the committee, which was held at Butler's legal chambers in late January 1870 (Forrest returned on 3 February). All members except Sheridan attended. McCarthy went on,

> Some wished to collect evidence in reference to the various allegations made against the regularity of discipline at St John's whilst others (who formed the majority) objected to such an enquiry as calculated to lead to unnecessarily offensive inferences and as insufficient to give a clear and just view of the management of the college from its foundation. The majority, of course, prevailed...

Despite this setback, McCarthy persuaded the Council to adopt his plan for improving college discipline through changes to the daily regime. A speech he wrote, probably for delivery at the August 1869 Council meeting, set out his case for change at great length, and with many oratorical flourishes.[34] The strict routine he proposed, and the more relaxed one it replaced, contrast starkly with twenty-first century attitudes and practice. It seems to have been assumed that students would do what was expected of them only if allowed no alternative.

Time to rise remained 6 a.m., but under the old regime, said McCarthy, students were 'not bound to present themselves before the Rector until the bell rings for morning prayer at ½ past 8 or for breakfast at 8'. Hence, 'if the morning be cold and dark and dreary they will feel the temptation to remain in bed and dream away in senseless comfort the happy hours of morn too strong to be resisted'. And if it 'be balmy and bracing' they may 'feel the invitations to go abroad and enjoy the merry scenes that surround them too pressing to be rejected'. A 'general licence' had 'unbarred the doors and gates', so they could 'ramble without the least fear of reprimand'. The new rules solved this problem by moving morning prayer and meditation to 6.30; students were then required to study for an hour before breakfast.

They would no longer be allowed to leave the college at any time without the Rector's permission, and absence at night during term would not be possible 'except at the written request of parents or guardians'. Currently, said McCarthy, the hours between 4 and 7 p.m. were at 'the capricious disposal' of the students. 'They can go whither their inclination impels them, whether the attractions of the city seduce them, or the pleasures of the playground allure them, or the amusements of their own rooms delight them, there is no obstacle to their gratification.'

Then, shortly after 7.30 p.m., following supper and evening prayer, the students were 'dismissed from the presence of the Rector and lost to his sight' until 8 the following morning.

> Now being aware that there is no special attention directed to their movements from 8 p.m. to 8 a.m., the students can easily devise ready means to spend many of these hours in occupations little in harmony with college discipline. And when we know what temptations of various kinds abound in and about the city, how largely the general licence to leave the college brings these seductions under the notice of the students, we have but too much reason to fear that every available opportunity may be used to their injury.

Sydney University – the original building in 1879.

The new rules did not affect activities between early morning and lunchtime, 1.30 p.m., because this period was occupied with lectures at the university. In the afternoon, the college lecture was moved from 3 to 5 p.m., with the students required to prepare for it for an hour beforehand. Recreation would be allowed between lunch and 4 p.m., giving students the 'proper buoyancy to grasp the abstruse subjects' dealt with in the lecture. After supper at 6 p.m., study was to resume at 7.30 and continue to 9.30, the new time for evening prayer and meditation. McCarthy proposed that lights go out at 10 p.m., but an amendment moved by Butler changed this to 11 p.m., with students returning to their rooms at 10. Silence was demanded during all study hours and after evening prayer.

Making his case, McCarthy argued that none of the 'three classes' affected – the servants, the students and the Rector – had cause for complaint. The servants would have to rise before 6 a.m., but this was expected of 'millions of their equals'. Students could not object to the 'judicious arrangement of their several duties'. Whether they came from homes 'where enlightened piety guides all the family movements' or from ones where 'no proper order reigned', the discipline at St John's should be such as would 'preserve in them what is good, eliminate what is vicious, develop what is virtuous, enlarge all their nobler faculties and return them to their parents with the dispositions and attainments becoming gentlemen, scholars, and Christians'.

And what of the Rector? McCarthy wrote that he had been told all his proposals would be adopted except the new times for morning and evening prayer, implying that Forrest objected to those. It would be said, he added, that, though the students would 'gladly receive this more perfect form of discipline', the Rector would 'find its observance an intolerable yoke, a slavery that will embitter his very existence'. McCarthy was unmoved. 'I candidly confess,' he wrote, that

> the faithful observance of this rule will entail the sacrifice of many social enjoyments, that it will oblige the Rector to spend his evenings at home with those committed to his charge and training, and necessarily bind him to a life of great order and regularity. But the very nature of his office insists upon strict regularity, continuous vigilance and willing readiness to advance the best interests of his pupils.

By overriding Forrest's objections, the Council implicitly endorsed McCarthy's criticism of the way he had been managing St John's. Forrest had seen his hopes for the college, which were starting to seem justified in the mid-1860s, dashed over the past few years as the supply of students from Lyndhurst was cut off. One can imagine that, after this new blow, he might have doubted the point of persevering. His six-weeks' escape to the wilds of New Zealand, which Garavel had probably told him much about, was well timed.

14

Strong words

St John's had only one resident student – Henry Sullivan, in the third year of his BA – in 1870. There were probably also two non-residents, who attended Forrest's lectures but lived elsewhere.[1] The atmosphere must have been somewhat desolate – scarcely ideal circumstances for implementing the new timetable or attracting more students.

Reflecting the prevailing gloom, Council meetings were poorly attended. Three Fellows lost their positions in April 1870 after being absent without leave from three consecutive meetings. One was Vicar-General Sheehy, another a foundation Council member, William Curtis. Lawyer and newly elected Member of the Legislative Assembly John Dillon replaced Curtis, becoming the second former St John's student on the Council. He had left the college only two years earlier. In July, the Fellows decided that future vacancies should be advertised in the Sydney press, probably a sign that willing candidates were proving hard to find.[2]

A March 1870 *Freeman's* report provides an indication of how much better things could have been for the college if Lyndhurst had not been allowed to usurp its role. Two Lyndhurst students had 'passed their BA degree examination with very great credit to themselves'. A third-year student had done equally well. And the school's new matriculant, William Hynes, had beaten more than twenty other candidates to win the £50 senior university scholarship.[3]

Seven St John's Fellows – McCarthy was a notable absentee – joined Forrest at the university's annual commemoration in the Great Hall in May. They had something to celebrate – especially Richard O'Connor, now sixty years old and in failing health. His son Richard E. O'Connor, a non-resident student at St John's, was awarded the Wentworth Medal for the best English essay. He went on to become one of the 'founding fathers' of Federation and a foundation High Court judge. Charles Coghlan, who enrolled in the college in 1869 and was probably a non-resident student in 1870, also did very well, winning the chemistry prize and a scholarship.[4] Both had finished their schooling at Sydney Grammar. (O'Connor was earlier at Lyndhurst.)

In a generally positive report on the state of the university, the Chancellor, Edward Deas Thomson, noted that numbers of matriculants were up a little (to eighteen), and they had done particularly well in the entrance exam. The Governor, the Earl of Belmore, bemoaned the low numbers at St John's and St Paul's (it had six students in 1870[5]). He thought that 'without residence a good deal of the advantage of a university career is likely to be lost'.

If mentions in the press can be taken as a guide, Forrest's life outside the college was quiet in the first half of 1870 and very busy in the second half. In June he joined a twenty-eight-man committee, headed by the Chief Justice, Sir Alfred Stephen, formed to raise funds for J.H. Plunkett's widow. Stephen told the meeting called to launch the project that Plunkett had 'left his affairs in a very embarrassed state'. A July subscription list shows Forrest gave £10 10s, the maximum contributed by any individual. Others who gave this amount included St John's Fellows Butler, Dalley and Ellis, and Archbishop Polding. The sum collected proved insufficient to provide Mrs Plunkett with an adequate annuity; she advertised in March and June 1871 that she was 'compelled by painful necessity to try to support herself, and is most anxious to receive pupils in Music and French'.[6]

Bishop Matthew Quinn visited Sydney in late June and, with Forrest, attended a banquet to mark the twenty-fifth anniversary of the Holy Catholic Guild of St Mary and St Joseph. Polding was unwell and unable to preside, which probably made for a livelier gathering. Rev. John Dwyer, the Darlinghurst Gaol chaplain sacked in 1868 after embarrassing Parkes, took his place.

J.K. Heydon was one of the main speakers; the controversial former

Freeman's editor recalled being part of the group the Archbishop called together in 1845 to establish the guild as a benefit society and Christian brotherhood. Forrest was not listed to talk, but rose 'in response to repeated calls from the meeting', a sign that, despite Polding's disapproval and the troubles at St John's, he remained a popular figure. He was not lost for words. 'It is sometimes asserted you are a political body – a secret society, a banded horde at the beck of the priests,' he told the members of the guild.

> Heed it not. They tell what is untrue and they know it. They bear false witness against their neighbour. Your lives, your works, your Christian forbearance under provocation without parallel in this country, are your most eloquent defence. When did the Catholic Guild undertake to exclude their fellow citizens from any place of honour or emolument in the country? When did they make their creed the touchstone of civil promotion? When did they administer a secret oath to any member about to join their society? Have they not published all and everything connected with the society? When their inoffensive dresses were objected to on a memorable public occasion, did they not forego their right and walk in the simple dress of the citizen in the sad procession which conveyed the dear old priest they loved so well to his last resting place?

That, no doubt, was a reference to the funeral of McEncroe at the height of the Fenian scare in 1868. Forrest concluded with praise for the Warden of the Guild, Edward Rubie, joking that he deserved 'the honour conferred lately on the Mayor of Melbourne, a gold chain of native gold – and so massive that the honour of bearing it would be counterbalanced by "the weight thereof"'.[7]

Two weeks later Forrest was Father Dwyer's guest speaker at a failed attempt to relaunch the Young Men's Society that had flourished at St Benedict's church, Broadway, in the early 1860s. Matthew Quinn and Dr McAlroy, Vicar-General of the Goulburn diocese and a St John's Fellow, were there, but few St Benedict's parishioners turned up and Dwyer admitted being 'rather taken aback' by the poor attendance. It was a far cry from the scene nearly ten years earlier at the same venue when an audience of a size and respectability seldom witnessed before in Sydney, according to *Freeman's*, cheered Forrest's first lecture in the colony (chapter 1). His main message this time, backed with 'many amusing illustrations and similes', was the one he promoted in Bathurst nine months earlier: acquiring knowledge required determination and a clear goal.[8]

Forrest was back in Bathurst in mid-August, to preach at the cathedral and speak at a gathering to mark the first anniversary of the Catholic library. Bishop Murray came from Maitland for the celebration, held in a room 'filled to excess' in which 'the greatest possible enthusiasm existed'. Murray spoke first, praising the library's role in placing Catholic books and newspapers within reach of all. He said Forrest had examined closely some of 'the secular books' used in public and denominational schools and found them 'totally unsuited for the purposes of education in this century' and 'in point of scientific knowledge considerably behind the age'.

Forrest concurred in a lively speech that the *Freeman's* reporter regretted not being able to record verbatim (although parts seem to have been taken down word for word). He claimed the Irish National system schoolbooks used in the colony were, in terms of both literary and scientific merit, 'the most defective and imperfect series in any civilised country'. He accused the Council of Education of violating the religious liberties of Catholics by making 'Protestant theology an essential part of secular education in all public schools'.

> Have you come over half the globe for this? Did the love of that old faith which is the glory of Catholics desert you on your arrival here? Your fathers suffered the loss of property, civil liberty and life. They endured the horrors of the dungeon, the transport ship, the pyre and the scaffold, rather than accept the honours and emoluments that awaited an unprincipled apostasy. Will you now permit this desertion of the old faith by your children because of the omnipotent will of five gentlemen called the Council of Education? Give me the old hearty proselytism when the head of a priest would have the legal price of the head of a wolf – £5. That is intelligible. But the sneaking, skulking proselytism of the public schools is an abomination to every honest, high-minded man.

He said 'the wildest and most irreligious doctrines' were being spread in the colony in the name of liberty, but he had no wish to see liberty curtailed. Civil and religious liberty was 'a glorious basis of any constitutional system, and is truly admirable notwithstanding its abuse'. But civil liberty would not survive long if religious liberty was strangled.

> This is the lesson taught by history. Some daring demagogue or military adventurer will crush religious liberty by imposing some new-fangled dogmas upon a people, and will then destroy their civil liberties. He who tyrannises over the soul will easily subjugate the body – a tyrant in religion will necessarily be a tyrant in law.'

Forrest again advised users of the library to focus their reading – to 'study one thing well'. Reading everything was not the way to knowledge, he said: 'Ballooning is not navigation.'[9]

In early October, he joined Quinn and Murray again, at the blessing of the Catholic church at Dungog, on the Williams River north of Maitland. Quinn performed the ceremony and Forrest preached. He noted that Protestants had contributed generously to the church's construction and had welcomed the bishops and priests to the district with 'unbounded hospitality'. The Catholic people would not forget this, he said.

> Would to God that the same spirit of union and charity prevailed in other places. May the waters of the Williams flow down smoothly and swiftly to other districts, bearing with them the same brotherly feeling, and cover the length and breadth of this colony, to calm and smoothen the disturbed waters of other less fortunate districts…[10]

Back in Sydney, he joined a St Francis Total Abstinence Society excursion to Clontarf at the end of October. Father Sheridan, St John's Fellow and former Prior of Lyndhurst, was in charge of the two to three thousand excursionists who, *Freeman's* reported, spent the day dancing with great vigour and playing various sports with gusto. 'The Very Rev. Dr Forrest, with several distinguished Catholic clergymen, gave an additional charm to the scene by their presence,' the paper added.[11]

Just over two weeks later, in mid-November, he returned to the Hunter with Matthew Quinn. His first engagement was preaching at the High Mass, celebrated by Bishop Murray, marking enlargement of the church at Morpeth. *Freeman's* published his sermon in full, the reporter claiming it 'would be useless to attempt to convey in a summary even a slight impression of the refined diction, the solid reasoning, and the profound theological learning with which the Very Rev. preacher carried conviction home to his hearers'. Possibly so, but his central message was that there is just one set of religious truths, that proclaimed by Christ and the apostles and taught by the Catholic Church.

Theology was not alone in being intolerant of error, he said. So were 'the physical, moral and mathematical sciences, chemistry and astronomy, law and physic… Only imagine how a man would be received by the British Association that would seriously deny the rotundity of the earth, or its diurnal rotation, or maintain that the sun was only a few feet in diameter… The rejection of a single corollary undermines the whole fabric of geometric truth…'[12]

The next day, he joined the two bishops at a concert given by the pupils of Maitland's Dominican convent. Some sang 'high class operatic music', but 'a fair proportion of the selections was of those simple touching airs which are more popular because they speak more distinctly to every heart', the local paper reported. Four pianos were in use, and 'the duets and trios were executed not by two or three players as the case might be, but by six, eight, or twelve, a pair or trio of fair musicians going to each instrument'. Their 'delicacy and precision of touch were only equalled by the exquisite time which they kept; the four pianofortes sounded like one instrument…'

An impressed Bishop Quinn gave the speech of thanks to the sisters and performers. The more he saw of young Australians, 'the more firm became his conviction that they possessed fine mental powers and great taste for music, which if properly developed will make a glorious future for Australia,' he said. He added that Forrest had just observed to him that the 'unspeakable charm' the young performers imparted to the music showed 'the most perfect training on the part of the teachers and a faithful correspondence on that of the pupils'. Compliments continued at the supper afterwards. Murray proposed the toasts, including one to

Forrest 'which was received with prolonged cheering, and acknowledged by the Very Rev. gentleman in a speech abounding in wit and humour'.[13]

The next evening Forrest had another engagement in Maitland, a lecture at the Schools of Arts, chaired by Bishop Murray, to raise funds for the Dominican Sisters' schools – tickets two shillings each. Under the title 'The Tendency of Modern Civilization', he essentially repeated the powerful talk he gave in July 1861 on the dangers he believed the advance of science, without corresponding moral progress, posed to the future of man (chapter 4). The 'large and intelligent' Maitland audience approved a proposal to publish the lecture as a pamphlet with the proceeds – one shilling a copy – also to go to the schools.[14]

As well as speech making, journalism was occupying some of Forrest's time. He probably wrote the review that appeared in *Freeman's* in August 1870 of a book that sought to show there was no conflict between the Bible's account of creation and geological evidence suggesting the Earth was unimaginably old. The review's lively style and clear exposition of the science and theology suggest this. The book's author was Dr Gerald Molloy, the man who beat Forrest for the post of Professor of Theology at Maynooth in 1857 (chapter 2).

Molloy argued, wrote the reviewer, that 'the Book of Genesis allows an indefinite period to have elapsed between the creation of the world and the work of the first so-called day, and that the days themselves were not days in our sense of the word but notably long intervals of time'.

> Now if any time be allowed to have existed before the first day, then the time may as easily have been millions of years as an hour, for Moses says nothing to determine its limit…
>
> To prove that by 'Day' Moses may have meant and probably did mean a long interval of time, we have the fact that the word *yom* which he uses is the very word that is so often employed in Scripture to signify an indefinite period…
>
> Again, Moses tells us that God created the world in six days, and rested on the *seventh day*. Now is this seventh day a period of twenty-four hours? Or is it not as St Augustine said fourteen hundred years ago 'a day without an evening and with no setting'… And if the *seventh day* is an indefinite period of time, why not also the *other six*?

Once more we have three 'days' mentioned in Genesis before the sun is said to have been created. These, therefore, could not well have been days of twenty-four hours, since the day of twenty-four hours depends for its existence upon the revolution of the earth in the sun's light. Therefore by 'day' is meant some other period of time, and if some other period, who will dare to limit its length?[15]

Forrest definitely wrote five articles, signed 'JF', that appeared in *Freeman's* between December 1870 and April 1871. The first lamented the occupation of Rome on 20 September 1870 by the forces of King Victor Emmanuel, the final step in the unification of Italy. The Vatican Council, whose main outcome was defining papal infallibility on matters of faith and morals, was still in session when the troops entered the city. Pope Pius IX suspended it a month later.

Forrest's response was probably influenced by a love of Rome developed during his studies at the Irish College from 1845 to 1847. His first lecture in Sydney (chapter 1) showed his admiration for the way the Papal States – now no more – had been run. And his Maitland lecture on the 'Tendency of Modern Civilization' revealed how he saw international politics. Force and fraud had become the ruling principles of nations, he said; 'the weak are crushed, insulted, robbed, exterminated'.

> 'The strong hand uppermost' is the watchword, but it has ever been the motto of barbarism. Are we lapsing into this with all our boasted progress? To protect the weak against oppression; to maintain right against brute force and violence; to adhere to truth, honour, justice, and religion, were at all times characteristic of civilisation… Who has the smallest reliance on the honour or truth of modern statesmen or politicians?[16]

His December 1870 *Freeman's* article was just as passionate. 'The Catholic King of Italy' [Victor Emmanuel] had bombarded the capital of a country at peace with all nations in a display of cowardice, cruelty and deceit, he wrote.

> Falsehood and deceit, violence and fraud and gigantic lying are the characteristics of modern statesmen. Every agency is utilised to mislead the nations. The peoples are duped, robbed, betrayed, under the plausible pretext of patriotism. But time will reveal all villainy, and history, if

not corrupt, will be obliged to write the following epitaph of Victor Emmanuel:– A professed Catholic, he robbed and imprisoned the Pope; a professed patriot, he impoverished his country; and in the name of Brutus, he grasped without remorse, and he wore without shame, the diadem of the Caesars.[17]

The capture of Rome occurred within days of Bismark's Prussian army laying siege to Paris, three months after the start of the Franco-Prussian war, which cemented German power in Europe and ushered in the French Third Republic. Emperor Napoleon III's troops had guarded the Papal state for the past three years; the war ended that protection. Forrest's second and third signed articles dealt with the broader situation in Europe, and painted a gloomy picture. He feared the present 'horrors that sicken Europe' were 'but the prelude to more extensive and appalling horrors yet to come'.

In Rome, the Pope, head of two hundred million Catholics, was 'a prisoner in his palace', deprived of 'all free communication with his spiritual children'. Cardinals dared not come to him as advisers except in disguise. 'A lawless and sacrilegious mob infests the city,' he wrote. 'Convents of nuns are forcibly entered by burglars under pretence of patriotism...' A 'red republic' was in prospect, like that, with all its atrocities, ushered in by the French Revolution.[18]

Forrest delivered a lecture on the Franco-Prussian war at Sydney's Masonic Hall in May 1871. *Freeman's* reported that he 'riveted the attention' of the 'very numerous and attentive assemblage'. Those on the platform included St John's Fellows Duncan, Ellis, Donovan, Dillon, Dr Gilhooley and Rev. D'Arcy (soon to take up his post as Vice-Rector), Rev. Dr Norbert Quirk of Lyndhurst, and Rev. Garavel, returned from his European travels.

Although saying he just wanted to make a 'few salient points' about the conflict, Forrest spoke at length on its causes, conduct and consequences. Faced with Prussia's dangerous ambition, France had spent four years preparing for the war that Napoleon III declared on 19 July 1870, he said. 'The civilized world stared in blank amazement, and the hereditary hostility of Frank and Teuton found expression in the brief but baneful words, To Berlin! To Paris!'

He was glad to be 'thoroughly ignorant' of the science of war, but blamed the collapse of the French armies on incompetent commanders. The French troops were heroes led by asses. 'There was Leboeuf, whose name aptly expresses his fitness for his functions. There were others just as incompetent.' He had no doubt both sides had perpetrated barbarities, which, although inevitable in any war, were to be deplored 'by all whose hearts are made of flesh not of stone'. Some committed by Prussians were such as 'to dishonour the lowest type of savages and degrade humanity'.

Fighting ended when an armistice was declared following the surrender of Paris, besieged since September 1870, on 28 January 1871. Under the Treaty of Frankfurt, signed in May 1871, the now republican France ceded Alsace and much of Lorraine to Germany. It had all happened very quickly; said Forrest, 'the ruin, absolute and sudden, of the French Empire is without parallel.'

> In one short month it vanished, as by the touch of some supernatural magician. There it was for twenty years, the wonder of nations and the arbiter of their destinies to a vast extent. It ornamented and beautified a capital which is a miniature capital of Europe, the chosen home of men of the most refined tastes, of the highest culture, of noblest aspirations, rich in treasures of art, as of literature, and imposing by its wonders of architectural beauty… It made France, from being the laughing stock of Europe, respected abroad and great at home – prosperous and happy…

He lamented the damage done to Paris – the immense 'destruction of beauty, of art treasures, of all forms of natural loveliness, heightened and finished to the last point of perfection by taste, by skill, by the labours of years'. And he said Prussia would never gain the loyalty of the people of the annexed areas; as long as the occupation continued 'there can be no peace for Europe'.

> One thing we know, that though we retire to bed in peace, we are reposing over a resistless volcano. As to international law in Europe and the sacredness of treaties, they are no more… Force and fraud, dark deception and treachery are the instruments of modern diplomacy… With all our boasted civilization we are lapsed back into barbarism; for surely there is barbarism where the weak are oppressed, robbed, slain by a lawless, powerful aggression.[19]

15
Exuberant charity

New South Wales experienced its own political drama at the end of 1870, fortunately confined to the Legislative Assembly chamber. The year-old Cowper government, for which *Freeman's* had held high hopes, fell to be replaced by another administration led by, in the paper's words, the 'greedy, unscrupulous leader of the Opposition', Sir James Martin. *Freeman's* was furious when John Robertson, whom it had praised as a principled opponent of Martin and Parkes, accepted office as Colonial Secretary under Martin. The 'poor forlorn old deserter' had drawn his sword against his own troops; 'will it be endurable for him to brag of his battles and his victories any more?'

But there was also good news. Henry Parkes had resigned his parliamentary seat after being declared insolvent with liabilities totalling more than £35,000. Justice at last, said *Freeman's*, which again detailed his deceits during the Fenian scare of 1868. 'It is well to think of these things; for life is so fast with us that crimes and services, treachery and patriotism, cowardice and valour are all soon buried in the same grave and alike forgotten.' It would be impossible for Parkes to become a government minister again, *Freeman's* added.[1] A little over a year later editor Thomas Butler backed Parkes's return to power heading a government elected with Catholic support and including his brother Edward as Attorney-General – such were the twists and turns of New South Wales politics.

Parkes resigned from the Council of Education when he left parliament – and was replaced by John Fairfax of the *Sydney Morning Herald*. *Freeman's* objected to the appointment not just because the Council was still without a Catholic member. People would believe, it editorialised, that to buy off a paper whose representations or attacks might endanger their power, an unscrupulous Ministry has placed as the guardian of our children's education a man whose utterances, wise or foolish, will have incomparably greater weight than those of the most experienced member of the board. Whatever view Mr Fairfax enunciates in the Council will, almost to a certainty, be reproduced in the *Herald*, of which he is the proprietor, and the ability or ingenuity of the *Herald*'s staff will be taxed to support it.[2]

Catholic claims that the Council remained heavily biased in favour of public schools and against their denominational competitors seem to have been justified. For example, only two of the thirteen applications for 'certification' – funding support – for Catholic denominational schools submitted to the Council up to 1872 succeeded.[3] In May 1871, *Freeman's* reported the rejection of an application by a Dubbo school that had 'at least 111' pupils – because 'the educational wants of the community were fully supplied'. It commented, 'The educational wants of a town over 300 miles from Sydney are "fully supplied", it is pretended, by a public school receiving 40 pupils, where there is...an uncertified school giving instruction to almost treble that number!'[4]

The statistics suggest, though, that the main reason for the decline of the colony's denominational schools was that most Protestants were happy to send their children to public schools. Between 1865 and 1879, the total number of certified denominational schools fell by nearly half, from three hundred and twelve to a hundred and fifty-nine. For Catholic schools, the reduction was much smaller – ninety-eight to eighty-three, or just fifteen per cent.[5] This helps explain the fact that the fight to retain the denominational system was waged mainly by Catholics.

Forrest had more to say on the subject in April 1871 in another signed *Freeman's* article. He claimed that, 'in an evil hour', parliament had given the incompetent Council of Education powers that were 'unsafe in any free country'. 'We here do not question the members of a Ministry', he wrote. 'They turn up like seaweeds after a storm, the result of a political accident or a fanatical excitement.' He complained that remonstrances, 'modest, firm and respectful', from the Catholic bishops about the books used in religion lessons in public schools had been ignored by the Council 'as if they had not been presented'. Denominational schools had been 'habitually' discouraged, and the taxes 'contributed by the Catholic people in proportion to the population' had been made 'the instruments of proselytising their children'.[6]

Numbers of Catholics – and Protestants – going on from primary school to higher education showed no sign of picking up as the 1870s began. Attendance at Lyndhurst had 'not been so numerous as in past years', the school's Prior, Norbert Quirk, reported at the 1870 speech day. And only fourteen new matriculants entered the university in 1871.[7]

Of these, at least five were Catholics, and three enrolled at St John's (the other two stayed on at Lyndhurst). Two – a school leaver from Brisbane and a thirty-seven-year-old recent immigrant from Ireland – entered St John's at the beginning of the year.[8] The Irishman, Daniel O'Lehane Creed, left the following October to try his luck as a prospector. He was in the news ten months later after exhibiting in Bathurst a twelve-carat stone that the town's jewellers declared 'a valuable diamond'.[9]

The college's third recruit of 1871, Francis Bede Freehill, enrolled in August. A former Lyndhurst student, he was the younger brother of Bernard Austin Freehill, whose name lives on in the national law firm Freehills. Francis ran the family legal practice after his brother died in 1880, became a St John's Fellow in 1883 and had a lifelong association with the college.[10] In 1937, his widow donated £15,000 to build its Freehill Tower, a shortened version of the structure planned by Wardell (chapter 5).

The new enrolments meant prospects for the college looked a little brighter in 1871 than the previous year. Nevertheless, Forrest probably knew he was just going through the motions when he asked at the March Council meeting that 'some arrangement be made to meet the expense of carrying on the college for 1871'. In earlier years the Fellows had recorded their gratitude to him for using his own money to keep the place running, but the atmosphere had changed. This time they carried a motion, moved by Butler and seconded by Rev. McCarthy, stating baldly that 'the Council having no funds at its disposal can make no arrangement to meet the expense of the College'.[11]

An offer by Forrest a month later to carry further costs allowed some new building work to be undertaken. The Council minutes do not reveal what this was, but the Rector's 1869 annual report probably provides the answer. The large dining room was still useless, he wrote then, but 'an outlay of £100 would suffice to fit it up for the present and one half of this sum can be had from the government'. After Forrest said he was willing to contribute the sum not chargeable to the government, the Council agreed that the work should proceed. Again there is no indication in the minutes that he was thanked for his generosity.[12] A report to the Council from the architect Blacket in July 1872 estimated the cost at £160, so Forrest presumably put in £80.[13]

In May 1871, the students faced their *viva voce* examinations at the college. Rev. McCarthy, initiator of this scheme, and W.A. Duncan tested their theological knowledge and two other Fellows, John Donovan and Patrick Healy, conducted the logic exam. How the students fared is not recorded; the Council minutes for July note simply that the examiners' reports were laid on the table by the Rector and read.[14]

In November, the Fellows considered, and were unmoved by, a letter from the students to Forrest complaining about the new college regulations initiated by McCarthy. A motion from Duncan declaring the Council willing 'at any time to consider any special grievance that may be felt by the students' was carried. But this went on to state that the students had not made clear which particular regulations they objected to, and the Council could not deal with 'a general complaint'.[15]

That seems to have been the end of the matter, possibly because most of the college residents in late 1871 were there only briefly. A parliamentary answer in November revealed that St John's had nine students then – two undergraduates and seven studying for the matriculation exam.[16] However, only two new matriculants appeared on the college roll the following year, and neither is recorded as having prepared for matriculation at St John's. So probably none of the seven proceeded to university.

Who were they? The college records provide no clues. Possibly they came from the Bathurst diocese with Rev. D'Arcy when he took up his post as Vice-Rector in the second half of the year. If they had gone on to become first year undergraduates in 1872, the problems of St John's would have been well on the way to being solved. But that was not to be.

D'Arcy had come to the colony in 1859, recruited by Archdeacon McEncroe during the visit to Ireland that also resulted in Forrest's appointment as Rector of St John's. The young priest, educated at St Patrick's College, Carlow, was stationed at Goulburn, Queanbeyan, Nowra and Bathurst under Polding. After the Bathurst diocese was formed, Matthew Quinn posted him to Peel, north of the cathedral town. His parishioners there presented him with a 'purse of 300 sovereigns' and a glowingly worded testimonial when he left for Sydney in August 1871.[17]

What special qualifications D'Arcy brought to St John's is unclear. A contemporary journalist and local historian, Robert Porter, described him as a gentleman and scholar for whom he had 'the highest respect, regard and esteem'. An important point in his favour was 'the fact that he is the only person I ever met, during my half century of experience as a printer, who thoroughly understood punctuation'.[18] Less complimentary are the recollections of Sister Angela Greene of the Sisters of Mercy, who was at Wellington, NSW, during D'Arcy's time as parish priest there from 1882. D'Arcy never got on with the people, she wrote. 'On Sundays he preached long sermons but he could scarcely be heard beyond the first bench.'[19] The recollections of a contemporary priest, preserved in the Bathurst Diocesan Archives, support the suggestion that he was not an inspiring speaker. He had a very thin voice and, while he 'wrote good English', he 'often read rather than preached'.[20]

D'Arcy could not have been attracted to St John's by the income available from McEncroe's bequest; this amounted to only about £90 a year. However, he also received £150 a year from the government under the old 'state aid' system that was phased out from 1863 (chapter 5).[21] Priests appointed before then retained their government salary for as long as they held a Church post in the colony; D'Arcy continued receiving his until his death, as pastor at Wellington, in 1907.

Outside the college, 1871 seems to have been a relatively quiet year for Forrest. In June he travelled to Goulburn to lecture at the town's Mechanics Institute on the 'spirit of the age'. Bishop Lanigan, six months back from the Vatican Council and the turmoil in Rome, took the chair and the audience of about two hundred 'listened attentively throughout', the local paper reported. Probably only Forrest knew that his talk was virtually a word-for-word repeat of his first Sydney lecture on progress in February 1861 (chapter 4).[22]

Towards the end of the year, Forrest probably saw a lot of Bishop Murray, who was in Sydney receiving medical attention for a persistent 'low fever'. This came on in August or September, the result, reported *Freeman's*, of hardship and exposure 'too great for his strength' experienced during extensive travels though the Maitland diocese earlier in the year. On his visitations, said the paper, Murray

> wished to meet with every member of his scattered flock, and loved to bring the blessings of his paternal ministrations as well into the shepherd's lonely hut as into the finest homestead. Anecdotes of the surprise of many of his people in thus meeting with their chief pastor, travelling as the humblest of his priests, are common. He loved to partake of the humble bush hospitality, to teach the devoted little ones, and to mix with them, in every sense, as a father in his own family.[23]

Bishops Lanigan and Matthew Quinn were also in Sydney in the last week of September 1871. With Murray, Polding, Forrest and other priests, they performed the sad funeral rites at St Mary's for Edward Butler's wife Ellen, who left behind eight young children.[24] Polding referred to Murray's illness in his letter to Gregory a week later, saying he feared the forty-three-year-old was 'done for, as regards missionary work'.[25] Murray departed for Rome and Ireland in early December, farewelled on the steamer by, among others, Polding, Quinn and Forrest. *Freeman's* reported that he left reluctantly, persuaded by doctors that the trip offered his only hope of recovery. Apparently it did the trick; Murray reported from Rome in early February 1872 that he had begun to improve at Suez and was gaining strength every day.[26] He returned to the colony in June 1873, and remained Bishop of Maitland until his death thirty-six years later.

In the letter to Gregory that expressed concern for Murray, Polding also remarked, uncharacteristically, that he was on good terms with all the bishops. Again he urged Gregory to return to the colony: 'Why not take a run over...and comfort the heart of your poor desolate father, now hastening on to his 77th year.' He was sure Gregory would attract the kind feelings of all the suffragans, and 'I would not despair of St John's – Rector and Fellows – and I think there are no difficulties we would not or could not tide over... Oh! Gregory, I have none to work with me...' In his previous letter, Polding had told Gregory that St John's was '*in statu quo* – a disgrace to us'.[27]

Surprisingly, Forrest was among the guests at the Lyndhurst awards ceremony, presided over by Polding, four days before Christmas. It would be interesting to have an account of his thoughts as Lyndhurst's Prior, Dr Quirk, and the Archbishop extolled the achievements of the school's university students. All three – two in first year and one in second year – had excelled in their exams, and two had won university scholarships. Said Polding,

> the success of Lyndhurst students at the university is, I consider, a genuine character of scholarly fruitfulness. Nothing has given me greater pleasure and hope in respect of the University of Sydney than the unmistakable decision of its superiors for the thoroughness and reality of learning as against shallow, superficial pretentiousness. And I have good reason, my dear children, to believe that this noble predilection of the university for what is true and genuine has found amongst us something on which it can rest. We have gained their honours, and their honours are worth the gaining because they are the stamp of real gold, and not the conventional promise to pay, that may be possibly a dishonour and a farce. That you should know what you profess to know is our aim, and I think we have realised this our aim when I see what you have done at this examination, and when I read, ah! I cannot tell you with what joy and thankfulness, what your old college fellows have attained before our university professors...[28]

After visiting Melbourne during the summer vacation, Forrest enrolled two new undergraduates at St John's in February 1872, a seventeen-year-old from the Hunter Valley and a twenty-two-year-old Victorian. Unfortunately, neither went on with his studies; when they left the college is not recorded, but it was certainly before the end of 1873. While the efforts of the Rector and Vice-Rector remained largely fruitless, Lyndhurst continued to bask in the success of its three university students (there was no addition to their ranks in 1872). All won scholarships in exams at the beginning of the year.[29]

March brought the death of the Bishop of Adelaide, Laurence Sheil, the target in 1868 of groundless rumours, apparently fanned by Parkes, linking the Church with the attempted assassination of Prince Alfred (chapter 11). Forrest, who had travelled to Melbourne for Sheil's consecration as bishop in 1866 (chapter 7), took part in the memorial Mass at St Mary's, celebrated by Polding.[30] Sadly, the amiable Sheil is best remembered as the bishop who excommunicated Mother Mary MacKillop. He took this extraordinary step in September 1871 following a dispute over control of the teaching order she founded in 1866, the Sisters of St Joseph. He also temporarily disbanded the Josephites, who by then were running thirty-five schools in South Australia. Sheil's odd behaviour in his last months has been attributed to his deteriorating health. He rescinded the excommunication five days before he died.[31]

The university's annual commemoration came around again later in March, and Forrest was there with D'Arcy and a few of the St John's Fellows.[32] They could take some heart from the fact that, of the nine young men awarded BAs, two had been at the college – Henry Sullivan and a winner of many awards during his university career, Charles Coghlan, who replaced Dalley on the college Council later in 1872.[33]

A week later, Forrest was in Bathurst again, delivering a lecture rejecting Protestant claims that the Catholic Church sought to deny people access to the scriptures in their own languages and thereby maintain, if not deepen, 'the darkness that hung over the minds of men'. He gave a long list of examples, dating back to shortly after the death of Christ, to show the Church had always supported the circulation of vernacular versions. But they must be translations authorised by the Church, not the work of 'illiterate men'. In typical Forrest style, he said the notion that insisting on correct translations meant denying people the scriptures in their own language was equivalent to saying 'that a man was opposed to dining because he refused to eat a Chinese dinner composed of puppy-dogs, etc'.[34]

On his return to Sydney he had the pleasure of catching up with his old friend from Irish College, Thomas Croke, who arrived from New Zealand on 12 April for a three-month Australian visit. Croke had been Bishop of Auckland since December 1870. He spent a weekend in Sydney, probably at St John's, before heading off to Bathurst with Matthew Quinn and another Irish College contemporary, Bishop Timothy O'Mahony, who had taken up his Armidale posting a year earlier.[35]

Forrest set out at about the same time with his brother-in-law Dr Gilhooley for Coppabella station, near Yass, to celebrate the marriage there of his twenty-five-year-old cousin and former St John's student, William Lehane (chapter 6). Five years earlier, he had presided at the marriage of William's sister at St Mary's, Sydney. Forrest spent at least three days with the family. Whether he also caught up with other relatives in the region is not recorded. Two sisters and a brother of Forrest's mother, Sarah O'Connor, had come to the colony in the 1840s and '50s. William Lehane's late mother Mary was one of the sisters; the other siblings had settled with their families near Boorowa.[36]

Croke's Australian visit, which included reunions with his sister who headed the Mercy convent in Bathurst and two brothers in Victoria,[37] began in the final stages of Henry Parkes's political resurrection. By the time he left in early July – seen off by Forrest, Bishop Lanigan, the old New Zealand hand Father Garavel and a few others[38] – Parkes had settled in as Premier. Some prominent Catholics, notably W.B. Dalley, were horrified at the turn of events, but many were pleased.

Parkes received his discharge from the Insolvency Court in September 1871, and soon re-entered the political fray.[39] When he stood for the seat of Mudgee at a by-election in early January 1872 *Freeman's* offered muted praise for his manifesto, saying his views on the 'great questions of the day – the land law, electoral reform &c' – were thoroughly liberal and consistent with those he had always held.

It called the current Martin–Robertson government the colony's 'most incapable and corrupt' yet.[40]

After easily defeating his only opponent, a Catholic journalist, J.G. O'Connor, Parkes delivered an acceptance speech that was a throwback to his stump oratory of 1868 and 1869. He told the cheering crowd he objected to Irishmen coming to the colony 'to distract the working of our political institutions by acting together in separate organised masses, not entering into the reason of politics, nor judging public questions on their merits, but blindly obeying the dictation of others as ignorant as themselves'. Who could those 'others' be but the Catholic bishops and priests? He went on,

> Until Irishmen learn to be Australian colonists – until they learn to tolerate free discussion – until they understand the uses of liberty, they must not be surprised if people regard their presence as something not very desirable. (Cheers.)… I object altogether to any class of men coming here, to set themselves in motion to extinguish freedom of speech and to impede the working of our free institutions. [A voice: You old baboon!][41]

Parliament resumed in late January, and the government soon fell. Governor Belmore called fresh elections – his last official act before returning to England in February.[42] Parkes, although not the official leader of the opposition, manoeuvred successfully with his supporters to have candidates elected who would back him as head of a new government. Edward Butler, who had resumed friendly contacts with Parkes the previous year, played a crucial role in organising Catholic support, and Bishop Quinn of Bathurst was a key ally. Further tacit support came from other unexpected quarters; 'We

Edward Butler.

213

are all right even to my surprise at St Mary's', Butler assured Parkes before voting day for the four-member East Sydney electorate. Parkes topped the poll and Martin was rejected.⁴³

The former government was routed, but power did not fall into Parkes's hands immediately. Opposition leader William Forster, who had taken a principled stand against Parkes during the Fenian scare, was called on first to form a government. Dalley, a member of the Legislative Council, and William Macleay reportedly agreed to serve with him, but he failed to muster the necessary support. Parkes, called on next, had no trouble doing so and was sworn in as Premier and Colonial Secretary on 12 May 1872. Butler took the oath of office as Attorney-General the next day.⁴⁴ Parkes had sounded him out about his willingness to take on the job as early as January; perhaps that contributed to his strong support for his old friend's campaign.⁴⁵

Why did Catholics turn to Parkes despite his notorious past, and his recent anti-Irish rhetoric? No doubt Butler, one of the colony's most successful barristers, had strong persuasive powers, but there must have been more to it. *Freeman's*, edited by Butler's brother, would have been influential. Highly critical of the recent short-lived Cowper and Martin administrations, it argued 'we can no longer do without a Government, a capable Government'. Parkes had 'done ever so many things to forfeit the confidence and esteem of the country'. However, 'we believe the country is inclined, in the present emergency, to condone his past sins, partly from the necessity of the case, partly in consideration of his known capacity'. It was confident 'the character of the men whom he has chosen as his colleagues, and their acceptance of office with him, will be a guarantee of some considerable worth for the future'.⁴⁶

To Dalley, Parkes's sins were unforgivable. Newly appointed ministers were required to face the electors again, and he used all his oratorical power to try to secure the Premier's defeat. He described the Parkes–Butler political alliance as 'infinitely the most odious and least pardonable that we have yet witnessed'. Catholics would find 'this dishonest and scandalous alliance will prove of no benefit to them, while it will not fail to be prejudicial to the religious liberty of the country'. He had little doubt that Parkes would be re-elected, but people would regret it. 'Irish Roman Catholics who, yesterday, regarded him with unspeakable horror, will on Wednesday lift him to power. But their day of remorse will come again...'[47]

Butler responded after his re-election, saying his joining the government should help promote peace and goodwill in the community and assure people that all denominations could expect 'full justice and impartiality'. He added that he knew from long intimate acquaintance that Parkes was no bigot, and the only political subject they had disagreed on over many years was the notion 'that a political conspiracy existed in this country to murder the Prince'.[48]

Parkes also spoke of the pair's friendship in an election speech. He had been Butler's first friend in the colony, he said, 'for when he first arrived in this country – now many years ago – he came to me'.

> I was then at the head of a great newspaper establishment, and he came to me as the first person he visited after his arrival. (Cheers.) For two or three years – I think more – we were associated night and day in the work of a great daily journal – (cheers) – and next to comrades on the battle-field, the position of comrades in the Press, perhaps, gives rise to the dearest and most gratifying recollections – (hear, hear) – and from that period until now we have at all times been friends.[49]

Butler commented on Parkes's Public Schools Act in his post re-election speech. He had been asked to help oppose its passage in 1866 but had refused, he said. Although the Act had defects, if rightly administered it was a measure 'that would be found productive of great benefit to the country'. Apparently Forrest agreed. While strongly critical of some of its provisions and the way it was administered, he had conceded from the start that the Act brought welcome advances (chapter 8).

Forrest shared the platform with Parkes and the Secretary of the Council of Education, William Wilkins, at the opening of a free public library at Camperdown in October 1872. He congratulated the local aldermen on inviting Parkes to open it, 'because to no man could the inauguration of this proceeding be more worthily trusted, and no-one had exhibited a deeper or a worthier zeal in the cause of education'. Forrest described himself as 'a plain, blunt man', and he 'dare say this, that the Premier deserved well and largely of this colony. (Cheers.)' Clearly he was on Butler's side rather than Dalley's in the argument over Parkes's fitness for office.[50]

At St John's, the atmosphere remained thoroughly depressing. Three more Fellows lost their Council seats in May 1872 after missing too many meetings, and in August a proposal to convene meetings only once a term rather than monthly was defeated only on Forrest's casting vote. Vice-Rector D'Arcy resigned at the end of the year, tactfully attributing his departure to Matthew Quinn's wish that he return to the Bathurst diocese because of a 'sudden and vast accession' to its population and the 'great want of missionary priests'.[51]

Some time before D'Arcy left – exactly when is not clear – Rev. McCarthy resumed his harsh critique of the college (chapter 13), this time focusing squarely on Forrest.[52] 'The condition in which we find ourselves is painfully humiliating,' his speech notes begin. 'Instead of exulting over the prosperity of the college, we are obliged to weep over the desolation which reigns through its magnificent halls.' He blamed the college's 'unsanctified discipline' for its failure to fill with students. There was no mention of the low numbers at the university generally, the smallness of the Catholic contingent, or the role of Lyndhurst in keeping students from St John's – or the earlier relative success of the college and Forrest's thwarted efforts to build on it.

What should be done, McCarthy asked?

> Shall we rest satisfied with closing the college as a college, and placing it at the disposal of the Very Rev. Dr Forrest to be used as a private residence, or as a mere boarding establishment, or as a billiard saloon, and live in the charitable hope that it may soon please the Lord to take the Rev. Dr to heaven, and once more place the college and its funds at our disposal?

This would be the easiest course for all parties, he wrote. 'It would relieve us from monthly meetings, from the annoyance of evil reports about café-frequenting students, and relieve the Rector from the drudgery of the daily and regular routine of spiritual and secular duties, and in a word terminate a bad and unsatisfactory business.' But the Fellows should ask themselves, 'what would they say of us at home [meaning, presumably, England and Ireland], ...throughout the Australian colonies...and wherever civilization is planted?'

Control of the college should be placed in the hands of 'men distinguished for learning, industry, and continuous regularity', McCarthy wrote. John Henry Newman had expressed the view when he set up the Catholic University in Dublin that 'men of great name' were required to 'attract students and form scholars', and he agreed.

> But why has not St John's flourished under a professor of great name? None is more willing or ready to bear testimony to his abilities than I am. I know in part the reputation in which he was held by men of learning in some of the first seats of learning. I believe he has a mind capable of investigating as far as the human mind can the most abstruse questions of theology and philosophy in its thousand branches. I believe he has a heart large enough to embrace all classes and conditions of society...

The problem was Forrest's 'unbounded' nature, he wrote. 'We want men of the Rector's mind without his exuberant charity, men of mind and lovers of the yoke of personal austerity, men whose sphere of happiness as well as of duties will be confined within the boundaries of St John's.' He suggested the Jesuits could provide such men, but did not address the question of what should happen to Forrest. The St John's College Act allowed 'removal and suspension' of the Rector by the Council 'for sufficient cause', subject to appeal to the Visitor.[53] It is hard to imagine Polding, as Visitor, interfering with any attempt to remove Forrest under this provision, but there is no sign that the idea was ever entertained.

McCarthy believed 'the occasion reprobates adulation, false delicacy and the suppression of honest convictions. We must trust each of us, unbosom ourselves to each other without fear of wounding each other's susceptibilities.' No evidence seems to survive of whether the other Fellows followed his lead.

Probably the sorry state of St John's was on Forrest's mind when, invited by Bishop Lanigan, he set out for Goulburn in mid-November to preach at the blessing of the just completed first stage of the new Saints Peter and Paul's Cathedral. More than a thousand people attended the ceremony, which began with Polding performing the traditional sprinkling of holy water outside and inside the bluestone walls. With him in the procession around the cathedral and at the subsequent Mass were, besides Lanigan and Forrest, Bishops Quinn of Bathurst and O'Mahony of Armidale and priests from the Goulburn diocese and Sydney.

Forrest's sermon focused on the transitoriness of life. He said the cathedral and the ceremonies conducted in it were outward signs of the homage people owed to God, 'in whose service they had to labour here for a short time'. It might fall to the next generation to complete the cathedral; if so, 'the example set to them would not be lost'.

> When that time came, their children would remember that the hearts, throbbing with exultation today for the work they accomplished, would be mouldering in the tomb – the hands that were so generous in furnishing assistance in the good work were no more – and they would consummate what their fathers began. They will remember that those who laid the foundation stone of this church were those most near and dear to them – that they handed to them unsullied [the] old faith…

Forrest said a philosopher, 'and one of no mean position', had compared man to 'the least of the animal creation – an ant, born at sunrise, that attained its maturity at noon and died at night';

> and how truly might it be said of man that this denotes his span of life! How little time has he to do good from the cradle to the grave, and how little valuable use is made of that short period![54]

16

Preparing for the coadjutor

Premier Parkes and Attorney-General Butler maintained their harmonious relationship into 1873. The year began for them with a trip to Queanbeyan. A brass band led their carriage into the town, 'and the rear was brought up by a long retinue of followers', *Freeman's* reported.

> Flags were flying from the principal hotels and stores, many of the residents congregated in the main street, and the advent of the Ministers was made the occasion of a sort of public holiday. In the afternoon the Premier and Attorney-General were accompanied on an excursion to the public buildings of Queanbeyan; and had opportunities of admiring, from almost every point of view, the beauties of this interesting little township, which is charmingly situated on the edge of the Canbury Plain...

After the tour, 'most of the leading men in the district' called on the pair at their hotel. At the banquet in the evening, 'one of the most successful affairs of the kind ever held in Queanbeyan', Parkes extolled the unprecedented 'harmony of opinion' that existed in his cabinet. 'We all think alike. I do not believe that has ever occurred in any former government.'[1]

A decision announced shortly before Parkes and Butler left Sydney, a major shake-up in membership of the Council of Education, won the applause of *Freeman's*. Best news was the appointment, at last, of a Catholic, W.A. Duncan. Sir James Martin and John Fairfax were among those the paper was happy to see depart. The university's Professor of Chemistry and Experimental Physics, John Smith, who, while perhaps not a 'very brilliant light', at least had a 'practical knowledge of the cogs and cranks of educational machinery', remained chairman. He had replaced Parkes in the position two years earlier. Other members were Forrest's friend Thomas Holt and, once more, Parkes, who 'may be trusted to administer the Act justly and impartially if it were only for his good name's sake as its author'.[2]

Freeman's was confident of the 'complete impartiality and competency' of Duncan, but must have harboured doubts about whether his appointment was good news for the denominational schools. He had been a member of the former National Schools Board and a consistent advocate of 'mixed' primary education. Any hopes that denominational schools would fare better under the new Council proved short-lived; in June the paper blamed abuses by the Council's secretary, William Wilkins, 'and his parasites' for decisions that it feared were leading inexorably to their 'extinction'.[3]

For Forrest, the year began with a visit to Tasmania at the invitation of Bishop Murphy to preach at the blessing of a new Presentation Sisters convent in Launceston. His subject was the importance of giving children moral and religious, as well as secular, education. The current tendency for God to be 'banished from the schools' and 'virtue put out of court, or sneered at' was very dangerous, he said. A child reared without moral training was 'a young barbarian', and a generation brought up without such training or instruction in religious truth would constitute a 'nation of barbarians'. It seemed strange that the source of light – science – should also be the source of darkness, he said. But it was so – as demonstrated by the French Revolution, which had 'dethroned God' and substituted worship of the 'goddess of reason'.[4]

Back in Sydney, he would have found the situation at St John's bleaker than ever. No undergraduates enrolled in 1873; it seems the only student residents during the year were two young men preparing, apparently without success, for matriculation.[5] Lyndhurst still had three resident undergraduates, all of whom were distinguishing themselves at the university. One of the two third-year students, Edmund Butler, a draper's son from Windsor, won two scholarships at the start-of-year exams and his brother Thomas, in his first year, won another. Both continued to shine after their student days, Edmund during his short life as a teacher and priest and Thomas as Professor of Latin at Sydney University, the first of the university's graduates to be appointed to one of its chairs.[6]

Polding presumably was kept informed on the state of St John's by his secretary, Thomas Makinson, still a member of the college Council, and in March 1873 he at last took some action. In a letter to Matthew Quinn (and probably the other suffragan bishops), he asked for 'an outspoken opinion' on the causes of 'the present lamentable state of St John's' and 'the probable and practicable remedy for such state'.

> No time is to be lost, and, whatever may be the result, we must not expose ourselves to the reproach of having stood by with folded hands whilst secularist statesmen were devising plans that whether it be intended or not must end in spoliation.

The letter, drafted by Makinson, claimed the college was 'almost universally accounted a failure' and noted that no students had matriculated there in 1873. 'This is a very sad result, not very creditable to our body, and certainly not of a tendency to give weight to our claims and hopes for Denominational teaching in primary or other institutions.' It added that all the bishops shared in 'the benefits and responsibilities connected with this College'.[7]

Replying, Quinn agreed that the college was in a sad state, but disclaimed any responsibility. 'I had nothing to say to the forming of its constitutions, and these constitutions do not recognise me. If I interfered in its concerns as a responsible agent, all parties concerned might justly say mind your own business.' However, as he took 'a warm interest in the welfare of the College', he would be happy to assist by offering his 'outspoken opinion' at a meeting of bishops. He urged Polding to call the bishops together to consider this and many other 'matters of great importance'.[8]

Rev. Dr Quirk of Lyndhurst joined Forrest and three St John's Fellows on the dais at the university commemoration in early April. Polding was there too, seated beside the Chancellor, Edward Deas Thomson. Of the university's twenty-three new matriculants, only one was from

Lyndhurst – scarcely cause for celebration. However, Quirk and Polding had an honours BA graduate as well as scholarship and prize winners from Lyndhurst to applaud. R.E. O'Connor was the only young man with a St John's connection on the awards list; he received his MA.[9]

Forrest probably found the parliamentary cricket match four days earlier a more enjoyable event. *Freeman's* noted that he and John O'Shanassy, the Catholic former Premier of Victoria, were among the guests at the between-innings luncheon. Sir James Martin chaired proceedings, with Parkes seated on his right and Forster on his left – a sign that political differences could be set aside on social occasions. Toasts were proposed to the Queen and the cricketer MPs, and responded to

Prize-giving at the last Sydney University annual commemoration in Forrest's time as Rector of St John's, April 1874.

heartily. Lord Belmore's recently arrived replacement as Governor, Sir Hercules Robinson, and his wife visited the ground in the afternoon, watching the game with about one thousand five hundred other spectators.[10]

At this stage, all in the colony apparently were still ignorant of important news from Rome – a Coadjutor Archbishop of Sydney, with right of succession to Polding, had been appointed at last. He was the man Polding had long sought for the post, the thirty-nine-year-old English Benedictine Roger Bede Vaughan. The decision was made in Rome in January and the consecration performed at Liverpool, England, on 19 March.[11] Since the completion of the telegraph link to England the previous year events on the other side of the world had been reported in the colony almost as soon as they happened, but it seems nobody thought to send news of Vaughan's appointment.

The first, brief, report in *Freeman's* appeared on 12 April. The following issue contained details of his aristocratic family background, his rise to the position of Prior of St Michael's Cathedral Monastery near Hereford, and his writings, notably a biography of St Thomas Aquinas. As a pulpit orator, he had few equals, displaying a familiar, easy and natural manner, the paper said. And his appearance was most impressive: 'He stands six feet two inches, and is straight and of full habit of body, and has a countenance which at once attracts and yet says "not too near".'[12]

Polding, of course, was overjoyed. He told Bishop Lanigan that God had 'at length answered my long, long prayer, and sent the man whom He has chosen'.

> In every respect, so far as I can judge, Dr Vaughan possesses the qualifications that all desire to see in a Missionary Archbishop, and my judgment is confirmed by all I hear and read of him, of his exceptional talent and learning, of his prudence and piety, of his loveable and genial character… You must sympathise with me, my dear Lord, in an especial degree for this special happiness of mine, over and above the good fortune that the Holy See is sending to all of us…[13]

In a note to Cardinal Barnabo in Rome, he wrote of the 'great joy' with which he 'was overwhelmed'. He assured the Cardinal, not entirely accurately, that 'the priests and the faithful' had received the 'happy news' of Vaughan's appointment with 'great joy and universal acclamation'.[14]

That certainly was not the response of the suffragan bishops, especially the Quinn brothers. Protests were quickly dispatched to Rome. Matthew Quinn told Barnabo he received the news of Vaughan's appointment 'with the most proper reverence and submission'.

> Yet my conscience obliges me to tell Your Eminence without reserve that considering that there is only one English priest and not more than a dozen English lay people under the Archbishop of Sydney's jurisdiction and the Archbishop's well known antipathy to the Irish and considering also the many grave and continually occurring scandals of many of the Benedictine Fathers of Sydney I feel the appointment of F. Bede Vaughan or any other English Benedictine will not have the support which the Sacred College so much wishes but quite the contrary...[15]

Polding called a meeting of bishops in Sydney in early May, and the Quinns, Lanigan and O'Mahony assembled at St John's; Murray was still away. According to their account of events, they called on Polding on their arrival 'and for ten days after the date specified in his Grace's summons; they had no business assigned and therefore could do nothing'.[16] Polding 'certainly is a most extraordinary old man', Murray told Cullen after hearing of these events from his fellow suffragans.[17] 'I am sorry that Dr Polding acted so unwisely about his coadjutor and brought the bishops together to look at one another without doing anything,' replied Cullen.[18] Presumably, the foreshadowed discussion of the state of St John's did not occur.

However, the time together at the college gave the bishops the opportunity to draft combined protests at Vaughan's appointment; possibly their anger at Polding's behaviour gave these added point. Murray told Cullen he had seen two letters they had sent to the Holy See, and every statement these contained was perfectly accurate.[19] The response from Rome brought no joy; James Quinn complained to Murray that he had received a letter saying, 'in substance', that 'the Cardinals believe it to be for the advancement of Religion to send "un Signore Inglese" as coadjutor'. Quinn went on, 'His Eminence has withheld our letter from the Pope, which seems to me a very extraordinary step to take.'[20]

The bishops also wrote, at some length, to Cullen in Dublin. They said Vaughan's appointment had 'caused dissatisfaction among Bishops, Priests and laity, with a few intelligible exceptions', and listed eight grounds for complaint. The fact that the coadjutor was English (or Welsh!) gave 'unqualified offence'.

> Irish Catholics and those of Irish descent have a long-abiding conviction of the want of sympathy between English rulers and Irish subjects. This fact cannot be denied. We regret it has been ignored. There is but one English priest in the Diocese of Sydney. The Catholics, not Irish, could be accommodated in one small church. The necessity of sending a Welsh Bishop here is not apparent to the Catholic people…

Most of the other objections related to the fact that Vaughan was a Benedictine. The 'past melancholy history' of the Benedictine Order in Australia would again come to the fore, with every old scandal revived, the bishops wrote. The bad consequences of Benedictine rule, under which 'the Order was everything, the Church was secondary', had been ignored. These included a failure to provide sufficient priests, churches and schools in country areas. Also, Benedictine institutions, despite their failure, enjoyed exclusive patronage and all other institutions were discouraged 'either by cold neglect or by something worse, when possible'. Examples were abundant; one was 'the inexplicable hostility' to St John's College.[21]

As well as preparing their written protests against Vaughan's appointment, the bishops decided while at St John's that, following his arrival, they would 'have nothing to do with him or say to him save on official business'.[22] Perhaps they also subtly let the public know what they were doing. A letter, signed 'A Catholic', appeared in *Freeman's* towards the end of their stay asking, 'is there any truth in the rumour that the suffragan Bishops of Australia have protested against the appointment of the Most Rev. Dr Vaughan?' The editor noted, 'We have heard the rumour alluded to by our correspondent, but we cannot vouch for its truth.'

Two letters in the next issue objected to 'A Catholic's' letter, claiming the writer's aim was to arouse prejudice against Vaughan. 'A Catholic' replied, saying 'ten or twelve days ago, a report was spread, whether maliciously...or not I am unaware', that the bishops had protested.

> I must confess, as an old colonist, I thought this report very probable. Every old colonist knows with what ardour, piety, and perseverance our venerable and venerated Archbishop endeavoured to establish in this colony the Benedictine family... All his efforts... were utter failures, although when he commenced he was in the full vigor of youth, much an abler man than the new Coadjutor, and had no impediment to remove. The new Coadjutor, to speak of no other difficulty, has to overcome the almost insurmountable difficulty of a previous failure... It is highly probable that the suffragan Bishops, though not old colonists, know of these facts, and, believing that the appointment of a Benedictine would renew these strifes... and believing that this would be sadly detrimental to the progress of religion in this colony, they might have petitioned Rome against the appointment of Dr Vaughan...

Freeman's closed the correspondence after publishing responses from 'A Catholic's' two critics and a letter complaining about the 'unseemliness' of the exchange.[23] Polding apparently did not know that the bishops had protested to Rome. But the sooner Vaughan came the better, he told Gregory in July, because his arrival 'will put a stop to this party work'.

> Some of our Bishops are frequently in Sydney, and, I fear, are not sufficiently discreet. F. [probably Forrest] has been rather free in his remarks upon Dr Vaughan. A very ugly set of letters were addressed to, and published in the *Freeman*...[24]

Forrest had a number of engagements outside the college in April and May at which he may have been overheard remarking on Vaughan's appointment; presumably his thoughts were similar to those of the Irish bishops. He and Judge Faucett constituted the welcoming party when Lady Robinson, the Governor's wife, and her family visited a fundraising bazaar at the Masonic Hall in late April. The good cause they were supporting was the Sisters of Mercy school and convent at St Patrick's, Church Hill.[25]

More likely his comments were noticed at the examinations and awards ceremony a week later at the nearby Marist Brothers school, established the previous year with funding support from McEncroe's estate. Polding presided, and many priests and prominent laymen attended. Forrest was the examiner in 'Euclid, mensuration and algebra'. *Freeman's* reported that 'the questions put, as those having experience of Dr Forrest as an examiner will readily testify, were searching and severe. But one or two questions were missed, and these were readily answered by the next in the class.'

The paper was highly impressed by the Marist school, saying pupils had 'flocked from all quarters of the city' to receive a 'real Catholic education' there. It proposed that scholarships be established so similar success could be achieved in higher education, but did not suggest where the money should come from. The scholarships would put students through Lyndhurst or other Catholic grammar schools, and then St John's. The 'effect for good would be incalculable' if the college constantly had fifteen scholarship holders, 'the very pick of our rising youth', enrolled. The alternative, *Freeman's* feared, was that 'we shall find ourselves (by our own fault entirely) without any higher Catholic education at all'. It noted that St John's had been 'in a languishing state…for some time back'.[26]

Forrest probably was among 'the many Sydney friends' who greeted the returning Bishop Murray, completely restored to health, on 3 June. 'Gentle in manner, easy of access, truly humble, though with talent of the highest order, with no pretence, zealously devoted to the interests of his flock, he wins all hearts,' noted the admiring writer for *Freeman's*.[27]

Although the youngest of the suffragans, Murray was recognised by Cullen and among themselves – certainly by Matthew Quinn and Lanigan – as the leader of the group (a letter written by Quinn in March 1872 expressed the hope that Murray would succeed Polding as Archbishop of Sydney).[28] He urged the others to calm down on the Vaughan issue. For example, he disagreed with James Quinn on the desirability of sending a strong response to the Vatican's rejection of their protests. Quinn proposed including a statement of 'the precautions we are obliged to take in order to prevent disrespect to our episcopal character' – essentially restricting communication with Vaughan to business matters.[29] Murray thought no reply was needed, and if one was sent it should 'be couched in the mildest terms…'[30]

A letter from Cullen to Murray towards the end of the year urged such an approach. 'I hope you have passed the winter safely, and that you shall have a pleasant summer whilst we shall be contending with the rain and damp and dreary weather of winter,' he began. 'I hope all your missionaries and nuns are quite safe. Here we have had a very wet harvest and the winter is already commencing to set in. The rain injured the harvest very much and a great part of the potatoes is destroyed. However we shall have enough of food for the country.' Then to the point:

> They say he [Vaughan] is a good and learned man. In any case, as he has been appointed by the Vicar of Christ, it is well to assist him… I think you would do well to throw oil on troubled waters and to quiet the other bishops of the province.[31]

Murray assured Cullen he would follow his 'good advice'. In fact, he had already acted according to it, and all the bishops would give Vaughan 'every assistance in their power'.[32]

Murray, Lanigan, O'Mahony, and James and Matthew Quinn gathered in Sydney again in early September before, with Forrest and a few other priests and laymen, setting out by 'special train' for Bathurst. The occasion was the opening of the first stage of the grand new premises of the Catholic secondary school, St Stanislaus' College, established by Matthew Quinn in 1867.[33]

The train took them to the then terminus of the western line, Raglan, just seven kilometres short of Bathurst. There, despite the bitter cold, nearly three thousand people greeted the party, *Freeman's* reported. Then an 'immense gathering of equestrians and vehicles' followed as they headed for town in two carriages each drawn by 'four magnificent greys'. At the cathedral, a 'concourse of people of all denominations', also 'immense', welcomed the procession, now headed by the town's Catholic school children marching with their banners and emblems.

The only ceremony on the day of their arrival, Thursday 4 September, was the presentation of an address to the bishops by the Catholics of Bathurst followed by responses from each of them. The visitors then had two free days before joining another 'immense throng', estimated by *Freeman's* at about four thousand, in 'genial and fine' weather at the cathedral. There, another procession formed – schoolchildren preceded by bearers of the banner of St John the Evangelist at the head, followed by members of the local Catholic guild and the thirty-five students of St Stanislaus' College. Next came Forrest and three St John's Fellows – Gilhooley, Donovan and Duncan – in academic costume, followed by the priests, bishops, and 'general body of Catholics'.

Their destination, five blocks away, was a very large marquee in the college grounds on a hill overlooking the town. Here Mass, with choral performances 'that kept the vast body of people spell-bound', was celebrated. After the sermon by James Quinn and the collection, which raised more than £1,000, about eight hundred people sat down to a 'sumptuous luncheon' in another marquee; the nine tables 'groaned under the abundance of the good things provided'. Then came the speeches.

Murray's was probably the most interesting of those by the bishops, and demonstrated his affection for his cousin Matthew Quinn. He spoke of the 'bounden duty' of bishops to cooperate in promoting 'the religious and educational interests of the faithful' – perhaps an allusion to Vaughan's impending arrival. He praised Quinn's achievements in seven years as bishop: 'I do not think there is another diocese in Australia, or perhaps in the world, where so much has been realized through the cordial union of bishop, priests and people.' And of Quinn, the man, he said,

when I was bowed down by sickness Dr Quinn, your worthy Bishop, took me from my own home to his house, and finding that I was not recovering, insisted on my taking a sea voyage to Europe to re-establish my health, and engaged to do for me the work of my diocese during my absence. That promise he nobly redeemed... I avail myself of this occasion to thank him most warmly...

Forrest spoke last, and broached the subject of the sorry state of St John's. 'Hitherto our success has not been what was reasonably expected,' he said.

...the fault is somewhere – not with the Fellows of the college, who have generously contributed money, and what is to most of them more valuable, time, to promote its interests. I venture to assert that the Fellows of St John's, as a representative body in the Catholic community, will be found to be equal in intelligence and social position to any equal number that may be named. Is the University to blame? No. The learned Professors, equal to the distinguished men of the European Universities, in their respective departments, do their work; they teach science and literature – not sectarianism.

Neither was 'the Catholic spirit' wanting; the 'splendid demonstration of today' was 'the best answer' to that proposition. He proffered no thoughts on where the blame lay.

'But you must not understand that the college has done nothing,' Forrest went on. 'We have produced, within a period of thirteen years, men who take a prominent place in the learned professions and in the Senate.' He was confident St Stanislaus' College, another 'splendid demonstration' of the Church's historic commitment to education, would increase the numbers of Catholics going on to university. 'This institution resumes here the work of our fathers of the sixth and seventh centuries in Ireland,' he concluded. 'Let us be worthy of our ancestors, true to faith, loyal in our just allegiance, and worthy citizens of a young, free, and flourishing country. (Applause.)'[34]

The visiting bishops and Forrest remained in Bathurst for a diocesan synod the following Tuesday, called by Matthew Quinn to promulgate to his priests the decrees of the Melbourne provincial council of 1869, ratified at last by the Vatican. Then all returned to Sydney, the suffragans summoned by Polding, under instruction from Barnabo, to a meeting to consider the establishment of new dioceses in Victoria.

The bishop with the greatest interest in the outcome, James Goold, was not present; Polding had just returned from discussions with him on the subject in Melbourne.[35] At that stage Goold had charge of the whole of Victoria, and was still one of Polding's suffragans. The two agreed that he should be elevated to Archbishop, and have his own suffragans in charge of two new dioceses. However, at the Sydney meeting, Murray, Lanigan, O'Mahony and the Quinns pressed for the creation of four new dioceses, arguing that, as Victoria had more Catholics than New South Wales, it should have at least as many bishops.[36]

Polding put his signature to this recommendation, and to a list of priests proposed by the suffragans for consideration by the Vatican as bishops of the four dioceses; in each case the first and second choice was an Irishman. Why did he sign? 'In order to avoid any hostility or spirit of dissension…and for love of peace', he told Barnabo after the meeting.[37] The suffragans had complained in the past about lack of candour by Polding in his dealings with them; this was another example.

Polding urged Barnabo to accede to Goold's wishes rather than accept the recommendation of the meeting, and in 1874 just two new dioceses, Ballarat and Sandhurst, were created. In line with the agreement reached in Sydney, but in opposition to Polding's advice to Rome, Irish bishops were appointed to both. Just before the Sydney meeting Polding had told Barnabo that to 'bring out all Irish Bishops would insult the Australian Church; the national Church in Australia would become an Irish Church'.[38] He evidently hoped his success in obtaining an English coadjutor would be followed by a further winding back of Irish influence.

In mid-October Polding called all the priests of the archdiocese – about sixty – together for a three-day synod. Amid much ceremonial, the decrees of the Melbourne provincial council were promulgated, as they had been in Bathurst a month earlier.[39] Forrest was there, but may have been distracted by news from parliament. In answer to a question on notice, Premier Parkes advised members that he had been informed by the Rector that there were 'two resident students not matriculated and two non-student graduates reading philosophy' at St John's. Opposition leader Sir James Martin was not impressed and brought on a brief debate.

He said that by law the role of the colleges was restricted to educating matriculated university students. They could not 'take such students as they might think fit, and educate them in any way they might think fit'. The Rector received a £500-a-year salary from the public purse, and 'it was his duty to see that no person was a student in his college unless he matriculated in the University'. Otherwise, 'how easy it would be for the governors of these colleges to convert them into private educational establishments of their own'.

Martin said he was not suggesting that the fact that 'there was not a single student at the college was any argument against the Rector'.

> It was not his fault. He was competent for the position which he held, and it was not his fault if students did not go there. They had no right to discharge the Rector on that account, or to deprive him of his salary, but he thought they ought to consider the propriety of paying £500 a year to the principals of these colleges unless there were a certain number of students. It was a perfect farce to pay this salary when there was not a single student in this college.

Edward Butler responded, suggesting 'some misunderstanding' existed over the requirement for students to have matriculated. Referring to the arrangement reached with the university in 1862 for admission of 'temporary residents' (chapter 4), he said he understood that 'the practice at one time' was that students could enter the college between matriculation exams, so long as they sat for the exam at the earliest opportunity. 'Whether this was the case in the present instance he did not know.'

The only other speaker was John Stewart, a supporter of Parkes during the Fenian scare. He said the colleges 'were nothing but sectarian institutions, for which the public paid a large sum of money and got no benefit', and wanted a parliamentary debate scheduled soon on whether they should be discontinued. This did not eventuate.[40]

Within weeks another matter arose that dominated political

discussion, and brought an abrupt end to the Parkes–Butler political alliance and to the pair's twenty-year friendship. Appropriately as it turned out, the long-foreshadowed retirement of the Supreme Court Chief Justice, Sir Alfred Stephen, took effect on Guy Fawkes Day, 5 November. By convention, Attorney-General Butler had first right of refusal of the position. Parkes recognised this and told him on a number of occasions that it was his if he wanted it. However, on 11 November, Parkes announced that Sir James Martin would replace Stephen. The fireworks commenced in parliament that evening.

Butler resigned as Attorney-General, and read into the record letters that had passed between the Premier and himself over the previous week. The first, written by Parkes on 5 November, told Butler in a remarkably unpleasant manner that he would not be getting the job. Parkes insisted that people who objected to Butler's appointment because he was Catholic had not influenced him.

> Day by day, however…I have become aware that the objections to you are not by any means confined to religious grounds, and that, in fact, they are entertained by intelligent persons of your own faith, and are founded on considerations which are reasonable and legitimate… These objections I find are widely, almost generally, entertained in your own profession, and they appear to be felt, so far as I can judge, by the great majority of the community, including all classes. Several days ago it was urged upon me by a Roman Catholic gentleman of influence as well as by others, that this really was the case… One and all regard your possible appointment with disfavour… They say very justly that the office of Chief Justice is the highest in the community… and that it ought to be filled by the member of the Bar possessing in the highest degree the qualifications of learning, professional character, liberal education, personal standing and social recognition; and that neither the Bar nor society will admit that you are pointed out by these considerations…[41]

Who was the Catholic 'gentleman of influence'? Perhaps, as Robertson suggested in parliament, he had as much reality as the 'Kiama Ghost' (chapter 11).[42] Some have assumed it was Dalley. He was friendly with Martin and Stephen, and the previous year had married a sister of Martin's wife in a Church of England ceremony – an event that strained his relations with his own Church.[43] However, his hostility to Parkes makes it unlikely that he would have personally 'urged' anything upon the Premier. Interestingly, there was opposition to Butler's elevation at St Mary's. In a letter to Gregory in June, shortly after Stephen announced his impending retirement, Polding's secretary, Thomas Makinson, wrote of Butler, 'He is, everybody says, a good lawyer, but not everybody thinks him fit for the first dignity on the Bench.'[44]

Butler's dignified response to his rejection, in his letters to Parkes and speeches in parliament, won much praise from the press, and Parkes's treatment of Butler was strongly condemned. However, Martin's appointment was generally supported. Butler acknowledged Martin's suitability for the Chief Justiceship; in fact, he thought him better qualified than himself 'provided that he would exercise sufficient industry'. In response to the claim by Parkes that the Bar opposed his appointment, Butler said he had asked the barrister Frederick Darley (who succeeded Martin as Chief Justice in 1886) for his assessment of barristers' views. Darley had said that 'he himself was in favour of Sir James Martin', and probably if the Bar was polled that would be the majority opinion. However,

> he had never heard expressed by any member of the Bar a single objection to him (Mr Butler) or to his qualifications, and Mr Darley authorised him to say that, if the Government had thought proper to appoint him to the office of Chief Justice, he believed the appointment would have been received with great satisfaction. (Cheers.) He hoped he would be pardoned for saying this. (Cheers.)[45]

Probably the real reason why Parkes broke his word to Butler was fear that appointing him Chief Justice would bring down the government. Such a concern seems to have been well based. During a censure debate on 30 October the government appeared headed for defeat, but then, as one member put it, 'a marvellous change' occurred.[46] Parkes's critics claimed he won over some members who were threatening to vote against the government by secretly promising them that Butler, whom they opposed because he was Catholic, would not be Chief Justice.

Freeman's deplored Parkes's 'wicked and cowardly breach of faith', and said Butler had been rejected 'simply and solely for being one of us'. It added pertinently, 'if he who has given proofs of fairness and freedom from bigotry cannot escape persecution for being a Catholic, which of us can?'

The government survived a censure motion over the affair two weeks later. William Forster delivered the speech of the debate, saying Butler's conduct had been 'in the highest degree creditable', but what had happened served him right for associating with Parkes, 'a perpetual traitor to friendship and to charity'. Replying, Butler said he did not form many friendships, but when he did form them 'he was very tenacious of them'. His long friendship with Parkes had continued 'under very many circumstances that might shake the friendship of one who did not hold friendship as firm as he did'. He now felt no personal hostility towards Parkes, but nothing more 'than the common courtesies of life' could ever again pass between them.[47]

17
Out of St John's

Despite Lyndhurst's prime role in the failure of St John's, it seems Forrest was on good terms with the Benedictine priests who ran it for Polding. In 1873, Rev. John Dwyer, who won fame as chaplain at Darlinghurst Gaol during the O'Farrell affair and later took charge of St Benedict's, Broadway, became Prior. Rev. Placid Quirk, the thirty-one-year-old younger brother of the former Prior, Dr Norbert Quirk, was head teacher.

Forrest had not examined at the school since 1866, but was back on duty at the end of 1873 and impressed by the performance of the top Latin class. The results were 'creditable to both masters and pupils', all students gained marks above seventy-five per cent, and 'in one or two instances' students produced English translations remarkable for their purity and accuracy, he wrote in his report. 'I have much pleasure in congratulating you upon the success of the college during the past year, and trust that the coming one will be no less satisfactory in its results.'[1]

Before the exams, he was a guest at the annual dinner given by the current Lyndhurst students for ex-students. Quirk proposed a toast to the examiners, many of whom, he said, were ex-students and others 'men of ripe scholarship and unimpeachable integrity'. Forrest, presumably in the latter category, responded with a 'humorous speech', *Freeman's* reported without giving much detail. He attributed the fact that he had not examined at the school 'as often as he had wished' to the timing of the exams, during his vacation. He praised the Lyndhurst alumni for their successes at the university as well as at school and 'paid a high tribute to the Very Rev. Dr Quirk [the former Prior, who was ill], to whom the institution was so deeply indebted for its success'.[2]

Forrest did not go to the Lyndhurst awards ceremony, a week before Christmas, having left on vacation for Hobart (he attended a school prize-giving there with Bishop Murphy on 19 December).[3] He also missed the arrival of Archbishop Vaughan, on the mail steamer *Nubia*, in the late afternoon of 16 December. None of the suffragan bishops was in Sydney to greet Vaughan either, but at least two, Murray and Lanigan, sent friendly notes of welcome to which he immediately replied in kind.[4]

As had long been the custom, harbour steamers packed with well-wishers met Vaughan's ship and escorted it to Circular Quay. The Archbishop was greeted with 'enthusiastic cheers, accompanied with energetic waving of hats and handkerchiefs', *Freeman's* reported. He 'repeatedly acknowledged' the greetings, and 'appeared to be as delighted at the scenery as he was pleased and touched at the "Cead mille fealthe" of his reception'.

At the Quay, a crowd estimated at fifteen to twenty thousand welcomed Vaughan and his companions, who included a French bishop, Monseigneur Vitte, on his way to New Caledonia. They stepped ashore to cheers from 'well-dressed' men, women and children 'crowded everywhere' and 'multitudes of spectators on the rigging of the adjacent ships'. Vaughan knelt before Polding, who greeted him warmly; then the two Archbishops and Mgr Vitte proceeded to St Mary's. A crowd set out after their carriages with 'the liveliest demonstrations of joy', but its enthusiasm 'and the very eccentric ideas of the drivers of carriages, cabs, and other vehicles altogether dissipated the last lingering notion that there could be any formal procession'.

Archbishop Vaughan.

Between three and four thousand people crammed into the pro-cathedral, 'all as quiet and orderly as their excitement and the intense heat would permit them to be'. After brief religious observances, the clergy and laity presented their welcoming addresses. Vaughan's responses showed he had done his homework and demonstrated his skill at winning an audience; *Freeman's* described them as 'a happy augury for the future'.

Replying to the clergy, he nominated completing the cathedral and education as priority issues. Then he said how glad he was that most of the priests of the archdiocese were Irish. He would have about him 'men who have the seal of the faithful upon their foreheads – (loud cheers) – men who have naturally from the persecution the nation has undergone received Christ into their hearts, and been brought to the foot of the cross. (Cheers.)' Responding to the laymen, he said coming from an old Catholic family that had gone through 'the persecuting days' gave him an affinity with the Irish, and added, 'Call me an Englishman if you will – I am one, but I am a Catholic first. (Cheers.)' He had been moved by his welcome:

> I saw one steamer crowded, and then another steamer crowded, and a third, and a fourth – indeed I did not count them all – I was so bewildered with the beauty of the scenery, and with the kindness of those around me. With such manifestations of kindness I cannot but feel that we have met together in a manner that will join us so that we shall not part.[5]

Bishop Murray was among those impressed by the way things had gone. Having read the newspaper reports, he wrote to Cullen two days after Vaughan's arrival. The reception had been 'really magnificent', he said. Everything seemed to have passed off 'very harmoniously and cordially', and there had been 'no allusion whatever to Benedictines by any one'.[6]

Vaughan also was pleased. In a letter to Cardinal Barnabo begun on the evening of his arrival he said he had 'made use of those words which have the power to conciliate all parties, especially the Irish'.[7] He told his father, in his first letter home at the end of December, that he had spoken in 'such a way as seems to have conciliated the Irish party and Irish clergy very much indeed to the fact of having an Englishman and a Benedictine to rule over them'. He went on,

This is a most beautiful city: the harbour is like fairy land – the whole thing far surpasses my expectations – not only the size and beauty and wealth of the city, but the power of the Church, the respectability and education of the clergy, and the prospects for the future Church... The weather is beautiful but very hot. I have been wet through almost ever since I have been here. Xmas Day was roasting. But fortunately the heat is not oppressive and I am in capital form.[8]

Two days after he arrived, Vaughan attended the Lyndhurst awards ceremony with Polding. This was probably his introduction to the strange fact that the Catholics who were making names for themselves at the university were residents of their former school rather than the Catholic university college. The Butler brothers had done extremely well again, and Rev. Quirk praised them highly. Polding presented Edmund Butler and the other student who had just completed his BA, Walter Edmunds, with a 'special prize'. Three of the final-year school students matriculated at the start of 1874, and stayed on at Lyndhurst for their university studies.[9]

Vaughan quickly made his presence felt in Sydney. A remark, in his speech at Lyndhurst, that the Church of England was 'falling to pieces' sparked heated controversy. In early January he took over as 'sole administrator, spiritual and temporal' of the archdiocese; Vicar-General Sheehy was dispatched to Windsor as parish priest.[10]

Whether this happened on Polding's initiative is doubtful. A newspaper article written long after the event by an unnamed person who claimed to have been present described a meeting between Vaughan and Polding at which the coadjutor demanded full control. A shocked Polding refused, but eventually bowed to Vaughan's pressure. A rejoinder from a supporter of Vaughan published soon afterwards appears to provide backing for the story. The writer claimed Vaughan had informed him of 'all the circumstances, facts, and motives' of his taking control. 'If the old archbishop, in his eightieth year, and at intervals of senile infirmity, may have been induced to hang on to an impossible state of things, it became all the more incumbent on his coadjutor to save him and the archdiocese from the consequences.'[11] Vaughan wrote to his father soon after the transfer, 'Archbishop Polding has got his diocese into such a deadlock with debt and confusion that he has handed the whole administration over to me.'[12]

Forrest returned from Tasmania on 27 January after 'assisting at several school examinations' and taking part in 'some religious celebrations of public importance'.[13] The fifty-three-year-old was in 'excellent health', *Freeman's* noted, which was fortunate in view of the trials ahead. His first engagement was a visit to Goulburn for the opening of Bishop Lanigan's new secondary school, St Patrick's College, on 1 February. This was the occasion on which three of the suffragan bishops – Lanigan, Murray and Matthew Quinn – first met Vaughan, who attended the opening with Polding. Forrest's first meeting with the coadjutor probably also took place there, although it is possible they had met a day or two earlier in Sydney.

As at the opening of St Stanislaus', Bathurst, five months earlier, proceedings began with a procession from the cathedral to the college, followed by Mass in a large marquee in the grounds. Then about four hundred sat down to lunch in another marquee. Lanigan presided at the top table, with Polding, Matthew Quinn, Forrest and St John's Fellows Duncan and Healy on his right and Vaughan, Murray and the Melbourne Jesuit, Rev. William Kelly, who had delivered the sermon, on his left.

The speeches contained much flattery, and Vaughan showed himself a master at it. He said he came as an Englishman amongst an episcopate largely composed of Irish prelates 'to unite his little stock of knowledge with their large experience'. Having met the bishops, he considered it 'a privilege to be allowed to identify my name and my interests with theirs'.

> Though I have known him but twenty-four hours, I have felt the attraction of the Bishop of Bathurst, and his gentleness, his piety, and his episcopal zeal have made themselves felt upon me during a pleasant but too short an acquaintance. As for his Lordship on my left (the Bishop of Maitland) we had but to be introduced to each other to know each other, if I may be allowed to say so, as friends; for, after all, men whose lives are identified with the same interests, and whose aims are simple and in the same direction,

do not require any great length of time to read each other's hearts and to take interest in each other's welfare... Nor do I exclude... the learned Dr Forrest, to look upon whose countenance is simply to be lit up by a reflection of wit, kindness, and generosity.

Vaughan also praised Lanigan: 'I reverence him for having in this place set up so beautiful a home where learning may not only dwell, but may spread its beneficent light abroad.' He said he saw in his dreams 'flourishing domes of learning arising in each of the dioceses of this great continent, and the choicest specimens of rising genius concentrating from each of them upon the great college of St John'. After distinguishing themselves at the university, they would take their places 'in the Senate and at the bar...'

> And through such elements as these being fused into the nerve and fibre of the ruling class, I perceive a strength in government, and an enlightenment in legislation, and a nobility and culture in the higher walks of life, which are the necessary and logical development of that system of education which is adopted by the Catholic Church.

Quinn returned the flattery, saying he found Vaughan open, manly and straightforward, and was pleased to call him his friend. Murray was more circumspect, but promised Vaughan the suffragans' most cordial cooperation and support. He also introduced a little levity. He noted a comment by Vaughan that he hoped the suffragans would allow collections for St Mary's Cathedral in their dioceses. 'He can have his fling throughout the length and breadth of the diocese of Maitland,' said Murray, 'provided, of course, the same privilege be granted to me, of having my fling in the diocese of Sydney. I flatter myself that neither I nor my people shall be losers in the transaction.'

Forrest spoke towards the end, offering his own vision of Australia's future. 'We are a young people, but we have a glorious inheritance in this sunny land,' he said.

> Let honour, intelligence, high cultivation of their natural gifts, with that Spartan chivalry which is, in the day of trial, the bulwark of freedom, be the aim and characteristics of young Australia... One hundred years hence

I see a great people, united by the common principle of freedom, proud of their descent and jealous of the cherished memories of the past, promoting every principle of moral and material progress...[14]

Vaughan did some more letter writing after his return to Sydney. His words reveal much about himself – including a strong sense of his own superiority and a tendency to be careless with the truth in making his points.

He told Cardinal Barnabo that the suffragans he met in Goulburn had promised to support him in everything: 'Being Irish, they are more swayed by the emotions than by the cold principle of truth, and so, having proclaimed against me vociferously before meeting me, now that they have seen me, they are proclaiming just as much in my favour.' He said Polding had 'begged' him to assume the role of administrator and vicar-general, and he could not 'in conscience refuse' because of the sorry state of the archdiocese's temporal affairs and ecclesiastical discipline. 'It is sufficient to state two facts,' he wrote.

> First, in regard to the administration: there is a debt for the payment of about 5,000 pounds sterling, and second, regarding the discipline: the account only for beer, wine and strong spirits for the Presbytery of St Mary's (the Pro-cathedral) for the past year is more than 600 pounds sterling.[15]

He wrote a long letter to his father on the same day. This combined enthusiasm for the task ahead with denigration of most of the people he had met. He believed the archdiocese was 'one of the finest in the world' and was full of hope: 'now that the people see that I am firm and intend to have no nonsense, and that the clergy find that they have got a master, I think that many threatening difficulties will subside, and that order will be brought into chaos'.

He said he had dined with the Governor and his wife – 'a very large lump of flesh, but very nice and sensible in all other respects' – two or three times already. They were the 'only real ladies and gentlemen' he had come across so far. 'I have also made acquaintance will the principal government people. But they are mostly h-less, and are very provincial, not to say Irish, in their manners and customs. A frightful want of culture and refinement, and the higher embellishments of life. Still, I get on with them very well, and am treated with the greatest courtesy and kindness.'

The Irish bishops, and 'some of the strong Irish laity', had been violently opposed to his appointment, he wrote.

> But as the Irish (Bishops included) appear to have the gift of acting more on impulse than on principle, it has not been a very difficult task to induce them to commit themselves as violently in my favour now as they did against me before. I have met several of the most antagonistic amongst the Bishops – and I find them to be rough, good-natured Irishmen, who are melted, like the sugar in their large glasses of whisky, by kind words and a little good-natured praise judiciously administered. In fact, in this short time I have got everyone worth having with me. The Irish are indeed a strange people! The nearest approach I have ever found grown men make to the simplicity and character of children! My great want is some real sterling men at my side – but I hope in time to get them.[16]

Two days after writing these letters, Vaughan – with Forrest, Rev. Coletti and a group of laymen including St John's Fellows Duncan and Dr Gilhooley – caught the morning train to Picton, south of Sydney, at the start of an expedition to the Burragorang Valley. The purpose of the visit was for the Archbishop to open a new church built by Rev. George Dillon, who had moved from Balmain to Camden in 1869, and confirm some of the local people, including several Aborigines. According to *Freeman's*, under Dillon's guidance the 'Burragorang tribe' had become the 'only complete Christian tribe' in eastern Australia.

The party entered the valley, now flooded by Warragamba Dam, on horseback via what Duncan described in an article in *Freeman's* as a 'zig-zag' cut into the face of a precipitous mountain. 'The view of the valley from the highest part of the zig-zag is beyond description beautiful. The wild rugged mountains on either side, the exquisite verdure of the valley beneath, with the Wollondilly meandering through it in lines of almost symmetrical beauty...' They arrived late in the evening of Saturday 14 February after, wrote Duncan, a few 'accidents by flood and field'. Sunday began with the church ceremonies, followed by the customary presentations, the most interesting of which was made by the 'Catholic tribe'.

The 'deputation advanced with the chief bearing a large opossum cloak in his arms,' *Freeman's* reported. 'Then came an intelligent aboriginal boy, named John Riley, dressed in the cassock and surplice of an altar boy, with an address in manuscript, which he read with great distinctness. The men of the tribe stood round.'

'Most Reverend Father', the address began,

> We are your children, every one of us… Before we were Catholics we were very wicked, but we did not know the evil we were doing. We do not leave our valley often now, and we do not sell the blankets our good Queen gives us for drink as we once used to. Our children are clothed, and many can read and write well. We still live in gunyahs, but we will build huts when we can get land to cultivate in our valley near the schools… The white man took all our land from us, and he shoots our 'possums for eating his corn, but he is very kind to us, and gives our men work in fencing, and stock keeping, and farming, and our women can wash, and sew, and fish… Our priest told us you would be our father, and try and get us land fit for corn and potatoes. If you do we will never leave our valley, and will be sober and good…

The visitors had much to think about as they headed back up the zig-zag after lunch. Duncan, in his *Freeman's* article, described 'the destruction of the aboriginal tribes' – the result of 'rum and gunpowder, strychnine and infectious disease' – as the 'blackest spot' in the history of the Australian colonies. It was to the 'immortal honour' of the people of the valley that 'their tribe' was increasing, and 'equally to the honour' of Dillon that all had been 'Christianised and baptised'. A leading article in the previous issue referred to a recent report of 'cold-blooded extermination' in Queensland, and described what was occurring there as 'but the repetition of what happened in New South Wales'. There was just one difference; 'in Queensland the Government would appear openly to organize and countenance means of extermination which New South Wales and Victoria only connived at'. Why did Aboriginal tribes 'disappear so fast before the white man wherever he comes with his so much boasted justice, and refinement, and civilization', the paper asked? 'This is a question which history will sharply investigate…'[17]

Vaughan made his first visit to Bathurst the following weekend, to preach at the close of a retreat. At a public meeting afterwards Quinn showered him with more praise, saying he had shown he possessed 'one of the greatest gifts of Heaven', candour and truth. An 'honest, straightforward, and simple line of action' was worth 'all the diplomacy in the world,' Vaughan replied.[18] Bishop Murray noted in a letter to Cullen in early April that Quinn had seen a good deal of Vaughan, 'and likes him very much'. Murray also was impressed, writing,

> Dr Vaughan is getting on wonderfully well and I think he will do an immense deal of good... We told him everything as far as we know about affairs here and about the Benedictines and happily he is a man that we can talk to. We shall be very glad to give him every assistance in our power, and the poor man will want it.[19]

Vaughan 'took up rooms' in St John's College towards the end of April, abandoning the residence that had been prepared for him before his arrival, Eveleigh House at Darlington, not far from the university.[20] A week later he paid his first 'official visit to the Rector and Fellows' accompanied by his secretary, the Very Rev. Anselm Gillett, a Benedictine priest who had come with him from England.

Proceedings began with Forrest reading a brief address of welcome from the Rector and Fellows that had been drafted by the long-standing Council members Sheridan, Donovan, Ellis and Duncan, and Rev. Dillon, who was elected to the Council in 1872.[21] This concluded,

> We deeply regret that, owing to causes which it would be out of place here to discuss, this college has not hitherto realized the aspiration of its founders. We trust, however, that your Grace's arrival will be a new era in its history, and that the Fellows of Saint John's and other liberal contributors to its erection may live to enjoy the full reward of their labours and munificence in seeing it filled with studious Catholic youth.

Vaughan had much to say in his response. He feared that the 'wave of infidelity' that was 'sickening Europe' would doubtless 'break upon these shores'. From the moment he first saw St John's – 'this noble pile of buildings' – he recognised 'with the quickness and vividness of light', that it was 'pre-eminently fitted to become the main fortress amongst us of Catholic Christianity'. At St John's 'the civil power' and the Church found themselves in perfect harmony, he said. 'I...hope that we may work together in this College during many years to come in advancing the interests of the purest and noblest cause which could be entrusted by God into the hands of man'.²²

Vaughan mingled 'with his usual winning familiarity' with the Fellows after his speech. Then all retired to the newly opened refectory – the dining hall that Forrest had said in his 1869 annual report could be brought into operation for £100 – for a 'champagne luncheon'. Polding, making what seems to have been his first appearance at the college as Visitor, was there with Rev. Coletti. At its April meeting, the Council had authorised the Rector 'to make all arrangements for supplying the lunch at a cost not exceeding £2 for each Fellow'. The Fellows subsequently agreed also to share the cost – £8 8s – of the illuminated address presented to Vaughan.²³

Probably by this stage all were aware that Vaughan, the college's newest resident, was on the verge of taking charge there. By late 1873, before the coadjutor's arrival, the view that Forrest must be replaced had spread beyond Rev. McCarthy and the Fellows who agreed with him. Perhaps prompted by Polding's letter in March (chapter 16), Matthew Quinn had reached the same conclusion. He had also overcome his reluctance to intervene, and entered into negotiations with the Superior of the Jesuit Order in Australia, Father Thomas Cahill, with a view to the Jesuits paying Forrest out and taking over.

A letter on the subject that Quinn wrote to Lanigan the day before Christmas 1873 provides an interesting insight into relations between the suffragans. He said he had mentioned the negotiations with Cahill in a letter to Murray, who

> told me to my great surprise that he disapproved of what I had done and he was sure the other suffragan bishops would also disapprove of it. I immediately desisted from further action in the matter. But I wrote to Dr Murray that I thought he was wrong...

St John's 'as it now stands is a scandal to the faithful and a reproach to the bishops', Quinn went on. Most of the Fellows were 'Forrest's creatures'; the rest were 'so disgusted and humiliated at the present sad position of the college that they will vote for any good man...' He said if a Jesuit was not put in charge immediately, Vaughan was likely to have Forrest 'removed before six months and a Benedictine in his place'. His first choice would be to have an able secular priest as Rector, but failing that a Jesuit would be vastly preferable to a Benedictine in the post, or to 'a continuation of St John's in its present sad state'.

'So much I wrote to Dr Murray, adding that I thought in acting as I did I was doing then everything the suffragans would wish me to do, otherwise I would not have moved an inch in the matter,' Quinn continued. He asked Lanigan for his opinion, and added: 'Of course all about St John's is strictly private.'[24] Remarks by Murray in August 1874 show he did not think Forrest was to blame for the state of the college (chapter 18). Quinn, like Rev. McCarthy, seems to have failed to consider a key question: would Polding support students from Lyndhurst going on to St John's if anybody – including a Jesuit – other than an approved Benedictine was in charge there?

Vaughan's arrival and his success in winning the approval of the bishops and influential priests and laymen transformed the situation. In early 1874 the St John's Council received a letter from Father Cahill saying that, unlike in 1870, it was now practicable to nominate a Jesuit professor for the college. The Fellows sought comment from the bishops; Vaughan's reply was the crucial one. He said Polding begged him 'to call your attention to the fact that the prospects of the future are not quite the same now as they were in 1870'. Therefore, 'whilst he feels very thankful to the Jesuit Fathers for the interest they are taking in the College of St John, he does not find himself in a position at the present moment to take advantage of their kind offer of assistance'. Doubtless, the opinions that the coadjutor attributed to Polding were his own.[25]

Vaughan wrote to his 'agent' in Rome, the Benedictine Dr Bernard Smith, from St John's three days after his official visit to the college. He now saw the suffragans as 'very zealous and earnest men', and did not 'anticipate any unpleasantness with them'. Of St John's he noted,

The college has not one student! Dr Forrest the Rector gets £500 per an. from Government and will I think agree to let me take his place if I provide for him otherwise. Anyhow I am going to try and set the College on its legs in one way or the other…

His diagnosis of the cause of the failure of St John's is brief but fair – in stark contrast to extravagant claims he made later (chapter 20). 'The Abp Polding & the Bps & Dr Forrest not having pulled together things have not succeeded as well as they might,' he wrote, 'but I really think that we are beginning a new era. I am determined to do all I can to unite all parties, and I even now see beginnings of success.'[26]

Forrest was still Rector on 11 May when he set out with Vaughan, the four New South Wales suffragans and Rev. Dillon on the long sea voyage to Brisbane for the opening of the first stage of St Stephen's Cathedral. Bishop James Quinn and an 'immense crowd' greeted them at the wharf when they arrived three days later, and 'loud and enthusiastic cheering' arose as they stepped ashore.

> A vast procession was then formed, nearly a thousand school children bearing flags, banners, &c., leading the way, and nearly three thousand persons following the carriages on foot. The Hibernian band took up a position immediately in front of the Bishops, and the procession marched to the Cathedral through the streets crowded with spectators, the windows of every house in the line of march being crammed.

The official program began two days later with welcoming addresses and a 'grand oratorio' in the cathedral. Vaughan performed the opening ceremony in the traditional manner the following morning, Sunday 17 May. A priest bearing the cross led the procession, 'attended by the acolytes and clerks'. The bishops and remaining priests followed, with Vaughan at the rear.

> The Asperges was intoned by the Archbishop, and the Psalm Miserere was chanted by the Bishops and priests as they proceeded round the building, the Archbishop sprinkling the exterior of the edifice – in each place at the base and a few feet immediately above, according to the ritual – with holy water. The procession having thus moved round the building, the main door was solemnly opened, and the edifice duly declared a place of worship for Roman Catholics.

Matthew Quinn was celebrant at the Pontifical High Mass that followed, and Forrest the priest assisting at the throne. Vaughan preached, filling in for an unwell Bishop O'Mahony of Armidale. The Brisbane trip apparently provided the first opportunity for the coadjutor to meet both James Quinn and O'Mahony. At the luncheon afterwards, in a marquee in the cathedral grounds, Vaughan praised Quinn's 'dignity, power, and influence', and said it was a privilege to be associated with the 'venerable and distinguished prelates' assembled beside him.[27]

The following evening the bishops were guests of honour at a public banquet at the town hall attended by the Governor of Queensland, the Marquis of Normanby, and many of Brisbane's leading citizens. James Quinn's old friend Dr Kevin Izod O'Doherty, the former Young Irelander, chaired proceedings. Vaughan offered more flattery, telling the gathering his early observations of Australians suggested 'the spirit of the intellect of these colonies' possessed 'many of the intellectual qualities of the Greeks of the time of Socrates.' There was 'a marvellous activity of temper, with a marvellous quickness of perception, a most striking clearness of vision, combined with the love of novelty and change, which reminded him of the representatives of the Greeks,' he was reported as saying. 'There was also one other thing in which they resembled this people, and that thing did not admit so much of praise – it was a want of reverence.'[28]

None of the visitors hurried home from Brisbane. While Murray and Lanigan boarded a steamer for Sydney the following Saturday the others headed for Ipswich, where O'Mahony celebrated High Mass and Vaughan preached to 'a crowded audience'. The following Monday they travelled by 'special train' to Toowoomba, then on Tuesday afternoon were back in Ipswich attending a school prize giving. They returned to Brisbane the next day and departed on the steamer *Lady Young* on Thursday 28 May.[29]

Forrest, *Freeman's* reported, became dangerously ill with bronchitis as a result of exposure during the return voyage. For a time, 'serious fears were entertained…as to his complete recovery'.[30] Probably this, rather than a falling out with his old friend, explains his apparent absence from farewell functions at St John's in early June for Matthew Quinn, who was about to leave on a visit to Rome and Ireland. Vaughan entertained Quinn and some of his clergy at midday dinner on the day he left. Those seeing him off, in addition to Vaughan, included Bishop Murray and St John's Fellows Butler, Duncan, Donovan, Ellis and Rev. Dillon.[31]

The St John's Council met again on Thursday 16 July. The minutes record that Forrest 'handed in a memorandum of the cost of the luncheon' given for Vaughan in May. Then, 'after referring briefly to the present state of the College', he 'announced that he was prepared, if it should meet the views of the Fellows, to resign the office of Rector'.

He left the room to allow the Fellows to deliberate. Then W.A. Duncan 'waited upon' him, and returned to the meeting room with his written resignation, which read,

> Gentlemen,
> I hereby resign my office as Rector of St John's College into your hands.
> Hoping your selection of a successor to me may be what I wish for the best interests of the College.

The Fellows formally accepted the resignation; then Rev. Dillon moved and Rev. McCarthy seconded a motion that Vaughan be elected Forrest's successor. 'After some discussion', this was carried unanimously. Duncan then waited upon Vaughan, who was introduced to the meeting, thanked the Fellows for his election, and announced his acceptance.[32]

The daily newspapers carried the news two days later. The *Sydney Morning Herald* commented, 'There is now every reason to believe that the college will rapidly progress.'[33] A 'Town Talk' item that appeared in Sydney's two other dailies, the *Evening News* and the *Empire*, treated Forrest somewhat harshly:

> The imposing-looking gentleman in the black wide-awake, with gold tassel, to whom the faithful touch their hats as Archbishop Coadjutor…seems to have a quiet but most effective way of doing things… Thus Dr Vaughan had no sooner recovered his land-legs…than he made a clean sweep of St Mary's. Then we heard that the most reverend, &c, &c, had taken up his abode at St John's College… It was explained that Dr Vaughan was, in his

new quarters, simply as the guest of the rector, Dr Forrest, who, with his one student, found life in this vast vacuum somewhat lonely. But there are guests as dangerous as a cuckoo in a thrush's nest, and we cannot say that we are surprised to read in this morning's papers, that Dr Forrest has resigned, and that Dr Vaughan reigns in his stead. It is certainly time that St John's College should have something more to show for the money it has cost and still costs the State… Dr Vaughan…will doubtless give the 'one student' some companions… As for the late Rector's opinion of the change, that is another matter. The reverend and learned gentleman once distinguished himself by a lecture upon the 'Spirit of the Age,' in which some of the latest steps in the world's so-called 'progress' were pretty roundly denounced as so many steps backwards. It would be interesting to know what, in a progressive point of view, he thinks of this step.[34]

Because of its weekly publication and early deadlines, *Freeman's* readers had to wait another week for the news. The paper kindly, but inaccurately, linked Forrest's resignation to his bronchitis attack, said the Fellows 'were fortunate in securing such a successor', and noted that Vaughan's secretary, Very Rev. Gillett, was to be Vice-Rector. A leading article said the news would be 'received with joy', and 'no other man we know of' was as well fitted 'to make the institution a great and complete success'. But it also praised Forrest:

> It is due to the late Rector…to say that the comparative failure of the College is not attributable to his having made himself inimical in any way, for the kindly good will and confidence in his ability which he inspired in all classes and sects on his arrival in the country, he has retained to the last.[35]

Forrest tried one last time to gain recompense for the large amounts of his own money he had put into keeping the college operating, submitting a claim to the Council in October 1874. The Fellows apparently found it difficult to deal with, and took more than a year to reach a decision. Edward Butler moved and Rev. Dillon seconded the resolution finally adopted, in November 1875:

> That this Council having had under consideration the claim of Dr Forrest dated 10th October 1874, as embodied in his memorandum of the same date, having also had under their consideration several minutes and proceedings of the Council in respect to keeping St John's College open

for students, and, recollecting also distinctly the statements made to Dr Forrest at many meetings of the Council and assented to by him to the effect that St John's College if kept open and carried on at all, should be kept open and carried on upon the personal responsibility of Dr Forrest, resolve that they cannot recognise his claim either against themselves personally or against the College.[36]

Clearly not a happy parting, but apparently Forrest was able to joke about it in later years. According to the fiftieth anniversary *Freeman's* published in 1900, a friend meeting him in the street

> remarked in a jocular way, 'You've been at the wickets a long time, but you're bowled at last.' 'Not at all, my good friend,' the Doctor replied; 'nothing of the kind. It is true that I have retired from St John's, but I have carried out my bat for 400.'[37]

Under the unannounced deal made with Vaughan, Forrest was to receive £400 a year from the £500 Rector's salary paid by the government. He was also promised a city parish – a commitment fulfilled in May 1875 when he took charge of St Augustine's, Balmain.[38]

18

More travels

Vaughan set off north by coastal steamer again on Friday 14 August, this time on his first visit to the Maitland diocese. His travelling companions, as before, included Forrest and Rev. Dillon; also on board were Bishops Lanigan and O'Mahony. Bishop Murray and 'hundreds eager to catch a glimpse of the distinguished visitors' greeted the party at the Newcastle wharf, *Freeman's* reported. Next day, they caught the midday train to Maitland 'where a truly magnificent sight presented itself'. People had flocked to the station from every population centre 'in the rich valley of the Hunter', and some five hundred horsemen joined the 'cavalcade' that escorted the ecclesiastics to the cathedral.

Saturday afternoon's formality was the reading of the welcoming address from the Catholics of Maitland and the bishops' responses. Next morning 'every inch of space within the Cathedral' was filled for the Pontifical High Mass; Vaughan preached for over an hour and 'was listened to with the utmost attention and reverence throughout'. The collection, for a school building fund, raised more than £1,100.[1]

The following evening, two hundred and sixty men and women assembled for dinner in a schoolroom decorated with flags, boughs, a scroll bearing the Irish greeting Cead Mille Failthe and a panel exhibiting Vaughan's coat of arms. Murray displayed his usual light touch in proposing the toast to the coadjutor. Vaughan had 'come here, as he has more than once expressed it, to sink or swim in the same boat with us,' he said. 'He has come to be our captain; and now, ladies and gentlemen, you have looked at him, you must admit that he is the making of a noble captain (laughter and prolonged applause).'

Vaughan was 'vociferously cheered' as he began his lengthy reply –

which was mainly about his ambition for St John's College to provide training to fit young Catholics for the most important positions in the colony. 'I say that if we properly constitute the college, and have a staff of professors fit for their important duties, we shall soon have an immense number of young men placed in a position to acquire the knowledge which is absolutely necessary for governing others,' he said. At the college,

> We shall be stamping our young men deeper and deeper with all that makes men noble and fine in character; all that makes man meet his fellow man in confidence and honour, and marks him as one also to be confided in; all that makes a man strong and powerful as an oak tree, fit to be used in any service, and always ready for any battle… I will teach there myself, for I love to stamp the souls of young men, and send them forth into the world to let people see what Catholics really are. I shall thank any of you who have children to send them to me; I will be their friend.

Vaughan proposed the toast to Murray, who responded 'in a feeling speech'; unfortunately, the newspaper account gave little detail. It noted that the bishop

> took occasion to refer to the resignation by Dr Forrest of the rectorship of St John's in favour of Dr Vaughan, and in reply to some newspaper strictures upon the occurrence, asserted that Dr Forrest lacked neither the ability nor the good will to promote the interests of the college. But circumstances had prevented him from being as useful as he desired to be, and perhaps the Bishops had not assisted him to the extent of their power.

Lanigan spoke next, saying 'the ill-success of the college under Dr Forrest had arisen from the absence of colleges in the different dioceses, which were now erected, and which would serve as feeders to St John's'. Forrest replied diplomatically,

> I really resigned the rectorship with a view, and only with a view, to making the college a greater success than could be expected in my time, under the circumstances (applause). I resigned it into no unworthy hands. Therefore I am proud of my resignation, because of my successor. I have to meet a popular prejudice. I meet it in that spirit of honesty and candour which will characterize the new rector, as I trust it has ever characterized me. I have not been compelled to resign the rectorship, or been cheated out of

it, but freely and voluntarily resigned it that it may be a great success, such as I wish it to be, and hope to live to see it become (applause).

He added that he had resigned 'on the most kindly relations' with Vaughan, and had never received 'anything but kindness and courtesy and affection' from both Polding and Vaughan, or had the slightest misunderstanding with either archbishop.[2] Forrest's comments were probably a genuine reflection of how he felt about Vaughan at the time. Like the bishops, he seems to have taken to the affable, eloquent and obviously able coadjutor. No doubt it is also true that Polding treated Forrest courteously at their rare meetings; his real feelings, and his actions regarding St John's, were another matter.

The reminiscences of John Lane Mullins, who finished his schooling at Lyndhurst at the age of sixteen in 1873 and remained there when he began his university studies the following year, provide an insight into the view of Polding and his supporters. Mullins described Polding 'as a great personal friend of my family'. He wrote that he had stayed on at Lyndhurst because 'in my father's judgment St John's College on account of its Rector did not present any attraction to Catholic students'.

According to Mullins, McEncroe on his visit to 'the Old World' in 1859 had been 'entrusted with the selection of a gentleman regarded as eminently fitted to adorn the position' of Rector, and been given that person's name. But when he declined the post, McEncroe selected 'apparently on his own judgment another ecclesiastic in the person of Dr Forrest whose name it is alleged was quite unknown in New South Wales'. Polding considered the appointment 'outside the order of leave' and 'refused to give it any formal ratification'.[3]

Mullins presumably had no way of knowing how false this account was. The choice of Rector was entrusted, at least in theory, to four eminent ecclesiastics of whom two, Cullen and Newman, provided glowing testimonials to Forrest's capacity (chapter 2). And Polding did ratify the appointment. In a letter to the St John's Council in September 1860, the then Vicar-General, Abbot Gregory, wrote,

> His Grace congratulates the Council on their success [in obtaining Forrest

as Rector] and authorizes me to notify to you that he has issued faculties to Dr Forrest which constitute him of course an approved Priest in this Archdiocese and give effect according to the St John's Bill of Incorporation to his appointment as Rector. With the sanction of his appointment His Grace also confers on Dr Forrest the title of Very Reverend.[4]

Vaughan wrote again to his agent in Rome, Bernard Smith, and to his father soon after returning to Sydney. He was now full of praise for the suffragan bishops. He told Smith he got on 'first class' with them and found them 'good, earnest, zealous men'. He told his father he had 'quite reconciled and united' the bishops, who were 'very zealous, self-sacrificing men – a harder-working set than our English Hierarchy, taking them as a body'.

These letters were Vaughan's first since he took over as Rector of St John's. Up to then, the college had been a 'dead failure', he told Smith, ignoring its relative success in the mid-1860s when numbers of students peaked at ten and some did very well. 'When I came there was not a student in it, and the place was going to rack,' he wrote. 'I hope before the year is out to have it in good working order. The Jesuits offered their late Rector £5,000 to get his place: I just came in in the nick of time, and offered him £40 [sic] a year – he resigned and the Fellows elected me.'[5]

Reporting the same news to his father, he made it clear that his current regard for the Irish bishops did not extend to Forrest. 'I am now Rector of St John's College within the University, and thus hold the reins and whip of the Educational department of the Church here,' he wrote.

> I bought my predecessor out – a most objectional [sic] whisky drinking, purple nosed little Irish priest. The Jesuits had offered him £5,000 down for his position – I offered him £400 a year for life and, as I get £500 from Government as Rector, I was able to afford to offer such a sum: and thus keep this most important position in my own control. Had I not done this my position now and in the future would be indefinitely weaker. I pay £100 to a Professor of Classics and thus my £500 per an. is got rid of! If my predecessor would only take it into his head to 'go up Jacob's ladder', as Dr Manning calls it when speaking of objectionable opponents, he would add so much to my power of doing good.[6]

Unfortunately for Vaughan, Forrest's demise was still some years off. However, he seems to have had little trouble raising funds for repairs and improvements at the college. *Freeman's* reported in April 1875 that more than £3,000 had already been spent 'putting the building in repair, furnishing it, and fitting it to become a worthy residence for our highest Catholic youth'. Vaughan had raised more than £800 of this personally by writing to 'lovers of education and of St John's', and would contribute another £800 himself.[7]

Jobs undertaken before the first five students under the new regime entered in October 1874 included making the students' rooms 'bright and cheerful looking', whitewashing the passage walls, building a large bathroom, improving the common room, and making the roof 'perfectly watertight'.[8] The students who moved in were, of course, John Lane Mullins and his four fellow undergraduates at Lyndhurst.[9] The Benedictine school's days as a residence for university students were over.

Forrest undertook more travel, no longer in company with Vaughan, before taking up his new appointment at St Augustine's, Balmain. In November, he attended a concert at the Dominican convent in Newcastle with Bishop Murray, and congratulated the young performers on their efforts in a 'humorous and lengthy' speech.[10] After examining again at Lyndhurst, he left in early December for another summer holiday in Tasmania. He preached at the reception of a novice into Hobart's Presentation Convent in mid-December and, with Bishop Murphy, examined at the convent a few days later. Bishop Murray, also in Tasmania to escape the summer heat, joined Murphy and Forrest at the reception of two more novices into the convent in January. Polding, with Rev. Coletti, joined the exodus south in January, and at the end of the month attended High Mass – featuring 'brilliant solos' by members of the 'Italian Opera Company' – at Hobart's St Mary's Cathedral with Murphy, Murray and Forrest.[11]

Vaughan told Smith in his September letter that Polding was 'getting rather deaf and losing his memory a little' but was otherwise 'in very good health'. Both Archbishops attended the Lyndhurst awards ceremony in mid-December, and heard Rev. Quirk claim that the school had trained twenty-five of the thirty Catholic students who had so far graduated from the university. He noted that the school leavers who continued their studies would in future do so 'under the fostering tutelage and banner of the College of St John'. Vaughan's response included, surprisingly, remarks that read like praise for Forrest's stewardship of St John's. Although the college had not 'turned out' many students,

> he had met some of them himself, and he was pleased to see that they had attained a high standard of education, both intellectually and socially; they were all gentlemanly, fine young fellows, and he thought if we could educate and bring up such as these, we could show that Catholics were as good as any other men, and that they would be able to take their proper place in society; and, instead of being despised, they would be looked up to.[12]

Accompanied by Bishop Murray, Vaughan left Sydney the next day for Bathurst to attend the awards ceremony at St Stanislaus' College. He would have been impressed to see that this school now had nearly eighty students, twice as many as Lyndhurst. He thanked the people of Bathurst for their donations – including one of £100 – to his appeal for St John's. 'From being a ruin and a desolation, I am bent on making St John's a pride, if so be, to the Catholic body – to those large-minded men and women who years ago so generously subscribed a princely sum for its erection,' he said.[13]

Two new matriculants from Lyndhurst entered St John's in February 1875. A month later, advertisements appeared for the 'Grand Opening' of the college on the morning of Wednesday 7 April.[14] Despite heavy early morning showers, the refurbished chapel and adjoining hall were 'thronged' by 10 a.m. when the Pontifical High Mass, celebrated by Polding, began. 'It was remarked that the venerable prelate rendered the solemn Gregorian music of the mass (as he is wont to do) in a clear and tuneful voice – loud enough to be distinctly heard by the large congregation present,' reported the *Sydney Morning Herald*.

Besides Polding and Vaughan, four bishops – James Quinn, Murray, Lanigan and Christopher Reynolds of Adelaide – were present. Forrest, recently back from another visit to Maitland where he had preached 'a most eloquent, argumentative, and impressive' sermon at the reception of a postulant into the Dominican convent,[15] was also there, as were about sixty other priests. Prominent laymen in the gathering included, besides the St John's Fellows, the Chancellor of the University Sir Edward Deas Thomson, Professor Badham, and William Forster, the new colonial Treasurer. The local political merry-go-round had completed another turn two months earlier with the defeat of Parkes and return to power of the fifty-eight-year-old John Robertson as Premier and Colonial Secretary; as well as Forster, his ministry included W.B. Dalley as Attorney-General.

After the Mass, James Quinn, leading a procession through and round the building, performed the traditional blessing. Then the archbishops, bishops, Forrest and other dignitaries assembled on a temporary balcony overlooking a grassy courtyard where a crowd of more than two thousand had assembled. Most either stood or sat on the grass as Vaughan delivered an oration that lasted nearly an hour and a half. He was 'listened to with much attention throughout', the *Herald* reported.

Much of his talk was a dissertation on education in ancient Greece and Rome and in early Christian times. He said St John's, 'like all institutions of learning destined to a glorious career', had had to struggle with many difficulties in its infancy, but he was confident of its future success. The roles of the university and college were complementary; while the university 'exercised the intellect and disciplined the will', at St John's 'the principal duty would be to inform, instruct, and educate the heart'. 'In proportion as this was successfully done', he added, St John's would turn out 'men of power, of real enlightenment, and true as steel.'[16]

Three of the visiting bishops were still in Sydney two weeks later when Edward Butler married his second wife, Marian Daintrey, in the St John's chapel. Vaughan performed the service, assisted by Bishops Quinn, Murray and Reynolds.[17] Another notable marriage had taken place two days before the college opening – that of Vaughan's brother Reginald to Norah Shanahan. She was a sister-in-law of Patrick Jennings, a wealthy

Bishop O'Mahony.

landowner and St John's Fellow who became, briefly, the first Catholic Premier of New South Wales in 1886. Both archbishops, James Quinn and Forrest were among those involved in this service, held at the pro-cathedral.[18]

A notable absentee from all these events was Bishop O'Mahony of Armidale. His stay in the colony was brief and unhappy. Accusations of over-indulgence in alcohol were made against him from soon after his arrival; then in May 1874 he was accused of seducing a young woman and fathering her child, born two years earlier. Eventually, in 1877, the authorities in Rome found O'Mahony had done no wrong. Long before then relations between Vaughan and the suffragan bishops had soured irrevocably, the Archbishop accused of bias and lack of candour in his handling of the allegations.[19]

The paternity charge was withdrawn before the end of 1874, but not before much damage had been done to O'Mahony's reputation. The accuser, Ellen Nugent, was in gaol for theft when she made the accusation and her mother demanded money from O'Mahony to support the infant. O'Mahony consulted Vaughan, who sought advice from Edward Butler. The lawyer made the obvious point that any payment would look like an admission of guilt, an argument also put strongly by Bishop Murray when he heard what had happened. Vaughan, however, encouraged O'Mahony to pay the Nugents on condition that they call off legal proceedings against the bishop and leave Armidale. They did both those things when £200 was handed over in October, after Ellen's release from gaol.

Within weeks, she withdrew her accusation against O'Mahony, and in declarations sworn in Melbourne named the real father and admitted an intention to extort money from the bishop. O'Mahony told Bishop Lanigan in a letter written in May 1875 that he was not informed of Ellen Nugent's recantation until March, four months after the event. Apparently Forrest passed the news on, after the politician Sir John O'Shanassy, who witnessed one of the declarations, 'accidentally mentioned the fact' to him. O'Mahony accused Rev. Martin Kelly, the priest he had chosen to deal with the Nugents, of concealing the information: 'He let the horrible slander circulate for six months and never once contradicted it.'[20]

Kelly, indeed, seems to have been the principal villain in the affair. What his motives were is unknown. However, information obtained by Moran in Ireland and passed on to Murray in early 1876 revealed a dubious past. Kelly had been expelled from Kilkenny after doing what O'Mahony was falsely accused of, fathering a child. This fact was not made known to O'Mahony when he recruited the priest from a seminary in France. Kelly left the Church in 1877 to marry.

According to the author of a detailed study of the O'Mahony affair, Rev. John Farrell, Kelly initiated the rumours about the bishop's drinking habits, revealed the payment made to silence the Nugents, and encouraged people to write to Vaughan with complaints about the bishop. Rumours of scandal were rife in Armidale when Vaughan sent two priests there in September 1874 to gather information while canvassing for funds for the St Mary's Cathedral building fund. After receiving their report, Vaughan and Polding advised the authorities in Rome that O'Mahony appeared to have lost the confidence of his people. Rome responded by directing Vaughan to conduct an investigation.

He immediately did so, sending letters to various laymen and priests requesting information and comments. As the people consulted were those recommended by Kelly and another priest opposed to O'Mahony, the response inevitably was biased. O'Mahony was ordered to Rome after Vaughan's report was received there. He told Lanigan in a letter written in February 1876, soon after arriving, that Barnabo's successor as head of Propaganda, Cardinal Franchi, had initially demanded his 'immediate and unconditional' resignation as Bishop of Armidale. However, he had managed to convince the authorities that the facts did not warrant this and 'the whole case' should be 'gone into *de novo*'.[21]

The next element in this complicated saga was perhaps the most extraordinary of all. Rev. Coletti, Polding's chaplain who had worried the Archbishop with stories of Irish intrigues against him (chapters 12 and 13), travelled to Rome as Vaughan's emissary, arriving about a month after O'Mahony.[22] Moran, then also in Rome, informed Cullen in April 1876 that the Italian priest had come with letters from Vaughan making allegations of intemperance against Murray and the Quinns.[23] Apparently his mission was not only to support the case against O'Mahony but also to damage the reputations of the other suffragans.

In March 1877, a Pontifical Commission declared O'Mahony innocent of habitual intemperance, the remaining charge against him, and criticised Vaughan's investigation. The adjudicating cardinals also, however, decided that the bishop should not return to Armidale because of the damaging publicity the case had aroused. Three months later, he succumbed to pressure to resign, in the mistaken belief that he no longer had the support of the New South Wales suffragans. Adverse opinions obtained by Vaughan from the Bishops of Sandhurst, Adelaide and New Caledonia had provided Franchi with grounds to give O'Mahony the misleading message that the colonial bishops were opposed to his return. When he learned he had been deceived – that, in fact, the Quinns, Murray and Lanigan held the opposite view – he appealed unsuccessfully to be reinstated.

O'Mahony was appointed an auxiliary bishop in Canada in November 1879 and spent the rest of his life there. Franchi had assured him when he resigned as Bishop of Armidale that Vaughan would be instructed to publish a statement declaring his innocence of all charges. Vaughan never did so – the final injustice in an episode that reflected very poorly on the Archbishop's respect for fair dealing, truth and natural justice.

19

At Balmain

The St Augustine's, Balmain, church hall was 'crowded to excess' on the evening of Thursday, 27 May 1875, for a farewell tea party and concert for Rev. L.B. Pacilio, who was about to return to Italy after four years as pastor. Forrest, his successor, presided and, after 'justice had been done to the good things sumptuously provided by the ladies in charge', gave what *Freeman's* described as 'one of his happiest, eloquent speeches' in praise of Pacilio. Responding amid 'deafening applause', the Italian promised his flock he would 'pray for them fervently on the glorious tomb of St Peter' in Rome.[1]

Forrest, it seems, had commenced duty at the historic church – blessed and opened by Polding in 1851 and presided over from 1856 up to his death in 1864 by Archpriest Therry – the previous month; his first entry in the baptismal register is dated 18 April 1875.[2] Five months later, a young nephew of McEncroe, Rev. Tom Keating, joined him as assistant priest. Around this time, Vaughan appointed Forrest one of four 'presidents' of 'theological schools' he had set up – an indication that, at this stage, the two were on good terms. In a letter to Cullen in 1864 (chapter 6), Forrest had observed that 'theological conferences for the clergy are badly wanted'; perhaps the 'schools' were his idea.

Letters from Vaughan to Forrest in the St John's College archives indicate what was involved.[3] In the first, dated 21 December 1875, Vaughan acknowledged receipt of 'cases' from Forrest. From the later letters it seems Vaughan sent a 'case' requiring a theological solution to the presidents perhaps four times a year. Each president then sent this on to the priests in his 'school' with a request that they prepare a 'solution'. The presidents subsequently sent 'reports' prepared from the solutions submitted, and their own solutions, to Vaughan.

263

One member of Forrest's 'school' was Rev. Dillon. Vaughan told Forrest in October 1876 that Dillon had written to him 'pleading, as an excuse for not sending you his Solution, a great stress of work'. Vaughan was not impressed: 'I told him that it would make his work all the more telling if he gave himself a short time to theological study.' All seven of Vaughan's letters – the last is dated May 1877 – are friendly in tone. Two invite Forrest to meetings on matters related to the theological schools with him and the other presidents; one of the invitations included dinner afterwards.

In August 1875, the centenary of the birth of the renowned Irishman, Daniel O'Connell, 'the Liberator', was the occasion of much celebration.

Archbishop Vaughan delivers the oration at Sydney's celebration of the centenary of the birth of Ireland's 'liberator', Daniel O'Connell.

Forrest was among the speakers at a 'most enthusiastic' public meeting at the end of June, attended by more than four hundred, that initiated arrangements for a 'grand demonstration' in Sydney on the anniversary, 6 August. Advertisements a week later announced that this would include an oration by Vaughan on the life and times of O'Connell, a grand concert of Irish music, a 'monster procession', and a program of athletic sports and amusements. In addition, donations were sought for an 'O'Connell scholarship' to be established at St John's College.[4]

Freeman's carried reports of many suburban and country meetings to raise funds and arouse enthusiasm for the coming celebrations. Forrest opened proceedings at a 'most influential and enthusiastic' gathering in Balmain with 'a forcible and eloquent address'. Then, after other speakers had promised the hearty support of the people of Balmain for the commemoration, he gave another 'very telling and humorous speech'. Unfortunately, no details were provided.[5]

The anniversary Friday dawned brightly. Proceedings began with the procession – numbers estimated at not less than twelve thousand – from the city to Prince Alfred Park, Redfern. Members of the Australian Holy Catholic Guild led the way, followed by contingents from other Catholic and workers' organizations, including the Seamen's Union. Marchers wore green and blue rosettes symbolising Ireland and Australia, and several groups carried large banners, the most conspicuous and imposing, according to *Freeman's*, belonging to the Hibernian benefit society. Among the images on this thirteen by eleven feet green silk extravaganza was 'a life-size figure representing Erin seated on a mound playing the harp, the Irish wolf-dog crouched at her feet; in the distant landscape may be seen the Round Tower, and ruined Abbey, reminding one of days long ago'.[6]

Five bands provided the music as the marchers made their way, over nearly two hours, along streets 'crowded with spectators'. When they reached the park, 'sports of all kinds' – including running, jumping, 'putting the stone', Irish jigs and reels, football and quoits – were indulged in 'with great zest'. Punch and Judy shows and a merry-go-round were 'extensively patronized', and dancing 'indulged in to an unlimited extent'. The *Herald* noted that, 'by a wise arrangement of the committee, no intoxicating drinks were allowed to be sold on the grounds, and in consequence there was nothing but sobriety and good order to be seen all around'.

In the evening people crowded into the hall built for the Intercolonial Exhibition of 1870, which marked the centenary of the arrival of Captain Cook, for the concert and Vaughan's oration. Among the dignitaries on the platform were Polding, 'whose appearance was the occasion of a general and spontaneous outburst of enthusiasm', Bishops Murray and Lanigan, and 'a large number of clergy' (who probably included Forrest).[7] Another was the English novelist Anthony Trollope, making a return visit to Australia. In his celebrated account of his first visit, in 1871–72, Trollope described Sydney as 'one of those places which, when a man leaves it knowing that he will never return, he cannot leave without a pang and a tear. Such is its loveliness.'[8]

First item on the program was a 'grand overture on the most beautiful melodies of Ireland' for organ and orchestra. Then a group of singers presented some 'gems of Irish melody', followed by a lengthy cantata in praise of O'Connell written for the occasion by Professor Badham and set to music by a Signor Giorza. The following chorus illustrates the style of the piece:

> Free as the thunderbolt scathing the offender,
> Spurning at surrender till thy race were freed;
> Dire in debate, and yet as woman tender,
> Counsellor, befriender of the sons of Need.

Freeman's noted that the exhibition hall's acoustics were very bad. Nevertheless, when Vaughan rose to give his lengthy oration his voice 'seemed to thoroughly permeate the vast area, and to be distinctly heard throughout'. Explaining why he had accepted the invitation to deliver the eulogy, Vaughan described O'Connell as 'the mighty champion of civil and religious liberty'.

It was not Ireland alone that was freed by him, but the Catholics of England also were, through his indomitable labours, lifted from their darkness and the shadows of death. The blow which broke for ever the chains and handcuffs of the sons of Erin shivered also, as if by sympathy, the manacles of the Catholics of England – and for the first time for three hundred years they stood upright, and began to learn that they were men.⁹

The oratory continued at a banquet at Sydney's Masonic Hall four days later. Forrest was among the two hundred there, with his old friend Dean (now Monsignor) Lynch and Rev. Placid Quirk of Lyndhurst. Patrick Jennings proposed the toast to O'Connell, describing him as 'the transcendent genius' and the 'greatest of Ireland's sons'.¹⁰ Despite all the enthusiasm, donations towards a St John's College scholarship commemorating O'Connell proved hard to attract; Vaughan's succession to the rectorship had not transformed the college into a popular cause. Jennings eventually came to the rescue, contributing £461 in 1878 to lift total collections to the required £1,000.¹¹

In the last week of September 1875, Rev. Dillon returned to Forrest's Balmain church to lead what seems to have been a highly successful Jubilee mission. The services each morning were crowded 'and in the evenings the throng was so dense that the building was altogether inadequate to afford standing room to the auditory,' *Freeman's* reported. Forrest and the five other priests who manned the confessionals 'were kept busy at their posts all day and generally until near midnight'. Many lapsed Catholics 'returned to the fervent confession of faith', and some Protestants were admitted into the Church. Polding attended the morning Mass, at which Forrest preached, on the Sunday the mission ended. A collection afterwards raised £750, nearly clearing the parish debt.¹²

As the opening of the new Catholic secondary boarding school in Maitland, Sacred Heart College, coincided with the last day of the Balmain mission, Forrest could not attend. Vaughan, Lanigan and Bishop Murphy of Hobart joined Bishop Murray for the celebration, conducted in similar style to the recent inaugurations of the equivalent institutions in Bathurst and Goulburn, St Stanislaus' and St Patrick's colleges.

Vaughan heaped more praise on Murray in his banquet speech, saying he 'not only respected, but loved' the bishop, who 'seemed to enjoy the sweetest communion with all men'. Reporting proceedings, *Freeman's* added its own accolades, writing of Murray's 'genial simplicity of character' combined with 'the foresight of true wisdom'. 'A good instance of this,' it went on, 'is furnished by his expressed aim in regard to this college. He does not start with the vain idea of making it a feeble competitor, but rather a feeder of St John's, knowing that no country foundation can possibly possess the advantages of a metropolitan affiliated college.' With those words the paper at last acknowledged, if obliquely, the role Lyndhurst had played, as a 'competitor' instead of a 'feeder', in the failure of St John's under Forrest.[13]

Bishop Murphy, on his way home to Hobart after the opening, returned to Sydney with Vaughan and visited St John's. Student John Lane Mullins recalled teaming up with Murphy's chaplain, Father Daniel Beechinor, to beat the bishop and a Captain Murphy – 'a very fine player' – at billiards on the college table. Also around this time, wrote Mullins, the Captain and an English visitor gave 'a very interesting demonstration of the points of the game'. Among those present, in addition to some of the students, were Vaughan, Vice-Rector Gillett and Forrest.[14] As well as providing further evidence that Vaughan and Forrest were on friendly terms at this stage, the episode suggests the coadjutor did not share Polding's aversion to socialising around the billiard table (chapter 6).

Vaughan visited St Augustine's in early December 1875 to administer confirmation to about one hundred and twenty children and twenty adults, and expressed pleasure at the large numbers receiving the sacraments there. The boys' school attached to the church was also doing well. *Freeman's* noted in its report of a ceremony at which Forrest distributed end-of-year prizes that attendance had doubled to more than sixty since a new teacher took charge five months earlier. 'This is another example of the fact that parents will send their children to Catholic schools, when such schools are well conducted,' the paper added.[15] No doubt the continuing decline of the denominational system – school numbers had fallen by one hundred and thirteen since 1868[16] – prompted that comment. Also causing concern was increasing talk of an end to government funding of denominational schools – as had been enacted in Victoria in 1872 and, recently, in Queensland.[17]

Forrest examined the top Latin class at Lyndhurst in early December, and was sufficiently impressed by one student's work to award full marks.[18] A week before Christmas he joined Polding, Vaughan and many other guests at the school's awards ceremony. As in earlier years, proceedings began outdoors where the students were 'put through several evolutions in military drill by Sergeant-Major McGarvie'. Vaughan took a particular interest in the sword exercise, *Freeman's* reported. Inside, before the two archbishops presented the prizes, Rev. Quirk reported positively on the school's progress. He noted that Lyndhurst was nearly twenty-five years old, and said that in its 'long stability' one might see 'the pledge of its future permanence and the fullness of its growth'. Addressing Polding, he added, 'A foundation like this of yours, when once it has taken deep root, is a permanent, an almost indestructible, thing.'[19] Perhaps Quirk had heard that Vaughan was contemplating closing Lyndhurst and was seeking support to stop this happening. The axe fell just eighteen months later.

In mid-February 1876, Vaughan returned to Forrest's parish to open a new school, St Joseph's, Balmain West. The pastor was absent, on another visit to Hobart with his friend Bishop Murray; Rev. Keating deputised for him.[20] Lending their support to an appeal for funds for urgent repairs to Hobart's St Mary's Cathedral, Forrest and Murray attended a public meeting – presided over by the Governor, Frederick Weld, a relative of Vaughan – in the crumbling edifice.[21] Those present may have been risking their lives; the partially built cathedral, opened in 1866, was apparently on the verge of collapse. A report commissioned from architects soon after the meeting confirmed the danger, and the building was immediately closed to the public.

The architects advised complete demolition of the cathedral's dominant feature, the thirty-metre-high 'central lantern tower', and a considerable lowering of the transept walls. 'And so correct did this opinion prove to be, that no sooner was a portion of the building disturbed than one entire wall came down with a crash,' *Freeman's* reported. In the event, the whole cathedral had to be demolished; 'it was found that almost the whole of the material used was simply rubbish'. The new St Mary's, able to accommodate about a thousand worshippers, was opened in early 1881 – eighteen months before Sydney's second St Mary's Cathedral.[22]

Back at Balmain, Forrest was host to Polding and Vaughan at a stone-laying ceremony on St Patrick's Day, Friday 17 March 1876. The building on which construction was about to begin, on land bequeathed by Archpriest Therry to the Jesuits and donated by them for the project, was a convent of the Sisters of the Good Shepherd. Edmund Blacket designed the three-storey structure overlooking the harbour and offering, according to *Freeman's*, 'as fine a view on every side as could be obtained'.[23] It was to replace inadequate rented accommodation.

A 'very large assemblage' watched Polding, assisted by Forrest and Keating, bless and lay the foundation stone. After Vaughan delivered the address he was presented with 'a genuine shamrock' to mark St Patrick's Day. 'This is an emblem of faith, and the stone laid here today is not only an emblem, but a monument of faith and religion,' he responded. 'The rock on which this stone is laid is no sham rock...'[24]

Life at St Augustine's proceeded smoothly as the convent rose. In September a 'very large audience' attended a 'grand concert and dramatic performance' to raise funds to further reduce the church debt.[25] About the same time Forrest took on additional duties as Catholic chaplain to Callan Park mental asylum. In return for a meagre government salary of £26 a year, he was required to hold a Sunday service there once a fortnight and 'attend all calls for his special services in case of sickness and the like'.[26] Time could still be found for light diversions; in November Forrest, Garavel and Lynch were among ten priests who joined the pupils of St Bede's school, Pyrmont, for a steamboat ride across the harbour and picnic at Chowder Bay.[27]

Forrest again tested the Lyndhurst students' progress in Latin at the end-of-year exams, and joined Polding and Vaughan at the awards ceremony. Vaughan's message to the boys was that they should try to make their mark. 'No one should suffer himself to be a drone, an idler,' he said. 'All should aim at something worthy, if not at something very high.' A few days later, Lyndhurst's headmaster, Rev. Quirk, took his turn as examiner, and found the Balmain Good Shepherd nuns had 'spared no pains in imparting a thoroughly sound education' to their pupils. After a musical performance by the children, Forrest presented the prizes 'and spoke at considerable length in a most amusing and witty speech'.[28]

The eighty-two-year-old Polding was, sadly, too ill to attend the celebrations in February 1877 marking twenty-five years since he opened and blessed Lyndhurst. 'Great numbers of old students loyally flocked together from all parts of the colony' for a special High Mass in the chapel on the jubilee Saturday, *Freeman's* reported. Two days later the Prior, Rev. Dwyer, chaired a dinner in the school's hall; Forrest was among the many guests.

Proposing the toast to Lyndhurst's prosperity, Judge Faucett praised its record in producing students who had taken 'the highest places and the highest prizes in the most open competition in the university'. Responding, Rev. Quirk noted that 'out of forty-five Catholic names on the roll of the university, no less than thirty-five were prepared and trained at Lyndhurst'. He was confident that the school 'would do still better in the future. (Cheers.)'

If Quirk had hoped for an endorsement from Vaughan, he was disappointed. The Archbishop offered no praise for the school's achievements. Instead, he nominated three essential qualities that 'such an establishment as Lyndhurst' should strive to develop in youth, and said he believed 'our young men at home' compared well with those 'reared in Australia' in these qualities. First was perseverance, and second accuracy of thought and expression. The third, and most important, was a quality he mentioned in a speech in Brisbane in 1874 (chapter 17) as lacking in the Australian character – reverence, looking up 'with honour and respect towards those who are greater and better than themselves'. It was 'in such a school as this that reverence could best be imparted or encouraged,' he said, implying that Lyndhurst had failed in this area.[29]

Forrest presided at a well-attended fundraising concert at St Augustine's, Balmain, the day after the Lyndhurst dinner. Two weeks later he travelled to Bathurst, invited by Bishop Matthew Quinn to assist at the installation of two prominent laymen – one from Bourke and the other from Orange – as Knights Companions of the Order of St Gregory. He was unable to take part in the ceremony, 'having unfortunately met with a very severe accident'. What that was is not recorded. It may have influenced the decision to postpone a raffle planned for 12 March in aid of the new Balmain convent, with a horse as the prize.[30] Probably it also accounted for the fact that Forrest was not listed among the priests present at the funeral of Archbishop Polding on Monday 19 March 1877.[31]

Polding, whose health had been failing for several months, took to his bed on 9 March. He retained intermittent consciousness for most of the period up to his death a week later, and received a stream of visitors – Catholic, Protestant and Jew, clerical and lay. W.B. Dalley, the Attorney-General and a man who, *Freeman's* noted, had always 'reverenced' Polding 'with a filial affection',[32] visited daily. Premier Robertson, the Anglican Bishop Barker and the Presbyterian Rev. John Dunmore Lang were among others who paid their last respects. Robertson recalled later that the Archbishop had told him he would like to see the seventy-seven-year-old Lang, who had ministered in the colony since 1823, twelve years before Polding arrived. Lang had agreed immediately to come, Robertson said. 'No one but God and those two saints know what passed between them, but when he came out there were tears on the dear old Doctor's face.'[33]

Freeman's observed that Polding's life was one of the few links connecting the colony's present and past.

> His daily visits to the gaols – his consolation of unhappy convicts – his nights spent in the condemned cells – the beauty of these things only lingers

here and there as a fast-receding memory... Those who have only looked upon the serene old man of latter days...can hardly realize the bright, brave, sensitive creature of thirty or forty years ago, for whom perilous duty had a fascination more intense than any human pleasure.[34]

Thousands paid their respects during the lying-in-state at the Presbytery. On the day of the funeral, the pro-Cathedral was packed long before the 10 a.m. start, and 'every avenue to the building was filled with vehicles of all descriptions – from the Governor's carriage down to the unpretending gig' – awaiting the procession to Petersham cemetery. Proceedings began with the entry of the priests – with Bishops Matthew Quinn, Murray and Lanigan and the now Archbishop of

Crowds line the route as Archbishop Polding's funeral procession turns from College Street into Park Street.

Sydney, Vaughan, at the rear – to the strains of Handel's Dead March. Quinn was celebrant for the Pontifical High Mass, and organ, orchestra, soloists and a chorus made up of several Sydney choirs combined to present Mozart's *Requiem*. 'Nothing could be more excellent than the execution of the music,' *Freeman's* observed.

Nearly a thousand members of the Holy Catholic Guild dressed in black, 'with sashes and bands round their hats', led the long funeral procession. Those on foot numbered about fifteen thousand, and two hundred and seventy-six carriages followed. Vaughan and the bishops, now joined by James O'Quinn (as the Bishop of Brisbane had styled himself since the O'Connell celebrations), performed the rites at the grave, and 'as those around took their last look at the coffin there was hardly a dry eye to be seen'. Vaughan concluded proceedings with a brief address praising Polding. One day, he said, he or somebody else would

> endeavour to set forth a brief history of his life in the great and exalted position to which he attained, and to exhibit that gentleness, that forbearance, and all those other qualities which take so many years to learn, and which were displayed by him with such great brilliancy. May his mantle indeed fall upon my shoulders, and may I learn from him those lessons I so much need...[35]

Gentleness and forbearance were certainly not on display in a cheerful letter that Vaughan wrote to his father four days after the funeral. Now that Polding, who had 'lived a spotless life', was dead, he felt 'somewhat like a donkey...with the log off his leg – not so easily caught!' He had spent the past three years studying his ground, taking stock of his men, and 'waiting till it came to my turn to take the box'. Having prepared for the 'real work', now he hoped to begin. 'I have the priests and people quite with me, and I believe I could, if necessary, talk any amount of opposition into a cocked hat!'

He noted the recent arrival in Sydney of his younger brother John, who served as his chaplain at the Polding obsequies. 'I am taking him under my especial care,' Vaughan wrote. 'He is too delicate a fibre to gain anything but harm from the society of priests – that is of the general run of them, for they are about the roughest and most unrefined portion of humanity, according to my experience.' He added that he was teaching his brother 'that to love God it is not necessary to turn oneself into a girl, and that the finest kind of male saint is one who is a man'. He concluded by suggesting a trip 'home' was unlikely in the near future; 'I must get a man I can trust to hold my place during my absence – a difficult thing to do where all are Irish…'[36]

In mid-April, Vaughan entertained seven Irish bishops at St John's – James O'Quinn, Matthew Quinn, Murray, Lanigan, Murphy, Reynolds, and Martin Crane of Sandhurst, Victoria. They had come to Sydney for the 'Month's Mind' ceremonies in honour of Polding.[37] Forrest, back on his feet, was one of about eighty priests who attended the Pontifical Requiem Mass, celebrated by O'Quinn, at St Mary's. At Vaughan's invitation, the Superior of the Jesuit Order in Melbourne, Very Rev. Thomas Cahill, delivered the panegyric. He was an interesting choice; one wonders what Polding, whose grand ambitions for his Benedictine Order in the colony were finally put to rest when he died, would have thought. Probably Vaughan was already in negotiation with Cahill on the establishment of schools to replace Lyndhurst; the first, St Kilda House in the city (now St Aloysius College), opened in 1879, and the second, St Ignatius' College, Riverview, on the North Shore, the following year.

On Sunday 22 April, three days after the Month's Mind, Forrest welcomed Vaughan and four of the visiting bishops, Murphy, Lanigan, Crane and Reynolds, to Balmain for the opening of the Good Shepherd – the name of the Order was changed soon afterwards to Good Samaritan – convent. A large crowd saw Vaughan perform the traditional blessing of the building, and heard him praise the Jesuits for donating the land and note with pleasure how quickly construction had proceeded. The collection, after an address by Bishop Crane, raised about £300 for the building fund; Vaughan put in £25, the bishops £5 each, and Forrest £20.[38]

St John's College remained Vaughan's residence; in fact he wanted to continue as Rector, but handed the job over to Vice-Rector Gillett after receiving legal advice that one person could not be both Rector and Visitor.[39] Other new arrangements included appointment of the Benedictine Felix Sheridan as Vicar-General and the creation of a nine-member 'Archbishop's Council', which included Forrest and the other three 'presidents of the theological schools'.[40] Vaughan wrote to Forrest on 15 May 1877,

> I know how busy you have been, still I trust you will soon be able to let me have your valuable 'Report' and 'Solutions' as I should be glad to call the Presidents together as quickly as possible.
> With every best wish, I am, dear V Rev. Dr Forrest
> Yours very faithfully in Christ
> Roger Bede
> Abp of Sydney[41]

If Forrest was busy around this time, Vaughan was probably more so. He had just completed a five-day 'apostolic visitation' to the Sydney Benedictines, a necessary step in implementing an apparently long-held intention to disband the Benedictine community and close Lyndhurst College. In letters written in 1874 and 1875, he expressed the opinion that starting afresh offered the only way ahead for the Order in Sydney, and commented that 'what is here is rotten dead'.[42]

A hint of what was soon to occur appeared in the *Evening News* on 5 May, two days before Vaughan's visit began. Some important changes were about to take place in the management of Lyndhurst, the paper said; it was reported that 'the president, Father Dwyer, has resigned, and the whole of the professors have received notice to leave, preparatory to new arrangements'. 'The reports are untrue,' Dwyer responded without elaboration in a letter to the editor written on the first day of the visitation.[43]

Freeman's reported that the school broke up for vacation on 21 June, after mid-year exams that had returned 'very satisfactory' results.[44] Classes never resumed. Placid Quirk was posted to the Cook's River mission and his brother Norbert to Campbelltown.[45] John Dwyer spent most of his seven remaining years at Rosebank, the Good Samaritan girls' school at Five Dock.[46] What became of the Lyndhurst students is not recorded; there was no alternative Catholic secondary school for them to attend in Sydney.

A decree from Propaganda in November 1874 had directed Vaughan to conduct the visitation and submit an 'accurate account' of the 'condition' of the Benedictines after Polding's death. Whether anything Vaughan learned from the 'manifestations of conscience' made to him influenced his conclusions is doubtful. He did not wait until he had completed his report, let alone received a response from Rome, before taking action.

The report, sent to Cardinal Franchi, head of Propaganda, at the end of October 1877, is a startling demonstration of Vaughan's willingness to set aside truth and natural justice in pursuing his goals. It contains no praise of individuals, only condemnation, most of it based on hearsay. There is not a word about Lyndhurst's successes, only stories of scandals – many exaggerated, if not entirely imaginary. Probably those most grievously wronged were the Quirk brothers who, whatever faults they may have had, apparently were gifted teachers.

An article published in 1983 by Terence Kavenagh of the Benedictine monastery at Arcadia, Sydney, contains the full translated text of the report – the original was in Italian – and a detailed commentary.[47] The first section, dealing with 'the past', comprises a long letter written at Vaughan's request by W.A. Duncan, whom he described as 'a great friend of the late Archbishop'. Duncan, in fact, was a long-time critic of the Benedictines and no friend of Polding. His introduction reveals with remarkable candour what Vaughan had asked him to provide: 'I gladly comply with the request of Your Grace to put down some notes on the irregularities which occurred at Lyndhurst...with the intention of assisting Your Grace in putting a remedy to the evils...'

Duncan, naturally, made much of the departure of Lyndhurst's prefect of studies, Rev. Anselm Curtis, with the housekeeper Mrs Granger in 1864 (chapter 6), an event that became public knowledge. Kavenagh makes the pertinent point that other scandalous episodes Duncan recounted, if true, would surely also have found their way into the press. For example, one Benedictine priest, in a drunken state, allegedly 'crashed his carriage into an Omnibus, broke the carriage and almost killed the horse. He was put in jail, but he managed to escape…' On another occasion this priest was seen in Pitt Street 'leading and being led by a public woman of the city. He was first seen by six persons, but gradually a crowd of about 200 persons surrounded them.'

Concluding his letter, Duncan said he could 'add other facts of similar character' but believed 'Your Grace will deem this sufficient for your purpose', a comment that makes even clearer the nature of his brief. As Kavenagh comments, the blackest picture possible was to be painted. 'No attempt at balance – (Benedictine virtues or past achievements) – was to be made, nor any effort to test or substantiate even the wildest allegations.'

Vaughan's shorter section on 'the present' was similar in approach. All he had to say about Placid Quirk, for example, was that many times he had been 'put to bed by his own pupils – being too drunk to walk'. This was the young man, 'deservedly a popular master' according to John Lane Mullins, who had set many of his students on the path to success at university. Mullins remembered him as 'a kind teacher who realised some of the difficulties that beset students'.[48] Kavenagh wrote of Quirk,

> He was only thirty-five when Lyndhurst was closed down, and is surely a tragic figure. Vaughan's Report, however, is no place for sympathy. The mouth of judgement opens, delivers its few, bald words of condemnation, and then snaps shut.

20
One of the ugliest blots

A month before Vaughan sent his report to Cardinal Franchi, Forrest received a letter that threw further light on the Archbishop's concept of justice. The writer was an Italian Franciscan priest, Rev. Octavius Barsanti, whose authority to perform priestly duties in the Sydney archdiocese had been revoked by the then coadjutor in May 1875. Addressed to the nine members of the Archbishop's Council, the letter sought support to have his case reconsidered.

At the time of his dismissal, Barsanti was assistant priest at St Benedict's, Broadway. Apparently he and the priest in charge, Dean Healy, had argued against Vaughan's plan to replace the lay teachers at St Benedict's school with Marist Brothers. Healy's less severe punishment was relegation to the distant parish of Bega.[1]

Polding had held the Italian in high regard. He sent him to Rome at the end of 1867 to try to discover the source of the complaints that had prevented Vicar-General Sheehy's installation as Sydney's Auxiliary Bishop (chapter 7).[2] Barsanti delivered the sermon at the laying of the foundation stone of the new St Mary's Cathedral in December 1868,[3] and the following year assisted the Archbishop at the provincial council in Melbourne. However, a letter he wrote to Polding in October 1875 objecting to the way he had been treated and advising that he planned to appeal to Rome brought no joy. Barsanti sent Forrest a copy with the notation, 'I am in poor circumstances. Can you assist me as your brother priest?'[4]

Barsanti claimed he had been 'abruptly and irrevocably dismissed' with no specific cause being given and 'no hearing and chance of self-defence'. In response to a direct appeal to the Pope, he wrote in his second letter, Franchi had requested Vaughan to reinstate him. After receiving advice of this in early February 1877, he had written to the Archbishop and Very Rev. Gillett saying he was ready to do anything 'deemed necessary for a peaceable understanding and friendly reconciliation'.

> But I had not reply from either. I called at St John's College on the morning of February 17, 1877, but I was told that His Grace and Father Gillet were out. I called on the evening of the same day, and they sent me a message by the servant that they would not see and speak to me upon any account at any time. I then engaged a gentleman, who desired me not to mention his name, and to him His Grace denied the fact of having received from Rome any communication in my regard. I engaged also the Superior of the Marists; and to him His Grace said that he had applied to the Pope for another decision.[5]

Vaughan stood firm. Barsanti eventually returned to active ministry – after the Archbishop's death in August 1883.

Some time in October or early November 1877, within weeks of receiving Barsanti's second letter, Forrest suffered the same fate as the Italian. No documents relating to the case seem to have survived, but Father Roger Wynne, a historian of the Balmain parish, pieced together the story, which he described as 'one of the ugliest blots in the annals of the church', from recollections of local people.[6] A charge of intemperance had been made by a parishioner, he wrote in an article published in 1983, 'and the unhappy priest was straightaway suspended and deprived of his parish'.

> Forty years ago, there were still to be found in Balmain a few old timers to whom the tragic events of 1877 were still very real. While some had fleeting memories of the 'silenced' priest, his old College gown draped about his shoulders, attending Mass each morning in the tiny porch of the old Church, at least one, the ninety-year old sister of the informant in the case, remembered 'as if it were only yesterday' the last public utterance of the deposed Pastor. He had been unjustly reported and unjustly condemned, he told his shocked parishioners, but he would leave it to God to judge his accusers.

The fifty-six-year-old Forrest had been very busy in the weeks before his downfall. He was Bishop Murray's guest again at Maitland in early September, preaching a 'most eloquent and instructive' sermon at a ceremony at the Dominican convent.[7] At the end of the month he welcomed Rev. Julian Tenison-Woods to St Augustine's to conduct a week-long mission. This remarkable priest's achievements included helping establish Mother Mary MacKillop's Sisters of St Joseph in 1866 (chapter 15) and publishing more than a hundred and fifty scientific papers on Australian geology, palaeontology and zoology.[8] Forrest's discussions with him probably covered science as well as religion; Forrest was a member of the Linnean Society of NSW and Tenison-Woods its president in 1880.[9]

Forrest was also busy helping organise a fundraising bazaar, to be held at the Guild Hall in the city, to help clear the £2,500 debt on the Balmain Good Samaritan convent, which was now home to ten nuns teaching more than four hundred children in three schools. *Freeman's* reported that he had worked hard to have the convent built, and was sparing no pains to make the bazaar a success.[10] Consistent with its policy of suppressing unpleasant Church news (for example, the closure of Lyndhurst was not reported), the paper did not subsequently note Forrest's humiliating dismissal. This had certainly taken place by the opening of the fortnight-long bazaar on Monday 19 November.

Vaughan did not open it as originally planned; he was visiting the Armidale diocese in his capacity as apostolic administrator following Bishop O'Mahony's resignation.[11] *Freeman's* provided detailed descriptions of the bazaar's thirteen 'very beautifully decorated' stalls and the articles offered for sale by the 'good lady stallholders' – including furniture, clothing, pictures of Vaughan and Mary Queen of Scots, and a bust of the Pope. Despite what had happened to her brother, Maryanne Gilhooley looked after a stall with her cousin Ellen Lyons, sister of William Lehane (chapter 15). Their offerings included chairs, fire screens, and English and Australian coats of arms.[12]

The *Freeman's* report did not mention Forrest, noting instead that Rev. Keating, 'the indefatigable pastor of the Balmain parish', had laboured hard to make the bazaar a success. Possibly someone suggested the paper had gone too far in turning Forrest into a non-person, because it noted later that many names had been 'accidentally omitted when mentioning those present at the bazaar, and among these was Dr Forrest's name'. It also reported that the event had been 'hardly so successful as was anticipated'; perhaps Forrest's removal had dampened spirits generally, not just at the Gilhooley/Lyons stall. Net proceeds totalled about £530, well short of the target.[13]

Vaughan appears to have been in a buoyant frame of mind as 1877 drew to a close. Causes for celebration included his success in preventing O'Mahony's return to Armidale and the arrival from Rome of his pallium, the traditional vestment symbolising the authority invested in an archbishop by the Pope. A letter to Bernard Smith in Rome reflected his mood. He boasted that he was much more popular with the colony's Irish than 'those Episcopi' who had protested against his appointment: 'The fact is I have knocked them into a cocked hat!'[14] His visit to Armidale in November seems to have provided support for this assertion; the town's cathedral was 'crowded to excess' with people eager to hear him preach. 'In fact', reported *Freeman's*, 'so great was the desire to hear his Grace that no service was held in the Church of England, and the other churches had but a very sparse attendance'.[15]

Three of the four bishops who protested to Rome when Vaughan was appointed – O'Quinn, Quinn and Lanigan (O'Mahony was the fourth) – came to Sydney for the Archbishop's investiture with the pallium on 12 January 1878. They joined four more bishops – Reynolds of Adelaide, Martin Griver of Perth, Ferdinand Vitte of New Caledonia, and Crane of Sandhurst – for the ceremony in the packed pro-Cathedral. Forrest was among the many priests present.[16] Notable absentees included Bishop Murray of Maitland, who was touring Tasmania with Bishop Murphy, reportedly recovering after renewed ill health.[17]

O'Quinn, as the senior prelate present, celebrated the special Mass. The body language would have been interesting to observe; of the bishops, probably O'Quinn had developed the deepest aversion to Vaughan. At his request, Rev. Dillon inquired in the Armidale diocese at the end of 1876 into the allegations against O'Mahony and reported that they were groundless. In a subsequent letter, which was published in the press, to Polding and the other suffragans, O'Quinn wrote of 'the foul play used by Dr O'Mahony's enemies in obtaining evidence against him'.[18]

Around this time, extraordinary allegations against O'Quinn by some Italian priests he had recruited after the Vatican Council came to light. The leader of the group, Rev. Eugenio Ricci, had been excommunicated in 1872 after physically attacking Vicar-General Cani (also an Italian), and subsequently threatened to shoot O'Quinn.[19] A letter to Cardinal Franchi signed by all the priests of the diocese in July 1877 forcefully denied the accusations. Among them were claims that 'The Bishop and the Irish priests are so addicted to wine that they are often afflicted with delirium tremens'; and 'On account of the women whom the Bishop has brought to Australia, one of whom left her husband, his reputation has been besmirched in public'.[20]

If O'Quinn is to be believed, Vaughan seized on to these allegations and spread them. A draft, written before Polding's death in March 1877, exists of a letter from O'Quinn to Rome in which he charges Vaughan with having 'falsely and maliciously accused me of habitual intemperance and fornication'. He asks for an investigation of Vaughan's charges against him and his against the Archbishop 'on the condition that whoever of us is found guilty shall be punished publicly'. He accuses Vaughan of, among other things, displaying 'vanity, pomp and ostentation to a scandalous degree' and 'violating the rules of ecclesiastical decorum' by 'habitually and publicly smoking'.[21] Vaughan offered his opinion of O'Quinn in a letter to Bernard Smith in Rome in May 1877; he was 'un imbroglione di prima classe', which translates from the Italian as a first class cheat or swindler.[22]

O'Quinn and the other bishops who had attended the pallium ceremony joined Vaughan again at the inauguration of the refurbished St John's College library three days later. Opening proceedings, the Rector, Very Rev. Gillett, said Vaughan had transferred the archiepiscopal library to the college, creating a very large collection. Previously the library had consisted of 'a fine large empty room – or almost empty'. Perhaps that qualification was an acknowledgement of the more than five thousand volumes donated by, among others, Plunkett and McEncroe in the early 1860s (chapter 6). Forrest was not present, or mentioned in the reported remarks of any of the speakers – Gillett, Vaughan, Sir Patrick Jennings, Judge Faucett and W.B. Dalley.[23]

Bishops Quinn and Lanigan returned to Sydney, and were joined by James Murray, in late March for 'Month's Mind' ceremonies in memory of Pope Pius IX, who had died on 7 February, and a Dirge and High Mass marking the anniversary of Polding's death.[24] The normally mild-mannered Murray took the opportunity to heatedly confront Vaughan over his misleading advice to Rome on the attitude of the bishops to O'Mahony's return to Armidale (chapter 18). Murray told the Archbishop he had lost the confidence of the suffragans.[25]

Soon afterwards, Vaughan received a letter from Franchi asking what he thought of the idea of sending an Apostolic Delegate from Rome to report on colonial Church affairs. Franchi also asked him to make some inquiries about O'Quinn's administration of the Brisbane diocese.[26] The way Vaughan dealt with the second request led Matthew Quinn to write after O'Quinn died three years later that the Archbishop had 'persecuted him to the day of his death. No lie was too gross or too base for him to catch at to serve his purpose.'[27] The first question produced a long and agitated response arguing – as it turned out, successfully – against the sending of a Delegate. With a changing of the guard after the election of the new Pope, Leo XIII, this was addressed to Franchi's replacement as head of Propaganda, Cardinal Simeoni.[28]

Vaughan's letter, in Italian, again gives the impression that he believed he could get away with anything in making a case; and it seems that he could. Parts are farcical; for example, Vaughan warned that if a Delegate wished to inspect the country dioceses he would have to travel through snake infested swamps.[29] Many of his statements are clearly untrue. And his comments on O'Quinn, Quinn, Murray and Lanigan contrast starkly with his description of them three years earlier as 'very zealous, self-sacrificing men' (chapter 18) and the praise he had showered on them at public gatherings.

After Polding's death, wrote Vaughan, 'this family Quinn, always with their cousin [Murray], aimed at taking control of the province of Sydney as their own property'.[30]

> ...the rural bishops – of Bathurst, Goulburn, and Maitland – being poor villages – these three looked with very greedy eyes at the beautiful city of Sydney, the only real city worthy of the name in this province. If a Quinn or Murray were to become Archbishop of Sydney, then the whole family would be in clover, but a foreigner, that is to say a non-Irishman, non-gang-member, someone hating whisky and lavish meals and the rowdiness that they generate, someone who preaches against drunkenness and condemns immorality, even amongst those wearing the mitre, someone of that ilk being made Archbishop of Sydney would never please this Irish family.

If 'that someone' were English, Vaughan went on, he would not be to their liking at all. 'They would be virtually banished from the pleasures of the big city: obliged, if they came to visit the Archbishop, to lead a quiet and sober existence, feeling like young lads under the school-teacher's gaze.' That was why the bishops had protested against his appointment as coadjutor. However, 'more than 40,000 of the Irish population' had given him an 'astoundingly enthusiastic welcome' to Sydney, wanting 'to make a solemn protest in this way against those Quinns whom they knew to have telegraphed against my appointment'. Vaughan doubled the contemporary estimate of the size of the crowd that greeted him in December 1873 (chapter 17), and his suggestion that the people were there in protest at the bishops' actions is absurd.

The Archbishop next turned his attention to St John's College and, incidentally, gave his reason for Forrest's dismissal from Balmain. 'The Rector, when I came to Sydney, was a certain priest named Doctor Forrest – a first class drunkard,' Vaughan wrote. He had now suspended Forrest 'for having gone into the pulpit drunk and having sprinkled the Holy Sacrament on the ground'. Perhaps this is true; more likely Forrest accidentally spilled the wine, someone complained, and Vaughan exercised his authority without giving the priest a hearing. The records of the two men suggest Forrest's denial is more plausible than Vaughan's accusation.

Vaughan went on, 'there was not a single student in the college when I arrived and the college was falling into ruin.' The government had decided to take it over,

> converting it into a hospital or something of the kind, because it was well known that the college was a store-house of whisky, where Doctor Forrest, together with Bishops Quinn and Murray, spent whole months amusing themselves and drinking spirits and even on Sundays doing nothing but riding in a carriage through the suburbs and visiting the seaside – my priests told me all of that, right after my arrival.

If so, how can we account for Vaughan's early praise of the suffragans, and why did he not mention any of this in his diagnosis of the cause of the failure of St John's in May 1874 (chapter 17)? If Forrest did abuse alcohol, why did his strident critic on the college Council, Rev. Callaghan McCarthy, not refer to this, and why did the Council refrain from exercising its power to sack him? But commentary is probably superfluous; many of Vaughan's claims are clearly ridiculous. He went on,

> What did I do? To save the college for religion and to save Catholicism from public shame, and at the same time to destroy this unedifying centre, I arranged for Doctor Forrest to leave: I was made Rector. I was then made Archbishop of Sydney and my friend, Father Gillett, a most holy man, replaced me as Rector: and he is still there, leading a rather monastic life, taking the Holy Sacrament after lunch and dinner, instead of whisky and other hard liquor, and at those meals, instead of rubbish and vulgar things that the Quinn family liked, there is reading of the Imitation of Christ and an excerpt from the Benedictine Rule.

'Having chased away the Quinns and their chief, Doctor Forrest – a man of very sharp mind – from the college, the scandal of Armidale broke,' Vaughan continued. He said the Quinns had done everything they could to sway him in favour of O'Mahony, but having seen the evidence against the bishop 'it was impossible in all conscience to defend him'. Vaughan described James O'Quinn as a 'past-master of cunning, intrigue and trickery that you would need a special schooling to understand'. With his prejudices so clearly on display, and his past form, it is hard to see how the Vatican could have imagined that Vaughan would conduct a fair inquiry into O'Quinn's management of the Brisbane diocese.

O'Quinn was a complex character, combining an autocratic leadership style inside the Church with a liberal, inclusive, approach in his dealings with the broader community. One consequence was that attitudes to him tended to polarise; he had staunch supporters and fierce critics. Vaughan located some of the latter to furnish him with complaints against the bishop.

Chief among these was the Queensland Parliamentary Librarian, Denis O'Donovan, who sent Vaughan a stream of letters over two years beginning in July 1878. Shortly before, Vaughan had erred in seeking an opinion from the Victorian politician Sir John O'Shanassy. He reported positively on the situation in Brisbane and told O'Quinn, an old friend, about the Archbishop's inquiry.[31] O'Donovan comforted Vaughan after this setback; O'Shanassy 'belongs emphatically to that large class in Australia which a Victorian politician once styled with much felicity "the wealthy lower orders"', he wrote.[32]

In a memorandum on Vaughan's investigation, O'Quinn noted that O'Shanassy was not the only one of his friends to whom the Archbishop had slandered him. He accused Vaughan of selectively seeking comment from people 'either hostile or supposed to be hostile' to him and encouraging the spread of libellous rumours. Vaughan was not a 'dolt' in matters of this kind, he added, 'as is proved by the successful way in which he handled Doctor O'Mahony's case'.[33]

It seems he had less success in tackling O'Quinn; Rome took no action against the bishop. After sending documents on the case to Rome in early 1880, Vaughan received a warning from Simeone. The Cardinal advised,

> it is good for Your Lordship to heed the laws of the strictest prudence in this matter in order that no pretext be given to anyone to believe that the opponents of Monsignor Quinn are being protected by Your Lordship or it will happen that the faithful have to suffer amazement at the disagreement between the two Bishops.[34]

21
Next door

On vacating the St Augustine's, Balmain, presbytery to make way for the new pastor, a returning Rev. Dillon, Forrest moved just a short distance – to a larger two-storey cottage on the other side of the church. It seems he received a stream of visitors there, but took little further part in public life. Receipts in the St John's College archives reveal a few of his retirement interests. He sent subscriptions to the Reform Club, Macquarie Street, in November 1878 and the Linnean Society in March 1879. He subscribed to the just-launched *Sydney University Magazine* in 1878; the best-known contributor to this substantial literary magazine was the poet Henry Kendall.[1]

Friends among Sydney's priests did not desert him after his suspension. With Garavel, Placid Quirk and others, he was a guest of Monsignor Lynch, then pastor at St Bede's, Pyrmont, on a steamboat excursion for the Pyrmont school children in mid-November 1877.[2] Interestingly, Lynch had sided with Bishop O'Mahony's accusers and was in favour with Vaughan. Despite this, he apparently remained on good terms with Bishops Murray and Quinn as well as with Forrest. Murray presided at Lynch's funeral in February 1884 and Quinn, then in Rome, wrote in reply to a letter from his cousin that he was glad the old priest had 'had so happy a death'.[3]

Later in November, Forrest, Lynch, Garavel and Rev. Slattery of St Benedict's, Broadway, attended a fundraising lecture at the Mount Carmel church, Waterloo. A week before Christmas, Forrest and Lynch were Slattery's guests at the break-up ceremony at St Benedict's school, run by the Marist Brothers. Forrest reportedly made 'a short but very amusing speech'.[4] Slattery was another priest who experienced

Steamers, large and small, plying Sydney Harbour in the 1880s.

Vaughan's wrath; he was sent to Cooma in early 1878 after, according to the historian Rev. Wynne, what was described as 'a stand-up fight with the Archbishop'.[5]

Subsequent mentions of Forrest in the press are sparse; most noted his presence at funerals and memorial gatherings. In August 1878 he joined the long procession escorting Rev. John Dunmore Lang from the Scots Church to his grave at the Devonshire Street cemetery. W.B. Dalley was one of the four pallbearers, a striking illustration of the regard and affection in which Lang was held, despite his often strident attacks on 'popery' and 'Romish superstition', by some broad-minded Catholics (two of the other pallbearers were the political rivals Parkes and Robertson).[6] Four years later Dalley and Forrest spoke at a meeting in support of the erection of a monument to Lang. Forrest said he was privileged to have enjoyed the Scotsman's friendship for more than twenty years, 'and over that friendship there never passed a shadow – not even theological. (Cheers.)' He had admired Lang for his indomitable energy, his pluck, his perseverance, his hatred of 'injustice under the name of the law', and 'the groundwork which, with Presbyterian solidity, he laid for freedom in this new colony'.[7]

In late October 1878, news arrived from Dublin of the death at the age of seventy-five of Cardinal Cullen – the man to whom Australia was mainly indebted, *Freeman's* observed, 'for the admirable selection' of its bishops. For his protégés Murray and the Quinns, Cullen's death was a political as well as a personal loss, removing their chief advocate with the Vatican authorities. Forrest's feelings can be inferred from the fact that, two days after attending a solemn Dirge and Requiem Mass for Cullen, presided over by Vaughan, at St Mary's, he joined his friend Bishop Murray at a grander ceremony in Maitland that included a lengthy panegyric.[8]

Another much-regretted departure was that of Edward Butler, who died of a heart attack while on his feet in court in June 1879. He was only about fifty-five. Vaughan, assisted by Bishops Quinn and Lanigan, presided at the large funeral; the procession from St Mary's to Petersham cemetery included nearly two hundred carriages and cabs.[9] Forrest, one of many priests present, made his regard for Butler clear in a heartfelt letter published in *Freeman's* in May 1882.[10] This was a response to criticism of Butler for his alliance with Parkes in the early 1870s (chapter 15) by a thirty-four-year-old parliamentarian, Louis Heydon, a son of the paper's former editor J.K. Heydon. 'Young as the writer may be', Forrest wrote,

> he is certainly old enough to know that the lamented gentleman's association with Sir Henry Parkes was not of Mr Butler's seeking, but was mainly brought about by those who vainly conceived that the union would have put an end to 'the war of creeds,' which the writer [Heydon]…affects to deplore… For…this object the distinguished lawyer sacrificed his personal wishes, his professional interests, his little leisure, and perhaps in the end his precious life. He exposed himself to the misconceptions of dear friends, to the misrepresentation of bitter enemies, not of himself personally – for he had none – but of his faith, and the suspicion of those who were neither, that he might do some good…

Referring to Parkes's breaking of his commitment to appoint Butler Chief Justice (chapter 16), Forrest wrote that 'it was notorious to the whole world' that Butler's religion was 'his single disqualification'.

He was a Catholic, and was dishonoured publicly for being so. His status as a barrister was, apart from his professional leadership of the Bar, the very highest. But his Church and his people were insulted in his person. To him the office to which he was entitled and from the occupation of which he was excluded was of no earthly consequence. It could only have been accepted at an immense material sacrifice; and could have added nothing to the universal reverence entertained for the greatness of his attainments, the serenity of his nature, the benevolence of his heart, and the probity of his character.

There was one Catholic, Forrest went on, 'as widely known as any man in these Australian colonies who, at the time of his friend's alliance with Sir Henry Parkes, warned the former of his peril and almost foretold the issue'. But 'on the day when all that was mortal of Edward Butler was lowered into his grave', that man, W.B. Dalley, had asked the Legislative Council 'to adjourn its sittings in honour of the stainless memory of his lost friend'. Forrest quoted Dalley's elegant adjournment speech, in which he described Butler as

> a colonist whose career in this country is eminently deserving of the attention of those who desire to fashion the generous youth of our times upon noble and affecting and unobtrusive examples. By the mere force of pure character, a clear and powerful intelligence, and an indomitable spirit he reached a high, if not the highest, place in a profession in which a signal success can only be achieved by patience, by labour, by courage, and by intellectual power... In the midst of that good fortune he was unchanged – the same simple, earnest, homely, compassionate man...

Butler's alliance with Parkes, castigated by Dalley at the time, followed another that had seemed just as unlikely, that of the conservative Martin and liberal Robertson. At the end of 1878, another strange coalition formed, between the perennial political adversaries Parkes and Robertson. After two years as Premier from February 1875, Robertson had given way to Parkes in March 1877, returned to power the following August, and four months later handed the reins to an unstable grouping led by fifty-year-old James Farnell. *Freeman's* described the new coalition, with Parkes as Premier, as a 'most remarkable political event', but thought it necessary, 'much as we dislike it', to restore capable government to the colony.[11]

It quickly became clear that reform of the education system would be on the agenda again soon. By 1879, government funding of church schools had ended, or an end had been signalled, in all other colonies except Western Australia.[12] Parkes hinted at what was in store for New South Wales in a speech in June 1879, saying 'whenever the education question is opened it will not be opened in favour of denominational schools'.[13]

In the meantime, a piece of good news captured the attention of Sydney's Catholic opinion leaders – Pope Leo's decision to honour the seventy-eight-year-old John Henry Newman by appointing him a Cardinal. The frail priest, whose writings had made him a revered figure in the Church and beyond, travelled to Rome in May 1879 for the ceremony creating him 'Cardinal-Deacon of the Title of St George'. Dalley took the initiative in calling meetings and forming an eighty-member lay committee to collect funds for a gift and congratulatory address. His proposal that Newman be sent a salver and goblet of pure Australian gold, with the salver bearing a suitable Latin inscription, was adopted.

Donations, mostly small, flowed in from the country as well as the city, and double the required sum was quickly collected. While clergy were not involved in the arrangements, some contributed – including, not surprisingly, Forrest. His £3 was one of the biggest donations; Bishop Quinn put in £2. The goblet and salver, whose inscription noted Newman's 'singular genius', 'wondrous subtlety of intellect' and 'rare felicity of imagination', was sent to the Catholic Duke of Norfolk, who presented it to Newman at a ceremony in London in May 1880.[14]

Forrest again demonstrated his affection for Father Garavel in July 1879 by making the biggest contribution, £10, to the testimonial purse presented to the Frenchman to mark his move from Waverley to St Bede's, Pyrmont (Lynch, the former pastor, was now at Campbelltown).[15] In the same month he attended the funeral of another of the colony's most notable early citizens, seventy-nine-year-old Sir Edward Deas Thomson.[16] The Scotsman, who arrived in Sydney in 1828, was Colonial Secretary for nearly twenty years from 1837 and Chancellor of the university from 1865 to 1878.

On the last Sunday in July, a joint pastoral letter by the New South Wales bishops – Vaughan, Quinn, Murray and Lanigan – on education was read in churches throughout the colony. It was intended to be provocative, and the outcry that followed ensured that few, inside or outside the Church, could remain ignorant of the bishops' message. They condemned public schools as 'seed-plots of future immorality, infidelity and lawlessness'. Catholic parents were told to send their children 'exclusively to Catholic schools'. Those 'so unhappy' as to be sending sons or daughters to public schools were told to withdraw them as soon as possible and

> examine their children's religious instincts and moral condition: and if, as is to be expected, they find faith and morals weakened, and the germs of lawlessness apparent, then let them, with great anxiety, do all they can to redeem the time and to remedy the evil.[17]

Vaughan drafted the document after a meeting with the suffragans in Sydney in May. Apparently, Quinn instigated the joint approach. He told Tobias Kirby, Rector of the Irish College, Rome, that Vaughan had been reluctant to join forces with the suffragans because he believed none of them had confidence in him. Vaughan had been persuaded that 'a portion of our duty is united action and no matter what our personal relations may be, we are bound to meet in order to carry out this duty'.[18]

Unfazed by the generally hostile press and political response to the joint statement, Vaughan issued five follow-up pastoral letters over the succeeding three months. In November, Premier Parkes introduced the expected new education legislation. Provisions of the Public Instruction Bill included abolishing the Council of Education – giving control of the school system to a minister and his department – and stopping funding of denominational schools on a date to be determined. The bill secured overwhelming support in parliament – the final vote in the Legislative Assembly in February 1880 was forty-two in favour and just six against – and 31 December 1882 was set as the date when support for denominational schools would end.[19]

Whether the bishops' intervention had any substantial effect on the timing or content of the legislation is doubtful. It certainly did have an impact on the faithful; numbers of Catholic pupils at seventeen public schools around Sydney dropped by twenty percent within a week of the joint pastoral's appearance. *Freeman's* estimated that about twelve thousand people attended a 'monster meeting' held in the grounds of the pro-Cathedral in November 1879 to protest against the legislation. It claimed the roll-up gave a 'decisive answer' to those arguing that the laity did not support the clergy on the question.[20]

In a speech at St Mary's in December, Vaughan said 'an indignant sense of galling injustice' had brought the bishops together to plan their joint response to the proposed destruction of 'the only class of schools' Catholics could use.

> What are we fighting for? For fair play, for equality with others. We claim to bring up Catholic children in Catholic schools, and to receive our share of State assistance for secular instruction, as tested by government inspectors. We are told this shall not be, that we must send our Catholic children to the State schools. We reply we cannot, and shall not.[21]

The work of Rev. Tenison-Woods and Mother MacKillop in South Australia in the 1860s showed that an alternative was possible – setting up networks of Catholic primary schools run by religious orders. Within five years of the establishment of the Sisters of St Joseph in 1866, the number of children receiving a Catholic education in that colony had risen from about one thousand three hundred to three thousand three hundred. Other jurisdictions followed the South Australian lead; for example, Matthew Quinn established thirty-three independent Catholic schools in the Bathurst diocese between 1866 and 1880.[22] The Sydney archdiocese lagged behind, but Vaughan was making a concerted effort to catch up. At a school foundation-stone laying ceremony in September 1880 he said teaching orders ran only three primary schools, teaching eight hundred and seventy-seven children, in the archdiocese in 1867; the figures were now twenty-four schools and four thousand and forty-three pupils.[23]

The bishops were confident the loss of funding for Catholic schools would he temporary – that the injustice involved in Catholics paying taxes that supported the public school system while receiving nothing for their own schools would be recognised and remedied fairly soon. 'We shall have to suffer for a time,' wrote Lanigan in 1884, 'but the kind feelings of others will not leave us always in our present oppressed condition.'[24] It proved a long wait; the Menzies government made the first move to restore state aid after the 1963 federal election.

Vaughan's other major project as the 1880s began was hastening progress on the new St Mary's Cathedral so the first section could be opened, with a temporary roof, in 1882. He told a meeting at the pro-Cathedral in July 1880 that £32,000 was needed, and called on Catholics to contribute generously over the next two-and-a-half years while government support for denominational schools continued. Then Catholic schools would have top priority.[25]

The first big meeting in the roofed and rapidly progressing cathedral took place in October 1881 when five thousand people gathered to take their first look at the interior and hear the annual report on the building's progress. The 'scene within the noble edifice', lit up by 'forty or fifty gas standards, and a flaming illumination at the rear of the platform', was 'at the same time intensely picturesque and imposing in the extreme', *Freeman's* said.[26] Vaughan had good news to report; as a result of his 'begging by pen and tongue', £16,409 1s 2d had been raised over the past thirteen months; this compared with annual collections of around £4,000 in earlier years.[27] Fundraising continued at a brisk pace, and when the Cathedral was opened the following September a debt of less than £3,000 remained.[28]

Vaughan travelled to Bathurst in June 1881 for the grand opening of St Charles' Ecclesiastical Seminary, a training college for priests established by Matthew Quinn. The luncheon was reminiscent of earlier gatherings attended by the Archbishop and suffragans (Lanigan was there, but not Murray, who was visiting Rome and Ireland again). Quinn said he could hardly find words to thank the Archbishop for coming, and Vaughan, after noting that it was a considerable time since he had been in Bathurst, renewed his praise of Quinn. He said the town's great Catholic works demonstrated Quinn's energy and perseverance and showed the people 'loved and venerated' their zealous bishop.[29]

The apparent reconciliation was short-lived. Bishop James O'Quinn died at the age of sixty-two on 18 August, sadly before his brother, who had been summoned and was on his way by sea from Sydney, reached Brisbane.[30] Quinn, who led the funeral service at St Stephen's Cathedral, invited Vaughan to come to Brisbane to officiate at the 'Month's Mind' Requiem Mass in September. 'I will personally regard it as the greatest favour you could confer upon me, and it will go far to lessen the grief I feel at the loss of my brother,' he wrote.[31] Vaughan declined; knowing what we do now about his efforts to undermine O'Quinn it is hard to see how he could have accepted.

Quinn appears to have been shocked by what he discovered when he went through his brother's papers. 'The Bishop of Brisbane has left most valuable documents after him,' he told Tobias Kirby in a letter written in October. 'They prove that almost from the day he put foot on Australian soil until the day of his death, the two English Archbishops sought his recall. At his death he was engaged in a hand to hand fight with Dr Vaughan.'[32] In another letter he said Vaughan had persecuted O'Quinn up to the day of his death (chapter 20).

The Month's Mind went ahead in a packed cathedral with Quinn as celebrant.[33] Two other bishops were there – Murphy of Hobart and O'Mahony's replacement in Armidale, Dr Elzear Torreggiani, who had taken up his post at the end of 1879. The fifty-one-year-old Italian, who had worked for many years in England and Wales and was nominated by Vaughan, proved a popular and successful bishop. Others who made the trip to Brisbane included Forrest, now nearly sixty-one years old, and Garavel. When the French priest died in 1885, *Freeman's* reported that one of his many endearing qualities had been the pleasure he derived from performing kindly acts, 'however arduous and fatiguing', for his brother priests.[34] Perhaps one such act was helping the apparently increasingly frail Forrest cope with this journey to honour an old friend.

The Jesuit Father William Kelly delivered the sermon, praising O'Quinn for spreading the work of the Church through his vast territory and providing for the future by amassing much property. 'The Church in Queensland might be said to be the best endowed of any on this ocean continent of ours,' he said. Obituaries quoted statistics to demonstrate O'Quinn's achievements. When he arrived in 1861, Queensland had a Catholic population of seven thousand six hundred and seventy-six served by two priests looking after four churches and three schools. In 1880, the figures were forty-seven thousand two hundred and fifty-six Catholics, thirty-one priests, forty-nine churches and thirty-three schools, plus twenty convents, two orphanages and two industrial schools. *Freeman's* claimed that O'Quinn had accomplished 'incomparably a larger work than has been undertaken or attempted by any man in these Australian colonies'.[35]

The southern visitors saw a little of this in the days after the Month's Mind. Their first excursion was to St Vincent's Orphanage at Nudgee, twelve kilometres by rough road from the city. After performances by the children and a distribution of prizes, Bishops Quinn, Murphy and Torreggiani, Forrest, Garavel and the other visiting priests, and lay guests including the former Young Irelander Dr Kevin O'Doherty and Chief Justice Charles Lilley sat down to a 'sumptuously provided' lunch. The venue was a house in the orphanage grounds that O'Quinn had used as a country retreat and named 'Rathbawn' after his birthplace in County Kildare. Speakers, including the Protestant Lilley who described O'Quinn as a dear friend, lavished praise on the late bishop. Then all set off for Brisbane in a downpour, which, the *Brisbane Courier* reported, made the journey 'very unpleasant'.[36]

Forrest had been scheduled to preach three days later at the consecration by Bishop Quinn of a new church at Sandgate, but perhaps became ill after the trip from Nudgee. The *Courier* noted that the Jesuit Father Joseph Dalton preached in his absence. Afterwards, Dr O'Doherty presented the three visiting bishops with an address from the 'Catholics of Brisbane' expressing the hope that Queensland would become a separate ecclesiastical province with Quinn as archbishop. Murphy and Torreggiani told O'Doherty they supported the idea, but Quinn demurred.[37] Responding to a similar address by twenty-four priests a few days earlier he had said the diocese needed a younger and more active man at the helm (he was sixty).[38] Quinn remained Bishop of Bathurst until his death in January 1885.

Back in Sydney, Forrest attended a concert in aid of the Balmain convent at the beginning of November with the new pastor of St Augustine's, Father John Carroll (Rev. Dillon was about to leave for Europe).[39] His next mention in the press was as one of those at the graveside when the Catholic MP for Yass Plains, Michael Fitzpatrick, who had died suddenly at the age of sixty-four, was buried at Petersham Cemetery on 12 December. The distressing events of that afternoon propelled the Church into a new controversy.

Fitzpatrick had not backed official Catholic policy on education, telling parliament during the debate on Parkes's Public Instruction Bill in November 1879 that he had always supported public schools. He said he respected the bishops profoundly, but deplored their contention that the schools were a breeding ground for infidelity and crime. Fitzpatrick voted against the bill at its second reading, arguing that, although he would have been glad had there never been any denominational schools, it was unjust to end funding to those that existed. Having made his point, he abstained in the final vote on the legislation.[40]

This history was widely believed to be the reason for the non-appearance of a priest to officiate at Fitzpatrick's burial. Large numbers of family, friends and political associates had gathered around the grave at the appointed hour. The former Premier James Farnell and MPs Sir Patrick Jennings and William Forster were among the mourners. 'Up to the time when the coffin was placed over the grave, the absence of a priest was not apparent,' the *Sydney Morning Herald* reported, 'but then there was a pause as if those conducting the arrangements were waiting for the priest to put in an appearance.'

The delay was to no avail; and, in a manner which showed that all hope of anyone coming to read prayers for the dead was abandoned, Sir Patrick Jennings directed that the coffin should be lowered into the grave. The deceased's sons and some other relatives knelt at the head of the grave, overwhelmed with grief; one of them in broken accents commenced the Lord's Prayer, which was joined in by the others.

Then 'a clerical friend' in his 'everyday dress' and acting on his own authority stepped forward, made the sign of the cross and pronounced the benediction. This was Forrest, whose presence and kind act doubtless went some way towards relieving the pain of the event.

'It is needless to say that when the funeral was over everybody was talking of what they had witnessed, and indignantly protesting against it,' the *Herald* went on. The paper was told, on inquiring, that Rev. Coletti, now the resident priest at Petersham, had promised to attend the funeral, and was willing to do so. However, 'the authorities of the Roman Catholic Church' in the city had stopped him on the grounds that Fitzpatrick had not complied strictly with the laws of the Church. A priest at St Mary's reportedly told a relative of Fitzpatrick, 'I'm afraid the unfortunate man has lost his soul.'[41]

Next day in parliament David Buchanan, eagerly seizing another opportunity to attack the Church, brought on a debate. Premier Parkes, also clearly enjoying himself, claimed the 'ecclesiastical government' was 'an organization for crushing the human soul under the pretence of saving it in the next world', and sought 'to perpetuate its own dominions' for the ends of its 'dark ambition'. Probably the most interesting contributions came from the Anglican Forster, who thought the Church's treatment of Fitzpatrick was no business of parliament, and the Catholic John Dillon, who had supported the Public Instruction Bill and now made a stinging attack on Vaughan.

Forster said he regretted that the Church authorities had refused Fitzpatrick the last rites of burial. But there had been a ceremony, although not the expected one, and everything had been done 'decently and in order'. A priest [Forrest] was present,

> and he kindly and good-naturedly pronounced the benediction [Mr Dillon:

Against instructions.]... Neither the hon. gentleman nor the House nor the community should think that their friend went to his grave without any ceremonial or rites at all. He went with rites which would be an honour to any man. (Hear, hear.)... He went there honoured and respected by all who were there, reverentially silent, which indicated the high character of the man, and the importance of the ceremony they were all performing.

Dillon said the Church's action was a studied insult, and he presumed the instruction to Coletti not to attend the burial had come from Vaughan. If it had,

> he only acted in accordance with the course of conduct which he has pursued ever since he came to the colony. We have had nothing but bigotry and intolerance ever since Archbishop Vaughan landed in the colony. He has used his position for the purpose of promoting dissension among the people, and everyone will confess, except those interested in concealing the fact, that the religious animosities existing throughout the country now are mainly due to the action of Archbishop Vaughan.

Vaughan's mind had been nourished on medieval learning, so it was not astonishing that his ideas on the duties of life were those of the Middle Ages, Dillon went on. 'When we find him ruling his clergy – a great number of whom are half-educated boors – with the utmost severity, what else can you expect but attempts like this to insult people, and to insult their remains after death?'[42]

The Church attempted to repair the damage. On 22 December, ten days after the burial, Coletti celebrated a Requiem Mass for Fitzpatrick at St Thomas's, Petersham. Then the priest, accompanied by family and friends of the MP, performed the burial service at the grave. The change of heart followed an exchange of letters between Vicar-General Sheridan and Coletti that confirmed that Fitzpatrick's attendance to his religious duties had made him eligible for a Church burial. Coletti told Sheridan he would have been present and read the service at the grave 'but for the interference of some over-zealous, though no doubt conscientious, persons'.

Freeman's demanded a clearer explanation, saying the episode had caused Catholics to suffer deeply 'in their interests as well as in their feelings'. Acknowledging that a mistake had been made and attempting to repair it were not sufficient: 'Somebody must be responsible, and the nature of the mistake and its effects upon society do not permit of any evasion of responsibility.' The paper said Coletti should not have allowed anyone who was not his 'official superior' to sway him and noted that the Vicar-General apparently had not been consulted.[43] Although Vaughan was away from Sydney at the time, the finger seemed to point at him. Nobody accepted the challenge to admit responsibility.

The thirty-three-year-old lawyer Dillon, who had been a student of Forrest's at St John's College in the 1860s, faced fierce condemnation. A letter writer to *Freeman's* called his speech cowardly and mean, and Melbourne's Catholic newspaper, *The Advocate*, was unable to 'recognise in him a single quality that is not degrading to human nature'.[44] He resigned his position on the St John's Council immediately after making his criticism of Vaughan. Probably not by coincidence, two other former students from Forrest's days, Patrick Healy and Richard E. O'Connor, submitted their resignations about the same time.[45]

William Forster – squatter, noted writer, and a member of the Legislative Assembly from the introduction of responsible government in 1856 – died less than a year after Fitzpatrick, in October 1882. In a leader probably written by Dalley, *Freeman's* mourned the sixty-four-year-old as 'the boldest, frankest, least selfish and most honourable man who has ever taken part in our public life'. The paper described him as a true friend of Catholics – an advocate and defender during 'our hour of darkest trouble and affliction', the Fenian scare of 1868.[46] Forrest was among the large group of mourners who travelled by special steamer to Ryde for the burial. One of the few singled out by the *Herald* for special mention, he was described as a friend of Forster's 'of over 20 years'.[47]

22

Farewells

Did Saint Patrick, patron saint of Ireland, come from Scotland or from France? Forrest, who spoke on 'the Life and Virtues of the glorious Apostle of Ireland' in one of his first sermons in the colony – at St Patrick's, Church Hill, on St Patrick's Day 1861 – probably enjoyed the discussion of this topic that filled many columns of *Freeman's* in early 1882. Dalley started the ball rolling at the St Patrick's Day banquet at the Town Hall, speaking of 'the saintly Frenchman' who had devoted his life's labour to the regeneration of Ireland. No, said Sir John Robertson, 'he left the enlightened country of the Scotchman and drove the snakes out of Ireland'. Saint Patrick was 'above all things in the world, a Frenchman', retorted Judge Faucett. The controversy continued for six weeks in letters to the editor, including four from W.A. Duncan who quoted authorities ancient and modern to prove the saint was definitely a Scot.[1]

While the claims flew back and forth, an event began on Easter Monday, 10 April 1882, in the nearly ready to open St Mary's Cathedral that was inspired by a precedent from New York's St Patrick's Cathedral. The New Yorkers had held a big fundraising fair in their cathedral shortly before its opening in 1879. Vaughan admitted he had doubts about the propriety of staging bazaars in cathedrals in the lead-up to their consecration, but decided it could not be unbecoming to 'follow in the footsteps of so great a man' as the Cardinal Archbishop of New York.[2] The 'Fayre of Ye Olden Tyme' at the new St Mary's ran for four weeks and was a great success, contributing nearly £6,000 to cathedral funds. A *Freeman's* reporter described the scene at the opening:

> the splendid galaxy of youth and beauty, the quaint but bright and charmingly pretty dresses of the shopkeepers; the rows of old-fashioned

and gorgeously painted little shops, with their curious sign-boards; the attractive and profuse display of beautiful and tempting wares; the gay bunting embracing all the colours of the rainbow, suspended from pillar to pillar; the endless variety of decorations; the great crowd of men and women in the gayest and smartest attire occupying every inch of room in nave and transepts; the noble building, with its stately columns, its lofty arches, and beautifully designed windows; the rich golden sunlight streaming into the edifice from the magnificent window at the northern end of the nave behind the dais, the brightness, the glitter, the dazzling brilliancy, the rich and harmonious blending of colours – all went to form a picture that was unique in its beauty, delightfully novel in character, and grand and imposing in the extreme.[3]

The 'Fayre of Ye Olden Tyme' in the new St Mary's Cathedral, four months before the building's grand opening.

The fair closed on 8 May, allowing four months to prepare the cathedral for its grand opening.[4] Proceedings on Friday 8 September, the feast of the Nativity of the Blessed Virgin, began at 7 a.m. with the formal blessing and dedication of the building, which was then about half its final length. Former Vicar-General Sheehy blessed the walls in the traditional manner as a procession moved slowly around the building, first outside and then inside. Then he celebrated the first Mass in the cathedral. *Freeman's* commended Vaughan for his 'gracious act' of inviting Sheehy – 'a companion in arms of the first Archbishop of Sydney' who had 'taken such an active share in the commencement of the building' – to perform these tasks.

The main event of the first day – ceremonies continued on the Saturday and Sunday – began at 11 a.m. with a procession of about one hundred clergy (who did not include Forrest) around the building and then in through the western entrance. As they entered, the orchestra struck up a march composed for the occasion. *Freeman's* described the scene:

> What a glorious and thrilling spectacle! And see in the very front of the procession is borne a superb banner of gorgeous beauty; a banner fringed with heavy gold, and with ornamental work of the richest kind encircling a picture of Mary Mother, the Immaculate Queen of Heaven. How it glitters! And there among the acolytes who follow is carried a banner of the Sacred Heart, and after that are others rich in artistic gold, and beautiful in design and finish.

The younger priests, 'full of zeal and fire, with bright face and light walk', led the way, followed by 'the old missioners with feeble frames and tottering steps'. Then came the seven bishops visiting Sydney for the occasion, and last of all the Archbishop 'with jewelled mitre, golden crozier, and embroidered cope, leaning now and then on his pastoral staff, and blessing the congregation, who kneel as he approaches'.

All four New South Wales suffragans were present; James Murray had returned to the colony in March 1882. Also there were the new Bishop of Brisbane, fifty-two-year-old Robert Dunne, who had been a friend and colleague of his predecessor James O'Quinn since Irish

College days; the first Bishop of Rockhampton, O'Quinn's former Vicar-General John Cani; and Francis Redwood, Bishop of Wellington, New Zealand. A notable absentee was Archbishop Goold of Melbourne. In an extraordinary incident three weeks earlier the sixty-nine-year-old had

Priests and bishops enter St Mary's for the inaugural Pontifical High Mass – Archbishop Vaughan, with golden crozier, at the rear.

been shot at and slightly wounded by a brother of the man who tried to assassinate Prince Alfred in 1868. The deranged P.A.C. O'Farrell, who had been Goold's solicitor in the early 1860s, claimed the Archbishop owed him money.[5]

Matthew Quinn, the senior bishop, celebrated the Pontifical High Mass. A chorus of nearly three hundred voices combined with organ and orchestra to provide a musical performance of a grace, dignity and brilliancy 'unique in the history of the Church and music in Australia', said *Freeman's*. The 'vastness of the structure' and 'splendour of the surroundings' made the ceremonial all the more impressive: 'Anything more affecting and beautiful it would be almost impossible to imagine.'

The inauguration of this grand building was followed swiftly by the loss of another. Fire destroyed the Garden Palace in the Domain, built for Sydney's International Exhibition of 1879, on 22 September. Not only was a spectacular venue for concerts, balls and public meetings lost, so were valuable records stored in various offices. These included many of scientific interest – including collections of the pioneer geologist and meteorologist Rev. W.B. Clarke, who was an Anglican minister, and of the Catholic priest and scientist Julian Tenison-Woods. Losses to the Linnean Society, including the whole of its library, were valued at more than £2,500.[6] Having known both clergy-scientists, and with his interest in science, Forrest no doubt felt the blow.

In December, he attended lectures by Professor Badham and W.B. Dalley held to raise money for the wife and children of Henry Kendall, who had died in August at the age of forty-three.[7] Forrest knew the troubled young poet, one of the first to celebrate the Australian landscape, when both were contributors to *Freeman's* (chapter 8). Apparently he was also part of the literary circle fostered by the lawyer N.D. Stenhouse, well known as a benefactor to Kendall and other colonial writers. A mention of Stenhouse, who died in 1873, in the fiftieth anniversary *Freeman's* in 1900[8] brought a generous letter of thanks from one of his daughters on behalf of the family:

> The tender and loving manner in which you refer to your glorious gallery

of writers, the brightest names of Australia's history, reflects a lustre upon your journal which we hope years will never dim. Our dear father must be pleased to find himself in the company of those he so loved in life, and we rejoice to find that you admire and love those who were his dearest friends – Dalley, Duncan, Deniehy, Badham, Kendall, Ven Archpriest Therry, Dr Forrest, and a score of others.[9]

With the new year, 1883, came a new government. The holy season 'never dawned upon fairer and more cheering prospects,' wrote *Freeman's* in its Christmas leader, hailing the election defeat of the Parkes administration. No longer would Catholics have to endure a government that 'owed its inspiration and its life to a policy of carefully fostered antagonisms of sections of society'. Alexander Stuart, a campaigner for reform of the land laws, widely regarded as long overdue, was the new Premier. His ministers included two Catholics – Dalley as Attorney-General and Sir Patrick Jennings.[10]

In early January, Archbishop Vaughan announced that he would be leaving in April to make his first reporting visit to Rome. Speeches at a public meeting the following month, which raised £550 towards a testimonial presentation, were full of praise for the Archbishop, although a common theme was that it was not necessary to agree with all his acts to appreciate the work he had done.[11]

Matthew Quinn left Sydney at the beginning of March on his second such visit (the first was in 1874), and was farewelled on the ship by, among others, Bishops Murray and Lanigan, and Forrest.[12] Demonstrating that relations with the Irish suffragans had not healed, Dr Torreggiani of Armidale was the only bishop in Sydney for Vaughan's departure six weeks later. The Archbishop authorised Torreggiani, the junior New South Wales suffragan and the one whose diocese was furthest from Sydney, to exercise episcopal functions in the archdiocese during his absence.

With hindsight – knowing that Vaughan was not to return – some of his words at the farewell gathering in a packed St Mary's on 17 April seem prophetic. Responding to the praise for him in the address from the clergy he said he was 'deeply impressed' by 'the mediocrity of my performance in every line of duty...' And something 'pierces far sharper and deeper into the chamber of my inmost spirit... what will my Judge say when I have to give an account of my stewardship before His court?' However, he made it clear that he planned to come back. 'I...feel as if I were leaving home in leaving you,' he said at the end of proceedings. 'I shall...come back to you who have made my life so happy in this colony, and who have given me an opportunity to do that which I love most – to do good to the people, to preach the high things of God...'[13]

With Very Rev. Gillett, he left on the steamship *City of New York* two days later, accompanied to the Heads by steamers full of well-wishers and all the way 'waving his hat in response to the cheers'. First destination was San Francisco; then after a slow crossing of the United States he set out for England in early August. He died of heart disease, apparently in his sleep, at the home of relatives on 18 August, shortly after arriving.[14]

As well as the modest Archbishop, a more typical Vaughan had been

Archbishop Vaughan and Dr Gillett set off for America, England and Rome, April 1883.

on display during the Sydney farewell in April. He praised his priests – whom he 'would not exchange…for any other body of Catholic clergy in the English-speaking world' – for their 'brave and consistent support'.

> Had it not been for this identity of spirit, this bond of union, this mutual and unclouded confidence, we should not have assembled in this great fane [the cathedral] to-night; we should still be worshipping mournfully in a miserable barn. Had it not been for your co-operation, your self-sacrifice, your appreciation of the Church's ordinary magisterium regarding education, the education question would not have been, as it is now, practically, solved.

One of the priests thought so highly of Vaughan that he wrote a gushing article about him, which appeared in May in *London Society* magazine.[15] This may have passed largely unnoticed had it not mixed derogatory comments about other prominent churchmen with the flattery. 'In the youngest of civilized lands, and in the nineteenth century, when our scientific guides and philosophers are never weary of telling us that religion is a thing of the past, by far the most important social personage is a Roman Catholic ecclesiastic,' the article began. That man, of course, was Vaughan.

After detailing his aristocratic pedigree and career in England, the writer turned to his Australian achievements. First was creating the zeal that resulted in funds for the cathedral pouring in from 'all the cities and townships of the vast Australian Continent… Little wonder that the poor Archbishop of Melbourne [Goold], a very worthy man, but hardly fit for the exalted position in which he found himself placed, should, so rumour said, feel "snuffed out" by his energetic brother prelate in Sydney.'

> Then Archbishop Vaughan found the Collegiate and Scholastic establishments for the education of Catholic youths in a somewhat neglected state. The good old Archbishop Polding had, if the use of a slang word may be forgiven in writing of such high and holy persons, let things 'slide' too much. Ill-conditioned people said that the worthy and reverend head of Sydney College [Forrest, no doubt] was addicted to the bottle; and others, that like one of the parish priests in Bouicault's plays, he took too kindly to party politics. [Dion Boucicault (1820–1890) was an Irish playwright and actor who had a successful career in England and the US.]

Vaughan sorted all of this out, even taking charge of 'one of the Sydney collegiate establishments' himself. 'It was an evil day for the self-indulgent priests when Archbishop Vaughan came to rule over them,' the writer commented. And the Archbishop was a very popular figure. On Sundays, Protestants as well as Catholics were drawn to St Mary's Cathedral by his 'singularly handsome and commanding presence' and the 'rare combination of culture and enthusiasm' that pervaded his every word and gesture.

> St Mary's is generally crowded with Protestant ladies. Flippant persons say it is simply because the Archbishop is so remarkably handsome. But this, like all flippant remarks, is only a portion of the truth. These ladies, as well as many of the sterner sex, who own allegiance to alien creeds, go to hear the Archbishop because they can revere his enthusiasm, his evident sincerity, and profound religious feeling, and at the same time they delight to hear the exquisitely chosen English and the full tones of the cultured voice by which he appeals so irresistibly to them.

When the article appeared in England, one of the Archbishop's brothers, Rev. John Vaughan, wrote to the Catholic *Weekly Register* noting two errors related to the Vaughan family history; he raised no objection to other sections.[16] The response at *Freeman's* was very different; the editor was outraged at 'the gross and offensive libel on the Catholic community of this country...disguised under the form of a panegyric of its religious chief'. A string of letters to the editor took up the theme.

Freeman's leapt to the defence of those slandered. Polding's 'life was a richer blessing' and his death 'a greater calamity' than 'we ever experienced'. Goold's 'blameless beautiful career' had been 'so full of spiritual advantages for the sister colony'. And Forrest was 'one of the most unselfish, honourable, humble, and accomplished priests of the diocese'.[17]

Who wrote the article? The comments on Polding and Forrest match sentiments expressed by Vaughan in letters to Rome and to his family, and it is easy to imagine him describing Goold in the way the writer did. The pseudonym used, 'Amiens', probably gives the author away; Rev. Adalbert O'Sullivan, a Benedictine priest based at Auckland between

1880 and 1888, is the likely candidate.[18] He was also known as Rev. A.M. Sullivan, and was mentioned by that name, as a visitor from New Zealand, among those attending the opening of St Mary's Cathedral in September 1882. After Vaughan's death he lobbied, in letters to the Vatican from Sydney, against the appointment of an Irish successor.[19] Letters that he wrote, as A.M. Sullivan, to newspapers in late 1883 and early 1884 indicate that he had been close to Vaughan and leave no doubt about his admiration for the Archbishop.

The first, to *Freeman's* in November 1883, defended Vaughan over claims by Rev. Sheehy that, by using inaccurate figures, he had exaggerated the progress made in church and school building since he arrived in 1873. Sullivan took responsibility for compiling the figures and for any errors in them.[20] In the second letter, to the *Evening News* in January 1884, he claimed Vaughan had 'minutely informed' him of 'all the circumstances, facts, and motives' behind his taking full administrative responsibility for the archdiocese in January 1874 (chapter 17).[21]

Forrest did not see the *London Society* article; it appeared in *Freeman's* the day after his death, at the age of sixty-two, on the afternoon of Friday 3 August 1883.[22] He had been 'gradually becoming enfeebled in health for a considerable time past,' *Freeman's* reported, 'but he looked so well and strong a week or two ago, that the unexpected announcement of his death caused a painful sensation among his friends'. The paper said the immediate cause of death, after a few days confined to his room, was 'paralysis brought on by cold'. The term used on the death certificate, presumably supplied by Forrest's brother-in-law and medico Dr Gilhooley, was apoplexy. Father Carroll of St Augustine's, next door, attended his fellow priest in his last hours, and the death was reportedly 'calm and peaceful'.

Nearly all the Catholic clergy of the city and suburbs, headed by Vicar-General Sheridan, assisted at the Dirge and Requiem at the cathedral the next morning; 'rarely have so many of the clergy gathered together before in St Mary's,' said *Freeman's*. Father Garavel was celebrant. Bishop Lanigan arrived from Goulburn in time to join the procession to Petersham cemetery and officiate, with Garavel, Placid Quirk and Carroll, at the burial.

Those who followed the hearse in a 'long line of carriages' and 'other private vehicles and cabs' included the political leaders Sir John Robertson and Sir Patrick Jennings. Judge Faucett, W.A. Duncan, John Donovan, Eyre Ellis, Dr Gilhooley and Thomas Butler, editor of *Freeman's*, were among other prominent people there. At least four of Forrest's St John's College students – Matthew Maher, Daniel O'Connell, Richard E. O'Connor and Frank Freehill – attended.

The Month's Mind on Wednesday 5 September, at which the former head of Lyndhurst John Dwyer celebrated the Requiem High Mass, brought about thirty priests back to the cathedral.[23] Those present included Monsignor Lynch, who had described Forrest as a dear friend in a note expressing his sorrow that ill health had prevented him attending the funeral.[24] Perhaps ironically, obsequies for Archbishop Vaughan prevented another good friend, Bishop Murray, attending this service. He wrote to Maryanne Gilhooley from Maitland,

> I cannot tell you how disappointed I am at not being able to attend the Month's Mind for poor Dr Forrest. On account of an old friendship and for many other reasons I would be most anxious to pay this tribute of respect to his memory.

However, he had arranged a Requiem Mass for Vaughan for the same day and sent invitations to the priests of surrounding districts, and so could not be absent from Maitland. He told Mrs Gilhooley he would say Mass for her brother on the morning of the ceremony.[25]

Freeman's noted the week after the funeral: 'It is remarkable, as showing the universal respect in which the late Very Rev. Dr Forrest was held, that all the daily newspapers of the city have published notices of the deceased clergyman couched in graceful and laudatory terms.' They had indeed. The *Herald* described him as a man of liberal and enlightened views 'whose sympathies were as broad as his heart was kind'.[26] To the *Evening News* he was 'a fine type of a cultured Irish gentleman, hospitable, charitable, witty, and broad minded...'[27] The *Daily Telegraph* wrote,

His learning, his great hospitality, his broad mind and big heart, combined with a humorous, good-natured manner, made him popular, not only with his own people, but with those who were, in a religious sense, opposed to him, and few men in the colony have made more friends among all sorts and conditions of men than "the fine old Irish gentleman" who has just passed from amongst us. Dr Forrest was a man of kindly and benevolent disposition, and in religious matters he displayed at all times, and often publicly, his broad spirit of toleration and liberality, scorning bigotry as he deplored sectarian strife, or discountenanced national animosities... So long as the good and generous in heart and mind are remembered, his memory will be kept green.[28]

Sydney had two Catholic papers in 1883, *Freeman's* and the 'official' *Express*, launched by Vaughan in 1880. 'As I have no newspaper on my side I have started one of my own in which I salt and pepper (red pepper) my opponents more freely than if I had to put my name,' he told his father in March that year.[29] The *Express* struggled for sales, and at the end of 1883, seeking to boost its appeal, declared itself a 'truly Irish-Australian' newspaper as well as 'a truly Catholic' one.[30] Vaughan may not have approved of this editorial direction, or of the fact that the unnamed author of the paper's 'Sundry Echoes' column had been a friend of Forrest. He wrote one of the nicest tributes:

Genial, generous, unaffected, he concealed a great deal of mental strength by his characteristic modesty and moderation. An able theologian of the best school, he was singularly competent to maintain his convictions in any pulpit or on any platform in the land, but he nervously shrank from purely polemical controversy through a whole-hearted desire that men and women of all sects should live at peace with one another... To one so esteemed and honoured – whom it was ever a pleasure to meet and regret to leave – it is not surprising that public feeling should be expressed, that his funeral should be attended by many of the worthiest men in the land. We will not conceal our personal regret at the loss of a gifted friend, whose very cheerfulness of manner often dispelled dull care...[31]

Freeman's devoted the best part of a page to its former contributor – a leading article as well as a long obituary and report of the funeral.[32] The obituary began,

For a few years our society has known but little of the bright, active, genial, and scholarly man who calmly passed away on Friday last. There was a time when no great public movement and no great social gathering were deemed perfectly representative in character without his presence. He was welcomed everywhere as one whose sympathies with all forms of goodness were without limit – whose generosity was far in excess of his means – and whose fidelity to his friendships and to his convictions was equally strong. He was one of the very few men in our midst who was such a shining example of perfect tolerance that the bitterest bigots exempted him from their animosities. For a considerable time he occupied a responsible office in connection with the higher education of our Catholic youth. How he discharged its duties may be learnt from the lips and from the lives of those whom he trained to be noble, straightforward, liberal, accomplished Christian gentlemen. He was prepared for his end by one detachment after another of his best affections. He saw those whom he had loved and honoured called away to their reward; and he had long ceased to regard the world as of old. But his relations with good men – his attachments – his affections – had a sacred sanction. A learned and devout priest, a courageous, sincere, cultured gentleman – a patriotic citizen – a delightful companion while health was given to him, and his friends were about him – a man who was never deaf to the cry of want or suffering – who loved justice and hated iniquity – such was the noble Irish priest whom we have lost.

In its account of his time at St John's College, the obituary hinted at the lack of support he had received from the Church hierarchy. Despite 'only a moderate amount of encouragement', and 'unaided', he had conducted the work of the college 'with marvellous success' in temporary accommodation up to 1863. Then, in the new building, 'his energy and his varied attainments' had enabled him to continue without the aid of professors. 'He taught mathematics, philosophy, classics, and logic as one who was master of all; and if proof were wanting of the success of his teaching it would be found in the fact that nearly every one of the students distinguished themselves at the University, and in after life…' The article did not mention the sad fact that only thirteen resident students took degrees during his fourteen years as Rector. That a few students living elsewhere chose to come to the college for tuition – the future High Court judge Richard E. O'Connor is the most notable example – probably confirms his attraction as a teacher.

The *Freeman's* leader mourning Forrest referred to the *London Society* article, which had appeared in the previous issue. 'Some silly, shallow, and yet malignant writer' had written 'a poor lie concerning a man who never said one ungenerous word nor harboured an unkind thought of any human being.' But it was a consolation that he had been 'grouped for purposes of calumny in so noble a company'. The leader's style suggests W.B. Dalley as the author.

> In the death of Dr Forrest the Catholic Church in these colonies has sustained a loss the proportions of which can only be justly measured by those who knew him intimately and were intellectually and morally qualified to appreciate his worth. Into his sum of sterling qualities entered many which are not ordinarily found combined in persons of very much higher pretensions. He was at once a solid theological student and in the best sense a thorough man of the world. He was familiar with books and with the society of men. He could enjoy with equal relish the seclusion of a scholar and the charms of social intercourse. And he was as highly prized by those who sought his sagacious counsel as by those who enjoyed the attractiveness of his society. He was one of the men whose kindly and valuable office was to dispel prejudice – to weaken meaningless hostility to our faith – and to remove misconceptions. And to accomplish this neither by controversy nor laboured exposition, but by the example of a bright winning manner and inoffensive life. These are achievements as great as those which are sometimes, but very rarely, the fruits of more serious labours and perhaps greater accomplishments. It is not an insignificant thing in a community like this to possess one who, while adorning society and defending his convictions, can quietly teach by his life that a man can be thoroughly true to his faith, and perfectly agreeable; that he may be a general favourite, and yet surrender nothing that is essential. The austerity of life which sacrifices liberality and even pity to an unattainable ideal of perfection may be regarded by some as heroic, but it is practically of little value in a mixed society. It discourages weaker and gentler creatures; and it provokes a worldly resistance which virtually leads of unfriendliness. There was a time in our history not very remote when it was the policy and advantage of schemers to fix upon us a stigma of impracticableness as citizens by reason of our alleged illiberality. Dr Forrest's life was a daily protest against such a slander, more eloquent and more effective than the most elaborate homilies. And while he was representative of our liberality in his demeanour, he did us no discredit in any walk of life by his attainments. He was on all subjects a widely-informed man; and on none an obtrusive

one. He preserved the bloom of a youthful and sympathetic nature almost to the last; and was as simple, as unpretending and as generous in age as he had been in youth. He had a natural antipathy strengthened by culture to mere grandeur – hated display – and had a priestly and scholarly sympathy with poverty. Those pleasures which were simple and graceful – which sprang from affection and demanded no sacrifice (except on his own part) – were those which he liked best. The pleasures he tasted at the hands of others he repaid a thousand-fold, by his humanity and by his humour. His time and his sympathy were the property of all who required consolation – his scantily-furnished purse was open to all who needed the alms of a poor but great-hearted gentleman – and he was ready to succour every variety of human misfortune. These are qualities not frequently found, and the loss of which is a great calamity.

23

If only...

Clearly, Forrest had made his mark. How sad it seems that, because Archbishops Polding and Vaughan were not among those who appreciated his character and talents, his career in the colony was so ill starred. He apparently loved life in Sydney despite all the setbacks. The optimistic spirit of the young, rapidly developing and beautifully situated city suited his personality.

Things could have been very different at St John's College. If the Council had opted for a less grandiose and expensive building, money would have been available to employ teachers and fund scholarships. If Lyndhurst had fulfilled its intended role as a feeder to St John's, a few talented students would have entered the college in most if not all years, maintaining a relatively stable, if small, undergraduate population. And if Polding had resigned as he said he felt tempted to do after Lyndhurst's headmaster took off with the housekeeper in early 1864 (chapter 6), he might have been replaced by somebody who supported Forrest's efforts.

That scandal can probably be credited with the college's relative success in the mid-1860s. Boosted by the matriculants and candidates for matriculation who came over from Lyndhurst in 1864, undergraduate numbers at St John's peaked at ten in 1865. They remained at relatively healthy levels over the next few years as these students moved through the university. But then the students were gone, leaving the college in dire straits until the supply from Lyndhurst resumed when Vaughan took over as Rector. Student numbers ranged from about ten to fifteen during the Vaughan-Gillett era (1875–1883).[1]

It is a measure of the man that Forrest retained high public regard, as well as self-respect, after his replacement by Vaughan at an empty St

John's and then his ignominious dismissal as parish priest at Balmain. If Vaughan had proved the open, straight-dealing man the Irish bishops, and apparently Forrest, first took him to be, Forrest's post-St John's career almost certainly would have had a happier ending. Who but Vaughan could have, on the one hand, engaged in pleasant correspondence with him as a 'theological school president' and on the other denigrated him in the harshest terms in letters home (chapter 18) and to Rome (chapter 20)?

Vaughan's relations with the suffragan bishops were at close to their lowest point in late 1877 when he suspended Forrest's priestly faculties. Probably there was a connection; an opportunity to act against the man he described to Cardinal Simeoni as the 'chief' of the 'family Quinn' was eagerly seized.[2] It is sad that Forrest did not live to see the arrival of Vaughan's successor, Archbishop Patrick Moran, in September 1884. Moran, nephew of Archbishop Cullen, was at the Irish College in Forrest's time, though ten years his junior. Like Bishops Murray and Quinn, Forrest doubtless would have warmly welcomed his appointment.

The St John's College Council noted Forrest's death at its meeting four days afterwards. In a motion proposed by W.A. Duncan and carried unanimously, the Fellows expressed 'their sense of his many good social qualities and of his great learning, classical and theological'. They also tendered 'to his much loved sister Mrs Gilhooley and the members of her family their deep condolence'.[3] It is a pity the motion said nothing about Forrest's efforts, against the odds, to make the college a success; however, in light of Duncan's treatment in his letter to Vaughan of those who had laboured at Lyndhurst (chapter 19), this perhaps is not surprising.

Bishop Murray visited St John's in November 1883, and reported to Lanigan that it was in a sad state. He had spoken to various Fellows, but avoided Duncan, 'who is rabid, I am told, and I would only make him worse'.[4] Gillett had resigned as Rector immediately after Vaughan's death; the question now was, who should succeed him? In December, a meeting of Fellows and graduates chose Father Daniel Clancy, a Jesuit, ahead of the young former Lyndhurst student Edmund Butler, who had been ordained a priest by Vaughan shortly before he left Sydney.[5] Clancy resigned two months later and was replaced by a Benedictine, Rev. David Barry.[6] He apparently had little success as Rector; Murray returned to the subject of St John's in May 1886, telling Lanigan that in its current state it was a 'disgrace to the Catholic body'.[7]

This echo of the past was one of a number that perhaps could be heard resonating through the grand sandstone halls over the next three decades. Up to the end of World War I, student numbers never rose above about twenty, funds were always scarce, and successive Rectors were expected, as Forrest had done, to use their government salary to balance the college budget.[8] In 1889, the Fellows objected to the fact that some ex-students of the Jesuit secondary school St Ignatius' College were allowed to continue living there while they attended university![9]

In a failed attempt to set the college on a more successful course, Archbishop Moran, now a Cardinal, arranged in 1887 for Dr James O'Brien, vice-president of the Dublin seminary All Hallows College, to take over as Rector from the man who had temporarily succeeded Barry, Very Rev. Dr Murphy. O'Brien arrived in February 1888, and was welcomed at a banquet at the college attended by the Archbishop and dignitaries including Bishop Lanigan, the first (temporary) Rector of St John's, Dean O'Connell, and most of the college Fellows. Interestingly, four of the Fellows present – Frank Freehill, Charles Coghlan, William Browne and Dr Michael Clune – had been Forrest's students. Three more graduates from his time as Rector were on the Council earlier (chapter 21). So about half his successful students served, at one time or another, as college Fellows.

The chief speaker of the evening was a now frail W.B. Dalley. His political career had climaxed three years earlier when, as Acting Premier, he offered Britain a contingent of New South Wales troops to help in the Sudan campaign. The offer, intended to show 'the readiness of the Australian colonies to give instant and practical help to the Empire', was accepted.[10] So, after a century free of Imperial military entanglements, the precedent was set that saw expeditionary forces set off, over the next decades, to the Boer War and the battlefields of World War I. It is one of the ironies of history that this gentle man who always sought harmony at home – *Freeman's* described him as 'Australia's peerless son... whom to know was to love' in its eulogy following his death at the age of fifty-seven in November 1888[11] – should be the first Australian political leader to send troops to a distant war.

Dalley used his speech at St John's, one of the last he made, to praise two men 'whose memory is, and ever ought to be, devoutly cherished'. First was the Benedictine Bishop Charles Davis, 'as liberal as he was saintly', who arrived in Sydney in 1848 as Polding's coadjutor, played important roles in the establishment of Lyndhurst and the university, and died aged only thirty-eight in 1854. Second was Forrest. Said Dalley,

for many years this house was the home of one who taught his pupils the difficult art of preserving and displaying the treasures of learning with the delights of refined social intercourse, of combining the gravity of scholarship with the gaiety of a bright happy sunny nature – who admired the accomplished man, but loved the generous one – who had a kindly winning word for his multitudes of friends and for the few unhappy creatures who were his enemies. (Great applause.) You who knew him and tasted his hospitality will remember how you carried away from his little festivals good things which made his feasts sweeter and his guests better. He was sent to you young natives of a new land from the dear old country where they grow and have ever grown such men to show you what a good sound scholar, what a dear friend – what a delicate humorist and a perfectly

The cross at Sydney's Waverley Cemetery, 'erected by a few of his old students and friends', marking Forrest's grave.

tolerant gentleman may be found in the person of an Irish Catholic priest. (Great applause.)[12]

The elaborate marble cross that marks Forrest's grave at Sydney's seaside Waverley cemetery is one sign that he was not soon forgotten. Petersham cemetery, where he had been buried, was resumed in the early 1900s, prompting the removal of his remains to Waverley in October 1904. An inscription below the cross records that it was erected – thirty years after he left St John's and twenty-one years after his death – by 'a few of his old students and friends'. Beside his grave are those of members of the Gilhooley family, including Forrest's sister, Maryanne, who came with him to Sydney in 1860, shared in the highs and lows and, after raising a large family, died at the age of seventy-nine in May 1916. Forrest is a given name of many of her descendants.

Sources

Archival collections
Bathurst Diocesan Archives (BDA)
Eris O'Brien Papers in Veech Library, Catholic Institute of Sydney – includes transcripts of Courtfield Letters (Archbishop Vaughan to his family)
Irish College, Rome, Archives (emailed response to request for information)
Lanigan Papers, copies held at National Library of Australia (NLA)
Maitland–Newcastle Diocesan Archives (MNDA)
Mitchell Library, State Library of NSW, for microfilm of Progaganda Fide records, SC Oceania, 1877–78
National University of Ireland, Maynooth, Library (written response to request for information)
St John's College, University of Sydney, Archives (SJCA). Holdings include an unpublished history of St John's College written by R.A. Daly in the 1950s.
St Stanislaus' College, Bathurst, Archives
Sydney Archdiocesan Archives (SAA)
University of Sydney Archives

Newspapers
Advocate, Melbourne
Australian, Sydney
Brisbane Courier
Daily Telegraph, Sydney
Empire, Sydney
Evening News, Sydney
Express, Sydney
Freeman's Journal (FJ), Sydney
Goulburn Herald
Illustrated Sydney News
Launceston Examiner
Maitland Mercury
Sydney Morning Herald (SMH)
Town and Country Journal, Sydney
Yass Courier

Journal articles
Cable, K.J., 'The University of Sydney and its Affiliated Colleges, 1850–1880', *The Australian University*, vol. 2, 1964, pp. 183–214.
Cahill, A.J., 'Lyndhurst and Sydney University Graduates', *Journal of the Australian Catholic Historical Society*, vol. 5, 1976, pp. 38–40.
Cahill, A.J., 'Archbishop Vaughan and St John's College, University of Sydney', *Journal of the Australian Catholic Historical Society*, vol. 14, 1992, pp. 36–49.
Daly, R.A., 'John Bede Polding and the Founding of St John's College, 1857–58', *Australasian Catholic Record*, vol. 35, no. 4, 1958, pp. 284–306.

Daly, R.A., 'Bishop Murray Settles into Maitland: 1867', *Australasian Catholic Record*, vol. 37, no. 3, 1960, pp. 189–201.

Duffy, C.J., 'The High Flying Eagle', *The Johnsman*, 1967.

Duffy, C.J., 'Archbishop Polding and his Critics', *Journal of the Australian Catholic Historical Society*, vol. 4, 1975, pp. 17–30.

Farrell, J.J., 'Archbishop Vaughan and the Resignation of Bishop O'Mahony, First Bishop of Armidale', *Journal of the Australian Catholic Historical Society*, vol. 15, 1993, pp. 7–23.

Forster, M., 'Lyndhurst and Benedictine Education', *Australasian Catholic Record*, series beginning vol. 23, no. 4, 1946, concluding vol 24, no. 3, 1947.

Guilford, E., 'Dean Lynch: Catholic Priest and Community Leader', *Journal of Hunter Valley History*, vol. 1, no. 1, 1985.

Haines, G., 'Reflections on Polding', *Journal of the Australian Catholic Historical Society*, vol. 4, 1975, pp. 1–16.

Hosie, J., 'Archbishop Polding: a rejoinder to Dr Haines and Monsignor Duffy', *Journal of the Australian Catholic Historical Society*, vol. 4, 1975, pp. 31–40.

Kavenagh, T., 'Vaughan and the Monks of Sydney', *Tjurunga*, no. 25, 1983.

McCallum, A., 'Fr. Patrick Smyth, Peacemaker at Eureka', *Footprints* – Quarterly Journal of the Melbourne Historical Commission, vol. 4, no. 6, 1982.

McCristal, J.E. (translator), 'Setting Diocesan Boundaries in Victoria (1874)', *Footprints*, vol. 1, no. 12, 1973.

O'Brien, J.M., 'The Religious and Social Fabric of Catholic Society in Mid-Nineteenth Century NSW', *Journal of the Australian Catholic Historical Society*, vol. 6, 1978, pp. 18–32.

Prendergast, A., 'The Benedictine Schools and Students of Colonial Sydney', *Journal of the Australian Catholic Historical Society*, vol. 21, 2000, pp. 67–79.

Roberts, C., 'James Quinn's Roman Background', *Australasian Catholic Record*, vol. 37, no. 1, 1960, pp. 11–16.

Roberts, C., 'Bishop James Quinn: From Dublin to Brisbane', *Australasian Catholic Record*, vol. 37, no. 2, 1960, pp. 116–121.

Rutledge, M., 'Edward Butler and the Chief Justiceship, 1873', *Historical Studies*, vol. 13, no. 50, 1968.

Wynne, R., 'Archdeacon John McEncroe (1795–1868)', *Australasian Catholic Record*, series beginning vol. 31, no. 1, 1954, concluding vol. 33, no. 2, 1956.

Wynne, R., 'Et Rigney Non Erit Finis', *Australasian Catholic Record*, vol. 51, no. 2, 1974.

Wynne, R., 'Dr John Forrest, First Rector of St John's College', *Australasian Catholic Record*, vol. 60, no. 3, 1983.

Books and theses

Australian Dictionary of Biography, Melbourne University Press, Melbourne, from 1966.

Australian Encyclopaedia, 10 vols, Angus and Robertson, Sydney, 1958.

Barff, H.E., *A Short Historical Account of the University of Sydney; in connection with the Jubilee Celebrations 1852-1902*, Angus and Robertson, Sydney, 1902.

Barker, T. (ed.), *A Century of Echoes: one hundred years of 'Echoes from St. Stanislaus'*, Crawford House Press, Bathurst, 1989.

Barton, G.B., *Literature in New South Wales*, NSW Government Printer, Sydney, 1866.

Birchley, D., *John McEncroe: colonial democrat*, Studies in the Christian Movement, Manly, NSW, 1986.

Birt, H.N., *Benedictine Pioneers in Australia*, 2 vols, Herbert and Daniel, London, 1911.

Bygott, U.M.L., *With pen and tongue: the Jesuits in Australia, 1865-1939*, Melbourne University Press, Melbourne, 1980.

Campbell, H.W., *The Diocese of Maitland, 1866-1966*, The Diocese, Maitland, 1966.

Compton, M.X., McKinley, M.P.D. and Dyson, D. (eds), *Documents and Resource Material relating to the Episcopacy of Archbishop John Bede Polding OSB*, vol. 2, Sisters of the Good Samaritan, Glebe Point, NSW, c. 2001.

Compton, M.X., McKinley, M.P.D., Kavenagh, T., Pullen, P., Forster, M.G., Dyson, D., Trower, U., and Condon, C. (eds), *The Letters of John Bede Polding OSB*, vols. 2 and 3, Sisters of the Good Samaritan, Glebe Point, NSW, 1996, 1998.

Cunningham, A., *The Rome Connection: Australia, Ireland and the Empire 1865-1885*, Crossing Press, Sydney, 2002.

Dowd, C.P., 'Papal policy towards conflict in the Australian Catholic missions: the relationship between John Bede Polding, O.S.B., Archbishop of Sydney, and the Sacred Congregation De Propaganda Fide, 1842-1874', PhD thesis, Australian National University, 1994.

Flannery, T. (ed.), *The Birth of Sydney*, Text Publishing, Melbourne, 1999.

Fogarty, R., *Catholic Education in Australia 1806-1950*, 2 vols, Melbourne University Press, Melbourne, 1959.

Gilchrist, A., *John Dunmore Lang: an assembling of contemporary documents*, 2 vols, Jedgarm Publications, Melbourne, 1951.

Haines, G., Forster, M.G. and Brophy, F., *The eye of faith: the pastoral letters of John Bede Polding*, Lowden Publishing, Kilmore, 1977.

Hall, J., *History of St Stanislaus' College Bathurst*, St Stanislaus' College, Bathurst, 1944.

Healy, J., *Maynooth College: its centenary history*, Browne and Nolan, Dublin, 1895.

Hellwig, E. (ed.), *Up She Gets, for Up She Must! An account of a journey from Kingstown, Ireland, to Maitland, Australia, in 1867 during the age of sail*, Dominican Sisters of Eastern Australia and the Solomon Islands, Sydney, 2001.

Keneally, T., *The Great Shame: a story of the Irish in the Old World and the New*, Random House, Sydney, 1998.

Lehane, R., *Irish Gold: a tale of two pioneer families*, Ginninderra Press, Canberra, 2002.

Livingston, K.T., *The Emergence of an Australian Catholic Priesthood 1835-1915*, Catholic Theological Faculty, Sydney, 1977.

Lyons, M.J., 'Aspects of Sectarianism in New South Wales circa 1865 to 1880', PhD thesis, Australian National University, 1972.

McLay, A., *James Quinn, first Catholic Bishop of Brisbane*, Church Archivists' Society, Toowoomba, 1989.

Maher, B., *Planting the Celtic Cross: foundations of the Catholic Archdiocese of Canberra and Goulburn*, B. Maher, Canberra, 1997.

Martin, A.W., *Henry Parkes: a biography*, Melbourne University Press, Melbourne, 1980.

Molony, J.N., *The Roman Mould of the Australian Catholic Church*, Melbourne University Press, Melbourne, 1969.

Molony, J.N., *An Architect of Freedom: John Hubert Plunkett in New South Wales 1832-1869*, Australian National University Press, Canberra, 1973.

Molony, J.N., *Eureka*, third edition, Melbourne University Press, Melbourne, 2001.

Moran, P.F., *History of the Catholic Church in Australasia: from authentic sources*, Oceanic Publishing, Sydney, 189-?

O'Donoghue, F., *The Bishop of Botany Bay: the life of John Bede Polding, Australia's first Catholic Archbishop*, Angus and Robertson, Sydney, 1982.

O'Farrell, P. and D. (eds), *Documents in Australian Catholic History*, vol. 1, 1799-1884, Geoffrey Chapman, London, 1969.

O'Farrell, P., *The Catholic Church and Community in Australia: a history*, Nelson, Melbourne, 1977.

Pawsey, M.M., *The Demon of Discord: tensions in the Catholic Church in Victoria, 1853-1864*, Melbourne University Press, Melbourne, 1982.

Porter, R., *History of Wellington*, W.C. Penfold & Co., Sydney, 1906.

Shanahan, M., *Out of Time, Out of Place: Henry Gregory and the Benedictine Order in Colonial Australia*, Australian National University Press, Canberra, 1970.

Suttor, T.L., *Hierarchy and Democracy in Australia, 1788-1870: the formation of Australian Catholicism*, Melbourne University Press, Melbourne, 1965.

Tierney, M., *Croke of Cashel: the life of Archbishop Thomas William Croke, 1823-1902*, Gill and Macmillan, Dublin, 1976.

Travers, R., *The Phantom Fenians of New South Wales*, Kangaroo Press, Sydney, 1986.

Travers, R., *The Grand Old Man of Australian Politics: the life and times of Sir Henry Parkes*, Kangaroo Press, Sydney, 2000.

Turney, C., Bygott, U., and Chippendale, P., *Australia's First – A History of the University of Sydney*, vol. 1, 1850-1939, The University of Sydney in Association with Hale and Iremonger, Sydney, 1991.

Vamplew, W. (ed.), 'Australians: Historical Statistics', vol. 10 of *Australians: a historical library*, Fairfax, Syme & Weldon Associates, Sydney, 1987.

Walker, R.B., *The Newspaper Press in New South Wales, 1803-1920*, Sydney University Press, Sydney, 1976.

Ward, W., *The Life of John Henry Cardinal Newman: based on his private journals and correspondence*, Longman's Green and Co., London, 1912.

Wilson, G., *Murray of Yarralumla*, Oxford University Press, Melbourne, 1968.

Zimmerman, B., *The Making of a Diocese: Maitland, its bishop, priests and people 1866-1909*, Melbourne University Press, Melbourne, 2000.

Other documents

Adams, W.M., *The Rhinoceros Ministry: a series of letters upon the principal decisions of the session*, F. Cunninghame, Sydney, 1867.

A Handbook to St John's College within the University of Sydney, F. Cunninghame, Sydney, 1881.

An Act to Incorporate Saint John's College as a College within the University of Sydney, Supplement to the NSW Government Gazette, 15 December 1857.

Bruce, R.C., *The first hundred years of St Augustine's Church, Balmain: centenary celebrations, September, 1948*, St Augustine's Church, Balmain, 1948.

Catholic College of St. John the Evangelist: a corrected report of the aggregate meeting in St. Mary's Cathedral on Monday the 3rd of August, 1857, with a complete list of subscribers, Sydney, 1857.

Dalley, W.B., *A speech delivered by Wm. Bede Dalley at the Masonic Hall, on Monday night, May 20 1872*, Edward F. Flanagan, Sydney, 1872.

Forrest, J., *Lecture on The Tendency of Modern Civilization*, Henry Thomas, West Maitland, 1870.

Funeral of the late Mr. Michael Fitzpatrick, M.L.A. (pamphlet), Sydney, 1881.

Moore, J.S., *University Reform, its Urgency and Reasonableness: an oration*, Henry Cole, Sydney, 1865.

Mullins, J.L., *Reminiscences of the Hon. John Lane Mullins M.A., M.L.C. covering the years 1857 to 1876*, 19? Manuscript in Fisher Library, University of Sydney.

O'Farrell Papers: a correct reprint of the Papers laid upon the Table of the Legislative Assembly by Mr Parkes, John Ferguson, Sydney, undated.

Report of inquiry into 'the present state of the Sydney University' by select committee appointed 13 September 1859. Votes and Proceedings of the Legislative Assembly, New South Wales, 1859-60.

St John's College Magazine, 1921.

Picture credits

Cover and p.38 *Town and Country Journal*, 10 April 1875, mfm NX 442, National Library of Australia

p.14 *Illustrated Sydney News*, 16 January 1866, PIC 079.44 ILL, National Library of Australia

p.20 Patrick Francis Cardinal Moran, *History of the Catholic Church in Australasia*, Sydney 189? N282.94 MOR, National Library of Australia

p.25 H.S. Sadd, *The Most Reverend John Bede Polding OSB, First Archbishop of Sydney*, PIC S8699 LOC 7871-7880, National Library of Australia

p.33 *Illustrated Sydney News*, 4 September 1868, PIC 079.44 ILL, National Library of Australia

p.43 Patrick Francis Cardinal Moran, *History of the Catholic Church in Australasia*, Sydney 189? N282.94 MOR, National Library of Australia

p.54 Patrick Francis Cardinal Moran, *History of the Catholic Church in Australasia*, Sydney 189? N282.94 MOR, National Library of Australia

p.57 Patrick Francis Cardinal Moran, *History of the Catholic Church in Australasia*, Sydney 189? N282.94 MOR,

p.65 *Illustrated Sydney News*, 16 January 1865, PIC 079.44 ILL, National Library of Australia

p.80 J.R. Clarke, *St John's College, University of Sydney*, ML ref. SPF/470, Mitchell Library, State Library of New South Wales

p.86 Patrick Francis Cardinal Moran, *History of the Catholic Church in Australasia*, Sydney 189? N282.94 MOR, National Library of Australia

p.89 *Illustrated Sydney News*, 16 December 1865, PIC 079.44 ILL, National Library of Australia

p.94 *Illustrated Sydney News*, 15 July 1865, PIC 079.44 ILL, National Library of Australia

p.110 *Illustrated Sydney News*, 17 March 1870, PIC 079.44 ILL, National Library of Australia

p.112 *Illustrated Sydney News*, 16 May 1866, PIC 079.44 ILL, National Library of Australia

p.119 Patrick Francis Cardinal Moran, *History of the Catholic Church in Australasia*, Sydney 189? N282.94 MOR, National Library of Australia

p.119 Patrick Francis Cardinal Moran, *History of the Catholic Church in Australasia*, Sydney 189? N282.94 MOR, National Library of Australia p.131 Patrick Francis Cardinal Moran, *History of the Catholic Church in Australasia*, Sydney 189? N282.94 MOR, National Library of Australia

p.136 *Illustrated Sydney News*, 16 August 1867, PIC 079.44 ILL, National Library of Australia

p.145 *Illustrated Sydney News*, 16 September 1867, PIC 079.44 ILL, National Library of Australia

p.146 *Illustrated Sydney News*, 22 February 1868, PIC 079.44 ILL, National Library of Australia

p.147 *Illustrated Sydney News*, 30 January 1874, PIC 079.44 ILL, National Library of Australia

p.156 *Illustrated Sydney News*, 14 November 1874, PIC 079.44 ILL, National Library of Australia

p.164 *The Bulletin*, 3 November 1888, mfm NX 141, National Library of Australia

p.171 *Illustrated Sydney News*, 28 December 1868, PIC 079.44 ILL, National Library of Australia

p.183 *Town and Country Journal*, 28 January 1888, mfm NX 442, National Library of Australia

p.189 Patrick Francis Cardinal Moran, *History of the Catholic Church in Australasia*, Sydney 189? N282.94 MOR, National Library of Australia

p.192 Charles Bayliss, University (Sydney), Album of photographs of the Sydney Exhibition Building and other Sydney buildings, PIC P2115/1-40 LOC Album 129, National Library of Australia

p.213 *Freeman's Journal*, 30 June 1900, mfm NX 43, National Library of Australia

p.222 *Illustrated Sydney News*, 2 May 1874, PIC 079.44 ILL, National Library of Australia

p.237 Patrick Francis Cardinal Moran, *History of the Catholic Church in Australasia*, Sydney 189? N282.94 MOR, National Library of Australia

p.260 Patrick Francis Cardinal Moran, *History of the Catholic Church in Australasia*, Sydney 189? N282.94 MOR, National Library of Australia

p.264 *Illustrated Sydney News*, 21 August 1875, PIC 079.44 ILL, National Library of Australia

p.273 *Illustrated Sydney News*, 31 March 1877, PIC 079.44 ILL, National Library of Australia

p.289 'Sydney Harbour from Shark Point', Andrew Garran (ed.), *Picturesque Atlas of Australasia*, Vol. 1, Sydney 1886

p.303 *Illustrated Sydney News*, 8 April 1882, PIC 079.44 ILL, National Library of Australia

p.305 *Illustrated Sydney News*, 30 September 1882, PIC 079.44 ILL, National Library of Australia

p.308 *Illustrated Sydney News*, 12 May 1883, PIC 079.44 ILL, National Library of Australia

Notes

1: Looking good
1. *Freeman's Journal*, 29 Dec 1860
2. FJ, 30 Jan 1861
3. Quoted in Flannery, p. 253
4. Quoted in O'Farrell, *The Catholic Church and Community*, p. 1
5. Vamplew, pp. 4, 5, 41
6. Bathurst Labour Market rates June 1862, FJ, 2 July 1862
7. Daly, ACR 35:4, pp. 284–306
8. Circular, 9 July 1858. In: *The letters of John Bede Polding OSB*, Vol. 2, p. 260
9. FJ, 12 Sept 1860
10. FJ, 3 Oct 1860, 19 Jan 1861
11. Prendergast, p. 72
12. FJ, 22 Dec 1860
13. FJ, 3 Feb 1864
14. FJ, 26 Sept 1860
15. FJ, 10 Oct 1860
16. ADB, Therry entry; O'Farrell, *The Catholic Church and Community*, pp. 18–29
17. ADB, McEncroe entry; Birchley
18. FJ, 1 Sept 1860
19. ADB, Plunkett entry; Molony, *An Architect of Freedom*
20. FJ, 13 March & 2 Oct 1861; *Goulburn Herald*, 28 Sept 1861
21. ADB, Butler entry; Keneally, pp. 159–62
22. FJ, 10 Oct 1860

2: Out of Ireland
1. FJ's Forrest obituary (11 Aug 1883) gives his birth date as 7 November 1820. 'Marlesford', the writer of a memorial poem in the St John's College archives (probably Gertrude Clara Woodhouse of Campbelltown), gives it as 19 November.
2. Information from NUI Maynooth archives.
3. Information on Irish College from website www.irishcollege.org and Roberts, ACR 37:1, pp. 11, 12. Comment on Cullen in Suttor, p. 65
4. FJ, 10 Oct 1860
5. References from Revs Justin McCarthy and M. O'Hea, SJCA
6. Roberts, ACR 37:2, pp. 117, 118
7. Ward, p. 354
8. Newman to Forrest, 22 July 1862, SJCA
9. Zimmerman, p. 14
10. Healy, pp. 435–36
11. FJ, 22 Aug 1860
12. In O'Farrell, *Documents*, pp. 199–205
13. Daly, ACR 35:4, p. 304
14. *Catholic College of St. John the Evangelist: a corrected report of the aggregate meeting...*
15. FJ, 16 Jan 1858
16. ADB, Polding entry; O'Donoghue
17. Maher, pp. 80–90
18. Polding to Bernard Smith, Rome, 21 Jan 1862, SAA Box O1735

19. O'Farrell, *The Catholic Church and Community*, p. 60
20. Letter in Birt, Vol. 2, p. 179; discussed in Birchley, p. 140 and O'Donoghue, p. 97
21. O'Donoghue, pp. 98–109
22. Birt, Vol. 2, pp. 232–33
23. Walker, p. 151. The book's section on *Freeman's Journal* has details of changes in owners and editors.
24. Daly, ACR 35:4, pp. 299–303
25. FJ, 23 Jan 1858
26. FJ, 20 Feb 1858
27. FJ, 6 March 1858
28. FJ, 14 & 21 April 1858
29. FJ, 28 April 1858
30. FJ, 12 May 1858
31. FJ, 19 & 22 May 1858
32. FJ, 26 May 1858
33. FJ, 9, 12 & 16 June 1858
34. Full text in O'Farrell, *Documents*, pp. 157–60
35. SMH, 17 June 1858, and FJ, 19 June 1858
36. FJ, 19 June 1858
37. SJC Council to Pius IX, 8 July 1858, SJCA
38. Polding letters, Vol. 2, p. 261
39. Polding letters, Vol. 2, p. 260
40. Birchley, pp. 187 & 195
41. SJC Council to McEncroe, 8 Nov 1858, SJCA
42. Letter dated 25 April 1859, SJCA
43. Birchley, p. 209; Wynne, ACR 33:1, p. 29; McEncroe to Polding 9 June 1859, Documents re Polding episcopacy, Vol 2, p. 20
44. McEncroe to Leahy, May 1867; Leahy to McEncroe, 1 Aug 1867, SAA Box U1208. An article about Croke in FJ, 14 July 1883, notes his 'intimate' friendship with Forrest.
45. Cullen and Newman references, SJCA
46. Report of SJC Council committee re agreement with Forrest, 21 Oct 1861, SJCA
47. FJ, 11 Aug 1883
48. FJ, 1 June 1916
49. As Ref 46
50. FJ, 19 Nov 1859

3: Sorting things out in Sydney

1. Wardell letters, University of Sydney Archives
2. Polding to Gregory 19 May 1868, Polding letters Vol 3, p. 299
3. *Australian Encyclopaedia* 1958, Vol. 9, p. 164
4. Duffy, 'The High Flying Eagle', p. 2
5. J.V. Gorman to Wardell, 5 Nov 1859, SJCA
6. Minutes, SJC Council, 1 Dec 1859, SJCA
7. Wardell letters, University of Sydney Archives
8. Daly, ACR 35:4, p. 295
9. J. Hart to Blacket, Aug 1860, SJCA
10. Daly, ACR 35:4, p. 305
11. Note, 2 Oct 1860, SJCA
12. Hart to Blacket, 16 Dec 1860, SJCA
13. Minutes, SJC Council, 9 May 1859, SJCA
14. Turney et al, p. 117
15. Cable, p. 184
16. Votes and Proceedings of the Legislative Assembly, Report of Select Committee, 8 June 1860

17. FJ, 3 & 10 March 1860
18. Minutes, SJC Council, 25 July and 1 Aug 1859, SJCA
19. Polding to SJC Council, 24 Aug 1859, Polding letters Vol 2, p. 305
20. FJ, 4 Jan 1860
21. O'Farrell, *Documents*, p. 160
22. Suttor, p. 181; O'Donoghue, p. 115; FJ, 2 March 1859
23. Suttor, p. 182; O'Farrell, *The Catholic Church and Community*, p. 104
24. FJ, 23 Feb 1859
25. FJ, 2 March 1859, contains a detailed report of the meeting.
26. FJ, 12 March 1859; this issue also contains responses to the threatened excommunications.
27. O'Farrell, *Documents*, pp. 184–88
28. Polding to Barnabo, c. 12 March 1859, Polding letters Vol 2, pp. 271–73
29. Polding to Barnabo, 12 April, mid April & 13 May 1859, Polding letters Vol. 2, pp. 276–89
30. ADB, Heydon entry
31. O'Farrell, *Documents*, p. 188
32. O'Farrell, *The Catholic Church and Community*, p. 117; O'Donoghue, p. 116
33. Duffy, 'Archbishop Polding and his Critics', pp. 19–22; O'Farrell, *The Catholic Church and Community*, p. 122; Molony, *An Architect of Freedom*, p. 263
34. Polding to Geoghegan, 9 July 1859, Polding letters, Vol 2, pp. 300–01
35. O'Donoghue, p. 133
36. Barnabo to Polding, 17 Aug 1859, Documents re Polding episcopacy, Vol 2, p. 27
37. O'Donoghue, p. 119; Birchley, p. 202; Shanahan, pp. 165–74
38. Polding to Barnabo, 14 April 1860, Polding letters, Vol 2, pp. 314–15
39. FJ, 22 Feb 1860
40. Polding to Barnabo, 11 April 1859, Polding letters, Vol 2, pp. 275–76
41. Birchley, p. 212
42. Polding to Gregory, 17 Feb 1861, Polding letters, Vol 3, p. 12
43. FJ, 17 Dec 1859
44. FJ, 31 March 1860
45. FJ, 2 & 6 June 1860
46. Polding to Barnabo, 21 July 1860, Polding letters, Vol 2, p. 325
47. Polding to Gregory, 23 March 1863, Polding letters, Vol 3, p. 106
48. O'Donoghue, p. 117; Suttor, p. 195
49. FJ, 30 Jan & 9 Feb 1861

4: Progress

1. *A Handbook to St John's College*, 1881, p. 50
2. Polding to Duncan, 8 March 1859, Polding letters, Vol. 2, p. 271
3. Report to SJC Council, 26 Nov 1860, SJCA
4. Daly, *History*, p. 9, SJCA
5. FJ, 5 Jan 1861
6. FJ, 9 Feb 1861
7. FJ, 20 April 1861
8. Student roll & Daly, *History*, p. 10, SJCA
9. Minutes, SJC Council, 20 May 1861, SJCA; Turney et al, p. 160
10. Polding to Goold, 20 Jan 1861, Polding letters, Vol. 3, p. 2

11. SJC Act of Incorporation, Section 10
12. Polding to Barnabo, 19 Feb 1861, Polding letters, Vol. 3, p. 13
13. Polding to Gregory, 20 Feb 1861, Polding letters, Vol. 3, p. 14
14. Polding to Gregory, 19 July 1861, Polding letters, Vol. 3, p. 27
15. Polding to Forrest, 28 Aug 1861, Polding letters, Vol 3, p. 35
16. SJC Council to Polding, 7 Oct 1861, Documents re Polding episcopacy, Vol 2, p. 68
17. Polding to Forrest, 6 Nov 1861, Polding letters, Vol 3, pp. 41–42
18. Polding to Lynch, 16 March 1861; Polding to Gregory, 20 March 1861; Polding to Lynch, 1 April 1861: Polding letters, Vol 3, pp. 15–18
19. FJ, 1 & 22 May 1861
20. Polding to Gregory, 19 April 1861, Polding letters, Vol 3, pp. 19–20
21. FJ, 19 June 1861
22. Polding to Gregory, 19 July 1861, Polding letters, Vol 3, p. 27
23. Daly, *History*, p. 16; Newman to Forrest, 22 July 1862, SJCA
24. FJ, 23 Feb & 2 March 1861
25. Keneally, p. 310
26. FJ, 13 March 1861
27. FJ, 20 March 1861
28. FJ, 22 & 25 June 1861
29. FJ, 24 July 1861

5: A bright start

1. FJ, 18 Jan 1862
2. FJ, 5 Feb 1862
3. Student roll; Daly, *History*, p. 27, SJCA; Cahill, Lyndhurst and Sydney University Graduates, pp. 38–39
4. Polding to Gregory, 21 Jan 1862, Polding letters, Vol. 3, p. 59
5. FJ, 27 & 30 March 1861
6. Polding to Gregory, 21 Sept 1863, Polding letters, Vol. 3, p. 127
7. Prendergast, pp. 68 & 72–77
8. Polding to Gregory, 17 June 1861, Polding letters, Vol. 3, p. 26
9. FJ, 21 Aug & 4 Sept 1861
10. Polding to Gregory, 19 May 1862, Polding letters, Vol. 3, p. 71
11. FJ, 20 Feb & 22 May 1861; *Yass Courier*, quoting the *Empire*, 14 Sept 1861
12. Forrest to Wardell, 10 June 1861, SJCA
13. Minutes, SJC Council, 18 Nov 1861, SJCA
14. FJ, 14 & 28 Dec 1861
15. FJ, 26 Feb 1862
16. Polding to Gregory, 20 Feb 1862, Polding letters, Vol. 3, p. 65
17. Quinn to Cullen, 19 May 1862, Box U1101 SAA
18. FJ, 8 March and 9 Aug 1862
19. FJ, 16 July 1862
20. FJ, 20 Sept 1862 (e.g.)
21. FJ, 23 & 30 July 1862
22. FJ, 23 Aug & 8 Oct 1862
23. FJ, 15 Oct & 26 Nov 1862
24. Gorman to Blacket, 21 June 1862, SJCA
25. Forrest to Nicholson and to Newman, 17 June 1862, SJCA
26. FJ, 21 June 1862
27. FJ, 11 & 21 June 1862
28. FJ, 20 Dec 1862
29. FJ, 5 July 1862; Turney et al, p. 109
30. Minutes, SJC Council, 13 Oct 1862, SJCA
31. FJ, 11 March 1863, contains the

Forrest–Polding correspondence, Polding's pastoral letter, and Blacket's report
32. Polding to Gregory, 23 March 1863, Polding letters, Vol. 3, p. 106
33. FJ, 14 March & 11 April 1863
34. Forrest to potential donors to St John's, March 1863, SJCA
35. Blacket to SJC Council, 14 Nov 1863; FJ, 29 April 1865; Turney et al, p. 109
36. Blacket's report in FJ, 11 March 1863
37. McEncroe, Feb 1864, circular letter, SAA Box L2416
38. Daly, History, p. 41, SJCA

6: Moving in

1. FJ, 20 Dec 1862
2. *Yass Courier*, 3 Jan 1863; Lehane, p. 62
3. Student roll, SJCA; Cahill, Lyndhurst and Sydney University Graduates, pp. 38–39
4. FJ, 21 March & 25 April 1863
5. Marriage certificate, BDM NSW
6. Daly, History, p. 35, SJCA; Polding to Gregory, 22 August 1863, Polding letters, Vol. 3, pp. 125–26
7. A Handbook to St John's College, 1881, p. 50
8. Cahill, Lyndhurst and Sydney University Graduates, pp. 38–39
9. FJ, 15 July 1863
10. FJ, 1 Aug 1863
11. FJ, 19 Sept 1863
12. Polding to Gregory, 21 Sept 1863, Polding letters, Vol. 3, p. 127
13. *Yass Courier*, quoting the SMH, 26 Sept 1863
14. Polding to Gregory, 20 Dec 1863, Polding letters, Vol. 3, p. 136
15. FJ, 26 Sept 1863
16. Daly, *History*, p. 32, SJCA
17. FJ, 23 Dec 1863
18. Minutes, SJC Council, 1 Feb 1864, SJCA
19. Terms and Regulations re admission of students, 19 Feb 1864, SJCA
20. Minutes, SJC Council, 29 Feb 1864, SJCA
21. Cahill, Archbishop Vaughan and St John's College, p. 39
22. *St John's College Magazine*, 1921
23. Forrest to Cullen, 20 Feb 1864, microfilm at SAA
24. Kavenagh, p. 194
25. Polding to Gregory, 20 Feb 1864, Polding letters, Vol. 3, p. 148
26. Polding to Gregory, 21 June 1864, Polding letters, Vol. 3, p. 157
27. FJ, 6 April 1864
28. ADB, Therry entry
29. FJ, 1 June 1864
30. FJ, 28 May 1864
31. FJ, 26 Oct 1864
32. *Australian*, 19 Sept 1839
33. FJ, 21 Dec 1864
34. Student roll, SJCA
35. FJ, 12 April 1865
36. FJ, 4 March 1865
37. Polding to Conway, 7 June 1864, transcribed letters no. 96, SAA
38. Polding to McEncroe, 18 May 1868, Box U1208 SAA
39. FJ, 31 Oct 1868
40. FJ, 7 April 1877
41. FJ, 15 & 18 March 1865
42. FJ, 17 Oct 1885
43. FJ, 12 April 1865

7: Disaster

1. Information on the fire and aftermath from FJ, 1, 8, & 15 July, 5 & 19 Aug, & 7 Oct 1865, & 9 & 16 Sept 1882
2. FJ, 29 April 1865
3. FJ, 8 July 1865
4. FJ, 12 April 1865
5. Moore, pp. 14–15
6. Matriculant numbers from reports of annual university commemorations: SMH, 23 May 1870; FJ, 8 April 1871; FJ, 30 March 1872
7. Lehane, p. 105
8. Tierney, p. xi
9. ADB, Sheil entry; FJ, 25 Aug 1866
10. Forbes to Forrest, 16 Sept 1865, SJCA
11. McCallum, pp. 25–32; indexed references to Smyth in Molony, *Eureka*
12. FJ, 21 Oct 1865
13. Minutes, SJC Council, 2 Oct 1865, SJCA
14. FJ, 18 Nov 1865
15. FJ, 25 Nov 1865
16. Dowd, pp. 242–52 & 320; Cunningham, p. 21
17. FJ, 27 Jan 1866
18. FJ, 17 Feb 1866; O'Donoghue, p. 151; Cunningham, p. 26
19. FJ, 21 April 1866
20. Dowd, pp. 262–69; O'Donoghue, pp. 121 & 151
21. O'Donoghue, p. 151
22. FJ, 19 Jan 1867
23. Therry to McEncroe, 25 Jan 1867, Box U1208 SAA
24. Cunningham, pp. 31–35; Kavenagh, pp. 196–98
25. Polding to Gregory, 9 Sept 1868, Polding letters, Vol. 3, p. 305
26. FJ, 13 Aug 1866
27. Moran, p. 478
28. Polding to McEncroe, 28 Feb 1867, Box U1208 SAA

8: Coming of the Irish

1. FJ, 30 Dec 1865
2. FJ, 23 Dec 1865
3. Prendergast, p. 73
4. Cahill, Lyndhurst and Sydney University Graduates, p. 39; Student roll, SJCA
5. FJ, 24 March & 7 April 1866
6. FJ, 30 June 1900
7. FJ, 26 April 1865 & 25 Aug 1866
8. FJ, 18 Nov 1865
9. ADB, Holt entry; FJ, 14 April 1866; SMH, 16 April 1866
10. Gilchrist, Vol 2, p. 693
11. FJ, 28 April 1866
12. *A Handbook to St John's College*, 1881, p. 50
13. Minutes, SJC Council, 7 May 1866, SJCA
14. FJ, 7 July 1866
15. FJ, 26 May 1866
16. FJ, 25 May 1861
17. Polding to Gregory, 20 March 1861, Polding letters, Vol. 3, p. 16
18. FJ, 4 Aug 1866
19. *Ibid*
20. FJ, 2 Dec 1865
21. FJ, 27 Jan 1866
22. FJ, 16 & 23 June 1866
23. FJ, 13 April 1864
24. FJ, 18 Jan 1868
25. Fogarty, Vol. 1, p. 110
26. O'Farrell, *The Catholic Church and Community*, p. 145

27. FJ, 28 July 1866
28. FJ, 8 Sept 1866
29. FJ, 22 Sept 1866
30. FJ, 13 & 20 Oct 1866
31. FJ, 27 Oct 1866
32. SMH, 27 Oct 1866; FJ, 3 Nov 1866

9: In Polding's absence

1. FJ, 10 Nov 1866
2. In Hellwig, p. 130
3. FJ, 10 Nov 1866
4. FJ, 8 Dec 1866 & 5 Jan 1867; Martin, pp. 224–25
5. FJ, 12 Jan 1867
6. FJ, 2 Feb & 6 July 1867
7. FJ, 10 Feb & 22 Dec 1866
8. FJ, 5 & 12 Jan 1867
9. Minutes, SJC Council, 3 Dec 1866, SJCA
10. Maher, p. 248
11. Cunningham, pp. 16, 31 & 39
12. Report to SJC Council 6 March 1867, SJCA
13. Copy sent to Bishop Murray is in MNDA
14. Daly, *History*, p. 48, SJCA; Quinn to SJC Council, 12 March 1868, BDA
15. Polding to Gregory, 24 Dec 1867, Polding letters, Vol. 3, p. 285
16. Birchley, pp. 213–14
17. FJ, 2 March 1867
18. Kavenagh, p. 156; Hall, pp. 32–35
19. Polding to Barnabo, 13 May 1859, Polding letters, Vol. 2, p. 285
20. Kavenagh, p. 199
21. Barker, pp. 6–7
22. Student roll, SJCA
23. Barker, p. 10
24. FJ, 23 March 1867
25. Polding to Gregory, 24 Aug 1867, Polding letters, Vol. 3, p. 274
26. FJ, 25 May 1867 & 13 Sept 1873
27. SMH, 13 June 1867; FJ, 15 June 1867
28. FJ, 22 June 1867; Moran, p. 359
29. FJ, 29 June 1867
30. SMH, 22 June 1867
31. FJ, 29 June 1867
32. FJ, 13 July 1867; Barker, p. 7
33. Minutes, SJC Council, 3 Dec 1866, SJCA
34. Polding to Gregory, 24 Aug 1867, Polding letters, Vol. 3, p. 274
35. FJ, 10 Aug 1867

10: Difficult times

1. FJ, 10 Aug 1867
2. Fogarty, Vol. 1, p. 177; FJ, 5 Oct 1867
3. Polding to Gregory, 24 Aug 1867, Polding letters, Vol. 3, p. 274
4. Polding to Gregory, 23 Oct 1867, Polding letters, Vol. 3, p. 278
5. FJ, 9 Nov 1867
6. Polding to Gregory, 23 Nov 1867, Polding letters, Vol. 3, p. 281; O'Farrell, *The Catholic Church and Community*, p. 170
7. Hellwig, p. 109
8. Murray to Moran, 22 July 1867, in Daly, ACR 37:3, p. 193
9. Hellwig, pp. 102–109
10. Murray to Moran, 22 July 1867, in Daly, ACR 37:3, p. 194
11. Letter in Hellwig, p. 132
12. Hellwig, p. 110

13. FJ, 21 Dec 1867
14. FJ, 28 Dec 1867
15. ADB, O'Sullivan entry
16. FJ, 16 March 1867
17. Polding to Gregory, 23 Oct 1867, Polding letters, Vol. 3, p. 278
18. FJ, 12 Oct 1867
19. FJ, quoting the *Empire*, 25 Jan 1868
20. FJ, 25 Jan 1868
21. SMH, 17 March 1868
22. Student roll, SJCA; Cahill, Lyndhurst and Sydney University Graduates, p. 39; Daly, *History*, p. 68, SJCA
23. FJ, 1 Dec 1866
24. FJ, 22 Feb 1868
25. Moran, p. 384
26. Murray to Moran, 19 April 1868, MNDA
27. FJ, 29 Feb 1868
28. *Empire*, 16 March 1868; FJ, 21 March 1868
29. FJ, 14 March 1868
30. SMH, 14 March 1868; Martin, p. 235; *Empire*, 16 March 1868
31. *Empire*, 17 March 1868; SMH, 18 March 1868
32. Polding to Gregory, 27 March 1868, Polding letters, Vol. 3, pp. 291–93
33. Polding to Gregory, 22 April 1868, Polding letters, Vol. 3, pp. 293–94
34. Polding to Gregory, 23 October 1867, Polding letters, Vol. 3, p. 278

11: Parkes on the rampage

1. Martin; ADB, Parkes entry
2. FJ, 28 March 1868, reprinting SMH report of 12 March 1856
3. Martin, p. 236; Travers, *Phantom Fenians*, pp. 42–50
4. Advertisement, eg *Yass Courier* 28 March 1868
5. FJ, 21 March 1868
6. FJ, 19 Dec 1868; O'Farrell Papers
7. FJ, 28 March 1868
8. FJ, 7 March 1868
9. Advertisement, eg *Yass Courier* 28 March 1868
10. FJ, 21 & 28 March, 4 April & 2 May 1868
11. FJ, 4 April 1868
12. Martin, p. 238; FJ, 21 March 1868
13. FJ, 11 April 1868
14. *Ibid*
15. Travers, *Phantom Fenians*, p. 94; FJ, 18 April 1868
16. *Illustrated Sydney News*, 25 March 1868; SMH, 18 March 1868
17. O'Farrell Papers
18. SMH, 31 March 1868
19. Travers, *Phantom Fenians*, p. 98
20. FJ, 25 April 1868
21. Martin, p. 242
22. FJ, 25 April 1868
23. Travers, *Phantom Fenians*, p. 102
24. Polding to Gregory, 19 May 1868, Polding letters, Vol. 3, p. 298
25. FJ, 23 Jan 1869
26. FJ, 9 May 1868
27. Published by F. Cunninghame, Sydney, 1867
28. FJ, 26 Sept 1868
29. Quoted in Travers, *Phantom Fenians*, p. 103
30. Martin, p. 244; FJ, 29 Aug 1868
31. FJ, 17 Oct 1868
32. O'Farrell Papers
33. FJ, 19 Dec 1868

34. *Ibid*
35. Dalley, speech at Masonic Hall, 20 May 1872
36. FJ, 13 & 20 March 1869, & 19 Nov 1870

12: Moving on
1. FJ, 29 Aug 1868
2. Polding to Gregory, 2 Sept 1868, Polding letters, Vol. 3, p. 302
3. SMH, 24 Aug 1868
4. Polding to Gregory, 27 March 1868, Polding letters, Vol. 3, p. 291
5. Polding to McEncroe, 18 May 1868, Box U1208 SAA
6. Polding to Gregory, 31 Jan 1868, Polding letters, Vol. 3, p. 287
7. Polding to Gregory, 9 Oct 1868, Polding letters, Vol. 3, p. 306
8. ADB, Bland entry
9. FJ, 8 Aug 1868
10. *Empire*, quoting *Southern Argus*, 28 July 1868
11. Wilson, p. 299
12. FJ, 31 Oct 1868
13. FJ, 12 Dec 1868
14. FJ, 9 Jan 1869
15. FJ, 16 Jan 1869
16. FJ, 5 June 1869
17. Student roll, SJCA; Report by Forrest to SJC Council, 3 Aug 1869, SJCA
18. FJ, 19 & 26 Dec 1868
19. Polding to Gregory, 6 Nov 1868, Polding letters, Vol. 3, p. 309
20. Polding to Lanigan, 10 & 26 Feb 1869, Lanigan Papers, MS 3718, NLA
21. J. Quinn to Polding, 23 Feb 1869, Lanigan Papers, MS 3718, NLA
22. M. Quinn to Polding, 16 March 1869, Lanigan Papers, MS 3718, NLA
23. Polding to Goold, 14 March 1869, Polding letters, Vol. 3, p. 322
24. Polding to Lanigan, 19 March 1869, Lanigan Papers, MS 3718, NLA
25. FJ, 17 April 1869
26. FJ, 24 April 1869
27. Coletti to Barsanti, 27 Feb 1868, Documents re Polding episcopacy, Vol 2, p. 196
28. FJ, 8 May 1869
29. FJ, 15 & 22 May 1869
30. Molony, *An Architect of Freedom*, pp. 140–47
31. Polding to Gregory, 14 June 1869, Polding letters, Vol. 3, p. 329
32. FJ, 15 & 22 May 1869
33. Reprinted in FJ, 15 May 1869

13: A changing guard
1. FJ, 19 June 1858
2. Daly, *History*, p. 54
3. Dalton to Forrest, 26 March 1869, SJCA
4. Minutes, SJC Council, 16 Feb 1870, SJCA
5. Polding to Forrest, 28 Feb 1870, Polding letters, Vol. 3, p. 338
6. Minutes, SJC Council, 3 May 1870, SJCA
7. Minutes, SJC Council, 7 & 12 Dec 1870, SJCA
8. FJ, 12 Aug 1871
9. Minutes, SJC Council, 3 Aug 1869, SJCA
10. FJ, 6 Feb, 29 May, 31 July & 14 Aug 1869

11. FJ, 15 May 1869
12. FJ, 22 May & 14 Aug 1869
13. FJ, 16 Oct 1869; SMH, 18 Oct 1869
14. FJ, 20 Nov 1869
15. FJ, 21 Feb & 3 April 1880
16. FJ, 31 July 1869
17. Farrell, p. 10
18. ADB, O'Mahony entry; FJ, 29 Jan 1870
19. FJ, 11 & 18 Sept 1869
20. FJ, 2 Oct 1869
21. FJ, 16 Oct 1869
22. *Ibid*
23. FJ, 25 Dec 1869
24. Polding to Gregory, 25 March 1870, Polding letters, Vol. 3, p. 339
25. Polding to Gregory, 20 April 1870, Polding letters, Vol. 3, p. 340
26. FJ, 11 Dec 1869
27. FJ, 22 Jan 1870
28. FJ, 25 Dec 1869; Martin, p. 268
29. *A Handbook to St John's College*, 1881, p. 51
30. Minutes, SJC Council, 14 May 1872, SJCA
31. FJ, 3 Nov 1894
32. Minutes, SJC Council, 3 Aug, 4 Oct, 2 Nov & 10 Nov 1869, SJCA
33. McCarthy speech notes, Box B2416 SAA
34. *Ibid*

14: Strong words

1. Student roll, SJCA; *A Handbook to St John's College*, 1881, p. 54
2. Minutes, SJC Council, 5 April and 5 July 1870, SJCA
3. FJ, 12 March 1870

4. SMH, 23 May 1870
5. Turney et al, p. 158
6. FJ, 4 June & 16 July 1870, 11 March & 3 June 1871
7. FJ, 25 June 1870
8. SMH, 5 July 1870
9. FJ, 27 Aug 1870
10. FJ, 22 Oct 1870
11. FJ, 29 Oct 1870
12. FJ, 3 Dec 1870
13. *Maitland Mercury*, quoted in FJ, 3 Dec 1870
14. Forrest J., *The Tendency of Modern Civilization*
15. FJ, 27 Aug 1870
16. Forrest, p. 16
17. FJ, 10 Dec 1870
18. FJ, 31 Dec 1870 & 14 Jan 1871
19. FJ, 6 May 1871

15: Exuberant charity

1. FJ, 10 & 17 Dec 1870
2. FJ, 7 Jan 1871
3. Fogarty, Vol. 1, p. 204
4. FJ, 27 May 1871
5. Fogarty, Vol 1, p. 136
6. FJ, 8 April 1871
7. FJ, 24 Dec 1870 & 8 April 1871
8. Student roll, SJCA; *A Handbook to St John's College*, 1881, p. 54; Cahill, Lyndhurst and Sydney University Graduates, p. 39
9. FJ, 10 Aug 1872
10. FJ, 31 Jan 1880 & 15 Dec 1883
11. Minutes, SJC Council, 7 March 1871, SJCA
12. Minutes, SJC Council, 4 April 1871, SJCA
13. Minutes, SJC Council, 2 July 1872, SJCA
14. Minutes, SJC Council, 4 April & 4 July 1871, SJCA

15. Minutes, SJC Council, 7 Nov 1871, SJCA
16. FJ, 2 Dec 1871 & 16 Nov 1872
17. FJ, 12 Aug 1871 & 25 April 1907
18. Porter, pp. 93–94
19. Sr Greene, *Annals*, Wellington Convent
20. Mons. Flanagan, Notes, BDA
21. FJ, 2 Dec 1871; Flanagan Notes, BDA
22. *Goulburn Herald*, 17 June 1871
23. FJ, 30 Dec 1871
24. FJ, 30 Sept 1871; ADB, Butler entry
25. Polding to Gregory, 6 Oct 1871, Polding letters, Vol. 3, p. 351
26. FJ, 9 Dec 1871 & 27 April 1872
27. Polding to Gregory, 14 June 1871, Polding letters, Vol. 3, p. 349
28. FJ, 23 Dec 1871
29. Student roll, SJCA; FJ, 6 Jan 1872 & 2 March 1872
30. FJ, 9 March 1872
31. ADB, Sheil entry; FJ, 16 March 1872
32. FJ, 30 March 1872
33. Minutes, SJC Council, 6 Aug 1872, SJCA
34. FJ, 6 April 1872
35. FJ, 20 April 1872
36. Lehane, *Irish Gold*, for Forrest's associations with these relatives.
37. Tierney, pp. 58–60, for details of Croke's Australian visit.
38. FJ, 13 July 1872
39. Martin, p. 265
40. FJ, 6 Jan 1872
41. FJ, 13 Jan 1872
42. FJ, 10 Feb 1872
43. Martin, pp. 272–75
44. FJ, 4 & 18 May 1872
45. Martin, p. 277
46. FJ, 18 May 1872
47. Dalley, speech at Masonic Hall, 20 May 1872
48. FJ, 1 June 1872
49. FJ, 25 May 1872
50. SMH, 16 Oct 1872
51. Minutes, SJC Council, 14 May, 6 Aug & 3 Dec 1872, SJCA
52. McCarthy speech notes, Box B2416 SAA
53. SJC Act, Section 6
54. FJ, 23 Nov 1872

16: Preparing for the co-adjutor

1. FJ, 11 Jan 1873
2. *Ibid*
3. FJ, 14 June 1873
4. *Launceston Examiner*, 4 Feb 1873
5. Parliamentary answer, SMH, 16 Oct 1873
6. FJ, 8 March 1873; Prendergast, p. 75; ADB, Thomas Butler entry
7. Makinson draft, undated, Box L2416 SAA
8. M. Quinn to Polding, 1 April 1873, BDA
9. SMH, 7 April 1873
10. FJ, 5 April 1873
11. Dowd, p. 335; ADB, Vaughan entry
12. FJ, 12 & 19 April 1873
13. Polding to Lanigan, 17 April 1873, Polding letters, Vol. 3, p. 366
14. Polding to Barnabo, 16 April 1873, Polding letters, Vol. 3, p. 365
15. M. Quinn to Lanigan, 24 April 1873, Lanigan Papers, MS 3718,

NLA. Includes English translation of letter in Italian by Quinn to Barnabo
16. J. and M. Quinn, Lanigan and O'Mahony to Cullen, 17 May 1873, microfilm at SAA
17. Murray to Cullen, 13 June 1873, microfilm at SAA
18. Cullen to Murray, 8 Oct 1873, MNDA
19. As Ref. 17
20. J. Quinn to Murray, 29 Sept 1873, MNDA
21. As Ref. 16
22. M. Quinn to Lanigan, 7 Dec 1873, Lanigan Papers, MS 3718, NLA
23. FJ, 17, 24 & 31 May & 7 June 1873
24. Polding to Gregory, 11 July 1873, Polding letters, Vol. 3, p. 369
25. FJ, 26 April 1873
26. FJ, 3 & 10 May 1873
27. FJ, 7 June 1873
28. Quinn to Tobias Kirby, Irish College, Rome, 25 March 1872, BDA
29. As Ref. 20
30. Murray to Lanigan, 13 Oct 1873, Lanigan Papers, MS 3718, NLA
31. Cullen to Murray, 8 Oct 1873, MNDA
32. Murray to Cullen, 18 Dec 1873, microfilm at SAA
33. FJ, 6 Sept 1873
34. FJ, 13 Sept 1873
35. O'Donoghue, p. 163; FJ, 6 Sept 1873
36. Proceedings in *Footprints*, Vol. 1, No. 12, Oct 1973
37. Polding to Barnabo, 17 Sept 1873, Polding letters, Vol. 3, p. 376
38. Polding to Barnabo, early Sept 1873, Polding letters, Vol. 3, p. 371
39. FJ, 18 Oct 1873
40. SMH, 16 Oct 1873
41. FJ, 15 Nov 1873
42. Rutledge, p. 218. This article gives a detailed account of the affair.
43. ADB, Dalley entry
44. Makinson to Gregory, 14 June 1873, Polding letters, Vol. 3, p. 369
45. As Ref. 41
46. Rutledge, p. 219
47. FJ, 29 Nov 1873

17: Out of St John's

1. FJ, 27 Dec 1873
2. FJ, 29 Nov 1873
3. FJ, 27 Dec 1873
4. Vaughan to Murray, 18 Dec 1873, MNDA; Lanigan to Vaughan, 17 Dec 1873, and Vaughan to Lanigan, 18 Dec 1873, Lanigan Papers, MS 3718, NLA
5. FJ, 20 Dec 1873
6. Murray to Cullen, 18 Dec 1873, microfilm at SAA
7. Vaughan to Barnabo, 16 & 29 Dec 1873, Box U1521 SAA
8. Vaughan to Colonel Vaughan, 29 Dec 1873, Courtfield Letters, transcripts at Veech Library
9. FJ, 28 Feb 1874
10. FJ, 3 & 24 Jan 1874
11. *Evening News*, 24 Nov 1883 & 5 Jan 1884
12. Vaughan to Colonel Vaughan, 12 Feb 1874, Courtfield Letters

13. FJ, 31 Jan 1874
14. FJ, 7 Feb 1874
15. Vaughan to Barnabo, 12 Feb 1874, Box U1521 SAA
16. As Ref. 12
17. FJ, 21 & 28 Feb 1874
18. FJ, 28 Feb 1874
19. Murray to Cullen, 10 April 1874, microfilm at SAA
20. FJ, 25 April 1874
21. Minutes, SJC Council, 3 March 1874, SJCA
22. FJ, 9 May 1874
23. Minutes, SJC Council, 7 April & 5 May 1874, SJCA
24. M. Quinn to Lanigan, 24 Dec 1873, Lanigan Papers, MS 3718, NLA
25. Minutes, SJC Council, 3 March & 7 April 1874, SJCA
26. Vaughan to Smith, 8 May 1874, Box O1735 SAA
27. FJ, 23 May 1874
28. FJ, 30 May 1874
29. FJ, 13 June 1874
30. FJ, 25 July 1874
31. FJ, 13 & 20 June 1874
32. Minutes, SJC Council, 16 July 1874, SJCA
33. SMH, 18 July 1874
34. *Evening News*, 18 July 1874; *Empire*, 20 July 1874
35. FJ, 25 July 1874
36. Minutes, SJC Council, 20 Oct 1874 & 2 Nov 1875, SJCA
37. FJ, 30 June 1900
38. Vaughan to Colonel Vaughan, 4 Sept 1874, Courtfield Letters; Wynne, ACR 60:3, p. 300

18: More travels

1. FJ, 15 & 22 Aug 1874
2. *Maitland Mercury*, 20 Aug 1874
3. Mullins, *Reminiscences*, pp. 2 & 18–19
4. Minutes, SJC Council, 1 Oct 1860, SJCA
5. Vaughan to Smith, 4 Sept 1874, Box O1735 SAA
6. Vaughan to Colonel Vaughan, 4 Sept 1874, Courtfield Letters
7. FJ, 3 April 1875
8. FJ, 22 Aug 1874
9. Mullins, p. 19
10. FJ, 28 Nov 1874
11. FJ, 19 Dec 1874 & 2, 9 & 30 Jan & 13 Feb 1875
12. FJ, 19 Dec 1874
13. FJ, 26 Dec 1874
14. FJ, 27 Feb & 20 March 1875
15. FJ, 13 March 1875
16. FJ, 10 April 1875; *Town and Country Journal*, 10 April 1875; SMH, 8 April 1875
17. FJ, 1 May 1875
18. FJ, 17 April 1875
19. Details of the 'O'Mahony Affair' in Farrell, JACHS, Vol 15, 1993, Cunningham, pp. 109–50, and McLay, pp. 193–97
20. O'Mahony to Lanigan, 8 May 1875, Lanigan Papers, MS 3718, NLA
21. O'Mahony to Lanigan, 19 Feb 1876, Lanigan Papers, MS 3718, NLA
22. FJ, 8 Jan 1876
23. Cunningham, p. 118

19: At Balmain

1. FJ, 29 May 1875
2. Bruce, R., St Augustine's, Balmain, centenary publication 1948
3. Vaughan to Forrest, seven letters re

theological schools, Dec 1875 to May 1877, SJCA
4. FJ, 3 & 10 July 1875
5. FJ, 31 July 1875
6. FJ & SMH, 7 Aug 1875
7. FJ, 14 Aug 1875
8. Quoted in Flannery, p. 303
9. FJ, 7 Aug 1875
10. SMH, 11 Aug 1875
11. FJ, 6 July 1878
12. FJ, 9 Oct 1875
13. *Ibid*
14. Mullins, p. 23
15. FJ, 18 Dec 1875
16. FJ, 26 June 1875
17. Fogarty, Vol. 1, pp. 248–49
18. FJ, 1 Jan 1876
19. FJ, 25 Dec 1875
20. FJ, 19 Feb 1876
21. FJ, 4 March 1876
22. FJ, 24 March 1877 & 5 Feb 1881
23. FJ, 28 April 1877
24. FJ, 25 March 1876
25. FJ, 9 Sept 1876
26. Letters re appointment, Sept & Oct 1876, Box L2207 SAA
27. FJ, 25 Nov 1876
28. FJ, 23 Dec 1876
29. FJ, 17 Feb 1877
30. FJ, 10 March 1877
31. FJ, 24 March 1877
32. FJ, 17 March 1877
33. Wynne, ACR 32:3, p. 216–17
34. FJ, 17 March 1877
35. FJ, 24 March 1877
36. Vaughan to Colonel Vaughan, 23 March 1877, Courtfield Letters
37. FJ, 14 & 21 April 1877
38. FJ, 28 April 1877
39. Minutes, SJC Council, 8 & 15 May 1877, SJCA
40. Council members named on letter to them by Barsanti, 17 Sept 1877, Eris O'Brien papers, Veech Library
41. Vaughan to Forrest, 15 May 1877, SJCA
42. Kavenagh, pp. 154 & 171
43. *Evening News*, 5 May 1877; FJ 12 May 1877
44. FJ, 7 July 1877
45. FJ, 10 Nov 1877
46. Kavenagh, p. 207
47. Kavenagh, pp. 183–206
48. Mullins, p. 15

20: One of the ugliest blots

1. Wynne, ACR 51:2, 1974
2. O'Donoghue, p. 148
3. FJ, 12 Dec 1868
4. Barsanti to Polding, 13 Oct 1875, MNDA
5. Barsanti to Archbishop's Council, 17 Sept 1877, Veech Library
6. Wynne, ACR 60:3, 1983
7. FJ, 29 Sept 1877
8. FJ, 22 Sept 1877; ADB, Tenison-Woods entry
9. Linnean Society receipt, SJCA; FJ, 1 May 1880
10. FJ, 29 Sept 1877
11. FJ, 17 Nov 1877
12. FJ, 24 Nov 1877
13. FJ, 8 Dec 1877 & 5 Jan 1878
14. Vaughan to Smith, 3 Aug 1877, Box O1735 SAA
15. FJ, 24 Nov 1877
16. FJ, 19 Jan 1878
17. FJ, 9 Feb 1878
18. FJ, 16 Dec 1876
19. McLay, p. 94
20. Syllabus of Accusations, Box U1524 SAA

21. O'Quinn to Vatican, undated draft, BDA
22. Vaughan to Smith, 11 May 1877, Box O1735 SAA
23. FJ, 19 Jan 1878
24. FJ, 30 March 1878
25. Cunningham, pp. 138–39
26. Cunningham, p. 140
27. Quinn to Tobias Kirby, late 1881, BDA
28. Vaughan to Simeoni, 11 May 1878, SC, Oceania, 1877–78, Vol II, folio 752, Mitchell Library
29. Cunningham, p. 141
30. Translation by M.R. Ovington, Canberra
31. Cunningham, p. 143
32. O'Donovan to Vaughan, 1 Aug 1878, Box U1524 SAA
33. O'Quinn, undated memorandum, Box U1524 SAA
34. Simeone to Vaughan, 31 May 1880, Box U1521 SAA

21: Next door

1. SJCA, Forrest papers
2. FJ, 17 Nov 1877
3. FJ, 23 Feb 1884; Quinn to Murray, 2 May 1884, MNDA
4. FJ, 24 Nov & 29 Dec 1877
5. Wynne, ACR 51:2, 1974
6. SMH, 12 Aug 1878
7. *Daily Telegraph*, 31 Oct 1882 & FJ, 4 Nov 1882
8. FJ, 9 & 16 Nov 1878
9. FJ, 14 June 1879
10. FJ, 27 May 1882
11. FJ, 28 Dec 1878
12. Fogarty, Vol. 1, p. 26
13. FJ, 28 June 1879
14. FJ, 21 June, 26 July & 2 Aug 1879, & 10 July 1880
15. FJ, 26 July 1879
16. FJ, 19 July 1879
17. FJ, 2 Aug 1879
18. ADB, Vaughan entry; Cunningham, p. 154
19. FJ, 8 Nov 1879 & 28 Feb 1880
20. Fogarty, Vol. 1, p. 251; FJ, 22 Nov 1879
21. FJ, 20 Dec 1879
22. Fogarty, Vol. 1, pp. 224 & 238
23. FJ, 25 Sept 1880
24. Fogarty, Vol. 1, p. 254
25. FJ, 10 July 1880
26. FJ, 22 Oct 1881
27. FJ, 10 July 1880
28. FJ, 16 Sept 1882
29. FJ, 18 June 1881
30. FJ, 27 Aug 1881
31. Cunningham, p. 191
32. McLay, p. 236
33. *Brisbane Courier*, 21 Sept 1881
34. FJ, 17 Oct 1885
35. FJ, 3 Sept & 3 Dec 1881
36. *Brisbane Courier*, 23 Sept 1881
37. *Brisbane Courier*, 26 Sept 1881
38. FJ, 1 Oct 1881
39. FJ, 5 Nov 1881
40. FJ, 29 Nov 1879 & 28 Feb 1880
41. SMH, 13 Dec 1881
42. SMH, 14 Dec 1881; Pamphlet, *Funeral of the late Mr. Michael Fitzpatrick, M.L.A.*, reprints contemporary newspaper reports and Hansard transcript of the parliamentary debate
43. FJ, 24 Dec 1881
44. FJ, 24 Dec 1881; *Advocate*, 17 Dec 1881
45. FJ, 28 Jan 1882
46. FJ, 4 Nov 1882
47. SMH, 2 Nov 1882

22: Farewells

1. FJ, 25 March, 15 & 29 April, & 13 May 1882
2. FJ, 3 June 1882
3. FJ, 15 April 1882
4. FJ, 9 & 16 Sept 1882
5. FJ, 26 Aug & 2 Sept 1882
6. FJ, 30 Sept 1882
7. FJ, 2 Dec 1882 & 6 Jan 1883
8. FJ, 30 June 1900
9. FJ, 7 July 1900
10. FJ, 23 Dec 1882 & 6 Jan 1883
11. FJ, 6 Jan & 17 Feb 1883
12. FJ, 3 March 1883
13. FJ, 21 April 1883
14. FJ, 25 Aug & 6 Oct 1883
15. FJ, 4 Aug 1883
16. *Express*, 21 July 1883
17. FJ, 4 Aug 1883
18. O'Sullivan was a monk of St Augustine's Abbey, Ramsgate (England), which belonged to the Cassinese Congregation of the Primitive Observance; information kindly supplied by Terence Kavenagh OSB
19. Propaganda Fide archives, SC, Oceania, Vol 14, 1882–84; information kindly provided by the late Mr A.E. Cahill
20. FJ, 13 Oct & 3 Nov 1883
21. *Evening News*, 5 Jan 1884
22. FJ, 11 Aug 1883
23. *Express*, 8 Sept 1883
24. FJ, 11 Aug 1883
25. Murray to Mrs Gilhooley, 3 Sept 1883, MNDA
26. SMH, 6 Aug 1883
27. *Evening News*, 4 Aug 1883
28. *Daily Telegraph*, 6 Aug 1883
29. Vaughan to Colonel Vaughan, 15 March 1880, Courtfield Letters
30. *Express*, 29 Dec 1883
31. *Express*, 11 Aug 1883
32. FJ, 11 Aug 1883

23: If only…

1. Numbers are given in *Freeman's Journal* reports of annual St John's College awards ceremonies.
2. Vaughan to Simeoni, 11 May 1878, SC, Oceania, 1877–78
3. Minutes, SJC Council, 7 Aug 1883, SJCA
4. Murray to Lanigan, 21 Nov 1883, Lanigan Papers, MS 3718, NLA
5. Livingston, p. 86
6. FJ, 10 Nov & 15 Dec 1883 & 8 March 1884
7. Murray to Lanigan, 21 May 1886, Lanigan Papers, MS 3718, NLA
8. Duffy, 'The High Flying Eagle', p. 2
9. Bygott, p. 36
10. ADB, Dalley entry
11. FJ, 3 Nov 1888
12. FJ, 25 Feb 1888

Index

A

Aborigines 178, 243
Adams, Walter M. 133, 161
Albert, Prince 111, 147
Alfred, Prince (Duke of Edinburgh) 145–1487, 150–153, 155–157, 162–165, 172, 183, 211, 306
Allen, Caroline 157, 159
Arnold, William 152
Aspinall, Butler Cole 157, 164
Athy, Rev. Edmund 104
Austin, Henry 78

B

Badham, Professor Charles 130, 259, 266, 306, 307
Barker, Bishop Frederick 111, 113, 272
Barnabo, Cardinal 32, 45–50, 55, 81, 104, 223, 224, 231, 238, 242, 261
Barry, Dr John 65, 69
Barry, Rev. David 319
Barsanti, Rev. Octavius 279, 280
Bassett, Dr 43, 45
Bataillon, Bishop Pierre 170
Beechinor, Rev. Daniel 268
Belmore, Earl of 146, 195, 213, 223
Benedict, Harry 161
Benedictine Order 24–32, 48, 82, 88, 98, 102–105, 129, 189, 223, 225–226, 236, 238, 245, 247, 257, 275, 276–281, 310–311, 319, 320
Bermingham, Patrick 126
Blacket, Edmund 39, 67, 71, 74, 76, 86, 207, 270

Bland, Dr William 168
Bland, Mrs 169
Bourke, Governor Sir Richard 16, 25, 70
Brennan, Rev. Michael 87
Browne, Andrew 55
Browne, William Charles 54, 65, 86, 319
Buchanan, David 187, 299
Butler, Edmund 220, 239, 319
Butler, Edward 16, 31, 43, 44, 47, 70, 73, 75, 109, 114, 152, 173, 183, 188, 190, 192, 195, 209, 213, 214, 215, 216, 219, 232, 233, 234, 250, 251, 259, 260, 290, 291
Butler, Thomas (brother of Edmund) 220, 239
Butler, Thomas (*Freeman's* editor) 109, 183, 204, 206, 312
Byrnes, James 155

C

Cahill, A.E. 83
Cahill, Rev. Thomas 246, 247, 275
Callaghan, James 129
Callan Park mental asylum 270
Cani, Rev. John 128, 283, 305
Carboni, Raffaello 100
Carroll, Rev. John 298, 311, 312
Catholic University of Ireland 20, 21, 34, 56, 92, 217
Catholic young men's societies 9–10, 13–15, 19, 45, 59, 61, 70, 89, 123, 196
Cheeke, Judge 157

Chisholm, Archibald 10
Chisholm, Caroline 10, 12, 59, 71
Christian Brothers 84
Clancy, Rev. Daniel 318
Clarke, Rev. W.B. 86, 306
Clune, Dr Michael 319
Coghlan, Charles 83, 195, 211, 319
Coletti, Rev. Vincenzo 176, 186, 243, 246, 257, 262, 299, 300, 301
Conway, Rev. James 89–91, 120, 167
Cook, Captain 15, 266
Corish, Rev. Mellitus 29, 31
Cowper, Charles 44, 69, 71, 78, 79, 95, 188, 204, 214
Crane, Bishop Martin 275, 282
Creed, Daniel O'Lehane 206
Croke, Bishop Thomas 34, 99, 148, 212
Croke, David 99
Croke, Mother Ignatius 148, 212
Cullen, Archbishop Paul 12, 18, 19, 21, 26, 32, 35, 48, 49, 69, 83, 84, 102–104, 108, 134, 224, 225, 227, 228, 238, 245, 255, 262, 263, 290, 318
Curtis, Rev. Anselm 14, 73, 84, 102, 104, 277
Curtis, William 31, 82, 194

D

D'Arcy, Rev. David 181, 202, 208, 211, 216
Daintrey, Marian 259
Daley, Victor J. 109
Dalley, William Bede 23, 67, 78, 93, 96, 108–109, 144, 151, 157, 161, 164, 173, 179, 183, 187, 189, 195, 211, 212, 214, 216, 233, 259, 272, 284, 289, 291, 292, 301, 302, 306, 307, 315, 319, 320
Dalton, Rev. Joseph 181, 297
Darley, Frederick 234

Darwin, Charles 11
Davis, Bishop Charles 320
Davis, W.M. 31, 43, 44,
Deniehy, Daniel 44, 45, 46, 61, 307
Denison, Governor Sir William 13, 42
de Lacy, Sister 47
Dillon, John 181, 194, 202, 299, 300, 301
Dillon, Rev. George 114, 161, 243, 244, 248, 250, 251, 253, 264, 267, 282, 288, 298
Dolman, William 50, 73
Dominican Order 141, 142, 199, 257, 259, 281
Donnellan, Sister M. Hyacinth 141
Donovan, John 82, 153, 202, 207, 229, 245, 250, 312
Duffy, Charles Gavan 144, 155
Duncan, William Augustine 26, 27, 28, 29, 52, 91, 125, 129, 151–153, 162, 190, 202, 207, 219, 229, 240, 243–245, 250, 277, 278, 302, 307, 312, 318
Dunne, Bishop Robert 304
Dunne, Rev. Patrick 126
Dwyer, Michael 161
Dwyer, Rev. John 161, 195, 196, 236, 271, 276, 312

E

Eagar, Geoffrey 162
Edmunds, Walter 239
Ellis, Eyre 81, 114, 152, 190, 195, 202, 245, 250, 312
Elloy, Bishop 114
Emmanuel, King Victor 201
Express 313

F

Fairfax, John 204, 219
Farnell, James 291, 298
Farrell, Rev. John 261

Faucett, Judge Peter 23, 31, 40, 44, 59, 75, 77, 78, 226, 271, 284, 302, 312
Fitzgerald, Edmund 67, 107
Fitzpatrick, Michael 298–301
Forbes, Andrew J. 99
Forrest, Benjamin 18
Forrest, Maryanne (Mrs Gilhooley) 13, 35, 78, 281, 312, 318, 321
Forrest, Sarah (née O'Connor) 18
Forrest, Very Rev. Dr John 7–8, 10, 12–16, 18–22, 34–35, 49, 51–60, 65, 67–69, 71–72, 74, 76–82, 84–85, 87–88, 90–92, 95, 97, 99, 101, 106, 108–110, 113–115, 118, 120, 122, 124–126, 128, 130–133, 135, 141–143, 147–150, 152, 158, 161, 167–168, 170–172, 174–175, 179–182, 185–186, 188–190, 193–194, 196–200, 202–203, 205–206, 208–210, 212, 216–218, 220–221, 226, 228–231, 236, 240–241, 243, 245–246, 248–251, 253–258, 260–261, 263, 265–269, 271–272, 275, 279–280, 282, 284–285, 288, 290–292, 296–299, 301–302, 304, 306–307, 309–313, 315, 317, 319–320
Forster, William 214, 222, 235, 259, 298, 299, 301
Franchi, Cardinal 261, 262, 277, 279, 280, 283, 284
Freehill, Bernard Austin 206
Freehill, Francis Bede 206, 312, 319
Freeman's Journal 8, 9, 15, 27–31, 50, 144, 147–148, 153, 183, 184, 306, 307

G

Garavel, Rev. Joseph 91, 93, 115, 120, 128, 176, 182, 193, 202, 212, 270, 288, 292, 296, 311

Geoghegan, Bishop Patrick 48, 69
Gilhooley, Dr James 78, 190, 202, 212, 229, 243, 311, 312
Gillett, Very Rev. Anselm 245, 251, 268, 275, 280, 283, 284, 286, 308, 317, 318
Giorza, Signor 266
Good Shepherd (later Good Samaritan) Order 71, 270, 271, 275, 276, 281
Goold, Archbishop James 42, 48, 55, 69, 79, 80, 99, 100, 175, 231, 305, 309, 310
Gorman, J.V. 31, 77, 114
Gorman, John 77
Gourbeillon, Jean 47
Granger, Mrs 84, 85, 277
Grant, Dean John 91, 128
Greene, Sister Angela 208
Gregory, Rev. Henry 25–28, 31, 41, 43, 44, 45, 47–50, 52, 55–58, 66, 67, 69, 75, 78–81, 84, 85, 102–105, 114, 126, 128, 130, 139, 140, 144, 153, 161, 166, 167, 174, 178, 187, 209, 226, 234, 255

H

Hall, Ben 81
Hart, James 43, 44, 91
Healy, Dean 279
Healy, Patrick Joseph 54, 65, 66, 77, 188, 207, 240, 301
Heydon, Jabez King 26, 27, 28, 29, 30, 31, 40, 43, 44, 45, 46, 49, 50, 52, 55, 140, 195, 290
Heydon, Louis 290
Holt, Thomas 109, 110, 111, 220
Holy Catholic Guild 195, 229, 265, 274
Hutchinson, Frank 109
Hynes, William 194

I

Irish College, Rome 18, 19, 20, 34, 58, 99, 148, 184, 201, 212, 293, 304, 318

J

Jennings, Sir Patrick 259, 267, 284, 298, 307, 312
Jesuit Order 32, 33, 180, 181, 217, 246, 247, 256, 270, 275, 319
Johnson, Robert 124
Joseph, Saul 96

K

Kane, Rev. Dr 34
Kavenagh, Terence 277, 278
Keating, Rev. Jerome 31
Keating, Rev. Tom 263, 269, 270, 281
Kelly, Rev. Martin 261
Kelly, Rev. William 240, 297
Kendall, Henry 109, 288, 306–307
Kenyon, Rev. 47
Kirby, Rev. Tobias 293, 296

L

Lalor, Peter 101
Lang, Rev. John Dunmore 111, 151, 160, 188, 272, 289
Lanigan, Rev. William 103, 120, 130–136, 140, 161, 166, 170, 175, 177, 184, 209, 212, 218, 223, 224, 227, 228, 231, 237, 240, 241, 246, 247, 249, 253, 254, 258, 261, 262, 266, 267, 273, 275, 282, 284, 290, 293, 295, 307, 311, 318, 319
Lawson, Henry 109
Leahy, Archbishop Patrick 34, 180
Leboeuf, General 203
Lehane, Jeremiah 77
Lehane, Mary (née O'Connor) 212
Lehane, William 77, 85, 99, 212, 281
Lenehan, Andrew 31
Lilley, Charles 297
Linnean Society of NSW 281, 288, 306
Lynch, Dean John 23, 32, 54, 57, 69, 141, 176, 184, 185, 186, 267, 270, 288, 292, 312
Lyndhurst, St Mary's College 13, 14, 41, 61, 65–68, 73, 77, 78, 80, 82, 84, 85, 88, 91, 98, 102, 104, 106–108, 125, 126, 129, 130, 148, 174, 175, 186, 193–195, 198, 202, 206, 210, 211, 216, 220, 221, 227, 236, 239, 247, 255, 257, 258, 267–269, 271, 275, 276–278, 281, 312, 317, 318, 320
Lyons, Ellen 281

M

M'Glone, Daniel 157
Macdonnell, Randal 31, 43, 44, 46, 52
MacKillop, Mother Mary 211, 281, 294
Macleay, William 159, 160, 161, 165, 214
Macquarie, Governor 15, 86
Magennis, Rev. Patrick 113
Maher, Matthew 91, 312
Maher, Rev. Brian 25
Makinson, Thomas 31, 58, 186, 189, 221, 234
Marist Order 115, 227, 279, 280, 288
Martin, Sir James 72, 78, 95, 106, 124, 146, 153, 157, 187, 188, 204, 213, 214, 219, 222, 232–234, 291
Mary Queen of Scots 281
McAlroy, Rev. Michael 126, 132, 196

McCallum, Austin 100, 101
McCarthy, Rev. Callaghan 189–193, 194, 206–207, 216–217, 246–247, 250, 286
McEncroe, Archdeacon John 15, 16, 23, 26, 28, 29, 31, 33–35, 48–51, 60, 68–70, 75–78, 81, 83, 85–92, 95, 103–107, 114, 115, 118, 119, 123– 125, 130, 131, 132, 135, 137, 140, 141, 142, 150, 151, 158–159, 166–169, 179, 180–182, 189, 196, 208, 227, 255, 263, 284
McEvilly, W. 44, 46
McGarvie, Sergeant-Major 269
McGirr, Michael 109, 129
McGirr, Rev. James 128, 129
Meillon, Joseph 66
Menzies, Sir Robert 295
Molloy, Rev. Gerald 21, 200
Moore, J. Sheridan 98, 99
Moran, Archbishop Patrick 19, 104, 133, 141, 149, 261, 262, 318, 319
Mullins, John Lane 255, 257, 268, 278
Murphy, Bishop Daniel 166, 175, 177, 220, 237, 257, 267, 268, 275, 282, 296, 297, 298
Murphy, Captain 268
Murphy, Very Rev. Dr 319
Murray, Bishop James 19, 21, 102–104, 119, 120, 123, 130, 132, 133, 134, 136, 139, 141, 142, 143, 144, 148, 149, 166, 170, 174–177, 184, 186, 197–199, 200, 209, 210, 224, 227, 228, 229, 231, 237, 238, 240, 241, 245, 246, 247, 249, 250, 253, 254, 257– 262, 266, 267, 268, 269, 273, 275, 280, 282, 284–286, 288, 290, 293, 295, 304, 307, 312, 318

Murray, John Hubert Plunkett 179
Murray, Sir Terence Aubrey 40, 60, 71, 169, 179
Murray, Thomas 130

N

Napoleon Bonaparte 18
Napoleon III, Emperor 202
Newman, Rev. John Henry 12, 19–21, 32, 34, 35, 58, 72, 217, 255, 292
Nicholson, Sir Charles 72, 74
Normanby, Marquis of 249
Nugent, Ellen 260, 261

O

O'Farrell, Henry 147, 151, 152, 155, 156–160, 163, 164, 236
O'Farrell, P.A.C. 306
O'Brien, Dr James 319
O'Connell, Daniel ('The Liberator') 16, 77, 264, 265, 266, 267, 274
O'Connell, Daniel (St John's College student) 77, 189, 312
O'Connell, Dean Maurus 10, 32, 109, 319
O'Connor, J.G. 213
O'Connor, Richard 24, 27, 29, 31, 41, 43– 47, 55, 69, 190, 194
O'Connor, Richard E. 194, 222, 301, 312, 314
O'Doherty, Dr Kevin Izod 59, 61, 249, 297
O'Donovan, Denis 287
O'Mahony, Bishop Timothy 19, 184, 212, 218, 224, 228, 231, 249, 253, 260–262, 281, 282, 283, 284, 286–288, 296
O'Mara, Tom 109
O'Shanassy, Sir John 176, 177, 222, 261, 287
O'Sullivan, Rev. Adalbert 310, 311

O'Sullivan, Richard 144, 156, 183, 184

P

Pacilio, Rev. L.B. 263
Parkes, Sir Henry 8, 16, 106, 117, 118, 124, 125, 134, 139, 146, 147, 153, 155, 156, 157–165, 166, 169, 187, 188, 195, 204, 211–216, 219, 222, 231, 232, 233, 234, 235, 259, 289, 290, 291, 292, 293, 298, 299, 307
Pell, Professor Morris 13, 68, 77, 82, 88, 108
Pickering, Thomas 97
Plunket, Archbishop Oliver 94
Plunkett, John Hubert 16, 23, 24, 28, 31, 39, 43, 47, 59, 70, 75, 77, 81, 91, 94, 113, 118, 120, 124, 135, 140, 171, 172, 178, 179, 180, 189, 195, 284
Plunkett, Mrs 195
Polding, Archbishop John Bede 7, 8, 13, 18, 22, 24–28, 30– 32, 34, 37, 38, 40–50, 52, 55–58, 66–71, 74, 75, 78, 79, 80–82, 84, 85, 87, 89– 91, 93, 95, 96, 102–104, 107, 114, 125–130, 133, 136, 137, 139–141, 143, 144, 153, 154, 158, 160, 166–168, 170, 172–179, 181, 182, 184, 186, 187, 189, 195, 208–211, 217, 221, 223, 224, 226, 227, 231, 234, 236, 237, 239, 240, 242, 246–248, 255, 257, 258, 261, 263, 266–272, 274, 275, 277, 279, 283, 284, 285, 309, 310, 317, 320
Pope Leo XIII 21, 284, 292
Pope Pius IX 26, 32–33, 172, 201, 225, 284
Porter, Robert 208

Presentation Sisters 220, 257
Propaganda Fide, Rome 32, 45, 261, 277, 284
Public Instruction Act 1880 293, 298, 299
Public Schools Act 1866 106, 117, 120, 123–125, 134, 139, 169, 180, 215
Pugin, Augustus Welby 37

Q

Quinn, Bishop Matthew 19, 21, 102, 104, 119, 120, 123, 128, 129, 132, 133, 134, 135, 139, 148, 158, 166, 170, 172, 174, 175, 176, 184, 195, 196, 198, 199, 208, 209, 212, 213, 216, 218, 221, 224, 227–230, 240, 241, 245–247, 249, 250, 272, 273, 275, 282, 284, 285, 286, 288, 290, 292–298, 306, 307, 318
Quinn (also O'Quinn), Bishop James 19, 20, 48, 57, 59, 68, 69, 71, 79, 84, 120, 124, 128, 130, 131, 133, 135, 139, 143, 166, 174, 175, 176, 177, 184, 186, 224, 228, 229, 248, 249, 258–260, 274, 275, 282–284, 285, 286, 287, 296, 297, 304
Quirk, Rev. Norbert 88, 107, 202, 206, 210, 221, 236, 276
Quirk, Rev. Placid 236, 239, 258, 267, 269, 271, 276, 278, 288, 312

R

Redwood, Bishop Francis 305
Reynolds, Bishop Christopher 258, 259, 275, 282
Reynolds, W. 44, 46
Ricci, Rev. Eugenio 283
Riley, John 244
Robertson, Dr 47

Robertson, Sir John 163, 179, 183, 188, 204, 213, 233, 259, 272, 289, 291, 302, 312
Robinson, Governor Sir Hercules 223
Robinson, Lady 226
Rosse, Lord 185
Rubie, Edward 196

S

Sacred Heart College, Maitland 267
Saint Patrick 60, 302
Savigny, Rev. W.H. 86, 147
Sentis, Louis de 44
Shanahan, Norah 259
Sheehy, Rev. Austin 69, 91, 102–104, 113, 115, 118, 119, 123, 124, 131–133, 137, 153, 168, 176, 183, 187, 194, 239, 279, 304, 311
Sheil, Bishop Laurence 99, 158, 175, 211
Sheridan, Rev. Felix 31, 85, 91, 107, 189, 190, 198, 245, 276, 300, 311
Shorthill, John 130
Sisters of Charity 47, 106
Sisters of Mercy 148, 150, 208, 212, 227
Sisters of St Joseph 211, 281, 294
Slattery, Rev. 288
Smidmore, Mrs 73
Smith, Dr Bernard 247, 256, 257, 283
Smith, Mr (orchardist) 10
Smith, Professor John 124, 219
Smyth, Rev. Patrick 100–101
Stenhouse, N.D. 306
Stephen, Sir Alfred 195, 233
Stephenson, H.H. 64
Stewart, John 232
Stuart, Alexander 307
St Aloysius College, Sydney 275

St Charles' Seminary, Bathurst 295
St Ignatius College, Riverview 275, 319
St John's College, University of Sydney 7, 8, 10, 12, 13, 22–24, 27, 30, 32–35, 37, 40, 41, 43, 44, 46, 49, 52–58, 66–69, 71, 72, 74, 76–79, 81, 82, 85, 87, 88, 90– 92, 95, 97– 99, 101, 107, 111, 113–115, 120, 123–130, 132, 135, 136, 141, 144, 148, 149, 151, 152, 159, 167, 169, 173–175, 179–182, 184, 188– 190, 192–196, 202, 206–208, 210, 212, 216, 217, 220, 224, 225, 227, 230, 232, 236, 241, 245–247, 250–252, 254–259, 263, 265–268, 275, 280, 283, 285, 286, 288, 301, 312, 314, 317, 318, 320
St John's College Act 55–57, 217, 256
St Laurence O'Toole's Seminary, Dublin 20, 21
St Mary's Cathedral, destruction by fire 93, 97, 115, 172
St Mary's Cathedral, opening of new building 170, 279, 295, 302–306, 311
St Mary's Seminary, Sydney 28, 31, 47, 61, 67, 102, 120, 135, 172, 173
St Mary's Cathedral, Hobart 269
St Patrick's College, Carlow 208
St Patrick's College, Goulburn 240, 267
St Patrick's College, Maynooth 18, 20, 21, 87, 200
St Patrick's College, Melbourne 66, 181
St Patrick's Young Men's Society 70, 89

St Paul's College, University of Sydney 39, 40, 55, 86, 88, 98, 124, 147, 195
St Stanislaus' College, Bathurst 128, 129, 174, 228, 229, 230, 240, 258, 267
Sullivan, A.M. (newspaper editor) 144
Sullivan, Henry 148, 194, 211
Sullivan, Rev. A.M. 311
Sumner, Rev. Bede 27
Suttor, T.L. 19
Sweeney, Rev. Norbert 48

T

Tenison-Woods, Rev. Julian 281, 294, 306
Therry, Archpriest John 15, 31, 32, 43, 75, 86, 87, 167, 182, 263, 270, 307
Therry, Judge Roger 23, 31, 103
Thomson, Sir Edward Deas 91, 98, 113, 114, 195, 221, 259, 292
Tole, Joseph 129, 135
Torreggiani, Bishop Elzear 296, 297, 307
Treason Felony Act 156, 157
Trinity College, Dublin 12, 18, 23
Trollope, Anthony 266

U

Ullathorne, Rev. Dr William 11, 12, 26, 32, 34, 35, 48, 49
University of Sydney, foundation and progress 12, 40, 55, 85–86, 91, 98, 133, 210

V

Vaughan, Archbishop Roger Bede 91, 103128, 223–225, 228, 229, 237–244, 246, 247, 249–254, 256–258, 260, 262, 263, 265–269, 271, 274, 275–278, 280–288, 290, 293–296, 299, 300, 301, 302, 304, 307–313, 317
Vaughan, Reginald 259Vaughan, Rev. Herbert 103
Vaughan, Rev. John 274, 310
Vitte, Bishop 237, 282

W

Wardell, William Wilkinson 37, 38, 39, 68, 71, 97, 136, 175, 206
Weld, Frederick 269
Wentworth, W.C. 44, 72
Whately, Archbishop Richard 139
Wilkins, William 124, 215, 220
Willson, Bishop Robert 42, 69, 78, 79
Wisdom, Robert 151
Wiseman, Archbishop 12, 32, 34, 35, 108
Woolfrey, Rev. Norbert 32
Woolley, Professor John 13, 68, 77, 82, 88, 108, 130
Wynne, Rev. Roger 280, 289

Y

Young, Governor Sir John 58, 73, 86, 95, 111, 114, 146
Young, Lady 71
Young and Williams, builders 39

www.ingramcontent.com/pod-product-compliance
Lightning Source LLC
Chambersburg PA
CBHW071803080526
44589CB00012B/665